Wagner Outside the *Ring*

ALSO BY JOHN LOUIS DIGAETANI
AND FROM MCFARLAND

*Stages of Struggle: Modern Playwrights and
Their Psychological Inspirations* (2008)

Inside the Ring: Essays on Wagner's Opera Cycle (2006)

Wagner and Suicide (2003)

*Carlo Gozzi: A Life in the 18th Century
Venetian Theater, an Afterlife in Opera* (2000)

Wagner Outside the *Ring*

*Essays on the Operas,
Their Performance and Their
Connections with Other Arts*

Edited by JOHN LOUIS DIGAETANI

McFarland & Company, Inc., Publishers
Jefferson, North Carolina, and London

LIBRARY OF CONGRESS CATALOGUING-IN-PUBLICATION DATA

Wagner outside the Ring : essays on the operas, their performances and their connections with other arts / edited by John Louis DiGaetani.
p.   cm.
Includes bibliographical references and index.

ISBN 978-0-7864-3400-8
softcover : 50# alkaline paper ∞

1. Wagner, Richard, 1813–1883. Operas.   2. Wagner, Richard, 1813–1883 — Performances.   I. DiGaetani, John Louis, 1943–
ML410.W13W125   2009   782.1092 — dc22   2009019477

British Library cataloguing data are available

©2009 John Louis DiGaetani. All rights reserved

No part of this book may be reproduced or transmitted in any form or by any means, electronic or mechanical, including photocopying or recording, or by any information storage and retrieval system, without permission in writing from the publisher.

On the cover: Act 3 of Otto Schenk's 2001 production of *Die Meistersinger von Nürnberg* by the Metropolitan Opera (photograph by Winnie Klotz)

Manufactured in the United States of America

*McFarland & Company, Inc., Publishers
Box 611, Jefferson, North Carolina 28640
www.mcfarlandpub.com*

For Elayne, Barbara, and Mary Ann

Acknowledgments

I would like to thank Hofstra University for granting me a sabbatical and travel funds to work on this book.

I would also like to thank Winnie Klotz of the Metropolitan Opera for the use of her wonderful photos. I am indebted to the other photographers for their Wagner production photos; I would especially like to thank the press department of the Bayreuth festival — Peter Emmerich, Friederike Emmerich, and Angela Nitzl — for the use of their photos and their expertise. Marie Burnett kindly helped me with editing and proofreading.

Finally, I would like to thank Elayne Horn, Barbara Rosenthal, and Mary Ann Spengler for their Wagnerian help and encouragement with this book.

Table of Contents

Acknowledgments vii
Preface 1
Introduction 3
Brief Chronology 7

I. The Individual Operas

1. Tradition and the Individual Talent in Wagner's Juvenilia
   YVONNE NILGES 9

2. *The Flying Dutchman*: An Introduction
   JAMES K. HOLMAN 23

3. Deciphering *The Flying Dutchman*
   GREGORY KERSHNER 31

4. Revelation and Obfuscation: Wagner's Readings in Romanticism
   for *Tannhäuser*
   STEVEN R. CERF 40

5. Romanticism in *Tannhäuser* and *Lohengrin*
   BARBARA JOSEPHINE GUENTHER 55

6. Don't Ask: Faith, Magic, Knowledge, and Sources in *Lohengrin*
   LISA FEURZEIG 80

7. *Tristan* and Ecstasy
   HANS RUDOLF VAGET 105

8. Infomercial in Three Acts: *Die Meistersinger von Nürnberg*
   NICHOLAS VAZSONYI 122

9. Relativities: Einstein, Wagner, and *Die Meistersinger*
   JAMES K. HOLMAN 141

10. Musical Characterization in *Parsifal*: A Study of Parsifal
    and Kundry
       JOHN J.H. MULLER 157

II. Wagnerian Opera and the Other Arts

11. Wagner and Dance: *Tannhäuser* and Beyond
       MARY CARGILL 175
12. "The Dream Organ": Wagner as a Proto-Filmmaker
       HILAN WARSHAW 184
13. Wagnerian References in the Fiction of Willa Cather
       RICHARD C. HARRIS 199

III. Wagnerian Opera in Performance

14. Michelle DeYoung: An Interview
       JOHN LOUIS DIGAETANI 217
15. Ben Heppner: An Interview
       JOHN LOUIS DIGAETANI 221
16. The Silver Age of Wagnerian Singing
       BARBARA JOSEPHINE GUENTHER 227

A Manichean Conclusion
       JOHN LOUIS DIGAETANI 251
Appendix: Discography and Videography of Recommended
       Performances 255
About the Contributors 259
Index 261

Preface

This collection of essays on the non–Ring operas of Richard Wagner is a companion to my *Inside the Ring: Essays on Wagner's Opera Cycle*. This book will interest the scholar and people becoming interested in Wagner's operas, and there are more such people as his operas are being staged by major companies more frequently around the world.

As Sarah Billinghurst, associate director of the Metropolitan Opera, has said, there is renewed interest in Wagnerian opera around the world. Thirty years ago, only the Met and the San Francisco Opera staged Wagner's operas in the United States, but these companies now have to compete for Wagnerian singers with opera companies in Chicago, Seattle, Washington, D.C., Los Angeles, Dallas, and Atlanta. Virtually every major world capital now has a Wagner society. We are living in a Wagner renaissance. *Die Fiegende Holländer, Tannhäuser, Lohengrin, Tristan und Isolde, Die Meistersinger von Nürnberg,* and *Parsifal* are being rediscovered as great works of operatic art as new designers, new directors, and new singers find new approaches to these classics.

The essays are by some of the major Wagner scholars and show the range of styles and approaches possible for the operas, and photographs of recent productions are included. This book will add considerable depth to an understanding of Wagner's complex but eternally fascinating operas. With its bibliographies, discography, and videography, this volume provides readers with resources to continue listening, reading, seeing, and experiencing Wagnerian opera.

There was a time when Wagner was a very tainted name because of his anti–Semitism and because of Adolf Hitler's horrible abuses of Wagner's ideas and operas, but that time has passed. Wagner's works need to be seen, experienced, and analyzed for their fascinating contents and multiple meanings.

Introduction

Coming from a theatrical family, Richard Wagner was immediately drawn to the theater and wrote plays as a teenager. Later he began taking music lessons in composition and eventually had the idea of combining Shakespeare with Beethoven since he wanted both theater and symphonic music in the same music-drama, as he came to call opera.

The first opera he wrote was *Die Feen*, based on Carlo Gozzi's play *La Donna Serpente*, and it was first staged in Munich in 1888, five years after Wagner's death. But it is certainly significant that he was immediately drawn to a mythic work. He wrote the work in 1834, when there was a Gozzi revival occurring in Germany and Austria, at a time when Gozzi's plays were not being staged in Italy. But Wagner could not get anyone to stage his first opera, and ultimately he came to think it was not worth staging since it remained so derivative of other composers of the time.

Wagner's second work, *Das Liebesverbot*, was staged in Magdeburg on March 29, 1836, and it was a resounding flop. Partially this was a result of the singers and the production, and ultimately Wagner denigrated the work as juvenilia, but modern productions of this work have succeeded with contemporary audiences. This opera is based on Shakespeare's *Measure for Measure* and has occasionally been revived. Both these early works clearly present ideas and musical themes that would appear in his later and more mature works.

Wagner's first real success in opera was his third opera, *Rienzi*, which was first staged in Dresden on October 20, 1842. Here Wagner finally tasted success. The Saxon king and his court applauded the opera, so it was repeated several times, and also staged at other opera companies in Germany. The overture become a hit all over Europe and was performed frequently, especially in Italy and France.

On January 2, 1843, Dresden was again the place for the premiere of Wagner's fourth, *Der Fliegende Holländer*. Wagner felt that this opera was his first mature opera, the first opera which was true to his soul and not trying to imitate other composers, but it was still a flop at its premiere. It must have seemed too startling and too gloomy to that Dresden audience, but Wagner revived it and it succeeded there eventually.

Dresden's royal opera house, now called the Semperoper, was also the place for Wagner's next premiere. On October 19, 1845, *Tannhäuser und der Sängerkrieg auf Wartburg* was performed. In addition to being placed in a historic fort in Germany, the Wartburg, this opera included the scandalous appearance of the Roman goddess Venus and her struggle to keep the Minnesinger Tannhäuser with her in her grotto while St. Elizabeth tries to return him to Christianity. Ultimately, the opera is many things, but surely it is also a critique of the Catholic hierarchy, since by the end we learn that the Pope in Rome has refused Tannhäuser forgiveness for his sin of living with the Roman goddess Venus, but the miracle at the end indicates that God forgives Tannhäuser even if the Pope will not.

Using the medieval technique of the miracle play, something Wagner would do in his next opera as well, Wagner had written a new kind of opera. The medieval theater troupes loved to reenact miracles on stage—for example, in the plays about the lives of the saints or even in the Catholic Mass. This Wagner provides at the end of *Tannhäuser* and *Lohengrin*.

Wagner's next opera, *Lohengrin*, premiered in Weimar on August 28, 1850, conducted by Wagner's dear friend Franz Liszt. Wagner could not be present at the premiere, despite Liszt's invitation, because Wagner was now persona non grata in all of Germany because of his involvement in the revolution in Dresden in 1849. Wagner associated with the other major revolutionaries there, especially Bakunin, which meant that the composer was lucky to escape with life and limb and avoid prison or even execution. Wagner was then living in Zurich, Switzerland, and trying to make a career when *Lohengrin* premiered.

Wagner's life was completely different and much improved when *Tristan und Isolde* had its premiere in Munich on June 10, 1865. Then he was the pampered darling of King Ludwig II, his patron in Munich, and the king of Bavaria. Ludwig became obsessed with Wagner's operas, and he even became obsessed with Wagner the man, so the king did everything he could to promote Wagner's operas with all the means at his disposal at his Royal Court Opera in Munich.

Die Meistersinger von Nürnberg had an even more glorious premiere on June 21, 1868, at the Royal Court Opera in Munich. This was certainly the most successful premiere in Wagner's career because Ludwig II was present in the royal box to receive the public ovation at

Die Meistersinger von Nürnberg, **Act 3, at the Metropolitan Opera (photograph by Winnie Klotz).**

the end of the performance, along with the composer. The date of June 21 was purposely picked since that was St. John's Day — Johannistag, or Midsummer Day in English. This reflected the connections between Wagner's opera and Shakespeare's play *A Midsummer Night's Dream*. St. John's Day figures prominently (and symbolically) in the final act as a celebration of the arrival of the summer solstice, the triumph of light over darkness. This makes a marked contrast to *Tristan und Isolde,* which celebrates the night and the lovers' yearning for oblivion.

Der Ring des Nibelungen had its premiere in 1876 in Bayreuth in the festival theater Wagner designed for this vast tetralogy. *Das Rheingold* and *Die Walküre* premiered separately at the Royal Court Opera in Munich in 1869 and 1870, but the entire four-opera tetralogy had its first viewing in Bayreuth, the small town near Nuremberg which Wagner chose to be the place for his own festival of Wagnerian performances. The Bayreuth festival, of course, is still going strong each summer. (For an analysis of the Ring cycle, see my companion volume, *Inside the Ring.*)

Placido Domingo as Parsifal at the Metropolitan Opera (photograph by Winnie Klotz).

Wagner's final opera, *Parsifal*, was first staged at Bayreuth on July 26, 1882, a year before the composer's death in Venice. Wagner intended *Parsifal* to be staged only at Bayreuth, primarily to support his wife, Cosima, and his large family and to also support his festival there. The Metropolitan Opera first staged *Parsifal* in New York on December 24, 1903 — the first performance of that work outside Bayreuth despite the strenuous efforts of Cosima Wagner to prevent it. According to American law, if not German law, the work was in the public domain and beyond copyright protection. Ten years later, *Parsifal* was beyond copyright protection in most of Europe so operas on the continent (and even Germany) staged Wagner's final work despite her objections. The work was just too important and there was too much audience interest to limit it to the Bayreuth Festival.

When Wagner died in Venice in February 1883, his amazing career finally came to a suitably dramatic end. His thirteen operas — not to mention his song cycle, the *Wesendonck Lieder*, and various other works — had indelibly changed the face of European music forever.

Brief Chronology

1813 Wagner is born in Leipzig, Germany.

1834 Wagner writes *Die Feen*, first staged after Wagner's death in Munich in 1888.

1836 *Das Liebesverbot*, first staged on March 29 in Magdeburg.

1842 *Rienzi*, first staged in Dresden on October 20, and Wagner's first success as a composer of operas.

1843 *Der Fliegende Holländer*, first staged in Dresden on January 2.

1845 *Tannhäuser*, first staged in Dresden on October 19.

1850 *Lohengrin*, first staged in Weimar on August 28.

1861 *Tannhäuser*, revised extensively and staged in Paris.

1865 *Tristan und Isolde*, first staged in Munich on June 10.

1868 *Die Meistersinger von Nürnberg*, first staged in Munich on June 21.

1869 *Das Rheingold*, first staged in Munich on September 22.

1870 *Die Walküre*, first staged in Munich on June 26.

1876 *Der Ring des Nibelungen*, first staged in its entirety in Bayreuth from August 13 to 17.

1882 *Parsifal*, first staged in Bayreuth on July 26.

1883 Wagner dies in Venice and is buried in Bayreuth behind his home, Wahnfried.

I. The Individual Operas

1

Tradition and the Individual Talent in Wagner's Juvenilia

Yvonne Nilges

> [M]y earliest efforts [... reflected] those general impressions of art which affect us from our youth up. The first artistic Will is nothing else than the contentment of the instinctive impulse to imitate what most attracts us.—Richard Wagner, *A Communication to My Friends* (*Prose Works*, vol. 1, 286)

I

If in all beginnings there dwells a magic force, in the case of Richard Wagner that allurement is effectively twofold. For the very first opera that the young Wagner completed in 1834—and which has, much like his second opera, hardly been accorded any attention in scholarship at all—engages, quite literally, with magic, whilst at the same time, it contains various presentiments, not to say pre-echoes, of Wagner's later works. Upon abandoning his first attempt to write an opera, *Die Hochzeit*,[1] Wagner, at the age of nineteen, decided to turn to a subject matter that had been dramatized by Carlo Gozzi and which, following E.T.A. Hoffmann's narrative "The Poet and the Composer" from the *Serapionsbrüder* cycle (1819–1821), was bound to generate an excellent "musical drama" or "Romantic opera" if set to music. Drawing on Gozzi's ten fairy tale plays or *fiabe dramatiche*, Hoffmann's fictional composer Ludwig advances his ideal of exemplary opera, according to which the music would emerge immediately from its literary source as a vital and indeed necessary product of the same. The young Wagner was familiar with Hoffmann's imaginary dialogue about the opera, and gladly took it as a personal model. By adapting one of Gozzi's magic fairy tales, *La donna serpente* (*The Serpent Woman*, 1762), Wagner composed a "grand Romantic opera in three acts" which he then called *Die Feen* (*The Fairies*), thereby initiating a long series of Gozzi operas that was to continue well into the twentieth century.[2]

Carlo Gozzi (1720–1806) ranks as the most important advocate of Italian improvised comedy, or *commedia dell'arte*, a genre that he both preserved and actively reformed. By the mid-eighteenth century, the *commedia dell'arte* had rigidified with the invariable repetition of the same stock situations. Whereas Gozzi's antipode Carlo Goldoni sought to remedy this problem by turning the *commedia dell'arte* into a more sophisticated, "academic" form of comedy involving a fixed text, Gozzi, on the other hand, defended its original spirit of improvisation, reviving the genre by introducing fantastical, tragicomic fairy-tale elements that were derived from themes and motifs from the *Arabian Nights* and an anthology of fairy tales by Giambattista Basile known as the *Cunto de li cunti* (1634–1636). In his preface to *La donna serpente*, Gozzi polemicizes against Goldoni's "so-called reformed and learned works," emphasizing that the most difficult thing in his own

> new genre [...] was avoiding repetitions, and inventing new and effective situations. [...] *The Serpent Woman* was my fifth Tale for the theatre. [...] When a "low" scene is developed on the stage with all the hallmarks of truth, and when it arouses interest and enthusiasm, causing people to attend the performance, it is no longer low. Rather, it is a useful and entertaining invention. To see if it is entertaining, you need only ask the audience. To see if it is useful, ask the actors, and you will find that such a scene is perfectly in keeping with the precepts of Horace [, whose famous dictum reads as follows: "Aut prodesse volunt aut delectare poetae"] [Gozzi 185f].

To the young Wagner as well, the idea of dramatic improvisation was without a doubt both useful and delightful, or, as Gozzi put it, "entertaining." Indeed, improvised theater was a concept which was to become even more intense and theoretically elaborated in his later years, although the role model he then referred to was no longer Gozzi (of whose plays Wagner remained fond all the same), but Shakespeare, whom Wagner could not praise enough for having created a "fixirte [...] Improvisation von allerhöchstem dichterischem Werthe" (a "fixed improvisation of the utmost poetic value").[3] Given the vast impact that Shakespeare had on Wagner's thought, and the supreme importance he attached to Shakespeare's theater — including the Elizabethan platform stage — it comes as no surprise that Wagner's second opera, *Das Liebesverbot*, should then in turn be based entirely on Shakespeare. But let us return to Gozzi's *Donna serpente* and *Die Feen* for the time being.

In his much later "Letter to an Actor on Acting" (1872), Wagner commended Gozzi for rehabilitating improvisation in his *fiabe dramatiche*. In Wagner's own adaptation of *La donna serpente* there was of course no room for merely sketched out scenes in the manner of an improvised scenario, and Gozzi's "low" elements such as food, hunger, stuttering or coitus, which are repeatedly turned into a laughing matter in the play, are missing in Wagner's "grand Romantic opera." So are Gozzi's satirical elements, which "prove that" Gozzi "viewed his [...] grand theatrical successes as far more than just a personal victory" against Goldoni: he also construed his plays as "the undeniable triumph of the principles put forth by the Granelleschi Academy" (DiGaetani 131). While Wagner's music was strongly influenced by the Romantic examples of Marschner and, principally, Weber, the names the young Wagner's characters bear do not lack humor: Gozzi's semi-oriental, semi–Venetian fairy-tale world is transferred to a fantastical, unidentifiable Nordic realm, in the process of which Gozzi's original masks, Truffaldino (i.e. Arlecchino) and Pantalone, are contracted into a single character called Gernot, of all names. Likewise, the humorous allusion to the heroes of the *Nibelungenlied* continues: Gozzi's Brighella and Tartaglia are reduced to a single character as well and now sport an equally incongruous name, Gunther. In general, most of the names were altered, whereas the plot remained broadly the same. In *A Communication to My Friends*, Wagner depicts the course of events in this first completed opera as follows:

> What took my fancy in the tale of Gozzi [...] was not merely its adaptability for an opera-text, but the fascination of the "stuff" itself.— A Fairy, who renounces immortality for the sake of a human lover, can only become a mortal through the fulfillment of certain hard conditions, the non-compliance wherewith on the part of her earthly swain threatens her with the direst penalties; her lover fails in the test, which consists in this, that however evil and repulsive she may

appear to him (in an obligatory metamorphosis) he shall not reject her in his unbelief [*Prose Works*, vol. 1, 293].

There is one major deviation from Gozzi's fairy tale which we shall elucidate in just a moment. Yet minor differences, however marginal they may appear to be, are often worth noting, since they effectively foreshadow — and in one case even refer back to — significant motifs encountered in Wagner's other works. In this context, the bare premise under which the fairy and her human lover have entered into marriage (and which conjures up the series of complications that constitutes the plot) becomes a decisive, virtually anticipating one: on the occasion of getting married to the fairy, in both Gozzi and Wagner, the human prince must not try to learn her name. In Gozzi's fairy tale, unaware of his wife's immortal background and out of curiosity, he nonetheless finally forces "her desk to find a letter with her signature" (Gozzi 192) — a comical, surreptitious action that is human, all too human. In contrast, in Wagner's opera the prince Arindal (cf. the Ossian tradition, with which the young Wagner had most likely been acquainted via Goethe's *Werther*) explicitly challenges his wife, urging her to let him fathom the mystery surrounding her otherworldly being. In both cases, the disobedience triggers the succession of unearthly ordeals; however, comparing this situation to *Lohengrin* ("Den Namen sag' mir an!"—"Thy name thou shalt tell me!"), here too it is the direct, outright confrontation comprising the very same question that causes Lohengrin's departure from his beloved Elsa.[4]

Another motif that Wagner added to *Die Feen* with reference to Gozzi's play is Arindal's madness in the third act. Unable to stand his wife's apparently malicious tests, which have in fact been imposed on her by the fairy king in order to prove Arindal's love, he lets himself get carried away and curses her, whereupon Cherestanì, or Ada in Wagner's opera, is in turn severely punished after having revealed her true identity. Whereas in Gozzi's fairy tale there are no signs of madness to be detected in the prince's behavior whatsoever, the young Wagner does not hesitate to make it clear that in addition to mere penitence, "Des Wahnsinns grause Nacht umhüllet ihn / und hält die leidensvolle Seel' umfangen" (XI, 48) ("The dread darkness of insanity has enveloped him / and holds his troubled mind enclosed within it"). The new-found motif of insanity can actually be traced back to Wagner's very first piece of writing: at the age of thirteen Wagner had enthusiastically indulged in writing a tragedy, *Leubald*. This very little known theatrical work is not yet set to music, but is based, in effect, on no less than nine Shakespearean plays. By compiling elements of Shakespeare's tragedies, comedies and histories alike, the young Wagner had arrived at his first use of (literary) *leitmotifs* in this maiden drama, employing detailed features from *Romeo and Juliet*, *Hamlet*, *Macbeth*, and *King Lear*, from *A Midsummer Night's Dream*, *The Merry Wives of Windsor*, as well as from the two parts of *Henry the Fourth* and from *Henry the Fifth*. As for the theme of madness in *Leubald* and *Die Feen*, here too Wagner applied a psychological plot device he owed to Shakespeare's *Lear*. Consequently, when in *Die Feen* Arindal's "wits begin to unsettle" (*The Norton Shakespeare: King Lear*, III, 4, vs. 139), we are dealing with a reminiscence not of Gozzi, but of Shakespeare, who, as mentioned earlier, also paved the way for Wagner's second opera, *Das Liebesverbot*.

However, the major modification that distinguishes Wagner's *Feen* from *La Donna Serpente* is implied in Gozzi's title and involves the imagery surrounding the fairy's punishment by the fairy king. Wagner recounts the conclusion of Gozzi's plot while underlining how far he chose to digress from it in his operatic adaptation:

> In Gozzi's tale the fairy is now changed into a snake; the remorseful lover frees her from the spell by kissing the snake: thus he [once again and ultimately] wins her for his wife. I altered this

denouement by changing the Fairy into a stone, and then releasing her from the spell by her lover's passionate song; while the lover — instead of being allowed to carry off his [... fairy] into his own country — is himself admitted by the Fairy-King to the immortal bliss of Fairyland, together with his fairy wife [*Prose Works*, vol. 1, 293].

Turning the fairy to stone, instead of into a snake, and her husband's method of breaking the spell were changes of which Wagner was particularly proud. *Die Feen* may thus be associated with the ranks of venerable classical examples, where the motif of a person who is turned to stone or becomes a statue reminds us, above all, of the myth of Pygmalion. The theme also occurs repeatedly in Gozzi — in *Il corvo* (*The Raven*) or *L'augelin belverde* (*The Green Bird*) — so that, in effect, Wagner "replaced one motif from Gozzi with another." However, "the way in which he interpreted it derives from elsewhere," i.e. from the myth of

> Orpheus, who not only tamed wild beasts with his singing but caused the very stones and trees to move [...]. (Musically and dramatically, the model for this scene is Hades in Gluck's *Orfeo ed Euridice*, where Orpheus's singing and playing melt the hearts of the unfeeling Furies [Borchmeyer 9f].

Nor should we forget the end of Shakespeare's *Winter's Tale* in this respect, where Hermione comes back to life precisely through the medium of music.

Not only are Ada and Arindal reunited at the end of Wagner's opera, but, unlike in Gozzi's fairy tale, they both become immortal: "Gegrüßt sei, Arindal, im hohen Feenreiche, / dir ist Unsterblichkeit nach deiner Kraft verlieh'n" (XI, 57) ("Welcome, Arindal, to the great fairy realm; / immortality has been bestowed on you because of your great courage"). Later on, Wagner alluded to what he then preferred to think of in terms of far-reaching transcendence and redemption:

> At the present time, this feature seems to me of some importance: though it was only the music and the ordinary traditions of opera, that gave me then the notion, yet there lay already here the germ of a weighty factor in my whole development [*Prose Works*, vol. 1, 293f].

Of course, if Ada and Arindal live happily ever after in the realm of fairies, any underlying tragic potential becomes itself transfigured and romanticized, with the result that one might ask oneself whether Wagner was not rather stylizing the facts by suggesting a coherent, pure, and "preordained" development from the operatic works of his adolescence.

An issue that was indeed to remain central to Wagner's thoughts and later theory, and which truly does manifest itself as early as in Wagner's *Feen*, is the composer's lifelong admiration for Shakespeare's *Midsummer Night's Dream* (later on, as had been the case before in *Leubald*, he would hark back to his favorite Shakespearean drama once again and make it one of the most significant sources for his *Meistersinger von Nürnberg*).[5] The enthusiasm Wagner expressed for Ferdinand Raimund's Viennese "Original-Zauberspiele" ("Original Magic Fairy Tales") in his late essay "On Actors and Singers" (1872) is part of the same context and belongs to Wagner's enduring fascination for inventive, "improvised" theater throughout his life.

On January 10 in 1835, the *Feen* overture was for the first time performed in Magdeburg, with Wagner himself the conductor. Nevertheless, and in spite of various efforts the young Wagner made in order to have the entire opera staged as well, he was not successful in doing so that year, whereupon he soon lost interest in the operation altogether and exclusively concentrated on his second opera instead. It is for this reason that the first full performance did not take place until five years after Wagner's death: *Die Feen* was first staged on June 29 in 1888 at the Royal National Theater in Munich. The same oblivion into which this first completed opera has sunk — quite undeservingly so — applies to Wagner's second opera, *Das*

Liebesverbot (*The Ban of Love*). The latter has been just as much neglected, although with even less justification, as is happens.

II

Jetzt gibt es Spaß, jetzt gibt es Lust! [XI, 111]   (Now let us jest and become sensuous!)

In *A Communication to My Friends*, we read about Wagner's mental state prevailing in his early twenties: "I had now attained that age when the mind of man, if ever it is to do so, throws itself with greater directness upon the immediate surroundings of life" (*Prose Works*, vol. 1, 294). Wilhelm Heinse's novel *Ardinghello* (1787), one of the last works that bears witness to the storm and stress movement, as well as Heinrich Laube's epistolary novel *Die Poeten* (1833, the first part of his *Vormärz* trilogy *Das junge Europa*) had left their hedonistic marks on Wagner's disposition, resulting in his musical conversion from German Romantic Opera to French *Opéra comique* and to Italian *Bel Canto* Opera, i.e. from Weber and Marschner to Auber and Bellini, respectively. In 1851, Wagner retrospectively commented on his conspicuous artistic change of mind:

> there was a possibility of my developing along two diametrically opposite lines: to the reverent earnestness [...] of my original promptings there here opposed itself, implanted by impressions gained from Life, a pert fancy for the wild turmoil of the senses, a defiant exuberance of glee which seemed to offer to the former mood a crying contrast. [...] The effect of the impressions produced on me by Life was still of general, and not of individual sort [...]. Whosoever should take the pains to compare this composition with that of the *Feen*, would scarcely be able to understand how in so short a time so surprising a reverse of front could have been brought about [*Prose Works*, vol. 1, 296].

As a matter of fact, it was in the same year—1834—that Wagner put final touches to the score of *Die Feen* while also beginning to work on the libretto of his second opera, which he completed in 1836. *Das Liebesverbot* is an adaptation of Shakespeare's dark comedy *Measure for Measure* (1604)—an extensively modified opera, however, which by no means adheres to the ethical, literally "measuring" principles of the original, whose title alludes to the New Testament (Gospel of Matthew: 7,1f.). Whereas the Shakespearean problem play powerfully revolves around justice and forgiveness, Wagner's subtitle, to begin with, reveals a considerable departure from Shakespeare's semi–Viennese, semi–Puritan (or English) setting as well as from Shakespeare's central themes of repentance and restraint: it was no accident that the young Wagner relocated the plot to what he considered to be fiery Sicily—a place where his vicegerent, a deadly serious German pedant, ridiculously seeks to spoil the enjoyment of its citizens. The full title of his comic opera subversively reads *Das Liebesverbot oder Die Novize von Palermo* (*The Ban of Love, or The Novice of Palermo*).[6] At first sight, it may indeed appear astonishing that Wagner would choose a Shakespearean problem play to inform his second opera, only to undermine the latter's constitutive tragic elements. Yet Wagner's attempt at a "revaluation of all values" was all but a misconstruction of, or even indifference towards, Shakespeare's "fundamentally deeply serious" original (*My Life* 113); rather, and in contrast to Wagner's earliest Shakespearean drama *Leubald*, the libretto of *Das Liebesverbot* illustrates a significant stage of development in Wagner's artistic self-conception, disengaging from mere mimesis and now embarking on a more inventive, by and large autonomous adaptation of Shakespeare's play instead. At the age of nearly twenty-three, Wagner thus finished his first artistic preoccupation with Shakespeare that was virtually all his own: his autobiography provides ample evidence that, nonetheless, Wagner was familiar with all the aspects of *Measure for Measure* which he himself deliberately neglected in his opera, and especially substantiates his profound understanding of Shakespeare's primary imagery, i.e. of gold coins and weighing human value on the scales:

> I took pains to interpret the solemn Shakespearean text strictly in this [altered] manner; [with reference to *Das Liebesverbot*, I considered it my task to] see only the somber, strait-laced governor, himself aflame with a frightful passion for the beautiful novice, who, while pleading with him to pardon her brother, condemned to death for illicit love, succeeds only in kindling in the rigid [... vicegerent] an even more fiery and dangerous infatuation by infecting him with the lovely warmth of her human feelings. That these powerful aspects of the drama are so richly developed in Shakespeare solely that they may be in the end weighed all the more heavily in the scales of justice was [for the time being] no concern of mine; all I cared about was to uncover the sinfulness of hypocrisy and the artificiality of the judicial attitude toward morality [*My Life* 83].

Consequently, Wagner took over less than a quarter of the original, i.e. merely five out of over twenty characters in Shakespeare, and only four scenes directly based on *Measure for Measure*, which itself consists of seventeen. It is above all the second half of Wagner's opera that deviates from Shakespeare's plot entirely. Instead, *Das Liebesverbot* boisterously celebrates an emphatically comical succession of events, in the course of which Wagner's apotheosis of the instinctual life, however, pays tribute to another Shakespearean character that was Wagner's favorite for life: Falstaff, the knight of the massive countenance. Live and let live, accordingly, serves as a motto for Wagner's purposefully carefree second opera, for the young Wagner was indeed following Falstaff's lead: starting from the latter's distinctive frame of mind commending the *conditio humana*—"Banish plump Jack, and banish all the world" (*The Norton Shakespeare: 1 Henry IV*, II, 5, vs. 438)—and ending with a judicial scene that resembles Falstaff's chatter with the Lord Chief Justice in the second part of *Henry IV* much more than it reminds us of its allegedly immediate examples, i.e. the two judicial scenes in *Measure for Measure*. "If sack and sugar be a fault, God help the wicked" (ibid., line 428f.), the ludicrous representative of whom Wagner leaves no doubt to be his narrow-minded, repressive German vicegerent.[7]

Compared to *Die Feen*, Wagner's *Liebesverbot* digresses from its original source in all sorts of ways: in fact, the digressions increase in inverse proportion to the degree that the opera as a whole arouses the impression of being uncomplicated due to Wagner's selective, strictly homogeneous approach that was to exclude all tragic, problematic elements. Yet despite Wagner's firm principle of reduction, his second opera is doubtless rich in content, as the libretto either modifies Shakespeare's imagery considerably or abandons the latter altogether by finding substitutes that served Wagner's own purpose. We shall direct our attention to these in a minute.

It is only the character of Wagner's vicegerent, Friedrich, that as a result of Wagner's "glorification of 'free sensuality'" becomes a mere type when "measured" against Shakespeare. In his autobiography Wagner recalled that he had named his all too meticulous governor "simply Friedrich in order to characterize him as a German," thereby contrasting this figure with the others, all of whom are Sicilians in Wagner's opera and full of zest for life (*My Life* 83 and 113). In contrast to Wagner's Friedrich, both the name and the character of Shakespeare's governor are far more complex and, indeed, render the problems of the problem play *Measure for Measure* in an exemplifying manner: the name that Shakespeare's vicegerent bears only sounds somewhat exotic, but the vicegerent himself is not intended to be a foreigner at all. The name in Shakespeare's drama, Angelo, alludes to the word "angel" which is ironically developed in numerous similes and metaphors in the play that associates Angelo with the devil — an imagery that Wagner did indeed take up, as he did also adhere to Shakespeare's imagery of ice, heat and boiling blood, though in a decidedly non-religious context. Shakespeare's Angelo is a believing Puritan who suffers existentially from his inability to keep his thoughts as untainted as an angel. Moreover, the connotation of "angel" in Shakespeare's *Measure for Measure* is an ingeniously ambiguous one, evoking the idea of a contemporary gold coin with an image of the archangel Michael (within this context, also cf. *The Merchant of Venice*, II, 7, vs. 55ff.: "They have in England / A coin that bears the figure of an angel / Stamped in gold"). Metaphors of gold, coins, and currency in the broadest sense run like a thread through Shakespeare's play, alluding to the chief theme of mere appearance and veracity, according to which the metals as well as human beings — and Angelo in particular — are tested as to their true value. Whereas Shakespeare's Angelo is an insistently tragic character who undergoes pitiful pain and experiences an existential crisis noticing that his literally angelic self-conception cannot live up to the "test made of my metal" (*The Norton Shakespeare*: *Measure for Measure*, I, 1, vs. 48), Wagner's German vicegerent of Sicily is all but "sicklied o'er with the pale cast of thought," and never even begins to question his desire for the novice Isabella (in both Shakespeare and Wagner, the young novice bears this name). Quite the contrary: the possession of Isabella, according to Wagner's governor Friedrich, would virtually absolve him of "alle Sünden, die ich kenne" (XI, 90) (exonerate him from "all sins I know"), so that the German censor Friedrich, unlike Angelo, becomes merely ridiculous in his desires and even goes so far as comically to plan to commit suicide afterwards, just so that his steely laws may be rehabilitated in the end. The psychological depth in Shakespeare, therefore, is missing altogether; so is the imagery of coins and weighing human value on the scales.

A fundamental element that Wagner added to his opera, however, is the motif of the Sicilian Carnival, as a result of which the second half of the opera in particular focuses on an imagery of disguise that could not be more dissimilar to Shakespeare's, whose drama conveys an utterly dismaying imagery of masquerade and of the theater. "Seeming, seeming!" exclaims Shakespeare's desperate Isabella in the face of Angelo's unwanted attentions, since she has considered Angelo to be a reputable, virtuous person:

> man, proud man,
> Dressed [!] in a little brief authority,
> Most ignorant of what he's most assured,
> His glassy essence, like an angry ape
> Plays such fantastic tricks before high heaven
> As makes the angels [!] weep, who, with our spleens,
> Would all themselves laugh mortal [II, 2, vs. 120–126].

This signifies a perverted topos of the *theatrum mundi*, and we may recall Macbeth's famous soliloquy in the fifth act in this respect, which presents itself as even more radical and disillusioning. Not so in Wagner's opera, where the carnival as an anarchic expression of sybaritic pleasure serves, quite on the contrary, as a symbolic, though exaggerated sensuous expression of liberty itself:

| Wer sich nicht freut im Karneval, | (If a man won't take pleasure in the carnival, |
| dem stoßt das Messer in die Brust! [XI, 111]. | You should thrust your knives deep in his breast!) |

As for the young novice Isabella, Wagner endowed her with a much more active role than she originally plays in *Measure for Measure*. "It was Isabella that inspired me," Wagner recollected the character in his later years: "she who leaves her novitiate in the cloister, to plead with a hardhearted Stateholder for mercy to her brother." In *Das Liebesverbot*, Isabella in fact contrives to paint her clemency plea "in such entrancing warmth of colour" that her plea becomes not merely an apology, but a veritable glorification of the love between the sexes and unrestrained sensuality, quite unlike in Shakespeare's original play (*Prose Works*, vol. 1, 295). Isabella's apotheosis of love therefore anticipates what Wagner was to write later on in his theoretical main work *Opera and Drama*: opposed to familial and, above all, brotherly or sisterly love, we read here that the love between the sexes is to be understood as a personified "revolutionary" ["Aufwieglerin"],

> who breaks down the narrow confines of the Family, to widen it itself into the broader reach of human Society. [The love between the sexes exceeds] Experience and Wont, and is therefore a view which takes us with all the strength of an insuperable feeling [*Opera and Drama* 182].

The notion of love as a fundamental turning point in life stirred up in a "revolutionary" manner is indeed central to all of Wagner's operas, and in the early case of *Das Liebesverbot*, Isabella too perfervidly advocates this same idea, thereby digressing substantially from Shakespeare. Unlike Wagner's Isabella, the novice in *Measure for Measure* adduces the concept of charitable love, of compassion and *agape* only when pleading for her brother's life; infused with a sincere notion of virtuousness that is even taken *too* seriously as it lacks an actual setting in life ("More than our brother is our chastity": *The Norton Shakespeare*, II, 4, vs. 184), she too has yet to find the appropriate "measure," as it were, and thus resembles Shakespeare's Angelo in so far as both characters adhere to a religious orthodoxy that is as problematic as it is (self-)destructive. Whereas Shakespeare's Isabella, at least in this respect, consequently serves as Angelo's *alter ego*, she categorically departs from her contemplative detachment from the world in Wagner's opera, where she becomes much more autonomous, even astute, and acts as Friedrich's direct antipode. It is worth noting that as a result, she herself takes up the role of Shakespeare's duke, who in *Measure for Measure* provides for a favorable denouement. In Wagner's opera the assistant function of the duke becomes superfluous due to tricks that are entirely Isabella's own. In the same fashion, Wagner's Isabella is a member of the convent for practical reasons — she has been orphaned, which is never mentioned in Shakespeare's drama — rather than out of genuine vocation. In the end, she is forever lost to the convent, following a young suitor in a triumphant procession that Friedrich is obliged to lead upon the duke's return to Sicily.

Wagner's reports of his arrangements to get his second opera staged testify how well he was aware of Isabella's much changed character:

> The police first of all objected to the title of the work [*Das Liebesverbot*], which, if I had not changed it, would have caused the complete collapse of all my plans for a performance. [...] Fortunately the sitting magistrate with whom I had to negotiate had not gone into the poem at all, and as I assured him that it had been adapted from a very serious Shakespearean play, it was deemed to be sufficient if I changed the title, which was startling in any circumstances, whereas the title *The Novice of Palermo* aroused no suspicions and its inaccuracy [with regard to the Shakespearean drama and the ever so differently characterized novice] caused no scruples [*My Life* 118].

Yet Wagner was to deprecate *Das Liebesverbot* in his later years, perceiving his second opera as a "childish" and embarrassing youthful transgression (*Cosima Wagner's Diaries*, vol. 1, 390). In 1866 — a year after his prose draft for *Parsifal* had been completed — he wrote a quatrain for King Ludwig II of Bavaria on the occasion of the presentation of the holograph score to his royal benefactor for Christmas. This stylized quatrain is written entirely in the spirit of Wagner's final opera, equating the earlier opera with Amfortas's transgression while hoping that the composer might be absolved by Parsifal-Ludwig:

Ich irrte einst, und möcht' es nun verbüßen;	(I once transgressed and now would fain atone;
Wie mach' ich mich der Jugendsünde frei?	But how can I cast off this youthful sin?
Ihr Werk leg' ich demütig dir zu Füßen,	I humbly lay its work before your feet,
Daß deine Gnade ihm Erlöser sei [XI, 59].	That it may find redemption through your grace.)

In spite of the cultic worship that devotees of a decadent Wagnerism granted Wagner as an accomplished composer in his later years — an "absolute" adoration based on *Kunstreligion* (religion of art) that Wagner visibly enjoyed, and which seemed to leave no room for more light-hearted works such as *Das Liebesverbot*— we have to bear in mind that Wagner had been utterly disappointed by the performance history of his second opera, a work of which he had originally been particularly proud. Wagner's later denunciation of *Das Liebesverbot* was therefore not least due to his thorough disenchantment, since, as had been the case with *Die Feen*, *Das Liebesverbot* was not blessed with success. Yet this time Wagner considered the fiasco even worse: unlike *Die Feen*, *Das Liebesverbot* was staged in Wagner's lifetime, and rather swiftly too; in fact, the debut performance (on March 29 in 1836, at the theater in Magdeburg) had been appointed to take place during the Holy Week, of all times, so that the opera suffered from severe interventions and abridgments. Later on, Wagner admitted that

> one could not blame the public for remaining completely in the dark about the outlines of the action sung to them throughout, because the management had failed to come up with booklets containing the text. With the exception of a few parts sung by the ladies [...], the whole thing, for which I had relied entirely on crispness and energy of action and language, remained no more than a musical shadow-play, to which the orchestra contributed inexplicable effusions, often of an overly loud nature [*My Life* 113].

This failed debut performance is but inadequately recorded: significantly, the only review it provoked at all was written by the young Wagner himself. It was published anonymously in Robert Schumann's *Neue Zeitschrift für Musik* and illustrates Wagner's great vexation (*Neue Zeitschrift für Musik* 4 (1836): 151f.). That debut performance was also to be the last in Wagner's lifetime. *Das Liebesverbot* did not achieve sustained success until the last fourth of the twentieth century;[8] a second performance in Magdeburg that Wagner was about to conduct had to be cancelled due to fisticuffs in the ensemble — a private, unintentionally comical "ban of love" imposed on the leading actress by her jealous husband finally crossed the whole performance. Wagner's attempt to have his opera staged that year in Berlin was doomed to failure as was his endeavor to succeed with a performance in Paris four years later in 1840: a French version of *Das Liebesverbot*, which Wagner himself had been participating in, did not progress beyond a fragmentary stage.

It was thus that Wagner wrote to Franz Liszt on September 8 in 1852 that he had not been

> rewarded [...] for my "Fairies," which I did not even have performed, or for my "Ban of Love," which witnessed only a *single* ghastly performance, or for my "Rienzi," which so little occupies my thoughts at present that I should not allow it to be revived, even if such a performance were to be planned [*Selected Letters of Richard Wagner* 269].

At that time, Wagner had of course already distanced himself from historical opera and turned to the primacy of myth instead. It is this third — historical — opera: *Rienzi, der Letzte der Tribunen* (*Rienzi, the Last of the Tribunes*), a "grand tragic opera in five acts," to which we shall now devote our attention.

III

> From his youth he was nourished with the milk of eloquence; a good grammarian, a better rhetorician, well versed in the writings of authors ... Oh, how often would he say, "Where are those good Romans? Where is their supreme justice? Shall I ever behold such times as those in which they flourished?" He was a handsome man ... It happened that a brother of his was slain, and no retribution was made for his death: he could not help him; long did he ponder how to avenge his brother's blood; long did he ponder how to direct the ill-guided state of Rome.

Thus Sir Edward Bulwer-Lytton (1803–1873), in 1835, begins his novelistic account of *Rienzi: The Last of the Roman Tribunes*.[9] Written in the Romantic tradition of Sir Walter Scott, this exceedingly conquering historical novel constitutes the source text of Wagner's third complete stage work (1840) that rounds off his juvenilia. While the plot dates back to fourteenth-century Rome, its degeneration from the virtues of the Republic and to the papal notary Cola di Rienzo (1313–1354), the literary discovery of the latter had — significantly — coincided with the French Revolution, whose cult of Republican Rome made it particularly receptive to Rienzo's vision of the Eternal City, as well as to his struggle with the nobili.[10] Correspondingly, the first drama dealing with Rienzo is the work of the Jacobin François Laignelot (1791), and the earliest English adaptation was written by Mary Russell Mitford in 1825. It was Bulwer-Lytton's novel, however, that unleashed a veritable flood tide of dramatizations in Italy, France, and most notably Germany — Wagner's *Rienzi*, among others, and even an operatic fragment written in 1841 by the young Friedrich Engels.

Following *Die Feen* and *Das Liebesverbot*, Wagner, who was now in his mid-twenties, thus once more took a turn in his development as a composer. *Rienzi* was an experiment in grand opera, the "most voluminous of all operas," as Wagner himself ambitiously remarked (*My Life* 187f.), aiming at nothing less than to "outbid" all previous examples of the genre "with all its scenic and musical display, its sensationalism and massive vehemence" (*Prose Works*, vol. 1, 299f.). According to Gerhart von Graevenitz, Wagner indeed arrived at a perfect imitation of a libretto by Scribe in writing *Rienzi*, a work famously, if inaccurately, described as "Meyerbeer's best opera."

Unlike the first historical drama in German literature: Goethe's *Götz von Berlichingen* (1773), Wagner's *Rienzi* neither avails itself of a pseudohistorical language nor of any storm and stress expletives, such as had been characteristic of his second fiery opera. Instead, the hero Rienzi is idealized in all respects — much more so than in Bulwer-Lytton's novel:

Das alte Rom, die Königin der Welt,	(Ancient Rome, the queen of all the world
Macht ihr [the nobili] zur Räuberhöhle, schändet selbst	You [the nobili] have turned into a robbers' den, desecrating
Die Kirche; Petri Stuhl muß flüchten	The Church; the See of Peter has to flee
Zum fernen Avignon;—kein Pilger wagt's,	To distant Avignon: no pilgrim dares
Nach Rom zu zieh'n, zum hohen Völkerfeste,	To come to Rome's high festivals,
Denn ihr belagert, Räubern gleich, die Wege;–	For you, like robbers, besiege the paths they'd take.
Verödet, arm — versiegt das stolze Rom,	Desolate, poor, proud Rome is exhausted,
Und was dem Ärmsten blieb, das raubt ihr ihm,	The pauper's last remaining crumbs you steal from him,
brecht Dieben gleich, in seine Läden ein,	Like thieves, breaking into his storehouse,
Entehrt die Weiber, erschlagt die Männer:–	Violating our women, killing our men:
Blickt um euch denn, und *seht*, wo ihr dieß treibt!	Now look around and *see* the harm you've caused!
Seht, jene Tempel, jene Säulen sagen euch:	Look, that temple, those columns plainly state

Es ist das alte, freie, große Rom,	That here you see the ancient, free, great Rome
Das einst die Welt beherrschte, dessen Bürger	That once subdued the world, whose citizens
Könige der Könige sich nannten!–	Could call themselves the kings of kings!
Banditen, ha! sagt mir, giebt es noch Römer?	Ha! Bandits! Say if Romans still exist?)
[I, 36].	

These verses are part of Wagner's introductory scene, where Rienzi blames the families Orsini and Colonna for Rome's ruin. The preceding offense encompassed a near rape of Rienzi's sister Irene, and it is thus that Wagner's papal notary exhorts the nobili to remind themselves of Rome's great heritage. Although Bulwer-Lytton's novel romanticizes its protagonist as well, one needs to differentiate between the degrees to which this is the case in the two works in question. Wagner's *Rienzi* opens with a scene that is neither historically authenticated nor suggested in the novel, although in the latter we read about a related episode: in the novel the Orsini plan to violate Rienzi's sister but are prevented from doing so by "Adrian di Castello, a distant kinsman of the Colonna" (Bulwer-Lytton, vol. 1, 30), who becomes the son of Colonna in Wagner's adaptation: Adriano. Yet, and most importantly, Rienzi himself does not appear in this episode at all, let alone deliver a speech as passionate as we have seen.

Likewise, and unlike both his historical and novelistic prototype, Wagner's Rienzi is (and stays) unmarried: his only bride, he claims, is Rome. Whereas for Bulwer-Lytton, Rienzi's historically authenticated marriage is of vital importance to the plot, Wagner, in his opera, chose to idealize his hero in such a way that the metaphysical cause of Rome virtually supersedes any other "revolutionary" love in terms of love between the sexes. Consequently, and along with *Parsifal* as an exception amongst all other operas that Wagner had written to this point and was yet to compose, *Rienzi* virtually replaces the "insuperable" power of love between the sexes by accentuating and, in fact, entirely transcending an idea instead: in this case, Rienzi's love for Rome.

Wohl liebt' auch ich!— O Irene,	(I loved indeed!— Irene, oh!
Kennst du nicht mehr meine Liebe?	Can you no longer recognize my love?
Ich liebte glühend meine hohe Braut,	How ardently I loved my high-born bride!
Seit ich zum Denken, Fühlen bin erwacht,	As soon as I could think and feel, I knew
Seit mir, was einstens ihre Größe war,	The greatness that had long ago been hers:
Erzählte der alten Ruinen Pracht.	The ancient ruins' splendor told me so.
[...]	[...]
Mein Leben weihte ich einzig nur ihr,	I dedicated my whole life to her alone,
Ihr meine Jugend, meine Manneskraft;	To her my youth, my manly powers;
Ja, sehen wollt' ich sie, die hohe Braut,	My only wish to see my high-born bride
Gekrönt als Königin der Welt:–	Crowned queen of all the world–
Denn wisse, *Roma* heißt meine Braut [I, 83f].	For you must know my bride is Rome!)

Bulwer-Lytton's work by and large adheres to the historical facts "with a greater fidelity than is customary in Romance" (Bulwer-Lytton, preface); despite various fictional episodes in the novel, this also implies a careful balance of both positive and negative character traits in the papal notary according to the greatest possible historical authenticity. However, Wagner's operatic approach to the subject was by its nature a categorically different one. The historical Rienzo's two periods in power, 1347 and 1354, are telescoped together; whilst the libretto alludes to several historiographical details,[11] it beautifies the tribune's allegedly altruistic motives in general, and the circumstances of his death in particular: unlike Wagner's heroic ending, the historical Rienzo did not die in the burning Capitol, but was murdered whilst fleeing from the same. So is Bulwer-Lytton's hero:

> Death lost all the nobleness of aspect it had before presented to him; and he resolved, in very scorn of his ungrateful foes, in very defeat of their inhuman wrath, to make one effort for his life! [...]
> Meanwhile the flames burnt fierce and fast [...]. The multitude were round him in an instant. [...] "Die, tyrant!" cried Cecco del Vecchio; and he plunged his dagger in [... Rienzi's] breast. [...T]he next moment the towers [...] had vanished from the scene, and one intense and sullen glare seemed to settle over the atmosphere,—making all Rome itself the funeral pyre of THE LAST OF THE ROMAN TRIBUNES! [Bulwer-Lytton, vol. 2, 368–371].

Thus ends Bulwer-Lytton's work. The novelistic account is closer to the facts than Wagner's opera, but nonetheless far from being accurate. In truth, the historical Rienzo's death was unequalled in cruelty and humiliation:

> Covered only with the remnants of his once magnificent costume and lacerated by the blows of a thousand swords and daggers, his body was dragged through the city, with his feet tied together, after which his head was torn off and his brain spattered over the street. [...I]n an act of gruesome symbolism, the leaders of the Colonna family then ordered the decaying body [...] to be taken to the Campo dell'Austa, or Augustus square. [...] Here the barbarically desecrated remains of the man [...] were handed over to the Jews, who burned him on a pile of dry thistles and scattered his ashes to the four winds [Borchmeyer 54].

When Adolf Hitler, for his part, took pleasure in regarding himself as a latter-day Rienzi, he thus misconceived the context as a whole. However, not only did he fail to comprehend the historical background of Wagner's opera, but also Wagner's work itself, whose overture was used to mark the beginning of his party rallies, and which he described as having had an enormous impact on him: "In that hour it began" (Kubizek 66). For in fact, Wagner's opera only affords examples of contrast between Hitler and Rienzi, who, after all, selflessly seeks to serve Rome and its citizens by effectively rejecting the offer of kingship and sparing his enemies for the sake of peace. In a similar fashion, particularly *Die Meistersinger von Nürnberg* was exploited during the Third Reich as part of the Nazi appropriation of Wagner's works.

Rienzi was finished at the end of 1840 and performed for the first

James Morris as the Dutchman in the Metropolitan Opera production of *The Flying Dutchman* (photograph by Winnie Klotz).

time on October 20 in 1842 at the Royal Saxon Theater in Dresden. Although this third completed opera of his proved to be much more successful than *Die Feen* and *Das Liebesverbot*, it reasonably "little occupie[d]" Wagner's "thoughts" in the time that was to follow, as we have already seen, since Wagner soon abandoned the genre of grand opera. His interest in history persisted, if we but think of his later projects *Die Sarazenin* [*The Saracen*], *Friedrich I.* and *Jesus von Nazareth*, or even of *The Flying Dutchman*. Yet in the case of the latter, history is already overshadowed by myth, a tendency that Wagner would then increasingly follow and, from the late 1840s onwards, raise to a matter of principle in his reform essays and *Opera and Drama*. Myth became a theoretically elaborate conception which gradually would outweigh historical opera in terms of the true music drama, and grow to be a distinctive feature of Wagner's later works.

Before putting a final touch to *Rienzi*, Wagner, at the age of 27, wrote a short poem which already seems to anticipate this very development; as humorously as affectionately, its few verses appear softly to bid farewell to Wagner's juvenilia, of which every single example must be regarded as a milestone along the way to his maturation as an artist and composer.

Nun ist es aus, das schöne Lied,	(Now it's passed, that merry song,
das Lied von meiner Jugend[.]	the song of my youth[.]
[...]	[...]
Ich wünsche Jedem gleiches Glück;	I wish to all a similar happiness,
ich gäb' es selbst nicht weiter;	I wouldn't pass up on mine;
doch denke ich zehn Jahr zurück,	but when I think back ten years,
so macht' ich's doch gescheidter.	I might have done it better.
(Paris, 4. August 1840) [XII, 350].	(Paris, August 4, 1840)

Notes

1. The completed libretto was unfortunately destroyed by the composer; however, those parts which had already been set to music have survived. The medieval subject matter of *Die Hochzeit* conspicuously resembles *Tristan* inasmuch as its chief motif, the *Liebestod*, plays a part. In fact, Wagner's *Hochzeit* stems from an anonymous short narrative written in verse entitled "Vrouwen triuwe" (A Lady's Faithfulness") whose ending is, in turn, obviously derived from the courtly branch of the Tristan legend (notably from Gottfried's predecessor, the Anglo-Norman poet Thomas of Britain). For a reprint of the late medieval "Vrouwen triuwe" cf. Friedrich Heinrich von der Hagen (ed.), *Gesammtabenteuer* [sic]*. Hundert altdeutsche Erzählungen: Ritter- und Pfaffen-Mären, Stadt- und Dorfgeschichten, Schwänke, Wundersagen und Legenden*, Stuttgart/Tübingen: Cotta, 1850, vol. 1, pp. 257–276.
2. Cf., for instance, the *Turandot* operas of Busoni and Puccini, Prokofiev's *Love for Three Oranges*, and Henze's *König Hirsch*. Hofmannsthal's and Strauss's *Die Frau ohne Schatten* is not directly based on Gozzi, but does take over numerous motifs and names as well as the general oriental atmosphere of the Italian playwright's fairy tales.
3. Subsequently, the German quotations from Wagner's works will pertain to the following edition: volume (roman figure) and page number (Arabic figure) of *Gesammelte Schriften und Dichtungen*, 2nd ed., Leipzig: E.W. Fritzsch, 1887; from volume XI onwards, they will refer to the *Volksausgabe*: *Sämtliche Schriften und Dichtungen*, 6th ed., Leipzig: Breitkopf und Härtel, 1911 (here IX, 143).
4. The two themes found here — a creature from the spirit world who longs to become human and who is prepared to foreswear his or her immortality for the sake of human love, and the tragic clash between the spirit and the human world — are symptomatic of many Romantic operas of the first half of the nineteenth century, ranging from Hoffmann's *Undine* (1816) to Marschner's *Der Vampyr* (1828) and *Hans Heiling* (1833) up to Wagner's *Logengrin* (1850). *The Flying Dutchman* (1843) is part of the same tradition. Additionally, in *Die Feen* and *Lohengrin* the linking element involves a test, however, according to which the human lover must not ask a question as to the partner's true identity: this was a classical motif, as Wagner was fully aware (cf. the myth of Zeus and Semele, or of Amor and Psyche, for instance).
5. With reference to this discovery and Wagner's ample response to Shakespeare in general, cf. Yvonne Nilges, *Richard Wagners Shakespeare*, Würzburg: Königshausen & Neumann, 2007.

6. It was not least the fact that Bellini, after all, was a Sicilian as well, that contributed to Wagner's choice of setting. Additionally, Egon Voss rightly remarks that the retention of Vienna, an approach that could certainly be regarded as appealing to the early Wagner given his oppositional mind-set at that time, would, on the other hand, have been synonymous with an obvious criticism of Metternich's repressive policy of restoration. Wagner's relocation therefore also implied a tactic sidestep to avoid prospective censorship.— Egon Voss, *Wagner und kein Ende: Betrachtungen und Studien*, Zurich/Mainz: Atlantis Musikbuch-Verlag, 1996, p. 53.

7. Wagner's indeed distinct sense of humor, which has unfortunately never been thoroughly investigated in the past, is perhaps conveyed most abundantly in this very response to Shakespeare's Falstaff. Wagner engages with this character from his earliest work *Leubald* up to only a few days preceding his death, when one of his last oral comments that have been recorded by his wife Cosima is, once more, devoted to Shakespeare's Sir John. To Wagner, Falstaff was the most original figure in world literature (and within this context, his aforementioned marked preference for improvisation becomes all the more prominent again); this said, it is not of little importance that in Wagner's favorite reading at that time, Laube's *Poeten*, recurrent allusions to Falstaff play a decisive role as well. For a detailed depiction of Wagner's relationship to Falstaff and Wagner's lifelong appreciation for humor in general cf. Yvonne Nilges, *Richard Wagners Shakespeare*, loc. cit.

8. The ultimate breakthrough of Wagner's opera was not until 1983, when *Das Liebesverbot* was directed by Jean-Pierre Ponnelle and conducted by Wolfgang Sawallisch in both Munich and Graz. Until the present day, the opera has never made its way to the repertoire, however, as has none of Wagner's juvenilia.

9. Quoted from a later edition: 2 vols., Edinburgh/London: William Blackwood & Sons, 1861, vol. 1, p. 1.

10. The correct spelling is "Rienzo," a popular corruption of "Lorenzo." Cf. John Deathridge, *Wagner's Rienzi: A Reappraisal Based on a Study of the Sketches and Drafts*, Oxford: Clarendon Press, 1977, p. 23.

11. As rumor has it, Rienzo supposedly was an illegitimate son of King Heinrich VII of Germany; the haste with which Riezo sought to implement his far-reaching political goals—and which actually forced him to abdicate and flee from Rome in 1347—is still indicated in the libretto, as is Pope Clement VI's antipathy with regard to Rome's dethroned liberator in Act Four.

Bibliography

Borchmeyer, Dieter. *Drama and the World of Richard Wagner*. Trans. Daphne Ellis. Princeton, NJ: Princeton University Press, 2003.

Bulwer-Lytton, Sir Edward. *Rienzi: The Last of the Roman Tribunes*. 2 vols. Edinburgh, London: William Blackwood & Sons, 1861.

Deathridge, John. *Wagner's Rienzi: A Reappraisal Based on a Study of the Sketches and Drafts*. Oxford, UK: Clarendon, 1977.

DiGaetani, John Louis. *Carlo Gozzi: A Life in the 18th Century Venetian Theater, an Afterlife in Opera*. Jefferson, NC: McFarland, 2000.

Gozzi, Carlo. *Five Tales for the Theatre*. Ed. and trans. Albert Bermel and Ted Emery. Chicago: University of Chicago Press, 1989.

Hagen, Friedrich Heinrich von der (ed.). *Gesammtabenteuer* [sic]. *Hundert altdeutsche Erzählungen: Ritter- und Pfaffen-Mären, Stadt- und Dorfgeschichten, Schwänke, Wundersagen und Legenden*. Stuttgart, Tübingen: Cotta, 1850. Vol. 1.

Kubizek, August. *Adolf Hitler: The Story of Our Friendship*. Trans. E.V. Anderson. Maidstone: Mann, 1973.

Nilges, Yvonne. *Richard Wagner's Shakespeare*. Würzburg: Königshausen & Neumann, 2007.

The Norton Shakespeare. Ed. Stephen Greenblatt. New York: W.W. Norton, 1997.

Voss, Egon. *Wagner und kein Ende: Betrachtungen und Studien*, Zurich, Mainz: Atlantis Musikbuch-Verlag, 1996.

Wagner, Cosima. *Cosima Wagner's Diaries*. Trans. Geoffrey Skelton. 2 vols. London: Collins, 1978, 1980.

Wagner, Richard. *Gesammelte Schriften und Dichtungen*. 2d ed. Leipzig: E.W. Fritzsch, 1887.

_____. [*Das Liebesverbot.*] *Neue Zeitschrift für Musik* 4 (1836): 151f.

_____. *My Life*. Trans. Andrew Gray. Cambridge, UK: Cambridge University Press, 1983.

_____. *Opera and Drama*. Trans. William Ashton Ellis. Lincoln: University of Nebraska Press, 1995.

_____. *Richard Wagner's Prose Works*. Translated by William Ashton Ellis. 8 vols. London: Kegan Paul, Trench, Trübner, 1892–1899.

_____. *Sämtliche Schriften und Dichtungen*. 6th ed. Leipzig: Breitkopf und Härtel, 1911.

_____. *Selected Letters of Richard Wagner*. Trans. and ed. Stewart Spencer and Barry Millington. London, Melbourne: J. M. Dent & Sons, 1987.

2

The Flying Dutchman: An Introduction

James K. Holman

It is a commonplace for Wagnerians to be transfixed by the historical context of the operas, how they relate to each over the fifty years from *Die Feen* to *Parsifal*. This is especially true of *The Flying Dutchman*, because of its critical place in Wagner's artistic development; it is at this point, after all, that Wagner's career emerges from the mediocre to the promise of great things to come.

A focus on context, however, can be a diversion. Seeing *The Dutchman* as simply the end of the past or the beginning of the future distracts from an appreciation of the inherent virtues and weaknesses of the work itself. As a matter of fact, the production and reception history of *The Flying Dutchman* was victimized by a kind of contextual tyranny from the 1860s until 1929, in that directors staged the opera in just this way — that is, as either past or future. The following is a brief survey of the opera's composition, its reception, and its performance history.

Inspiration: Norway, Paris, and Homeland

It is entrenched Wagner lore that in 1839 he and his wife, Minna, (and their substantial Newfoundland dog, Robber), fleeing Cossacks and creditors in Riga on the schooner *Thetis*, encounter a violent and memorable sea storm en route to Paris (via London).

Wagner has famously written about the voyage: As the captain of the *Thetis* sought shelter in a Norwegian fjord, "the passage among the crags made a wonderful impression on my fancy; the legend of the Flying Dutchman, as I had heard it confirmed from the seaman's mouths, took on within me a distinct and peculiar colour, which only the sea-adventures I was experiencing could have given it" (Newman 9).

In his luggage Wagner carried the work, composed in Riga, that he hoped would (and in fact did) make his name, but it wasn't *The Dutchman*. Rather it was *Rienzi: The Last of the Tribunes*. This opera and Wagner's destination both reflect the composer's miscalculated ambitions.

Paris in 1840 was still the glittering capital of Europe and the center of European opera.

Rienzi was a work in the French manner, a five-act historical grand opera intended to appeal to the current tastes of the French capital. In coming to Paris, Wagner believed that he was leaving behind all that was petty in the backwaters of the provincial German states. *Rienzi* would be his ticket to fame and fortune.

How did Paris react to this unknown Saxon of twenty-six years? The way Paris still greets its unknowing visitors — with contempt, rejection and humiliation. The Wagners came to Paris with *Das Liebesverbot* and *Rienzi* in hand, and also a list of people who might help them. The Théâtre de la Rennaissance actually accepted *Liebesverbot*, but went bankrupt before staging it.

Wagner was indeed received by important people, who in turn arranged for his initial, if less than penetrating, introduction into the musical world of Paris. Wagner made friendships, generally among a corps of struggling artists, and many of their friendships survived for years.

But the two-and-a-half years in Paris were emphatically a period of dashed hopes. The Wagners were poor — there are even claims of debtor prison. He put a few *sous* on the table by writing musical criticism in insignificant journals, and by copying and arranging the scores of inferior but more successful musicians. Even Robber ran off one dark night; Wagner describes a lonely and fruitless search in the empty streets.

Poverty and failure were exacerbated by living amidst the triumphs of others. Wagner attended performances of works by Hector Berlioz, extraordinarily innovative pieces that had an emphatic and productive impact on his subsequent creative life, but resulted also in an unhappy, competitive relationship between the two men for years afterward. Wagner also absorbed the colorful stagecraft of Fromental Halévy, whose wildly successful *La Juive* (1835) was at the center of the Parisian repertory at the time.

A more fruitful, but eventually disturbing encounter was Wagner's relationship with the king of the French grand opera, Giacomo Meyerbeer. As late as his autobiographical sketch of 1852, Wagner had nothing but kind words for Meyerbeer, and his generous efforts to help the young Wagner.

But years later, to his shame, Wagner would demean both Berlioz and Meyerbeer (but not Halevy). He would forget that he had learned much from Berlioz's revolutionary orchestration and liberated tonalities, and from Meyerbeer's genuine talent for stage spectacle — all of which had positive influences on Wagner's artistic development. But he would not forget that the less talented, more successful Meyerbeer was neither Italian nor French, but rather a rich, German Jew born Jakob Liebmannn Meyer.

Paris was the crucible, the transformative cauldron, of Wagner's life. Rejection became humiliation, and Paris the antipode, the enemy against which he forever felt the need to prove himself, and to vanquish, for most of his life. It was in Paris that darker forces — of envy, vindictiveness, and a seemingly unquenchable need to dominate — began to crowd in on his otherwise convivial nature.

Had Wagner been ordinary, the matter might have rested there, and he might have faded into a bitter obscurity. But Paris unleashed other forces in Wagner, beyond his astonishing will to persevere. Brooding in Paris, he somehow found within himself an almost spiritual solution to his artistic frustrations. As described by the musicologist, Thomas Grey, Wagner somehow rescued himself "from the career of a mere hack critic and arranger by the revitalization of his authentic creative impulses, and specifically, the impulse to (musical) *composition*" (Grey 2).

This re-commitment to creating music would no longer involve imitating the French style, as in *Rienzi* (or the Italian, as in *Liebesverbot*). In what he described as a condition of "utter homelessness," Wagner turned back to his distant homeland, no longer viewed as a backwater, but now as the sturdy and sacred cradle of the German masters—Mozart, Beethoven, Weber. Wagner now yearned "for the maternal bosom of 'German music' ... as the redemptive agent ... of his own artistic repatriation" (Grey 7).

And what was to be the vehicle of this transformation? Only now did the memory of the sea voyage—the violent storms and safe harbor of the Norwegian fjords—flood his imagination. He grasped that it would no longer be historical subjects, but mythology, and the weird and intoxicating legend of the Dutch sea captain, that would stimulate the onset of his real and original work. In the Paris suburb of Meudon he rented a piano, and flung himself into the composition, which he later claimed to have finished in seven weeks, the Overture written last. The result was *The Flying Dutchman*, a work redolent of newfound energy, and brimming with the surging vitality of the sea itself.

1842 brought Wagner good fortune. With Meyerbeer's help, both *Rienzi* (in Dresden) and *The Dutchman* (in Berlin) were accepted. Wagner left Paris, returning to Germany in the expectation that *The Dutchman* would be greeted as the future of German music. Dresden was indeed to be the triumph that Wagner had hoped for, but hardly as he had anticipated.

The Berlin *Rienzi* was cancelled, but Dresden took it, and the opera was premiered at the Königlich Sächsisches Hoftheater on 20 October 1842. And so, in a remarkable irony, it was *Rienzi*, not *The Dutchman*, which provided the composer's first triumph.

The Saxon audience was thrilled by the latest grand opera in the Parisian style. It was *Rienzi* that launched Wagner's reputation and career, leading to his appointment as Kapellmeister to the Saxon King. Nor would *Rienzi* fade away in the face of the ensuing music dramas; the Wagner scholar Barry Millington has written that "to the composer's embarrassment on account of its stylistic nature, *Rienzi* was one of Wagner's most successful works in the latter years of his life and up to the end of the century" (Millington 51).

To Wagner's disappointment, *The Dutchman* encountered a very different response. Premiered in the same theater on 2 January 1843, it survived a mere four performances, and was abandoned. This was not the opera audiences had hoped for from the composer of *Rienzi*. On the one hand, it seemed a regression from the current vogue of French grand opera back toward provincial German pieces, specifically toward German *Schauer-romantik*, or gothic romances, of passé composers like Marschner, Spohr and Lortzing. On the other hand, its forward-looking "symphonic" passages and psychological intensity were equally disconcerting.

Performance and Reception, 1860 to 1901: A Repertory Opera

The Dresdeners have not been alone in their ambivalence, for it has taken the world a long time to come to terms with *The Flying Dutchman*. The opera is indeed a hybrid, which looks Janus-like backward in the use of traditional forms and conventions—French, Italian and German—as much as it anticipates the revolutionary music dramas to come. And the more it has been probed, especially in the last eighty years, the more complex—and rewarding—it has emerged. This is aptly demonstrated by its performance and reception histories.

Due to Wagner's eventual ascendancy in the 1860s, *The Dutchman* would not remain abandoned for long. A dozen or so years after the success of *Rienzi* in Dresden, the taste for French grand opera had withered, while Wagner's two subsequent operas, *Tannhäuser* and

Lohengrin, were being regularly performed throughout Germany. At his death in 1883, and through the end of the century, Wagner and Wagnerism had become the most dominant artistic forces in Europe.

As a result, opera houses began to go back to *The Dutchman* simply because it was a Wagner opera. During this initial period of popularity through the end of the century, *The*

Hildegard Behrens as Senta in the Metropolitan Opera production of *The Flying Dutchman* (photograph by Winnie Klotz).

Dutchman was received as a standard "repertory opera": a reliable romantic melodrama, and a showcase for singers. (Carnegy in Grey 51) It is filled with set pieces—arias, duets, choruses—which the most bourgeois audience could enjoy. Daland's aria from Act 2, pleasing as it is, might have been written by Marschner, or Meyerbeer himself, and is jarringly interjected into the high tension of the Dutchman/Senta encounter.

The "retrograde" quality of *The Dutchman* was not lost on Wagner himself, and like *Rienzi*, was a subject of some embarrassment to the composer of *Tristan* and *The Ring*. He made significant, but less than extensive, revisions in 1846, 1852 and 1860, and later in his life made some effort to argue that *The Dutchman* was more consistent with his emerging theories and mature musico-dramatic styles than it really was.

Bayreuth, 1901: A Music Drama

This position was reinforced by his widow, Cosima Liszt Wagner, after the composer's death in 1883. Ruling the Bayreuth Festival with something like an iron hand until her own death in 1930, she brought *The Dutchman* to Bayreuth for the first time, in 1901.

Cosima took a revisionist, even polemical approach to *The Dutchman*—she wanted to prove that the opera was not an embarrassing throwback, but a genuine music drama, part and parcel of her husband's development of the "music of the future," and not inconsistent with the later masterpieces.

To accomplish this, she personally supervised significant changes. (It is common today to underestimate both her intelligence and grasp of her husband's intentions.) First, she cut much of the vocal ornamentation of the set pieces, such as the cadenza to Erik's cavatina in Act 3. She also staged the opera as continuous music, with no break between the three acts. Wagner had originally proposed that the work be performed this way, but early on recast it in three separate acts (Millington 51).

Cosima meticulously researched Norwegian locales and costumes in order to suppress flamboyant "operatic" qualities in favor of a more sober, authentic dramatic context. The 1901 production included Wagner's own revisions, especially in orchestration, which gave the work a more polished veneer.

Cosima also used Wagner's revised endings of both the Overture and the final act—the so-called "redemption" music—which clearly echoes the "transfiguration" music at the conclusion of *Tristan und Isolde*. The original score had ended with a sequence of abrupt chords, without the musical apotheosis. The important revision was written in 1860, in preparation for *The Dutchman*'s "return" (another notable irony) to Paris. As in *Tristan*, the surging climax suddenly softens, drops into a minor key, and resolves itself into a kind of redemptive transcendency.

In many ways, it can be argued that Cosima's treatment for 1901 was correct; *The Dutchman* is not a period piece like *Rienzi*, and it contains much that becomes characteristic in the mature music dramas. There are advances toward the composer's eventual, and particular, use of leading themes, or leitmotifs.

Senta's theme is interesting in this regard, as it illustrates Wagner's use of remarkably short musical "modules"—they can hardly be called phrases—of just two or three notes. The three descending notes at the beginning of Senta's theme is a transformation of the same module in the sailors' chorus in Act 1, which Wagner claims to have heard the sailors shout as the *Thetis* put in to safe haven. The same module forms a kind of closing affirmation at the end of the opera.

The Bayreuth Festival staging for *The Flying Dutchman* (courtesy Bayreuth Festival).

The final two notes of Senta's theme are also heard, repeatedly, at the beginning of the sailors' chorus. Wagner was hardly the first composer to make use of representative themes, but in *The Dutchman* we begin to hear elements of compression and transformation in ways that characterize the later operas.

Cosima also staged the 1901 Dutchman without interruption, as a single act. Wagner had originally presented the piece this way, perhaps to facilitate its acceptance at the Paris Opera, but later gave up on this notion, as it was not relevant to the Dresden premiere. "His later claim that it was in order to focus on the dramatic essentials rather than on 'tiresome operatic accessories' may be retrospective rationalization" (Millington 51).

The transitional music between Acts 1 and 2, consisting almost entirely of the development of the two-noted module cited above, is a powerful reminder of Wagner's emerging skill at transition, of which he was especially proud. In any case, Cosima embraced Wagner's later rationalization as part of her effort to project *The Flying Dutchman*, not as romantic opera, but as a full-fledged "music drama," or as musicologist Patrick Carnegy has put it, part of the "Wagner canon." (Carnegy in Grey 51) Cosima succeeded; her innovations, and the potent authenticity of Bayreuth, transformed and subsequently constrained the way *The Dutchman* was staged for many years.

The Flying Dutchman at the Bayreuth Festival (courtesy Bayreuth Festival).

Performance and Reception: 1929 to the Present

The most telling break with this tradition occurred nearly thirty years after the 1901 Bayreuth staging when, in 1929, Otto Klemperer, no great Wagnerian, staged a ground-breaking interpretation at the radical Krolloper in Berlin. This was a time of cataclysmic upheaval — of cultural, political and economic turmoil in the Weimar Republic — and battle lines were already being drawn between the republican avante-garde and the proto-fascist reaction.

Klemperer and his team staged the work in a style they called the "New Objectivity." The set were stark and minimally representative. The stage bore not a trace of the Norwegian folk, nor Cosima's meticulously researched bric-a-brac. Klemperer restored Wagner's original, brassier scoring, and returned to the abrupt denouement, without the transfiguration music. This attempt at a direct, ahistorical staging had the effect of letting the opera stand on its own, giving free reign to its original shapes and sounds, outside of the invented elaboration, by the composer and his widow, of its supposed context as precursor to the music dramas.

During the 1920s, Adolphe Appia, the reform-minded Swiss director, continued to open the opera to its own inner possibilities, and the process reached an authoritative peak in a 1955 Bayreuth production by Wieland Wagner. The opera was staged in the "New Bayreuth" mode: not much scenery, moods conveyed by dramatic lighting, and the focus on the psychology of the characters as they exposed their inner conflicts. Once again, the original score was used, and there was no transfiguration.

Once New Bayreuth had wiped the board clean, the gates opened to every possible interpretation. At the Berlin Komische Oper in 1962, the profoundly influential director Walter Felsenstein gave *The Dutchman* a provocative Marxist treatment. The action is dreamed by Senta, who wakes at the end to break free of capitalist constraints. The production was converted to film two years later by Joachim Herz, filmed along the sea in the style of an Ingmar Bergman film.

In 1975, Jean-Pierre Ponnelle took things a step further by presenting the drama as a dream — not Senta's, but that of a peripheral character, the Helmsman, who wakes at the end apparently happy to have avoided the entanglements with a woman as demented as Senta.

Ulrich Melchinger's 1976 production in Kassel offered a black mass of sexual and other depravities. Carnegy has reported that the ritual throat-cutting of a live chicken "excited even (Kassel's) well-schooled audience into hysteria and tumult" (Carnegy 118).

In Bayreuth in 1978, a production which is available in DVD, Harry Kupfer had the remote and unhinged Senta moving between fantasy and reality, conjuring the Dutchman in her mind, without realistic hope for redemption for either character.

Herbert Wernicke's 1981 Munich staging presented the Dutchman as an outsider seeking nothing more than middle-class comforts, while Senta, was moving in the opposite direction, a malcontented insider trying to escape the conventions of *bourgeois* society. Thus unfulfilled by the Dutchman, she stabs herself to death, at which point he drops anchor from his armchair.

The point is not whether or not these productions illuminate or obfuscate, but simply that the opera world has moved beyond treating *The Flying Dutchman*, as it once did, either as a romantic warhorse or as a mature and sacrosanct music drama. In that sense, even the most bizarre stagings have been a powerful homage to this opera, now given credit for more intellectual grip, psychic complexity and emotional depth than was imagined by the Dresden audience in 1843.

Conclusion

In the introduction to the first volume of his collected writings, Wagner wrote: "I am unable to cite in the life of any other artist such a striking transformation accomplished in so short a time" as occurred with him between the composition of *Rienzi* and *Holländer*, "the first of which was scarcely finished when the second one, too, was nearly complete" (Grey 3). In this, as in a great deal of what Wagner wrote, he was correct.

Yet, it is not quite right to say that Wagner's sea voyage inspired the composition of *The Flying Dutchman*. Rather, it was the psychic brutality of his failure and humiliation in Paris that ignited his creative imagination. His turn back toward musical composition, and his German homeland, propelled him toward an as yet unexplored universe of mythological insight and inner truths, a "phantom vessel" within which he would begin to give rein to his increasingly flawless artistic intuition. In that short step between *Rienzi* and *The Dutchman*, Wagner found the path to his authentic musical and dramatic voice.

BIBLIOGRAPHY

Grey, Thomas, ed. *Der fliegende Holländer*. UK: Cambridge University Press, 2000.
Levin, David J., ed. *Dutchman* Issue. *The Opera Quarterly* 21:3 (2005).
Millington, Barry. *The New Grove Guide to Wagner and His Operas*. UK: Oxford University Press, 2006.
Newman, Ernest. *The Wagner Operas*. New York: Alfred A. Knopf, 1963.

3

Deciphering *The Flying Dutchman*

GREGORY D. KERSHNER

Wagner briefly defined opera as a "sheltering asylum for all the madness of the world (Narrenhause für allen Wahnsinn der Welt)."[1] When a composer uses certain words and music to express his despair, the symbols he uses are not conventional but idiosyncratic. In short, in Wagner's works as a librettist and composer — and in so-called neurotic illness — the characteristic symbols are personal rather than social. Wagner in the *Flying Dutchman* does not communicate facts, but he employs music and text to express his inner feelings. The aim of this essay is to provide a systematic semiological analysis of Wagner use of language beyond the limits of discursiveness, venturing into the terrain of neurosis. The sociological and psychological have to be drawn upon in order to analyze aspects of the social whole. Their spheres are interdependent in *The Flying Dutchman*, but irreducible to each other, for the opera is a "unity of identity and difference with society." Obviously, German society reached into Wagner's psyche, but with him, it was translated into a language quite distinct from that of everyday life —"the language of the unconscious," or the primal scene of opera. The German language of his time and the language of his operas are related but separate entities.

Act I of *Der Fliegende Holländer* climaxes with a monologue by the Dutchman. Reflecting that once again his term of seven years' wandering is at an end, he bitterly laments his fate:

> The time is up, and once again seven years
> have elapsed. The sea, sated, casts me
> up on land ... Ha! Haughty ocean!
> Shortly you must bear me again!
> Your stubbornness can be changed, but my doom is eternal!
> Never shall I find the redemption I seek on land!
> To you, surging ocean, I remain true
> until your last wave breaks
> and your last waters run dry!—
> How often into ocean's deepest maw
> I have plunged longingly;
> but alas! I have not found death!
> There on the reefs, fearful graveyard
> of ships, I have driven my ship;
> but ah! the grave would not take me!

> Mocking, I challenged the pirate
> and hoped for death in fierce affray:
> "Here," I cried, "prove your deeds!
> My ship is filled with treasure."
> But ah! the sea's barbarous son
> crossed himself in fear, and fled.—
> How often into ocean's deepest maw
> I have plunged longingly.
> There on the reefs, fearful graveyard
> of ships, I have driven my ship:
> nowhere a grave! Death never comes!
> This is the dread sentence of damnation.
> I ask thee, blessed angel from heaven
> who won for me the terms for my absolution:
> was I the unhappy butt of thy mockery
> when thou didst show me the way of release?
> Vain hope! Dread, empty delusion!
> Constant faith on earth is a thing of the past!
> One single hope shall remain with me,
> it alone shall stand unshaken:
> long though the earth may put out new shoots,
> it yet must perish.
> Day of Judgment! Day of doom!
> When will you dawn and end my night?
> When will the blow of annihilation resound
> which shall crack the world asunder?
> When all the dead rise again,
> then shall I pass into the void.
> You stars above, cease your course!
> Eternal extinction fall on me!

The direction of spirit and main rhetorical gestures of the Dutchman's plaint are unmistakable. But only a close reading will exhibit the details and manifold energies at work. Freudianism enables us to pose the question of the relation between society and the unconscious in this passage, and I want now to examine it in terms of this concrete literary example. Even conservative critics, who suspect such phrases as the "death drive" as alien jargon, will admit that there is something at work in this passage which resembles Freud's famous discussion of it in *Beyond the Pleasure Principle* published in 1920. In the years leading up to his writing of the prose sketch in 1840, Wagner was suffering from acute depression. In 1835, he wrote that he was "filled through and through with melancholy and tears" and that he can "find pleasure in nothing, in nothing,—nothing!"[2] After a series of failed love affairs, Wagner finally married Minna Planer in 1836, who then left him for a merchant named Dietrich in the following year. Earlier in 1834 he avers that his "soul is awash in emptiness and idiocy"; gambling away his money, he has "allowed" his love affairs to grow cold.[3] In a letter to Robert Schumann, he mentions the "delightful delusion" that Schumann may believe that he no longer exists. He behaves at time like a madman.[4] Reflecting on his recent behavior, he concludes "I was insane, I tell you, I did not understand either myself or my position in the world. The result was a whirlpool of chaos & misery whose complexities I can look on only with horror ... it is scandalous and inexplicable into what an abyss I have fallen."[5] His appointment as musical director in Riga was not renewed in 1839, and he decides to learn French and attempt his fortunes in Paris. In order to avoid creditors, he and Minna departed clandestinely from Riga: "I'll write a French opera in Paris, and God alone knows where I'll end up then!"[6] In a letter to Meyerbeer composed in May 1840 when he gave the prose sketch of *Der fliegende Holländer* to Scribe and in June to Meyerbeer, Wagner speaks of his "abyss," his "recklessness," and threatens that if his patron Meyerbeer does not financially assist him, he "shall simply go to ruin" and bring his wife down with him.[7] In an earlier letter to Meyerbeer, written in January 1840, Wagner refers to his future "incredible fame" and success as a composer. It is in this unstable state of mind, developed over several years, that stamps the above passage with its characteristic tenor.

Confessional narrative lies somewhere close to the heart of Romanticism and its desire to know what it is like to be a unique and particular human being. Modern opera, from Romanticism on, begins to accord importance to confessional narrative, and Wagner practiced it extensively in *The Flying Dutchman* and in prose writings and letters composed at the same time. Romantics get their main impetus from Jean-Jacque Rousseau's *Confessions* and epistolary novels of the eighteenth century such as Richardson's *Pamela*. As William Hazlitt noted, Rousseau's writings exhibited an "extreme sensibility, or an acute and even morbid feeling of all that related to his own impressions, to the objects and events of his life."[8] These more or less intimate first-person narratives, whether memoirs, letters, diaries, or novels, provided a confessional narrative framework which eventually found its way into Romantic art.

Romanticism represented a new interest in and valuation of the individual that stands at the inception of modern conceptions of selfhood and introspection. Wagner fully embraced this new function of art. His letters written between 1835 and 1845 testify to his need to confess and express his bitter and deeply felt anguish about life. Wagner first began making notes for a projected autobiography in 1835. His *Autobiographische Skizze,* written in 1842–3, is a testimony to his self-consciousness as an artist and much of which served as the basis for *Eine Mitteilung an meine Freunde* (*A Communication to my Friends*) in 1851 and *Mein Leben* in 1865.

***The Flying Dutchman*, produced by August Everding at the Metropolitan Opera (photograph by Winnie Klotz).**

Viewed alongside his enormous corpus of letters and diaries entries, Wagner offers a portrait of an artist obsessed with his own personal development. What I wish to assert in this essay is that confession — as opposed to letters, diaries and memoirs — implies that Wagner wished or even needed to reveal something that is hidden, possibly shameful, and difficult to articulate. The confessional moment in Wagner's operas rest upon the assumption that they contain mental pathologies he found impossible to express in any other form, and which is captured in tropes of metaphor and metonymy in a manner of displacement and condensation as described by Freud in his *Interpretation of Dreams*. In *Der Fliegende Holländer*, Wagner dramatizes neuroses that he would in normal diary and letter writing wish to keep hidden. Other examples of this type of writing include Benjamin Constant's *Adolphe* (1816), a novel of self-loathing and, at the same time, narcissistic self-preoccupation and Ivan Turgenev's *Spring Torrents* (1872), characterized more by nostalgia and regret. Wagner, the omniscient narrator in *The Flying Dutchman*, engages us a kind of hide-and-seek, where the audience finds what is confessed by him.

Nevertheless, Wagner's confessional tendencies in *The Flying Dutchman* are predicated on self-awareness and his search for self-knowledge; he involves us in an unending deciphering and dialectics of confession. The case-histories of Freud confirm the lesson that the self as conveyed in language is not wholly transparent to itself, that in the story of *The Flying Dutchman* Wagner tells lies as well as truths.[9]

If narrative is viewed as rhetoric — as the telling of a story by someone to someone for a purpose and on some occasion — then Wagner's operas as staged, performed narrative can be

The Flying Dutchman at the Bayreuth Festival (courtesy Bayreuth Festival).

seen as the embodied telling of a story by a phalanx of performers and producers for a live audience on a public occasion in a social setting. Wagner's operatic narratives are "told," therefore, through what Keir Elam[10] calls their dramatic texts — the verbal/dramatic libretto and the musical score — and their performance text — the production that at the one and the same time interprets, visualizes, and brings to aural and physical life those dramatic texts. In a sense, *The Flying Dutchman* "shows" even as it "tells."

Operatic narrative may lack prose fiction's description of people and places, it explications, its narrative point of view, and its easy ability to shift time and place, but *The Flying Dutchman* offers instead direct visual and aural presentation of figures and places, enacted action and interaction as explanation, and a strikingly vivid sense of time in the here and now. In short, Wagner's *Flying Dutchman* depicts as it narrates. To all this, however, opera adds music. Like stories, music is central to Wagner's operas and in particular his employment of the technique of Leitmotif. It is central to his ordering, shaping, and meaning-making needs. As a narrative dimension to the opera, music speaks directly to the audience, not to the characters in the story, and hence conveys in a manner entirely unmediated Wagner's emotional states of mind. Only in self-consciously sung pieces like Senta's ballad do the characters share our ears and hear the music we in the audience enjoy. As a dimension of operatic narrative, Wagner's music reinforces or contradicts, supports or undermines the message of the dramatic and verbal story we see and hear on stage — as the use of Leitmotif in *The Flying Dutchman* makes evident. When Senta[11] in her famous ballad in Act II wonders where the Dutchman could be, the music tells the audience, but not her, of her impending fate through the "redemption motif."

Senta's Ballad and the Dutchman's soliloquy "Die Frist ist um" describe two traumatic episodes, opposing poles, around which the entire opera is constructed. In both a trauma is depicted and left unresolved until the drama's tragic denouement. The Ballad relates the legend of the Flying Dutchman, but is essentially a song of obsession, expressing her irremediable attachment to the idea of the Dutchman. Her entire being is dominated by thoughts, feelings of the fix idée. She has abandoned herself to rumination and brooding. The poem relates her meditations, reflections, and musing. In the course of her recounting the legend, Senta springs up and exclaims:

> Let me be the one whose loyalty shall save you!
> May God's angel reveal me to you!
> Through me shall you attain redemption!

Her narrative account possesses something of a ritual quality. All her mental effort is engaged in finding a solution by thinking, but a conclusion is avoided, and Wagner starts the process over again repeatedly essentially until her demise.

The same pattern of obsessive neurosis is expressed in "Die Frist ist um." The pathology of the doubting, rambling, repetitiousness, are symptomatic of an unresolved trauma:

> There on the reefs, fearful graveyard
> of ships, I have driven my ship:
> nowhere a grave! Death never comes!
> This is the dread sentence of damnation.

The Dutchman is pathologically disturbed, and the recollection of his doomed fate is presented in such a way that it cannot be dealt with or assimilated in a normal way. His ego is overwhelmed and has lost its mediating capacity. In this traumatic experience, a state of helplessness prevails, ranging from total apathy—"Eternal extinction fall on me!"—and withdrawal to emotional storm accompanied by disorganized behavior bordering on panic: "Vain hope! Dread, empty delusion!" His traumatic state fluctuates both in intensity and duration in his lament which closes with an incapacitating traumatic event, namely suicide.

For it is surely the case that *The Flying Dutchman*, without appearing to be at all aware of it, is a profoundly psychotic opera: the Dutchman reveals himself in the passage above as *non compos mentis*, entirely failing in reality testing. He feels a strong animosity towards life, and in the end achieves release from his condition by killing himself in an ambiguous act of self-love, revenge, and self-liberation. In this passage, Wagner is engulfed in a mythical state of mind, the whole death instinct is turned against the subject himself (both the Dutchman and Wagner)—but this is not yet what Freud calls primary masochism. It falls to the lot of the libido to divert a large portion of the death instinct on to the external world: "A portion of the instinct is placed directly in the service of the sexual function, where it has an important part to play. This is sadism proper. Another portion does not share in this transposition outwards; it remains inside the organism and, with the help of the accompanying sexual excitation ... becomes libidinally bound there. The death instincts, which are opposed to the life instincts, strive towards the reduction of tensions to zero-point. The death instincts are to begin with directed inwards and tend towards self-destruction, but they are subsequently turned towards the outside world in the form of the aggressive or destructive instinct. This instinct is held to represent the fundamental tendency of every living being to return to the inorganic state. This instinct is then called the destructive instinct, the instinct for mastery, or the will to power. A portion of the instinct is placed directly in service of the sexual function, where it has an important part to play. This is sadism proper."[12] The Dutchman activates the death instincts throughout the opera; moreover, he seeks the total "sadistic" annihilation of the village society.

The deeper investigation of the meta-psychological problems raised by these phenomena, the advances made in his thinking about sadomasochism, and the introduction of the death instinct enable us to circumscribe and differentiate the self-punishing behavior of the Dutchman. In "Analysis Terminable and Interminable" (1937), Freud puts forward the hypothesis that it is impossible to account adequately for the need for punishment, as an expression of the death instinct, by invoking the conflictual relationship of the super-ego and the ego. If it is true that one portion of the death instinct is "psychically bound by the super-ego," other portions, "whether bound or free, may be at work in other, unspecified places."

The question of the Oedipus complex is utterly central to an understanding of *The Flying Dutchman*. In Freud's theory, it is not just another complex: it is the structure of relations by which means the Dutchman comes to be what he is. It is the point at which Wagner in the figure of the Flying Dutchman is produced and constituted as a subject; one problem for him is that it is always in some sense a partial, defective mechanism. It signals the transition from the pleasure principle to the reality principle; from the enclosure of his ship to the Norwegian village at large, since he turns from incest to extra-familial relations; and from Nature (the heaving seas) to Culture (village life), and the post–Oedipal Dutchman assumes a position within the cultural order as a whole. Moreover, the Oedipus complex is for Freud the beginnings of morality, conscience, law, and all forms of social and religious authority. Daland's real or imagined prohibition of incest is symbolic of all the higher authority the Dutchman destroys, and by seeming to "introject" (making his own) this patriarchal law, the Dutchman forms momentarily what Freud calls a "superego" (das Über-ich), the awesome, punitive voice of conscience within us.

But the unruly, insubordinate unconscious of the Dutchman reasserts itself. He has developed an individual identity, a particular place in the sexual, familial, and social networks of the village; but he could do this only by appearing to have split off his guilty desires, repressing them into the unconscious. The Dutchman who emerges from the Oedipal process is a split subject, torn precariously between conscious and unconscious; and the unconscious returns to plague him in suicide.

The Flying Dutchman at the Bayreuth Festival (courtesy Bayreuth Festival).

The picture of melancholia presented in *The Flying Dutchman* reveals the violence of a compulsion to self-punishment that can go as far as suicide. But it is also one of the contributions of Freud and of psycho-analysis to have shown that self-punishment is the true motive of types of behavior where punishment is only apparently the unwished-for consequence of certain aggressive and criminal acts ("The Ego and the Id" (1923). In this sense we may speak of "criminals out of self-punishment" without necessarily implying that this process is the only motive for what is inevitably a complex phenomenon.

The term "narcissism" appears in Freud's work for the first time in 1910, when it is called upon to account for object-choice in homosexuals, who "take themselves as their sexual object. That is to say, they proceed from a narcissistic basis and look for a young man who resembles themselves and whom they may love as their mother loved them." The discovery of narcissism leads Freud — in the Schreber case — to posit the existence of a stage in sexual development between auto-erotism and object love. The subject "begins by taking himself, his own body, as his love-object," which allows a first unification of the sexual instincts. This view of the matter is again put forward in *Totem and Taboo* (1912–13). In general, all the figures in the *Flying Dutchman* are narcissistic since they are all poorly integrated into a larger social entity, guided by their own drives for gratification.

The unconscious is a place and non-place, which is indifferent to reality, which knows no logic or negation or causality or contradiction, wholly given over as it is to the instinctual play of the drives and the search for pleasure. Wagner's *Flying Dutchman* presents a crisis of human relationships, and of the human personality, as well as a social convulsion. Anxiety, fear of persecution, and fragmentation of the self are found throughout Wagner's works. What is significant is that in Wagner's works such experiences become constituted in a new way in the history of opera as a systematic form of expression. The harsh necessity Wagner repeatedly faced in his life was his need to repress his tendencies to pleasure and gratification. He had to undergo this repression of what Freud named the "pleasure principle" by the "reality principle," but his repression became excessive and made him ill. This form of sickness in Wagner was a neurosis. It is important to see that such a neurosis is involved with what is creative in Wagner's *Flying Dutchman*. The way in which Wagner coped with his desires which he could not fulfill was by sublimating them, by which Freud means directing them towards art. Wagner found an unconscious outlet for sexual frustration in writing operas. It is by virtue of such sublimation that his operas came about; by switching and harnessing his instincts to this higher goal, Wagner became the creative artist he is.

If many studies of Wagner have examined the social relations, social classes, and forms of politics which they entailed, this essay looks at their implications for his psychical life as reflected in his operas. The paradox or contradiction on which his work rests is that he came to be what he is only by a massive repression of the elements which went into his making. He was not of course conscious of this since the place to which unfulfilled desires are relegated is known as the unconscious. Sexuality for Freud is itself a "perversion" — a "swerving away" of a natural self-preservative instinct towards another goal. Wagner was never a citizen who could be relied upon to do a hard day's work. He was anarchic, sadistic, aggressive, self-involved and remorselessly pleasure-seeking, under the sway of what Freud calls the pleasure principle. He surges with sexual drives, but this libidinal energy recognized in his operas no distinction between masculine and feminine.

The Wagner who emerged from the pre–Oedipal states was not only anarchic and sadistic but incestuous; Wagner's close involvement with his mother's body leads him to an unconscious desire for sexual union with her. What persuaded Wagner to abandon his incestuous desire for the mother is the father's threat of castration. This threat was not spoken in the opera; but *The Flying Dutchman*, in perceiving that all women are "castrated" — including Senta — imagines that this is a punishment that must be visited upon himself. He thus represses his incestuous desire in anxious resignation to a life of aimless wandering, adjusts himself to this "reality principle," submits to the father, Daland, detaches himself from Senta, and comforts himself with the unconscious consolation that he cannot now hope to oust Daland and possess Senta. Daland symbolizes a place, a possibility, which he himself will be able to take up and realize for a brief span of time. If he is not a patriarch now, he will be shortly. The Dutchman makes peace with Daland, identifies with him, and is thus introduced into the symbolic role of manhood. He thus becomes a gendered subject, surmounting his Oedipus complex; but in doing so he has, so to speak, driven his forbidden desire underground, repressed his death drive into his unconscious; however, Erik was not ready and waiting to receive such a desire: it is produced by this act of primary repression. For a brief time, the Dutchman thrives in those images and practices which the Norwegian village defines as "masculine." He becomes in their minds and his own a husband/father himself, thus sustaining the illusion this society has of him by contributing to the business of sexual reproduction. The Dutchman's earlier diffuse libido has become organized through the Oedipus complex in a way which centers it upon sexual gratification with Senta.

The "royal road" to the unconscious is dreams, Freud maintained. Senta's day-dreaming allows us a privileged glimpse into her (Wagner's) unconscious. Clearly her day-dreaming of the Dutchman is essentially a symbolic fulfillment of her unconscious wish; it is cast in symbolic form because if this material were expressed directly to herself it would be shocking and disturbing to her, as it is to her friends. In order for her to love the Dutchman, her unconscious charitably conceals, softens, and distorts his reality, so that her dream become symbolic texts which we, the audience, need to decipher. Her watchful ego is still at work even within her day-dreaming, censoring an image here or scrambling a message there; her unconscious itself adds to this obscurity by its peculiar mode of functioning in the opera.

In order to explore questions about the relation between Wagner and society as represented in *The Flying Dutchman*, Freudian theory provides concepts and theorems which reveal much about the socio-psychological formation of his self. Psychoanalysis is argued to have shown how the lack of independence, the deep sense of inferiority that afflicts most men, the centering of their whole psychic life around the ideas of order and subordination, their cultural achievements, are all conditioned by the relations of child to parents or their substitutes and to brothers and sisters.

NOTES

1. Richard Wagner, *Opera and Drama, Richard Wagner's Prose Works* (London: Kegan Paul, Trench, Trübner & Co.) vol. 2: 12.
2. Richard Wagner, *Selected Letters* (New York: Norton, 1988): 24.
3. Letters 22.
4. Letters 29.
5. Letters 28–29.
6. Letters 24.
7. Letters 68.
8. "On the Character of Rousseau" in *The Portable Romantic Reader*.
9. Peter Brooks, *Troubling Confessions* (Chicago: Chicago University Press, 2000).
10. *The Semiotics of Theater and Drama* (London: Routledge, 1980).
11. See Linda Hutcheon and Michael Hutcheon, *Opera: Desire, Disease, Death* (Lincoln: University of Nebraska Press, 1996).
12. Sigmund Freud, "The Economic Problem of Masochism."

BIBLIOGRAPHY

Brooks, Peter. *Troubling Confessions: Speaking Guilt in Law and Literature.* Chicago: Chicago University Press, 2000.

Elam, Keir. *The Semiotics of Theatre and Drama.* New York: Routledge, 1988.

Freud, Sigmund. *The Standard Edition of the Complete Psychological Works of Sigmund Freud.* Trans. James Strachey. 24 vols. London: Hogarth Press and the Institute of Psycho-Analysis, 1953–1974.

Hazlitt, William. *The Round Table: A Collection of Essays on Literature, Men, and Manners.* 2 vols. Edinburgh: A. Constable and Co., 1817.

Hutcheon, Linda, and Michael Hutcheon. *Opera: Desire, Disease, Death.* Lincoln: University of Nebraska Press, 1996.

Wagner, Richard. *Richard Wagner's Prose Works.* Trans. William Ashton Ellis. 8 vols. London: Kegan Paul, Trench, Trübner, 1893–1912.

_____. *Selected Letters of Richard Wagner.* Trans. and ed. Stewart Spencer and Barry Millington. New York: W. W. Norton, 1987.

4

Revelation and Obfuscation: Wagner's Readings in Romanticism for *Tannhäuser*

Steven R. Cerf

Wagner was a voracious reader and a voracious reader with a mission — which would often revolve single-mindedly around whatever stage work he was creating. During his *Tannhäuser* mission, which took him in a new direction, this voracity was at its height.

What made his libretto to *Tannhäuser* a major turning point is that here, for the first time, Wagner set an opera squarely in the Middle Ages — a milieu that had not appeared in his previous four operas, but would be central to every one of his eight subsequent stage works. In fashioning his libretto, he exhaustively studied the major German Romantic writers of the nineteenth century's first four decades: both those who belonged to the circle of the *Frühromantik* (Early Romanticism) at the beginning of the century and those who exemplified the late Romanticism (*Spätromantik*) of the 1830s. Anything in print that related to Wagner's evolving creation of the world of the eponymous Tannhäuser was fair game for this, his first project back on German soil after two and a half years in Paris (1839–1842).

Three of the specific Romantic literary sources key to Wagner's basic structuring of *Tannhäuser* have a special significance. These are the first volume of *Der Sagenschatz und die Sagenkreise des Thüringerlandes* (*A Treasury of the Tales of Thuringian Legends and Legend Cycles*) (1835) by Ludwig Bechstein (1801–1860), *Der Runenberg* (*The Mountain of Runes*) (1802) by Ludwig Tieck (1773–1853) and the ballad "Der Tannhäuser" (1836) by Heinrich Heine (1797–1856). In Bechstein's travelogue/folk-history, Wagner found two elements crucial for his opera: a description of the prominent role of the fortress castle of the Wartburg (not only in regional Thuringian history, but in German history as a whole) and the author's melding of the Tannhäuser myth with the Wartburg minstrel contest. In the Tieck novella, Wagner saw a gripping psychological study of a protagonist torn between two worlds: the pagan world of sensuality that he finds in the mysterious female figure associated with elevated terrain of the eponymous mountain and the pure, but flat, world represented by the piety of his wife, tellingly named Elisabeth. In Heine's ballad, the extended opening portion underscores Tannhäuser's plaintive longing to be free of Venus's ensnaring blandishments — not out of moral guilt, but to escape his all-encompassing paralytic emotional state. What these three seminal sources have in common is that Wagner never publicly acknowledged his creative debt to them.

One might ask why Wagner needed these mediating Romantic texts to gain access to the medieval topics that he would spend forty-plus years mining. As scholars today point out, Wagner was able to read Middle High German literature and to make out Old Norse. His personal library in Dresden contained excellent philologically-grounded Middle High German and Old Norse editions (Mertens 237). The answer to this question is that Wagner also required the perspective provided by such Romantics as Bechstein, Tieck, and Heine, whose historical and national bent led them to rediscover and celebrate the richness of Germanic medieval thought and culture. Through the Romanticists' lens, Wagner was able to align himself with his contemporary artistic world in tapping those six-hundred-year-old national roots that had been neglected by the German eighteenth-century Enlightenment thinkers' adherence to classical antiquity. Steeped as Wagner was in this nineteenth-century Romantic reception of the medieval legend, it is not surprising that he would classify *Tannhäuser* on the score's original title page as: "Grosse romantische Oper"—"Grand Romantic Opera" (Csampai and Holland 33). He was, thus, challenging the hegemony of French grand opera with his own first embrace of a German historical period.

We know from Wagner's autobiographical account that at the end of June of 1842, he took his leave from his wife Minna, who was at the baths in Teplitz, and in true Romantic fashion set out on a solitary hike through the Bohemian mountains, carrying the works of a variety of German Romantic writers in his rucksack. That he had gathered these sources months earlier in Paris, before returning to Germany, is clear from an extended entry in his *My Life* (*Mein Leben*) written close to twenty-five years later (1865): "All I regarded as inherently German had attracted me with ever-increasing force and impelled me to look for its deepest meaning with enthusiastic longing, and here I suddenly found it in the simple retelling of the legend based on the ancient, well-known ballad of Tannhäuser." Wagner did not indicate whose "simple retelling" of the tale he read—a significant omission that will be examined later. Wagner continues: "Of course I already knew the basic outlines of the [Tannhäuser] story from Tieck's version in his *Phantasus* [collection of artistic fairy tales published in 1812]; yet his conception of the subject had led me back in the direction of fantasy, as evoked for me by Hoffmann, and I had in no way felt myself tempted to undertake an adaptation of the material for dramatic purposes. The element of the folk book [i.e. the simple retelling] which made such an impact on me was the connection, if only fleetingly set forth, of Tannhäuser with the contest of the song at the Wartburg. I was also familiar with this [contest] through Hoffmann's story in his *Serapionsbrüder*; but I felt that [Hoffmann] had a distorted view of this old material and I now wanted to form a more authentic picture of this attractive legend for myself. Then [in Paris, Samuel] Lehrs (1806–1843) brought me the annual proceedings of the Königsberg Germanic Society, which included C.T.L. Lucas's critical study of the 'Wartburg Contest,' even giving the text in the original language. Although I could use virtually none of the material from this authentic version for my own purposes, it nonetheless showed me the German Middle Ages in a significant coloring I had not yet dreamed of. In the same [folk book] volume I also found, as a continuation of the Wartburg poem, a piece of criticism about the poem *Lohengrin*, together with a lengthy narrative of the principal content of this rambling epic" (*My Life* 212–13).

What is revelatory about this passage is Wagner's self-claimed departure from both of Tieck's *Der getreue Eckhart und der Tannenhäuser* (*Faithful Eckart and Tannenhäuser*) (1799) and E.T.A. Hoffmann's *Der Sängerkrieg* (*The Contest of the Singers*) (1818). Also illuminating

Jessye Norman portrays Elisabeth in the Metropolitan Opera production of *Tannhäuser* (photograph by Winnie Klotz).

is his rejection of the Lucas chronicle for its lack of imaginative scope and possibly the writer's view that the two contemporary minstrels Tannhäuser and Heinrich von Ofterdingen (actually a fictional creation) were related. But what of the folk book? Wagner names no author but does, tellingly, mention the interconnection between the folk book and *Lohengrin*. This oblique reference incontrovertibly establishes his source as Bechstein's Tannhäuser narrative, which also connects the hero—caught between Venus's domain near the Wartburg and the Wartburg itself—to the Wartburg song contest. Bechstein's account tellingly closes with a Middle High German Tannhäuser ballad (Bechstein 141–45).

During this 1842 hike, Wagner began to outline the seminal prose-draft-outline-version of the libretto for a three-act opera, *Der Venusberg* (*The Mountain of Venus*) while jotting down a number of musical themes. The composer was veritably "continuing the work of Carl Maria von Weber whose friend Clemens Brentano had begun to fashion a [librettistic] work on the Tannhäuser legend, but had laid it aside" (Gutman 85).

In the spring of 1843, Wagner completed the *Tannhäuser*-libretto. The original artistic fairy-tale working title had by now metamorphosed into the two-part: *Tannhäuser und der Sängerkrieg auf Wartburg—Tannhäuser and the Contest of the Singers at Wartburg*. This contextual title immediately places the conflicted hero both with his fellow minstrels and in the fabled castle fortress—and, further, reveals the protagonist's status as a national artist. The use of the word "und" ("and") instead of the traditional word in such double titles "oder" or "or" is key: by employing "und," Wagner literally announces that he has conjoined the Tannhäuser myth with the myth of the singers' contest. Also, the word Wartburg in the original German title is not introduced with the modifying definite article in the dative case, "der." Instead, the absence of a restrictive definite article immediately underscores the Wartburg as an icon of surmounting national importance.

Wagner was doubtless attracted to the self-taught cultural anthropologist Bechstein because that writer repeatedly interwove the theme of the Wartburg into the stories of *Treasury of Legends*. Reflecting Bechstein's attention to that *topos*, Wagner has set each act, or part of each act, in or just outside of the Wartburg. The first act's third scene takes place in a sun-splashed spring landscape "from which in the background right, the Wartburg can be seen" (Pahlen 47). The second act is entirely set "in the hall of the minstrels in the Wartburg" (Pahlen 61). The third act unfolds first "in an autumn landscape near the Wartburg" and then "in the valley in front of the Wartburg just as at the conclusion of Act One" (Pahlen 103).

Significantly, when Wagner and his wife returned to Dresden from Paris in April of 1842, their trip took them past the Wartburg. In *My Life*, it is the Wartburg that literally invites the composer to turn to his first artistic project back again on German soil: "The one real ray of light was our view of the Wartburg, past which we drove during the only sunlit hour of this journey. The sight of the mountain-top castle, clearly visible at great distance to those approaching from the Fulda side, stirred me very warmly. I at once mentally christened a neighboring ridge the 'Hörselberg' and thus constructed, as we drove through the valley, the scene for the third act of my *Tannhäuser* in an image so clear that I could always recall it vividly.... It seemed a particularly prophetic indication that I should first sight the Wartburg, so rich in history and myth, at precisely this moment" (*My Life* 219).

Three thematic features made Bechstein's *Treasury of Legends* just as welcome to the thirty-year-old composer/librettist three months later: not only the two already discussed—the prominence attached to the Wartburg (19–27); and the section featuring Tannhäuser being waylaid by Venus, just as he is about to enter the singers' contest (137–38)—but also Bechstein's emphasis on the timelessness of medieval saga (Bechstein 13–18).

Richard Cassilly stars in the title role of *Tannhäuser* at the Metropolitan Opera (photograph by Winnie Klotz).

The third act of *Tannhäuser* at the Bayreuth Festival (courtesy Bayreuth Festival).

Bechstein, a pharmacist, turned ducal librarian, a devout soul, naturalist, Freemason, and father of six saw himself directly in the line of those eighteenth- and nineteenth-century tale and verse collectors in the field: e.g. Herder, Brentano, Arnim and the Grimm brothers. Traveling into the hinterland of his native Thuringia, geographically at the heart of the German lands, he collected oral history via homespun legend-like tales chiefly from the older citizenry in the remote corners of the countryside. As Bechstein rhapsodizes: "The saga is the mother of History: it is the purple-colored dawn at morn which precedes Historia's sun. The saga is the sanctified and collective property of the people which it guards faithfully and in peace in its natural habitat of meadows and forests and mountains" (13).

As already suggested, the Wartburg's central role in Bechstein surely fascinated Wagner. The autodidact evokes not only the castle fortress of medieval times, but states in his personalizing prefatory poem: "Du, Wartburg schaust herunter vom Berg, Du stolze Zier, /Ein Greisenbild, doch munter naht frohe Jugend Dir." ("Thou Wartburg, gazest down from the mountain, thou proud ornament, /A picture of old age, yet happy youth energetically approach you") (Bechstein 9). Here he alludes to the longevity of this German architectural icon: to its age-old significance within German thought and culture. Containing one of the few well-preserved Romanesque palaces in existence, the Wartburg during the Reformation provided refuge for Martin Luther, who completed his translation of the New Testament there. On October 18, 1817, less than three decades before the first performance of *Tannhäuser*, the fortress served as the site for the student celebration or *Wartburgfest*, hosted by liberally progressive university students from Jena and their cohorts from many other German-speaking lands to celebrate the tercentenary of Luther's Reformation and his posting of the ninety-five theses — and, moreover, the fourth anniversary of Napoleon's defeat at the Battle of the Nations in Leipzig. At that *Wartburgfest*, the seven to eight hundred youths referred to by Bechstein

Tatiana Troyanos as Venus in the Metropolitan Opera version of *Tannhäuser* (photograph by Winnie Klotz).

unfurled their own newly adopted tricolor of black, red, and gold, the German flag, as we know it today. For the first time in public they revealed the three color banner representing the uniforms they had worn only a few years before, when operating behind the French lines during the Napoleonic Wars: red for their uniform coats, black for the trim, and gold for the buttons (Schulze 110). In fact, the assembly turned into a demonstration for a unified and centralized Germany with a growing national consciousness, not unlike Landgrave Hermann's resounding call against the Guelphs in Wagner's *Tannhäuser* midway through Act Two (Pahlen 73). This politically progressive, Young German slant informs Wolfram's later reference to nationalistic heroes as being "tapfer, deutsch und weise"—"brave, German and wise" (Pahlen 75). Such Middle High German writers as Wolfram von Eschenbach and Walter von der Vogelweide (another character in the opera) referred in their verses to the crowds of people in the Wartburg and the "people's noise." Even in the monarchic middle ages, the Wartburg served emblematically as a house of the people. As Richard Wagner told his second wife, Cosima in 1873, "In medieval times priests and monks despised life, and [the minstrel] knights rescued it through their poetry, the outward symbol of this was the Wartburg" (Cosima Wagner v. I 645–46).

Most significantly for Wagner's opera, it is Bechstein who, as mentioned earlier, brings together the Venus-Tannhäuser myth with the Singers' Contest in the Wartburg (Bechstein 137–140). Just as Bechstein's Tannhäuser is about to enter the Wartburg, he hears the beguiling song of the beautiful siren, who is none other than Venus (138). In this account, the Venusberg of the opera's original title and, tellingly, the "lower depths" from which the love goddess's song emanates are at the foot of the Wartburg. Bechstein's Tannhäuser is so smitten by Venus that he remains at the Venusberg for close to a year before becoming sated. Finally out of desperation, he pleads with Venus to be released. Just as in the medieval ballad included

Tannhäuser, Act 1, the Philippe Arlaud production at the Bayreuth Festival (courtesy Bayreuth Festival).

in Bechstein, when Tannhäuser cries out the name of the Virgin Mary and Venus feels compelled to release him (Bechstein 143) — Mariology [the worshipping of the Virgin Mary] triumphing over the pagan goddess — so, too, does the Wagnerian hero gain his physical release by crying out the Virgin's name (Pahlen 47). In addition, in both Bechstein and Wagner, Venus's parting threat centers on Tannhäuser; despite his physical departure from her realm, she bewitches him into continuing to sing her praises, which he, of course, does in the opera's second act (Pahlen 87). What must have fascinated Wagner in reading Bechstein was clearly not only the conjoining of the two different myths, but the geographical proximity of these two antipodes, the Venusberg and the Wartburg (Bechstein 138); for they both occupy simultaneously psychically and emotionally the same inner-being of Tannhäuser. To convey Tannhäuser's torn state, Wagner carefully crafts his stage directions linking the two different stage settings of the first act in the opera's original Dresden Version: "Venus collapses with a scream and disappears. With lightning speed — ['Blitzschnelle'] the scene is changed. Tannhäuser who has not altered his position, finds himself suddenly transported into a beautiful valley" (Pahlen 47). The two conflicting worlds that Tannhäuser synchronistically occupies are shown without having the hero physically move, thus underscoring his residence in both.

That Wagner gave no credit to Bechstein is scarcely surprising. As a populist, in-the-field-cultural-literary investigator, the Thuringian did not have the cachet of such imaginative poets as Hoffmann and Tieck. Nor, as an autodidact, did Bechstein have the academic standing of a Lucas. Furthermore, as the extended quotation from *My Life* indicates, Wagner wanted to highlight his direct contact with original sources, and it would not serve Wagner to reveal that Bechstein acted as the intermediary compiler of the original folk book. Another reason for this cover-up would be that Bechstein's account of medieval Brabant was conceivably a source for his next opera, *Lohengrin* (1848) (Bechstein 83–88). When writing *My Life* in the 1860s, Wagner might have thought it embarrassing to connect Bechstein to two of his consecutive stage works, even though Wagner there makes oblique reference to *Lohengrin*. Such a slight to Bechstein was to be repeated by Wagner's own most famous student decades later, when Engelbert Humperdinck (1854–1921) kept publicly mum about having heavily drawn from Bechtsteinian source-material for his *Hänsel und Gretel*-opera (1893), thus allowing the world of opera erroneously to believe that he was setting the Grimms' fairy-tale to music (Cerf 15–17).

If Bechstein, as late–Romantic anthologizer, provided Wagner with the encouragement of employing such nationalistically conscious icons as the Wartburg and the singers' contest together with the Tannhäuser legend, it was the early Romantic, Ludwig Tieck, whose prose fiction provided the composer with the theme of Tannhäuser's psychological struggle. On that crucial 1842 hike, Wagner took along Tieck's path-breaking collection of earlier works with a fantastical and non-judgmental interior psychological streak running through them. Wagnerian critics have repeatedly fixated on one of the works in this collection, *Der getreue Eckart und der Tannenhäuser* or *Faithful Eckart and Tannenhäuser* (1799), but they have sadly ignored another work in the collection that was more important for Wagner's inner conception of Tannhäuser.

The final third of the *Eckart* tale (the last ten pages, comprising the second section) deals with the Tannhäuser legend (*Tannenhäuser* 48–58). Tieck, however, places an emphasis more on rivalry (between the sensualist Tannenhäuser and his childhood and grounded friend Friedrich, both of whom love the same chaste beauty, Emma) than on Tannenhäuser's conflicted attraction both to Venus and the virginal Emma. The tale begins with the upstanding knight, Friedrich von Wolfsburg, encountering his long-lost friend, who has suddenly returned after years away — so rumor has it — in the Venusberg. After much beseeching on Friedrich's part, Tannenhäuser recounts how he, years before, had loved a girl named Emma, and had murdered his rival for her affection. He then states that he entered Venus' grotto and has just now found the need to flee from there. Friedrich, upon hearing this multi-page-long narrative (49–57), explains that it is he, Friedrich, who has married Emma — that Tannenhäuser had not, in fact, murdered his wife and must be, in fact, delusional (57).

Tannenhäuser, upon hearing this, takes leave for Rome to seek papal absolution. Months later, he returns to Friedrich, reporting that the Pope had denied him his wish. Tannenhäuser then disappears and Friedrich immediately discovers that his wife has, in fact, just been murdered. Overtaken by Friedrich in wild pursuit, Tannenhäuser places a burning kiss on Friedrich's lips, which the reader is told at the very end of the tale, causes Friedrich to follow Tannenhäuser into the Venusberg — from which neither ever returns (*Tannenhäuser* 57–58). As J.W.Thomas has stated, Tieck presents Tannenhäuser as archetypal Romantic hero "estranged from society and himself, driven by nameless longings, more at home with pain than with joy, and hovering on the brink of madness." The Venus Mountain in this tale, the critic emphasizes, "has a three-fold ambiguity. It represents nature and the epitome of beauty and natural joys; it is the essence of evil and all that is forbidden; it is as much a product of emotional delirium and mental confusion as of magic" (Thomas 79). Clearly, Wagner was moved enough by this particular novella to mention its title in *My Life*, and Tannenhäuser's disoriented appearance as he returns from Rome is practically identical to the stage directions in the opera: "Tannenhäuser ... is wearing the tattered garb of a pilgrim, his face is pale and distorted, and he walks haltingly, leaning on his cane" (Pahlen 111). In the Tieck tale, we read that Tannenhäuser enters Friedrich's chamber "barefoot, pale and emaciated in tattered pilgrim's garb" (*Tannenhäuser* 57).

It turns out, however, that Tieck's *Der Runenberg* appealed to Wagner along with the Eckart story — and arguably had a greater effect on the interior direction Wagner went in relating his own operatic drama. *Runenberg* presents a grippingly integrated psychological portrait. In Tieck's artistic fairy tale, Christian the work's protagonist is not juxtaposed to another figure. Christian is so arresting that, unlike Tieck's Tannenhäuser, he can be presented on his own terms, and requires no contrasting figure or foil, like Friedrich, to amplify or deepen his characterization. He is portrayed as a conflicted figure wrestling with his simultaneous attraction to the virginal beauty, Elisabeth, and to a nameless mountain siren of Venus-like pulchritude and power. By the end of the work, Christian's inner conflict between sensual and chaste love — or, in the Middle High German terms, between "hohe Minne" (an elevated form of idealized love) and "niedere Minne" (an earthy low form of exclusively physical and appetitive love) — leads to his final psychological breakdown, because he is unable to sustain a committed conjugal existence with his wife without being obsessed with the possessive mountain spirit. Christian is one of the first neurotic personalities in German Romantic literature, for Tieck's genius renders him in a non-moralistic or judgmental manner. The storyline alone dictates Christian's ever increasing metaphorically geographical struggle, at major turns in the work, betwixt and between the eponymous mountain of runes (primeval runes being the earliest forms of the German alphabet dating from the third century) or the *Runenberg* and the quotidian flatlands or plains with their conventional regularity. Clearly, Wagner was himself under Tieck's *Der Runenberg* spell, for, as mentioned, he thought of calling his new piece *Der Venusberg* before settling on the *Tannhäuser* title.

The struggle between the polarities of physical and idealized love, *Eros* and *Agape*, stands at the center of both *Runenberg* and Wagner's distinctly autobiographical opera, *Tannhäuser*. In the beginning of the Tieck, Christian is sitting alone on a mysterious mountain, where a ravishing woman bestows a golden tablet upon him. He returns to the flatlands — this area being on the opposite side of the mountain from the plains where he was brought up — and marries a chaste beauty, with the sainted name of Elisabeth. During years of fidelity, he raises a family: only once does he utter a subtle and mysterious outburst unfavorably comparing his wife's beauty with that of the sensual woman of the mountain (*Runenberg* 71). Then he is visited by a nameless stranger who leaves seductive gold in his trust and departs, never appearing to reclaim it. Christian becomes manically obsessed with this treasure during the final third of the story and, consciously remembering the nameless mountain beauty, feels abruptly compelled to abandon his family and the order it signifies to seek for more treasure (74–82). Only years later does he briefly return home, old and demented, with pebbles that he is convinced are gold nuggets. At the end of the tale, he disappears for good. The remarkable aspect of this psychological story is its concentration on Christian's breakdown — as the protagonist shifts from the Venus figure to Elisabeth (71), from Elisabeth back to the Venus figure (78), and for one last time to his abandoned wife (who has since remarried), before he is forever lost (81). This synchronicity of the lone hero's monomaniacal love-obsession for the two women standing in marked opposition to each other is mirrored in Wagner's Tannhäuser and particularly in his return to Elisabeth in act two — between his stay at the Venusberg in the beginning of the first act and his homage to the love goddess at the end of the second act. The incessant *perpetuum mobile* of both Tieck's Christian and Wagner's Tannhäuser reflects their inner turmoil: they cannot fall in love with one woman and also forget the other.

Tannhäuser, Act 2, at the Bayreuth Festival (courtesy Bayreuth Festival).

Tieck's fascination with the individual psyche is apparent from the very beginning of the novella, when a torn Christian—"zerrissen" in German, a favorite adjectives of the Romantics—is sitting, as a forester's assistant, atop a mountain—symbolic of his charged and heightened state of emotions—and "yearning for those flatland regions of his youth that he had voluntarily left behind" (62). In ways strikingly similar to Wagner's solitary Tannhäuser after he has been propelled out of the Venusberg, Christian is a lone soul at the crossroads of his very existence. However, in the Tieck, this opening scene is immediately followed by the appearance of the Venus-figure who we hear "has removed Christian from the familiar circle of his parents and relatives with a strange and foreign force." As Christian states, "mein Geist war seiner selbst nicht mächtig"—"My own inner spirit was not in control of itself" (63). Thus from the very beginning, Christian, like Tannhäuser, is a flesh and blood psychological study and not a didactic figure with a moral exemplary tale appended to him.

In both Tieck and Wagner, we are confronted with a protagonist, the opposite poles of whose dual nature literally struggle with each other to produce breakdown. The striking non-judgmental modernity of both protagonists not only anticipates the Nietzschean struggle of the Dionysian versus the Apollonian, but also looks even further ahead to Claude Lévi-Strauss's discussion of the pathological: "From any non-scientific perspective (and here we can exclude no society), pathological and normal thought processes are complementary rather than opposed. In a universe which it strives to understand but whose dynamics it cannot fully control, normal thought continually seeks the meaning of things which refuse to reveal their significance. So-called pathological thought, on the other hand, overflows with emotional interpretations and overtones, in order to supplement an otherwise deficient reality. For normal thinking there exists something which cannot be empirically verified and is, therefore, 'claimable.' For pathological thinking, there exist experiences without object, or something 'available.' We might borrow from linguistics and say that so-called normal thought always suffers from a deficit of meaning, whereas so-called pathological thought (in at least some of its manifestations) disposes of a plethora of meaning.... [Society] calls upon the neurotic to furnish a wealth of emotion heretofore lacking a focus" (Lévi-Strauss 181). Clearly, Christian's wanderings throughout the novella reify a dualistic struggle, as do Tannhäuser's travels from the Venusberg to the Wartburg and then to Rome and back again to the Wartburg. Tieck as Romantic in his 1802 work has taken Goethe's Faustian dilemma of "two souls residing in one breast" and psychologized them—and so does Wagner. Crucial in both is the actual interface or space between both worlds. The spaces between Christian's predictable parental world of gardening, the routinized flatlands of his wife's family and the intervening mountain separating both worlds from each other geographically symbolize the profound rupture that he feels in his inner core; and it is the tension between these irresoluble realities that provides the psychological profundity of the work. Similarly crucial in Wagner's opera is the tension between the mountain of Venus—with her grotto and the limitless carnal pleasures she provides—and the Wartburg, bastion of redemptive courtly love, where the Virgin Mary's goodness and chastity are reflected in Elisabeth's Beethovenian Leonore–like self-sacrifice as she defends Tannhäuser at all costs. The modernity of Tieck and Wagner is that they come down on neither side as they present the on-going conflict of each protagonist, in both of whom two polarities simultaneously vie for exclusive positioning. As Father Owen Lee has stated: "[Tannhäuser is] ... a man torn not between good and evil, but between two opposing sets of values, each important and essential to him" (Owen Lee 21).

What is compelling in both *Der Runenberg* and *Tannhäuser* is the abrupt or explosive departure that each protagonist makes from one sphere to get to the next; no institution whether that of the family or of the church in Tieck or that of the minstrel guild or the Church in Wagner can help the protagonist — in each of his cleft worlds, each protagonist is on his own. Only at the very end will Wagner's Tannhäuser find solace and that through the personal intervention of Elisabeth — not through papal absolution. In Tieck and Wagner, the medieval constructs of sin and guilt are replaced emotionally by that nineteenth-century Romantic inner urge that Lévi-Strauss would call "the plethora of meaning" of the pathological; the tumultuous personal struggle each of these two figures faces is unique to his very being.

In Cosima Wagner's private diaries, which were not published during the composer's lifetime, it is clear in how high a high regard the composer held the interiority of *Der Runenberg*. In October of 1877, Cosima makes the following entry: "In the evening R. reads us *Runenberg* which casts a fine spell over us; R. says that it made a tremendous impression on him in his youth" (Cosima Wagner v. I 987). Less than a year later, Cosima writes: "We take a pleasant walk to Birken, a conversation about the mountains reminds R. of Hoffmann's story *Die Bergwerke von Falun*.... R. feels it must have been influenced by Tieck's *Runenberg*" (Cosima Wagner, v. II 142). Revealingly, Wagner did not confess his own creative indebtedness to Tieck's work, and there is no record of his ever singling out *Runenberg* in public, but in the above entry it is clear that he was projecting his own artistic indebtedness onto the earlier Romantic, by mentioning ETA Hoffmann's debt to Tieck. Obviously, the composer felt more secure, though not entirely forthright, in the earlier cited 1865 passage from *My Life*, when he drew a negative comparison between the less sophisticated Tieck *Tannenhäuser*-novella and his opera. Evidently, he did not feel secure enough to point to Tieck's more refined Christian-figure as a possible literary antecedent of his own Tannhäuser.

Wagner's great ambivalence towards Heinrich Heine can never be denied. In a single Cosima Wagner diary entry, we encounter both Wagner's repulsion and attraction to the poet simultaneously. In the following 1869 quote, the composer has been reading in a volume of late Heine works and has to confess that Heine's irreverence is, in fact, attractive: "'He is the bad conscience of our whole era, the most unedifying and demoralizing matters one can possibly imagine, and yet one feels closer to him than to the whole clique he is so naïvely exposing'" (Cosima Wagner v. I 172). The composer obviously felt this attraction a quarter of a century before when he was drawn to Heine's mature "Tannhäuser" ballad for his same-titled opera. Heine's own self-promoting short prose introduction to the poem in the French translation of the work could easily have captured Wagner's immediate interest: "In reading these two versions, the medieval [from *Das Knaben Wunderhorn*] with my modern version simultaneously, one sees how the ancient sense of faith predominates in the older version; whereas in the modern version, a skepticism of this epoch is revealed: no establishment or institutional authority reins in the poetical voice of the modern version, whose single aim is to express pure human emotion in verse" (Heine Werke, v. I 513).

When comparing the "Tannhäuser" ballad from the *Knaben Wunderhorn* collected by Clemens Brentano and Achim von Arnim in the first decade of the nineteenth century with the Heine version, immediate differences in thematic concern become evident. The folk-ballad's hero wants to leave Venus' realm because of his guilt over the carnal sin he has committed, and the eternal damnation he will, as a consequence, suffer: "I would have to remain in Hell's fiery glow, / that burns eternally" (*Des Knaben Wunderhorn* v. I l. 23–25). In the defense of his exit he states that he is becoming physically ill (l. 37) and in his moral outrage, he has called Venus a "Teufelinne" (l. 48), a "she devil" who has done him "harm" (l. 45). Heine's protagonist, by contrast, seeks his freedom because he is bored from the stupor of endless physical embrace. As he states in the seventh stanza: "we have amused ourselves and laughed too much, /I long for the tears, / and instead of roses/ I would like to crown my head with the pointed tips of thorns" (*Neue Gedichte* l. 25–28). Much of the vigor of the first extended third of the Heine ballad comes from the poet's use of *Rollenlyrik*: Tannhäuser and Venus (just as in the opening scene of the Wagner opera) alternate in articulating their respective roles of seductress and captive. In both Heine and Wagner, Tannhäuser addresses the love goddess with force and is unencumbered by a moralistic sense of guilt: the knight wants his freedom.

In the central portion of the Heine ballad, during the knight's confession to the Pope in Rome, Tannhäuser, in very much his own voice, articulates his overriding personal dilemma: even though he has physically escaped from Venus, he has not been successful in fleeing from her emotionally: "I finally did from her mountain escape,/ Yet I am still on the rack,/ For those eyes are pursuing me everywhere/ And call to me, come back!/ By day, I am a mere ghost,/ My life begins at night;/ Then I dream of this beautiful woman/ who sits laughing at my side" (*Neue Gedichte* l. 101–108). This, the dichotomous Tannhäuser, the modern-day neurotic, unhappy if he is with Venus and unhappy if he is without her, speaks with the same directness as Wagner's Tannhäuser does towards the end of Act Two during the song contest. In both cases, the personal avowals of these eponymous characters provide an unmitigated dramatic immediacy to their plight. Wagner's Tannhäuser — with his avowal to Venus in the song contest, followed immediately by his contrition and his preparation to visit Rome at the end of the second act — clearly echoes the duality of Heine's protagonist (Pahlen 87–99).

That Wagner did not mention the connections between his protagonist and that of Heine's comes as little surprise. As with Bechstein, Wagner did not wish to credit Heine with inspiring two of his successive stage works. Heine's *Schnabelewopski* memoirs and their depiction of the ghost-like sea captain doomed to travel around the globe had helped prompt the creation of *Flying Dutchman*, when Wagner read them in Riga in the 1830s (Taylor 94). That Wagner recognized the literary achievements of Heine is seen in general laudatory terms, just two years before Wagner completed his *Tannhäuser* libretto. In his article for the Dresden *Abendzeitung*, dated the fourth of August 1841, Wagner avers: "Any youngster who picks up his pen today, for good or ill, consciously or unconsciously, tries to imitate Heine, for never before has a writer who appeared so suddenly, so quickly and so quite unexpectedly come to dominate his field so irresistibly as Heine has his" (Barth, Mack, Voss 163). But again, as in the cases of Bechstein and Tieck, no specific word of gratitude to Heine was ever to be uttered.

Ironically, these three writers did have their encounters, perhaps as poetic revenge on the ever so strangely silent Wagner. They were to engage one another, on their own terms, with regard to Tannhäuser. In the humorous parodic third section of the Heine Tannhäuser ballad, Heine in his own voice writes a hard-hitting critique of the dearth of significant culture on German soil. As part of his hard-hearted criticism, he mentions "a poor old cur who made quite a stir in his youth; / But now he can only bark and piss, /having lost his one last tooth" (l. 197–200). This unkind reference was directly aimed at the sixty-three-year-old Tieck, who in his later years, in fact, lacked the path-breaking creativity of his youth.

That Bechstein and Heine should have known each other validates the term "The Romantic School," "die romantische Schule" — not a formal institution, but a nineteenth-century school of thought with many a diverse participant. Bechstein was fascinated by Heine and much aggrieved that Heine's writings were banned in the Germany of the 1830's because of his liberal political views. In early 1836, Bechstein sent Heine his anthology of Thuringian sagas while reminding the poet of their personal encounter and their ensuing interview in Paris the year before. In a published account of that interview, Bechstein quoted Heine's response after he had asked him whether the poet would ever again reside in Germany — he had been living in Paris since 1831. Heine, relates Bechstein, "smiled in a melancholy manner and answered: 'That would be difficult. I am Tannhäuser, who sits a captive in the Venusberg; the magic goddess will not free me'" (Hirsch and Vortriede III 256).

Despite the disparate nature of such sources as Bechstein, Tieck, and Heine, it is the way that Wagner drew inspiration from them that underscores their commonality. As tortured as his Tannhäuser himself, both in the credit he gives to his sources and that which he withholds, Wagner, concealing and revealing, was able to find creative stimuli in these cohorts and distill what he needed to dramatize his own Tannhäuser as a unique protagonist. As Harold Bloom states in his tellingly titled *The Anxiety of Influence*: "But poetic influence need not make poets less original; as often it makes them more original, though not therefore necessarily better. The profundities of poetic influence cannot be reduced to source-study, to the history of ideas, to the patterning of images. Poetic influence, or as I shall more frequently term it, poetic misprision, is necessarily the study of the life-cycle of the poet-as-poet" (Bloom 7). Ultimately, the dichotomy of irreconcilable opposites that racks Wagner's minstrel Tannhäuser makes him consistent in one major area: like his librettist/composer he is a Romantic first and foremost.

BIBLIOGRAPHY

Arnim, Achim von, and Brentano, Clemens. *Des Knaben Wunderhorn*. Vol. I. Stuttgart: Reclam, 1987.
Barth, Herbert, Dietrich Mack and Egon Voss. *Wagner: A Documentary Study*. Trans. P.R.J. Ford and Mary Whittall. New York: Oxford University Press, 1975.
Bechstein, Ludwig. *Der Sagenschatz und die Sagenkreise des Thüringerlandes*. Vol. V. Hildesheim: Olms-Weidmann, 2004.
Bloom, Harold. *The Anxiety of Influence: A Theory of Poetry*. 2d ed. New York: Oxford University Press, 1997.
Cerf, Steven R. "Too Grimm For Words." *Opera News* 61 (1996): 14–17.
Gutman, Robert W. *Richard Wagner: The Man, His Mind, and His Music*. New York: Harcourt, Brace & World, 1968.
Heine, Heinrich. *Werke*. Vol. I. Frankfurt am Main: Insel, 1968.
Hirsch, Rudolf, and Werner Vortriede. *Dichter über ihre Dichtungen: Heinrich Heine*. Vol. III. Munich: Heimeran, 1971.
Köhler, Joachim. *Richard Wagner: The Last of the Titans*. Trans. Stewart Spencer. New Haven, CT: Yale University Press, 2004.
Lee, M. Owen. "To See Your Soul: Tannhäuser Holds The Mirror Up to Man's Duality." *Opera News* 46 (1982): 20–22.
Lévi-Strauss, Claude. *Structural Anthropology*. Trans. Claire Jacobson and Brooke Grundfest Schoepf. New York: Basic, 1963.
Mertens, Volker. "Wagner's Middle Ages." *Wagner Handbook*. Eds. Ulrich Müller and Peter Wapnewski. Trans. John Deathridge. Cambridge, MA: Harvard University Press, 1992. 236–268.
Schulze, Hagen. *Germany: A New History*. Trans. Deborah Lucas Schneider. Cambridge, MA: Harvard University Press, 1998.
Taylor, Ronald. *Richard Wagner: His Life, Art and Thought*. London: Panther, Granada, 1983.
Thomas, J.W. *Tannhäuser: Poet and Legend*. Chapel Hill: University of North Carolina Press, 1974.
Tieck, Ludwig. *Die Märchen aus dem Phantasus*. Vol. II. Munich: Winkler, 1963.
Wagner, Cosima. *Diaries: 1869–1877*. Eds. Martin Gregor-Dellin and Dietrich Mack. Trans. Geoffrey Skelton. New York: Harcourt Brace Jovanovich, 1978.
_____. *Diaries: 1878–1883*. Eds. Martin Gregor-Dellin and Dietrich Mack. Trans. Geoffrey Skelton. New York: Harcourt Brace Jovanovich, 1980.
Wagner, Richard. *My Life*. Ed. Mary Whittall. Trans. Andrew Gray. New York: Da Capo, 1992
_____. *Tannhäuser: Textbuch, Einführung und Kommentar*. Ed. Kurt Pahlen. Munich: Piper. 1989.
_____. *Tannhäuser: Texte, Materialien, Kommentare*. Eds. Attila Csampai and Dietmar Holland. Reinbek bei Hamburg: Rowohlt, 1986.

5

Romanticism in *Tannhäuser* and *Lohengrin*

BARBARA JOSEPHINE GUENTHER

Great artists are not static. As they seek to find their own voice, they move from early, usually derivative work, to middle-period works in which their distinctive idiom begins to emerge, and finally to the masterworks that are the culmination of their career. Wagner is no exception to this. When, between 1833 and 1840, he wrote *Die Feen*, modeled after Weber; *Das Liebesverbot*, "determinedly imitative of Rossini and Bellini" (Plantinga 259); and *Rienzi*, a grand opera in the French style, he cannot have known the extent to which he would in time revolutionize opera. Wagner began with a genre that was "half ceremonial pomp, half entertainment," and, through the strength of his personality and the genius of his music, forced upon an initially unwilling public the idea that what happened on the operatic stage could be art in the highest sense of the term (Dahlhaus, *Nineteenth-Century Music* 195). The masterwork in Wagner's career is, of course, the great *Ring* cycle. Not only is it the fullest embodiment of his musical ideas; its libretto is thoroughly animated by Romanticism.[1]

Between those first three experiments and the monumental *Ring* lie three operas (*Der Fliegende Holländer*, *Tannhäuser*, *Lohengrin*) that show Wagner moving toward the music drama[2] as well as the full expression of Romanticism found in the *Ring*. The librettos of *Tannhäuser* and *Lohengrin* demonstrate the dynamic interplay among a phenomenal and strong-willed artist, source materials created by other poets, and German Romanticism.

Before examining the librettos of these two operas, we need to consider the way in which ideas—whether of German Romantic writers, philosophers, or, in his theoretical writing, Wagner himself—seem to have made their way into the operas. We cannot know the extent to which Wagner was *consciously* influenced by Romanticism, but closely examining the complex and ultimately mysterious interaction between ideas and the operas can yield important insights.

First let us consider Wagner's own ideas. Do the librettos of *Tannhäuser* and *Lohengrin* demonstrate a causal link to Wagner's theories? Determining this depends on having a clear view of those theories—which is not so easily done. Even if James Plaskitt's contention that Wagner's major theoretical works are a "linguistic labyrinth" (156) is a gross overstatement—that is, even if Wagner's written thoughts are clear—there remains a problem of inconsistency. Leon Plantinga, for instance, discussing the two-year period immediately after the

Simon Estes as Herman in the Metropolitan Opera's *Tannhäuser* (photograph by Winnie Klotz).

completion of *Lohengrin*, when Wagner wrote *Art and Revolution*, *The Artwork of the Future* (both in 1849), and *Opera and Drama* (1850–51), states that the composer's mind at this time was "a welter of confused ideas drawn from diverse and incongruent sources" (269).[3] Even if both Plaskitt and Plantinga are overstating — that is, even if Wagner's theoretical writings are both clear and consistent — the operas of the 1840's demonstrate that Wagner did not consistently apply his theories of opera to the works themselves. He was "too good a musician and too experienced a man of the theatre to be completely fettered by theories, even his own" (Longyear 174). Though we cannot know to what extent Wagner was conscious of this inconsistency, we do recognize that far from being a flaw, this gap between theory and practice is a tribute to Wagner's exceptional dramatic instincts.

The soundness of these instincts is also seen in the way that the ideas of others made their way into the operas. The German Romantics, writes Stewart Spencer, were of "seminal importance" to Wagner's operas, as were the writers of the Young German movement and (among others) the philosophers Hegel and Feuerbach. True, it is often difficult "to disentangle the strands of literary, political and philosophical influence" (Spencer, "Literary Tastes" 149), but we can see that these writers and thinkers have left their imprint on the operas. This imprint was made in a creative interaction described insightfully by Roger Hollinrake: "Wagner's attitude to [these thinkers] was one of imaginative, retrospective identification rather than of literal dependence" ("Philosophical Outlook" 145). An important word in this statement is *retrospective*— a concept that Byron Magee elaborates upon.

Magee points out that Wagner first wrote *The Ring*, and then read Schopenhauer, discovering that the two men shared an important idea. This led Wagner to state, "I am convinced Schopenhauer would have been annoyed that I discovered this [concept] before I knew about his philosophy" (*Cosima Wagner's Diaries*, qtd. in Magee 180). Magee believes that the discovery of Schopenhauer

> ... had raised the unconscious realm of [Wagner's] creative intuitions as fully and explicitly to the level of his consciousness as could be done. In doing this it had provided him with a philosophy available to his conscious mind that was in harmony with his own existing insights, apprehensions and intuitions.... His consciously held philosophical beliefs were now ... in organic unity with his creative intuitions, and also, therefore, with the preconscious and unconscious drives from which those intuitions sprang [182].

Magee's point can be applied to other philosophers read by Wagner — Feuerbach, for instance — and other operas, such as *Tannhäuser* and *Lohengrin*. Wagner did indeed absorb the ideas of others, but in a way that is perfectly congruent with Romanticism's celebration of the creative power of the individual artist's deepest intuitions.

Understanding that the creative interaction between Wagner and Romanticism is just as indirect as, but no less real than, the interaction between Wagner and the philosophers he valued, we can now look specifically at the librettos of *Tannhäuser* and *Lohengrin*. In terms of Romantic ideas, the two operas are transitional; the later works, particularly the *Ring* cycle and *Tristan und Isolde*, are more thoroughly grounded in the Romantic worldview. Several of the important themes in *Tannhäuser* and *Lohengrin* are central to Romanticism; other elements in the two operas seem to be Romantic but, when scrutinized, are not.

The Romantic view of nature as numinous and oracular may have originated in Schelling's belief that there was a *Weltseele* (World Soul) that could be seen most clearly in the visible phenomena of nature. This pantheistic notion went far beyond merely seeing nature as picturesque. Goethe's Werther, for instance, felt his heart flooded by "bliss" as nature's outer forms revealed to him "the inner, glowing, sacred life of Nature" and all her "unfathomable forces" (64–65). In England, Wordsworth's vision of the moonlit ocean as he stood on the summit of Mount Snowdon is one of the most exalted and awe-filled descriptions of a vital and profound Nature. That "Vision," it seemed to him, was "the type/Of a majestic Intellect":

> There I beheld the emblem of a Mind
> That feeds upon infinity, that broods
> Over the dark abyss, intent to hear
> Its voices issuing forth to silent light
> In one continuous stream; a mind sustained
> By recognitions of transcendent power
> In sense conducting to ideal form;
> In soul, of more than mortal privilege [*The Prelude*, 14. 66–67, 70–77].

This Romantic sense of nature, so evident in the *Ring* cycle, is not present in either *Lohengrin* or *Tannhäuser*. Leon Plantinga notes that the setting of the latter opera "in the picturesque German countryside," is one reason to term it a Romantic opera (264), but he is speaking of a particular musical genre, not of the Romantic worldview. In a few places, *Tannhäuser* seems to view nature as the Romantic writers did. After Tannhäuser rejects Venus in Act 1, he suddenly finds himself transported to a beautiful valley under a blue sky and bright sunshine, complete with a shepherd ("Tannhäuser ... befindet sich plötzlich in ein schönes Tal versetzt. Blauer Himmel, heitere Sonnenbeleuchtung"). The somber third act is set in the same valley, but in autumn. At the beginning of that act, day is declining into evening ("Der Tag neigt sich zum Abend"), and by the beginning of the third scene, night has completely fallen. Later in that scene, when Tannhäuser calls upon Venus, Wagner's stage directions specify "Dark night; light clouds gradually veil the scene ("Finstere Nacht; leichte Nebel verhüllen allmählich die Szene"), and as the minstrel turns again and calls upon Elisabeth, the clouds gradually darken. Immediately after Venus states her defeat—"Alas! Lost to me!" ("Weh! Mir verloren!")—the valley is illuminated by dawn.

This correspondence between aspects of nature and narrative plot and character is a feature of many Romantic novels. In Charlotte Brontë's *Jane Eyre*, for instance, a chestnut tree symbolizing the love between Jane and Rochester is split by lightning just before the two are to marry, portending the devastating discovery that Rochester was already married. Throughout that novel, images of fire and ice reinforce the narrative, as do the moors in Emily Brontë's *Wuthering Heights*. There is a significant difference, however, between the function of nature in those novels and in *Tannhäuser*. Even a casual reader of either Brontë narrative cannot miss the extent to which the nature/human correspondence suffuses each work. In *Tannhäuser*, one must go searching for a relatively few examples that point less to a truly Romantic attitude toward nature than to good nineteenth-century showmanship. Even Venus's description of her grotto as "the warming depths of the earth's womb" ("der Erde wärmenden Schoß") is a passing description; consider, in contrast, the emotional depth and resonance of the figure of Erda in the *Ring*.

Another trait of Romanticism not found in *Tannhäuser* or *Lohengrin* is the yearning for transcendence and the concurrent value placed on striving in and of itself, whether "tentative progression and development" or "pure endeavor" (Hugo, "Masterpieces" 248). One encounters this striving for the infinite—*Streben nach dem Unendlichen*, or in Shelley's phrase, "the desire of the moth for a star"—again and again in Romantic writing. Coleridge, probably echoing A.W. Schlegel's *Lectures on Art and Literature*, characterized the literature we now term Romantic as "the infinite, & indefinite as the vehicle of the Infinite ... Sublimity" (qtd. in

Bone 124). Bone notes that both Schlegel and Coleridge speak "confidently of the Romantic as a will to escape the confines of the finite material world, and wander in the freedom of the infinite sublime" (124). In *Lohengrin* and *Tannhäuser*, there is no shortage of struggle — within the self, against other characters, and, especially in *Lohengrin*, against society — but these are the age-old struggles, not the distinctively Romantic striving toward transcendence.

Not only is the Romantic yearning for transcendence absent from these two operas, Wagner actually turns that idea on its head. Bryan Magee points out that the young Wagner believed that "this world — what philosophers call the empirical world, the world that can be experienced by human beings — is the only world there is. There is no transcendental realm" (56). The presence of a transcendental realm in *Lohengrin* — Montsalvat — simply reflects the worldview of Wagner's sources. In his Grail narrative, Lohengrin describes Montsalvat as "inaccessible" ("unnahbar") to the onlookers, a place that gives those who have seen the Grail freedom from the shadow of death ("wenn ihn er sieht, weicht dem des Todes Nacht"). In the bridal chamber he tells Elsa that he left a place of "splendour and delight" for her love, in which he could find all his happiness:

Be near my ardent heart,	Sei meines Herzens Glühen nah,
that the eyes in which I saw all my happiness	daß mich dein Auge sanft bescheine,
may shine upon me softly!	in dem ich all mein Glück ersah!

Lohengrin, as Carl Dahlhaus states so aptly, is "an Undine in knightly guise" (37). He may have begun with a limited mission to stand in combat for Elsa, but, with the dream logic of a fairy tale, he almost immediately asks Elsa to become his wife. At the end of the opera, with his dream of love shattered, he returns to the transcendent Montsalvat not in joyful anticipation, but with his head sunk in sorrow on his shield ("er steht mit gesenktem Haupte traurig auf seinen Schild").

At first glance, *Tannhäuser* might seem to be grounded in the Romantic yearning for transcendence, with Tannhäuser's longing to leave Venus and unite with Elisabeth, embodying the classic turn from sensuality to the Romantic idea of absolute love. However, Tannhäuser's longing is not so neatly schematized. Barry Millington, for instance, maintains that in this opera the spheres of sensual love and spiritual love should not be regarded as "polar opposites," with "the acceptance of one implying the rejection of the other"; instead they should be seen as "dialectically interrelated." Each sphere has both positive and negative traits, and the opera's action represents an unsuccessful struggle for a synthesis — unsuccessful because "the hero is destroyed in the attempt" ("Introduction" 30).

Carl Dahlhaus reinforces Millington's implication that the relationship between Tannhäuser and Elisabeth is not what the Romantic writers meant by absolute love. He contrasts this opera with *Der fliegende Holländer*, seeing *Tannhäuser* as a drama of redemption whose "threads" have become "tangled" because of the "emotional delusion and confusion from which there was no escape route." One is not sure whether the minstrel's love of Elisabeth is "stamped by demonic possession or pious longing for salvation"; one is convinced, Dahlhaus maintains, that the love is not "truly human" (*Wagner's Music Dramas* 24).

Scholars and impresarios agree on this point. The "impulsiveness," "extraordinary amnesia," and "abrupt oscillation between extremes" that Dalhaus notes in the character of Tannhäuser (*Music Dramas* 25) were echoed in comments by Elijah Moshinsky shortly before his 1984 production of the opera opened at Covent Garden. Moshinsky saw Tannhäuser as being "outside his own experiences; he only observes them and is never fully at one with his feelings" (964).

One does not feel that the Romantic writers who sought transcendence were in any way removed from their feelings. They often expressed emotional extremes — typically, the polarities of joy and dejection — but not both within a single work. When they were caught up in the imagination, they were rhapsodic. Consider, for instance, Coleridge's "Kubla Khan," in which the poet presents himself as a bard so inspired that he would inspire "holy dread" in those listening to his words:

> And all should cry, Beware! Beware!
> His flashing eyes, his floating hair!
> Weave a circle round him thrice,
> And close your eyes with holy dread,
> For he on honey-dew has fed,
> And drunk the milk of Paradise [lines 49–54].

"One cannot live at concert pitch," scholar and professor Alvin Whitley once remarked when discussing the Romantic polarities. One is not surprised, then, to find the Romantic writers describing their feelings of dejection. The poet who wrote "Kubla Khan" also wrote the magnificent "Dejection: An Ode," describing the "dull pain," the "smothering weight" descending upon him when his poetic powers fail him:

> A grief without a pang, void, dark, and drear,
> A stifled, drowsy, unimpassioned grief,
> Which finds no natural outlet, no relief,
> In word, or sigh, or tear — [2.21–24].

Although both *Lohengrin* and *Tannhäuser* present men and women experiencing extreme changes of mood, these oscillations are the result of the action. When there is no Romantic transcendence, there can be no fall from transcendence to dejection.[4]

If *Tannhäuser* and *Lohengrin* are not animated by a sense of nature as numinous and oracular, a longing for the transcendental, and Romantic polarities, in what ways do they embody other Romantic themes? One Romantic theme that is present in both operas though tangential to the central concern of each is nationalism. More important is the role of magic and the fairy-tale world, especially in *Lohengrin*. Most important is a cluster of Romantic themes that are central to these operas: in *Tannhäuser*, world-weariness and the alienated artist; and in both, the Romantic fascination with the exotic — specifically, the medieval world. We will see that Wagner, like other Romantic writers, re-envisioned the medieval world, imbuing the older stories with the Romantic value of individualism, and significantly modifying much of the conventional religiosity of his sources.

The Enlightenment had set a value on being "a citizen of the world," and Rousseau, a transitional figure moving toward Romanticism, had stressed the importance of personal uniqueness. Across the Channel, the English Romantics were profoundly moved by political events and the thinking behind those events: for the earlier Romantics, the French Revolution; for Byron, Greek independence. Throughout Europe, the concept of liberty carried reverberations it had not in earlier times. In time, Rousseau's claim for the importance of the individual was expanded to apply to the nation, an idea that was most congruent with Hegel's theories of history. When describing the dialectical progress of the world-spirit ("Weltgeist"), Hegel went so far as to say that "the state [of modern Prussia] is the Divine Idea [i.e., God] as it exists on earth" (Hollinrake, "Philosophy" 53). Although Wagner certainly would not have subscribed to every one of Hegel's ideas and although questions of influence are best treated by understatement, the information we have suggests the soundness of one scholar's contention that "the pervasiveness of Hegel's influence on 19th-century thought ... should not be underestimated. It is probable that, directly or indirectly, Wagner's debt to the philosopher was far greater than his own subsequent testimony—and the contents of his libraries at Dresden and Bayreuth—would leave us to believe" (Hollinrake, "Philosophical Outlook" 143).

Hollinrake's summation of Hegel—"he bestowed a Teutonic identity, intelligence, will and purpose on the world-historical process" that he had termed the *Weltgeist*, or world-spirit ("Philosophy" 53)—leads one to think of Wagner's own ideas. It is true that most of the composer's later theories about art and music would be "predicated upon an assumed centrality of the German nation, its culture and language" (Plantinga 261), and Wagner's biography alone demonstrates that he was thinking in political terms long before he wrote the later treatises. Always the individualist, Wagner did not join those associated with the popular cult of national supremacy (Hollinrake, "Social and Political" 143), but he was most definitely concerned with the German national identity and the identity of German art. It is not surprising, then, to find a nineteenth-century concern with the German state in both *Tannhäuser* and *Lohengrin*, despite the medieval setting of both operas.

In *Tannhäuser*, there is only one reference to the German state, in the Landgraf's welcome to the minstrels just before the beginning of the song contest. After expressing his gratitude for the many times their songs have cheered him, he draws a parallel between the victories on the battlefield and those in the hall of music:

If our sword in stern bloody battles	Wenn unser Schwert in blutig ernsten Kämpfen
fought for the supremacy of the German State,	stritt für des deutschen Reiches Majestät,
if we withstood the savage Guelphs	wenn wir dem grimmen Welfen widerstanden,
and held disastrous discord in check,	und dem verderbenvollen Zwiespalt wehrten:
you won no less a prize.	so ward von euch nicht mindrer Preis errungen.

This national reference—so brief and so tangential to the action of the opera—suggests that German matters were very much on Wagner's mind when he wrote the libretto.

The nationalism in *Lohengrin* is more evident. The second utterance in the opera is the Herald's introduction of Heinrich as "King of the Germans" ("der Deutschen König"). After the Brabantians repeat their welcome, King Heinrich's long speech mentions "the Empire's plight," and the "scourge/that has so often visited German soil ["die deutsches Land"] from the East": the wrathful Hungarians. The king reminds his listeners of his military accomplishments over the past nine years, but warns the Brabantians that once again the Empire needs to be defended:

East and West, to all I say:	ob Ost, ob West, das gelte allen gleich!
Let every acre of German soil put forth troops of soldiers,	Was deutsches Land heißt, stelle Kampfesscharen,
never again shall anyone abuse the German Empire!	dann schmäht wohl niemand mehr das Deutsche Reich!

Though political concerns drive much of the action, many historical settings could easily have accommodated with ease this outline: a nobleman seeks power by marrying the daughter of a dead ruler; a resentful noblewoman[5] now out of power makes the primary heir disappear and, by discrediting that heir's sister, finesses her marriage to the man who will become the ruler. Wagner, of course, was working from sources that gave him this particular setting, and even if those sources had not existed, he would have been unlikely to use a non–Germanic setting. This was the age when national independence was seen as "a necessary prerequisite

Peter Hofmann as Lohengrin and Eva Morton as Elsa in the Metropolitan Opera production (photograph by Winnie Klotz).

to individual freedom," a time when creative artists were eager to develop national themes in their works (Horton and Hopper 362–63).

Once the psychological action has largely run its course, Wagner inserts another reminder of German nationalism. Lohengrin tells King Henry that he cannot lead them in battle but predicts German victory not only for the upcoming conflict but also for all time:

... mighty King, this do I foretell:	... großer König, laß mich dir weissagen:
a great victory awaits you, O pure one!	Dir Reinem ist ein großer Sieg verliehn!
Never, not even in the most distant future,	Nach Deutschland sollen noch in fernsten Tagen
Shall the hordes from the East rise up	des Ostens Horden siegreich nimmer ziehn!
in victory against Germany!	

The historical setting with its German nationalism is in the opera not simply because the idea was important to Wagner. Ever the dramatist, Wagner saw that the historical setting could serve important dramatic functions. The opera's external action is rooted in a definite historical period; the historical level contrasts with the inner, psychological level. It is the contrasting background of knights and their ruler fighting a particular enemy that throws into relief the absolute and timeless central character (Holland 20). Carl Dahlhaus makes the point even more strongly: "The setting of an unhistorical, fairy-tale world would nullify the conflict that destroys Lohengrin" (*Wagner's Music Dramas* 37). The historical setting serves a further aesthetic purpose as well: it justifies the tragic ending. In mid-nineteenth-century opera, tragic endings were acceptable only in the grand operas of Meyerbeer and Halévy with their historical subjects (Dahlhaus, *Wagner's Music Dramas* 37). In *Lohengrin*, we see Wagner using the Romantic concern with nationalism not simply for its own sake, but for important dramaturgic purposes.

Another Romantic concern, especially in Germany, was magic. Nineteenth-century readers welcomed the Gothic novel and other literature that contained "ghosts, witchcraft, occultism, and other eerie phenomena" (Hugo, "Masterpieces" 255). This may have been in part a reaction to the rationalism of the Age of Enlightenment; it was also an understandable outcome of other Romantic ideas. Romanticism placed a high value on nature and the natural human being; at the same time, the Romantics had a renewed interest in antiquarianism. These tendencies, combined with the ever-present human desire for novelty, help explain the Romantics' attraction to the exotic. Romantic literature is filled with this love of past times and distant lands: the fantastic Polar seascapes of Poe's *The Narrative of A. Gordon Pym* and Coleridge's *The Rime of the Ancient Mariner*, and the ancient Greek and medieval European settings of many of Keats's works, for example. It was one short step from a love of the exotic to a fascination with magic, and it was a step taken by the German Romantics again and again. E.T.A. Hoffmann's explorations of abnormal psychology, a variant of the Gothic, led Heinrich Heine to call his work a "cry of terror in twenty volumes" (Hugo, "Masterpieces" 240). Heine was proud of this feature of German Romantic literature, recognizing that in their tales of terror, the Germans had far surpassed the English novelists who had inspired them: "[Hoffmann's novel *The Devil's Elixirs*] depicts the most dreadful, the most terrible things the mind can conceive. How weak, compared with such a work, is M.G. Lewis's *The Monk*, which treats the same themes! In Göttingen, it is said, a student went mad after reading Hoffmann's novel" (*Letters from Berlin*, qtd. in Prawer 16).

There are fantastic, magical, fairy-tale elements in both *Tannhäuser* and *Lohengrin*, particularly the latter. Wagner includes them not for the sake of novelty; they always are integral in forwarding the drama.

Tannhäuser lacks dramatic coherence. The action, as Elijah Moshinsky notes, is not resolved: "it comes to a conclusion with the portrait of a man who projects his feelings towards opposing ideals" (964). In fact, says Moshinsky, the motives of both Tannhäuser and Elisabeth are "puzzling" (966). Carl Dahlhaus also notes "a casualness about motivation" (How did Tannhäuser get into Venusberg in the first place? What was the origin of the hero's love for Elisabeth?) In addition, Dahlhaus finds the opera filled with abrupt movement between extremes: "memory turns into forgetting and forgetting into memory at a stroke, without transition" (*Wagner's Music Dramas* 26). These are not complaints against the opera, for, as Dahlhaus points out, to demand stylistic uniformity and consistency is a classic, not a Romantic impulse. In *Tannhäuser*, these "stylistic discrepancies" serve an important dramatic function: "they can be seen to express the conflict between the everyday, natural world, to which Tannhäuser longs to return, and the artificial paradise where Venus seeks to keep him" (28).

In such a universe, magic is almost to be expected. When Tannhäuser tells Venus that he wishes to leave her, a sign from her produces a magic grotto ("eine zauberische Grotte"), and when he insists on leaving, Venus disappears and the Venusberg is swallowed up ("Der Venusberg versinkt"). Near the end of the opera, when Tannhäuser calls out to return to Venus, light clouds appear and the minstrel experiences "gentle breezes ... sweet fragrance ... [and] rapturous voices," becoming increasingly excited as the spell ("der Zauber") comes nearer. When movements of dancing forms become visible, the horrified Wolfram exclaims, "Black [evil] magic is abroad!" ("Böser Zauber tut sich auf!"). Then, in another of Tannhäuser's "magic" utterances of a name, Elisabeth's (see Moshnisky 964), the clouds gradually darken, and not only Venus but the entire magic vision ("die ganze zauberische Erscheinung") disappears. Such movement between extremes would be a flaw in most narratives, but, as Dahlhaus has noted, in *Tannhäuser* they are dramatically important to the opera.

In *Lohengrin*, the non-realistic element is even more pervasive, since the central narrative (set against the foil of the historical, nationalistic outer action) is a fairy tale. Fairy tales generally include magic, and *Lohengrin* is no exception. Most notably, Gottfried is turned into a swan by Ortrud and then back into human form by Lohengrin, with the aid of the white dove of

Tatyana Troyanos as Venus in the Metropolitan Opera's *Tannhäuser* (photograph by Winnie Klotz).

the Grail. Lohengrin leaves for Gottfried the magic horn, which will assist him in danger; and the sword, which, like Siegfried's Nothung, will bring him victory in battle.

Even in the outer, historical action of the opera, the characters recognize that magic exists and must be guarded against. Announcing the trial by combat in Act 1, the Herald says, "Let not the deceit and cunning of magic ["bösen Zaubers List und Trug"] spoil the nature of the ordeal!" Certainly Friedrich believes in magic; one of the first things he says to Lohengrin is "I know not what magic ["Zaubern"] brought you here." Ortrud later exploits this belief in the power of magic as she manipulates both her husband and Elsa. In Act 2 Ortrud tells her husband that Lohengrin's power comes not from God but from magic alone, which causes him to transfer his anger from Ortrud to Lohengrin.

By convincing her husband that tearing off the smallest part of any creature made strong by magic will make it powerless, Ortrud not only deflects his anger against her, but, more important, incites him to attack the knight. By publicly accusing Lohengrin of having defeated him by the cunning of magic, Friedrich causes the crowd as well as Elsa to begin to doubt the mysterious stranger:

Johanna Meier as Elisabeth in the Metropolitan Opera's *Tannhäuser* (photograph by Winnie Klotz).

[Friedrich]
    The trial by combat was defamed, deceived!   Gottes Gericht, es ward entehrt, betrogen!
    You are beguiled by the cunning of magic!   Durch eines Zaubers List seid ihr belogen!
    ...

[the crowd]
    What secret must the knight harbour?   Welch ein Geheimnis muß der Held bewahren?

[Ortrud and Friedrich, observing Elsa]
    I see her brooding wildly,   In wildem Brüten darf ich sie gewahren,
    doubt is stirring within her breast!   der Zwiefel keimt in ihres Herzens Grund!

Perceiving the first sign of Elsa's doubt is not wishful thinking on the part of Ortrud and Friedrich, for Lohengrin repeats their words: "I see her brooding wildly!" and Elsa herself states that she is torn with doubt ("Im Zweifel doch erbebt des Herzens Grund!") — in Wagner's stage directions, "overcome with worry, confusion and shame" ("Unruhe, Verwirrung und Scham").

Elsa had dismissed Ortrud's initial attempt to exploit her vulnerability:

[Ortrud]
    may he never leave you   der nie dich möge so verlassen,
    as he came to you — by magic!   wie er durch Zauber zu dir kam!

[Elsa — with "horror" and "indignation," then "sadness and compassion"]
    Piteous creature, can you not understand   Du Ärmste kannst wohl nie ermessen,
    how a heart can love without harbouring doubts?   wie zweifellos ein Herze liebt?

However, Elsa ultimately capitulates. When, in the bridal-chamber scene, her husband says that he had come from "splendour and delight," she accuses him of intending to enchant ("betören") her and says that he will want to leave her. In Act 1, the men and women had hailed Lohengrin's appearance as "a miracle" ("ein Wunder"), but when Elsa repeats that thought in Act 3, it is clear that "miracle" has become attached to the notion of a threat — reinforced by the word *magic*:

[Elsa]
    Full of magic is your being   Voll Zauber ist dein Wesen
    a miracle brought you here;   durch Wunder kamst du her;
    how can I ever hope to be happy,   wie sollt' ich da genesen,
    how can I ever be sure of you?   wo fänd' ich dein' Gewähr?[6]

In the central figure of *Tannhäuser*, Wagner conflates several favorite Romantic themes. One, the importance of the artist, is typical of Romantic writers who sometimes write in almost mystical terms of the poet-seer-prophet: Hölderin and Shelley, for instance. For Shelley, poets are "the unacknowledged legislators of the World." ("A Defense of Poetry," final sentence). Beethoven expressed his high regard for the Romantic imagination when he wrote to Bettina von Arnim that "when two such as I and Goethe meet, these grand gentlemen [kings and princes] are forced to note what greatness, in such as we are, means" (263). Other Romantics combined this high notion of the artist with the sense of the artist's alienation from society. In an article for the *Paris Music Gazette*, Franz Liszt contrasted artists, "elected men who seem to be chosen by God Himself to bear witness to the grandest feelings of humanity," with "a forgetful and materialistic society." With typical Romantic vividness and intensity, he described the pain of their alienation:

> ... to relate [artists'] woes and miseries, their exhaustion and their disappointments — to rip off the bandages from all their ever-bleeding wounds and to protest with energy against the oppressive iniquity or the stupid insolence that brands them, tortures them and, even worse, deigns to use them as playthings ... would be a beautiful and noble task to undertake [qtd. in Hugo, *Portable* 586–87].

Artists, Liszt contends, are "predestined men, struck down and chained, who have stolen the sacred fire of Heaven, who have given life to inanimate matter, form to thought."[7]

In his libretto for *Tannhäuser*, Wagner integrates these Romantic themes with two others: Romantic hedonism, and that particular variant of the Romantic intensity of feeling known as *Weltschmertz*: a feeling of world-weariness with overtones of frustration and melancholy.[8]

That Tannhäuser is an artist is clear; he is not only a minstrel (Sänger), but a remarkably gifted artist, as Wolfram acknowledges:

Was it magic, was it a divine power	War's Zauber, war es reine Macht,
by which you wrought such a miracle,	durch die solch Wunder du vollbracht,
enchanting that maid of matchless	virtue an deinen Sang voll Wonn und Leid
by your song of joy and sorrow?	gebannt die tugendreichste Maid?

Further, Tannhäuser is an artist who suffers. In the opera's first act, he tells Venus that he yearns for the ineffable, but because he is a mortal, subject to change, he cannot sink into joy forever:

My heart yearned, my soul thirsted	Nach Freude, ach! nach herrlichem Genießen
for joy, ah! for divine pleasure:	verlangt' mein Herz, es dürstete mein Sinn:
what once you showed only to gods	das, was nur Göttern einstens du erwiesen,
your favour has bestowed upon a mortal.	gab deine Gunst mir Sterblichem dahin.—
But alas! I have remained mortal,	Doch sterblich, ach! bin ich geblieben,
and your love overwhelms me.	und übergroß ist mir dein Lieben;
Though a god can savour joy for ever,	wenn stets ein Gott genießen kann,
I am subject to change;	bin ich dem Wechsel untertan;
I have at heart not pleasure alone,	nicht Lust allein liegt mir am Herzen,
and in my joy long for suffering.	aus Freuden sehn' ich mich nach Schmerzen!

Typical of so many Romantic figures, Tannhäuser is filled with longing, so much so that he will exchange the pleasures of Venusberg for "strife and struggle" ("Kampf und Streite"). Demonstrating the "emotional delusion and confusion" that Dahlhaus finds in this opera (*Wagner's Music Dramas* 24), Tannhäuser first tells Venus that he seeks freedom, then that he seeks death; in the next scene he echoes the words of the older pilgrims, saying that he sees

Act I of *Tannhäuser* at the Bayreuth Festival (courtesy Bayreuth Festival).

"neither rest nor repose," but instead "pain and toil." But after hearing the name of Elisabeth, Tannhäuser suddenly "recognize[s] again/ the beautiful world from which I fled." Despite the respite from strife that Elisabeth affords him, Tannhäuser remains a tortured soul throughout the opera.

Barry Millington maintains that the creative artist needs "to suffer, to feel pain and sorrow, to experience emotions which he can transmute into art" ("Introduction" 32) — a thoroughly Romantic view of the suffering artist. Elijah Moshinsky echoes Millington when he states that Wolfram's third-act aria, directed to the evening star, is musically superior to Tannhäuser's "ardent but rather banal Hymn to Venus"; Moshinsky suggests that Tannhäuser's Rome narration cannot match the beauty of the music given to Wolfram. Moshinsky's interpretation is that Tannhäuser "is the greater artist because he suffers more" (965).

Certainly, Wolfram has his own suffering. In love with Elisabeth and aware of her love for Tannhäuser, he nevertheless encourages the errant singer to return to the company of minstrels. Observing the impassioned reunion of Tannhäuser and Elisabeth, Wolfram, in a rare moment of self-pity, laments that "every ray of hope/evades me in this life!" ("flieht für dieses Leben/mir jeder Hoffnungsschein!"). As discouraged as he may be, however, his disappointment is not at all the anguish of the suffering artist. The most important dramatic function of this character (whom Moshinsky describes as "a bit pedestrian," 965) may be as a foil to Tannhäuser, which is clearly seen when considering Wolfram's two arias addressing the star of heaven. The contrast also demonstrates the theme of Romantic hedonism found in *Tannhäuser*.

When one considers that Romanticism extolled political and artistic freedom, rebellion from the reason-based strictures of established society, and the importance of feelings, it should not be surprising to find that a number of Romantic writers — Byron, Shelley, and Victor Hugo, for instance — found in erotic love a way to achieve the transcendence that they so valued. In Germany, it was the philosopher Ludwig Feuerbach, the greatest philosophical influence on Wagner until the mid–1850's, whose "extravagant glorification of love," as Friedrich Engels termed it, helped reinforce this Romantic theme (Magee 48, 50). Romantic hedonism is more than reveling in the senses. It does celebrate *eros*, love rooted in the human sexual instinct, but contains "a distinctively human idealism" as well (Frye 20), seen perhaps most clearly in Shelley's *Prometheus Unbound* and Keats's *Endymion*.

In *Tannhäuser* the erotic element may lack the societal idealism of full-fledged Romantic hedonism, but the protagonist's striving for a union beyond the merely physical is thoroughly Romantic. It is important to distinguish Elisabeth's love for Tannhäuser as more complex than Wolfram's notion of love. The words that Elisabeth uses when welcoming Tannhäuser have erotic overtones. Singing of her "unnamed raptures" ("Wonnen, die noch nie genannt"), she tells Tannhäuser,

... what a strange new life	... welch ein seltsam neues Leben
your song aroused in my breast!	rief Euer Lied mir in die Brust!
Now I was as if wracked with pain,	Bald wollt es mich wie Schmerz durchbeben,
now as if pierced with sudden joy.	bald drang's in mich wie jähe Lust;
...	...
In dreams I felt dull pain;	im Traume fühlt ich dumpfe Schmerzen,
Waking, I was filled with troubled fancies.	mein Wachen ward trübsel'ger Wahn.

Wolfram's notion of love has no such suggestion of eroticism. The sentiments he expresses in his song contest aria demonstrate a one-dimensional view of love that would be corrupted by physical contact. He first idealizes the women in the hall as "ladies lovely and virtuous,/a

Hakan Hagegaard as Wolfram in the Metropolitan Opera's *Tannhäuser* (photograph by Winnie Klotz).

Act 3 of *Tannhäuser* at the Bayreuth Festival (courtesy Bayreuth Festival).

fair garland of most fragrant flowers" ("hold und tugendsam erblick ich Frauen,/lieblicher Blüten düftereichster Kranz") and then addresses the single star shining down on him, stressing its "distant radiance" ("jeder Ferne"). In the third act, after Elisabeth has walked away, he again sings to the star, with its "gentle light from afar" ("dein sanftes Licht entsendest du der Ferne"). This image of a distant star brings to mind Keats's "Bright star" sonnet, which expresses a quite different attitude to love.

Like Wolfram, Keats's speaker begins by admiring the star, particularly its steadfastness. He notes the "lone splendor" of the night in which it hangs, and even compares it to a hermit ("eremite") helping nature in the "priestlike task" of moving the oceans' waters to cleanse the human shores:

> Bright star, would I were stedfast as thou art—
> Not in lone splendor hung aloft the night,
> And watching, with eternal lids apart,
> Like nature's patient, sleepless eremite,
> The moving waters at their priestlike task
> Of pure ablution round earth's human shores [lines 1–6].

He imagines the star looking on parts of nature that are cold, remote, and isolated: "gazing on the new soft-fallen mask/Of snow upon the mountains and the moors." To this point in the sonnet, the sentiment resembles Wolfram's; in both arias he sings of the star's distance, its remoteness.

In the second part of his sonnet, however, Keats rejects his admiration of remote purity and, unlike Wolfram, speaks no longer as a lone human looking up at the night sky. Keats's speaker still wishes to have the steadfastness of the star, but he wishes to lie so close to his lover that he can feel the rise and fall of her breast as she breathes:

> ... yet still stedfast, still unchangeable,
> Pillow'd upon my fair love's ripening breast,
> To feel for ever its soft swell and fall,
> Awake for ever in a sweet unrest,
> Still, still to hear her tender-taken breath,
> And so live ever — or else swoon to death [lines 9–14].

This is a flesh-and-blood longing, not an idealization of the woman. In Wolfram's first aria, the star is a symbol of a love that delights his "soul" and "spirit," a delight that he must be careful not to "sully" with "impure thoughts." His second aria associates the star with Elisabeth, whom Wolfram believes will soon become "a blessed angel in heaven."

The view of love expressed in Keats's sonnet, typical of the Romantic hedonism found in the second generation of English Romantic poets, is close to that described by Tannhäuser in his contest song. The minstrel first points out the impotence that he sees in Wolfram's notion of love:

| If so timid is your longing, | Wenn du in solchem Schmachten bangest, |
| your world will truly run dry! | versiegte wahrlich wohl die Welt! |

He then justifies his glorification of erotic love, the importance of "human contact" that "inclines to [him] in soft flesh," a contact that is near to his "heart and mind" because it was created from matter like his own:

... that which deigns to human contact	... was sich der Berührung beuget,
which lies near to my heart and mind,	mir Herz und Sinnen nahe liegt,
that which, created from like matter,	was sich, aus gleichem Stoff erzeuget,
inclines to me in soft flesh	in weicher Formung an mich schmiegt,
I boldly take from the fount of pleasure	ich nah ihm kühl, dem Quell der Wonnen,

Of course this pleasure is not without its pain, as Tannhäuser's desire for both Elisabeth and Venus leaves him in agony. There is no question that in Tannhäuser Wagner has created a protagonist who embodies a number of Romantic themes: Romantic hedonism, world-weariness, and the alienated artist. There *is* a question about Lohengrin representing an artist, however, even though the claim was made by Wagner himself.

In 1851, in *A Communication to My Friends*, Wagner included the following statements as he offered his interpretation of the Grail knight:

Admiration and adoration were what he did not seek; only one thing could release him from his isolation and satisfy his yearning: love, to be loved, to be understood through love. All his highest thinking, his most conscious knowing, were filled with no other desire than to be a complete, whole human being, swayed by and received with the warmth of human emotion, to be a human entirely, not a god, i.e. an absolute artist [qtd. in Dahlhaus, *Wagner's Music Dramas* 40].

Wagner's statement leads Dahlhaus to state that "*Lohengrin* is the tragedy of the absolute artist" (40). He is not the only one to take Wagner at his word; in an essay accompanying the 1987 Decca CD of the opera, Dietmar Holland contends that Wagner used "the allegory of the artist" in writing *Lohengrin* (18, 22). He quotes Wagner's definition of tragedy, which also interprets the knight as an artist: "Now I come to the essence of tragedy in the situation of the true artist living in the present age — a situation to which I gave artistic shape in my opera *Lohengrin*:— the most urgent, most natural demand of such an artist is to be accepted and understood unconditionally through feeling..." (18) Extending Wagner's interpretation of Lohengrin as the absolute artist, Holland states that the Grail "epitomizes the realm of art" (19).[9]

Wagner's pronouncements are sometimes unclear and sometimes inconsistent, but the statements quoted by Dahlhaus and Holland are in fact both clear and consistent. Whether they are sound, however, can be judged only by looking closely at the opera itself—which simply does not support this interpretation. Wagner's equation of the Grail knight with the artist does not illuminate the opera, though it does remind us of the composer's practice of mythologizing himself.

Although *Lohengrin* is not animated by the Romantic theme of the misunderstood artist, it does reflect, along with *Tannhäuser*, another important Romantic theme: the fascination with the exotic — in the case of these operas, with the medieval world. The Romantic movement had emerged as a reaction against the Enlightenment's skepticism, its utilitarian spirit, and its rigid rationalism. Because the Romantics were painfully aware that the present was inadequate, they felt a powerful nostalgia for the past, particularly ancient Greece and their own medieval past (Spencer, "Wagner's Middle Ages" 165).

What the Romantics fell in love with, however, was not the medieval world as it actually seems to have been. One need only leaf through Novalis's *Christendom or Europe: A Fragment* (1799), Chateaubriand's *The Genius of Christianity* (1802), Sir Walter Scott's *Ivanhoe* (1819), or any of William Morris's historical fictions about the Middle Ages, to see that these writers, by no means uninformed about the Middle Ages, were recreating, not replicating, the period.[10]

Before examining how Wagner colored the medieval past in both *Tannhäuser* and *Lohengrin*, we should consider how he came to choose medieval subjects; certainly, not *every* Romantic writer dealt with the Middle Ages. Wagner's exposure to German medievalism, as well as to German Romanticism, can be traced to the influence of his uncle, Adolf Wagner, an expert on Shakespeare and the Greeks, and a person steeped in the writings of the Romantics, particularly his associate E. T. A. Hoffmann, Fouqué, and Tieck (Furness 56). We know that Wagner read a great deal of Tieck, who was the first Romantic to revive medieval genres and themes (Watanabe-O'Kelly 236). Were the twenty volumes of Tieck's works on the shelves of Wagner's Dresden library simply for display? Raymond Furness maintains that the composer's libraries "were no mere ostentation but bore witness to a remarkable desire to remain abreast of literary and philosophical developments," a statement supported by the many entries in Cosima Wagner's diaries recording evenings spent in reading and discussion (Furness 55–56). Stewart Spencer modifies Furness' view, asserting that in the 1830's Wagner was "a fitful reader" ("Literary Tastes" 149).

Whether Wagner was an avid or a fitful reader, biographers agree that a turning-point seems to have come in Paris in the winter of 1841–42, when a series of conversations between the composer and the classical and medieval scholar Samuel Lehrs revived Wagner's love of Greek literature and, more important for *Tannhäuser* and *Lohengrin*, renewed the composer's interest in the German Middle Ages (Spencer, "Literary Tastes" 149).[11] Whether Wagner was influenced more by his uncle than by Lehrs, the fact remains that the chief sources he used in composing *Tannhäuser* were by German Romantic writers: Eichendorff, Fouqué, Heine, Hoffmann, and Tieck.[12]

In composing *Lohengrin*, Wagner went directly to older sources, though it is a sign of the times that he first became acquainted with the Lohengrin legend in the form of a synopsis and commentary in the annual proceedings of the Köningsberg Germanic Society. This

Peter Hofmann, left, with Eva Marton in the Metropolitan Opera's *Lohengrin* (photograph by Winnie Klotz).

occurred during the same winter when the composer was talking with Samuel Lehrs (Millington, *Compendium* 283–84). In both operas, Wagner significantly altered the medieval worldview. In creating *Tannhäuser*, writes Millington, the composer "conflated the legends to weave a story that gives us not an authentic view of 13th-century ideal and *mores*, but a technicoloured one in which the medieval world is refracted through a Romantic lens" (*Compendium* 281). The central figure of that opera is marked by the kind of individuality characteristic of Shakespeare as well as Romanticism. Additionally, the Christian surface of both operas is significantly undercut.

As dramatists creating characters, Shakespeare and Wagner are almost polar opposites. In Shakespeare's notion of character and psychology, writes Bryan Magee, "everything is unique," whereas in Wagner's "everything is universal. [Wagner's] insight is not so much into individuals as into the human condition" (85). Nevertheless, Shakespeare's influence on the developing composer was significant. The young composer was surrounded by theatre, as several of his siblings were associated in one way or another with the stage, and he was able to see performances of Shakespeare, whose works had been translated into German by Schlegel and Tieck. The influence of the English playwright on German literature was great enough, claims Furness, that "it cannot be overemphasized" (56). Many Germans regarded Shakespeare as "a liberator, a writer who was closer to the German spirit than to the French," and Wagner later stated, "[Shakespeare] is my only spiritual friend" (qtd. in Furness 56). This regard for Shakespeare may have come as well from Wagner's high regard for Hegel, whose *Lectures on Aesthetics* saw art as having passed through various great stages, culminating in the Renaissance (Danto 538). In *Opera and Drama*, Wagner suggests that it was the struggles of the individual that caused the movement from the compliant docility of a truly medieval character like Wolfram to a new era that Romantics like Wagner could value:

> Searching the history of the world, since the decay of Grecian art, for an artistic period of which we may justly feel proud, we find that period in the so-called "Renaissance," a name we give to the termination of the Middle Ages and the commencement of a new era. Here the inner man is struggling, with a veritable giant's force, to utter himself [124].[13]

Certainly, Tannhäuser embodies the individuality so prized by both Renaissance and Romantic writers. Wagner's minstrel demands artistic expression to an extent that alienates him from Wartburg society, but even before his shocking paean to eroticism in the song contest, he tells Venus that he longs above all for freedom:

for freedom I am consumed with longing,	nach Freiheit doch verlangt es mich,
for freedom I thirst;	nach Freiheit, Freiheit dürste ich:
to strife and struggle will I go,	zu Kampf und Streite will ich stehn,
even though it be to downfall and death!	sei's auch auf Tod and Untergehn!

In the song contest, Tannhäuser persists in his praise of Venus despite drawn swords, charges of blasphemy and audacity ("Kühnheit"), and "general disruption and horror" ("allgemeiner Aufbruch und Entsetzen"). As the narrative plays out, Wagner's sources leave him little choice but to present the medieval interpretation of the minstrel repenting, seeking forgiveness, falling again under the spell of Venus, and finally being saved — just barely — by the intercession of Elisabeth.

Nevertheless, the overriding impression that Tannhäuser makes is less a repentant sinner than a rebellious individual, "a force for anarchy in a would-be ordered society," a force "for individuality against regimented rule and social assumptions" (Moshinsky 966). Wagner wrote the Dresden version of the opera when he was absorbed by the anarchic personality of Bakunin (Moshinsky 966) and strongly influenced by the Young German writers who, impatient with what they saw as the reactionary values of the Biedermeier era, were eager to denounce religious and political constraints (Millington, "Introduction" 29). Like other Romantic writers, Wagner imbued the medieval setting of *Tannhäuser* with his own worldview, producing a character standing in anguish between two worlds, "one of the greatest nineteenth-century romantic rebels in revolt against artistic as well as religious authority" (Kestner 19).

Wagner transformed the Middle Ages in another way. To a casual observer, both *Lohengrin* and *Tannhäuser* might seem quintessentially Christian. In fact, however, in both operas the Christian worldview is modified, almost undercut. Secularism was in the air in Wagner's Germany. By the turn of the century, Kant, the founder of Idealism, had been succeeded by disciples such as Fichte, the early advocate of atheism and nationalism; and Schleiermacher, who "reduced religion to intuition and feeling ('Anschauung und Gefühl') independent of doctrine and dogma" (Hollinrake, "Philosophy" 52). Feuerbach, an important influence on all the theoretical tracts of Wagner's Zurich period and on the text of the *Ring*, believed that God was "the unconscious product of human consciousness: The question of the existence of God is for me nothing but the question of the existence of men" (qtd. in Hollinrake, "Philosophical Outlook" 144).[14]

One did not need to be an atheist to welcome radical changes in German thought. The poet Heinrich Heine, writing in 1833, declared that "with Faust, the medieval epoch of faith ends and the modern critical age of science begins." What knowledge, reason, and science now offer, Heine states, is "the pleasures which faith, Catholic Christianity, has for so long cheated us of." Declaring that "the German people is itself that learned Doctor Faust," Heine predicted that in time, Goethe's prophetic poem would enable the German people to "[vindicate] the rights of the flesh" ("The Romantic School" 41, 42).

Tannhäuser represents just such a vindication. True, he is torn between Venus and Elisabeth, but, as discussed above, in this opera sensual and spiritual love are not mutually exclusive; they are dialectically interrelated, with the opera striving—unsuccessfully—for a synthesis.[15] And it is not the two women, Venus and Elisabeth, who present the strongest contrast; as we have seen, it is Wolfram, not Elisabeth, who unambiguously embodies spiritual love. Certainly, the opera is built on contrasts; among them, writes Joseph Kestner, is "medieval conformity and Renaissance individualism" (16), which might initially seem strange since the early-thirteenth-century setting of *Tannhäuser* is two and a half centuries before the Renaissance would have begun to reach Germany. But it is not so strange after all. Wagner's sources were Romantic works (though the legends of Tannhäuser predated those sources), but even had the composer been working from medieval sources, his libretto would have reflected his own time. We have also seen how his familiarity with Shakespeare reinforced the notion of individual freedom that was so important to the Romantics. The result is an opera that is an amalgam of medieval piety, pagan abandon, Renaissance self-determination, and Wagner's own secular, Romantic worldview.

Lohengrin is set much earlier than *Tannhäuser*, in the early tenth century, and Wagner used much older sources: Johann Joseph von Görres's edition of the anonymous epic *Lohengrin*, and two poems, *Parzivâl* and *Titurel*, by Wolfram von Eschenbach, composed near the juncture of the twelfth and thirteenth centuries (Millington, *Compendium* 283–84). These facts might lead one to expect a more authentic presentation of the Middle Ages; however, Wagner's interpretation of Eschenbach is "individualistically selective and psychologically tinted" (Kester 134). The most important way in which Wagner alters the medieval worldview is to temper the sense of the transcendence represented by Montsalvat. Bernard Hoeckner may be overstating when he says that the dramatic effect of the Grail narration "falls flat." He quotes Wagner's contemporary, the German composer and teacher Joachim Raff, who argued on musical grounds that "The mystic content of [Lohengrin's] narrative is exhausted in the prelude" (129). And if there is an element of overstatement in Hoeckner's statement that the Grail knight delivers his narration "lonely, lamely, and too late" (131), there is no denying that Lohengrin leaves for Montsalvat profoundly saddened.

Looking at how Wagner modified the medieval worldview in both *Tannhäuser* and *Lohengrin* requires an important caveat. Regardless of the lack of true resolution in *Tannhäuser*, regardless of Lohengrin's dejection as he sails away, those experiencing the opera are caught up by the transcendence of the music. Because of the great wash of sound that ends each opera, the spectator cannot help but feel, more than anything else, a triumphant affirmation of the medieval worldview.

No caveat is needed in seeing the importance of the Romantic worldview to *Tannhäuser* and *Lohengrin*. True, Wagner stopped using the term *romantic* after 1849; by 1851 he doubted whether even *Lohengrin* could be described as "Romantic" and, in later revisions of *Tannhäuser*, no longer added the designation "grand Romantic opera" (Deathridge 64). However, that is simply a matter of terminology and has more to do with music than with ideas. Wagner can easily be considered "German Romanticism's most favoured beneficiary," as Roger Hollinrake points out, for "he responded with enthusiasm to the world of spirits, medievalism, artist-figures and outsiders which that movement delighted in portraying. Romanticism in Germany lasted some thirty years, and Wagner absorbed it as no other musician" ("Philosophy" 56).

The timing could not have been more felicitous. At a crucial point in his artistic devel-

Lohengrin, the August Everding production at the Metropolitan Opera (photograph by Winnie Klotz).

opment — after the first three derivative experiments and before the full mythic and musical accomplishments of the later operas — Wagner was enriched by the great Romantic writers and philosophers. If he was a beneficiary of Romanticism, he gave back to the arts much more than he took. Only eighty years after the composer's death, William Blissett described the cultural phenomenon of Wagnerism as "arguably the greatest single fact to be reckoned with in the arts during the past century" (qtd. in DiGaetani 12). A strong assertion, certainly, but one that is proven true over and over again in opera houses around the world.

Notes

1. See Barbara J. Guenther, "Romanticism in the *Ring.*" *Inside the Ring.* Ed. John Louis DiGaetani. Jefferson, NC: McFarland, 2006. 95–124.

2. John Deathridge and Carl Dahlhous point out their agreement with most of Wagner's biographers that *Lohengrin* can be claimed as a musical drama whereas *Tannhäuser* "is still an opera" (*The New Grove Wagner* 130). Dahlhaus states this even more directly in *Richard Wagner's Music Dramas*: "*Tannhäuser* is an opera, not a music drama" (31). In terms of ideas, however, both operas are similar in the extent to which they reflect the Romantic worldview.

3. Alan David Auerbach's analysis of Wagner's political writing and his actions notes "the considerable inconsistencies" (96) of "the remarkably inconsistent Richard Wagner" (410). Auerbach's explanation is that Wagner "was prolific in his prose and so emotionally involved in everything that he wrote and said that he did not always think out carefully what he was saying or appreciate where his arguments were taking him" (333).

4. Peter Thorslev reminds us that a rapturous awareness of transcendence, a tradition of thought found in the major philosophical works of German Idealism and in much of what Thorslev calls "High Romantic" literature, is not typical of every Romantic writer. He points out that the mature poetry of Shelley and Byron,

for instance, fails to show "evidence of any settled faith in a transcendent 'idea' realizing itself in nature and in history, driven by an inexorable will" (93).

Drummond Bone also notes that the later works of Byron and Goethe "share a secular ironic relativism which is sympathetic to the twentieth century." The "revolution of thought" usually applied to the typically Romantic writers is, in Byron and Goethe, "a revolution which has little to do with transcendent categories" (130).

5. Ortrud is introduced by her husband as "scion of Radbod, Prince of Friesia." The designation *Prince*, used in two modern English versions of Wagner's libretto, is a translation of *Sproß*, meaning *descendent* or *scion*. Regardless of how Wagner's term is translated, the meaning is clear: Ortrud is of noble blood. This is reinforced a few lines later, when Friedrich states that Ortrud "is of the house that once/gave its princes to these lands " ("mein Weib dazu aus dem Geschlecht, das einst/auch diesen Landen seine Fürsten gab").

6. In addition to magic objects, spells, and events, the opera is suffused by such words as "spell," "enchant," "enraptured," and "beguiled," spoken not only by Elsa but by the onlookers and even Friedrich. A related strand running through the opera is Elsa's waking visions, emotional transfigurations, and "dreamy state" ("träumerischer Mut"). Although this is not part of the opera's theme of magic, it does remind one of other Romantic works, such as Keats's "The Eve of St. Agnes," which, like *Lohengrin* is set in the Middle Ages. Keats's heroine, Madeline, is so caught in "an azure-lidded sleep" that even when her lover wakes her, we are told

> Her eyes were open, but she still beheld
> Now wide awake, the vision of her sleep:

Caught between reality and the dream world, Madeline "look'd so dreamingly" that her lover "fear[ed] to move or speak."

The English Romantics were not drawn to magic as so many of the German Romantics were, with the notable exception of Coleridge (e.g., *Rime of the Ancient Mariner, Christabel*), who was thoroughly conversant with German literature and philosophy. However, with the exception of Byron, the English Romantics were often drawn to write of visionary experiences.

7. This description suggests a favorite image of Shelley, treated most extensively in *Prometheus Unbound*. Shelley treats the figure of Prometheus idealistically; Mary Shelley, in the title of her novel *Frankenstein; or, The Modern Prometheus*, uses the figure of the mythic fire-bearer ironically. Victor Frankenstein is "decidedly not the champion of humankind" (Abrams 15).

8. Related to the notion of the alienated artist afflicted with world-weariness is the Byronic hero. This protagonist is not simply a figure separated from society because he had rejected it or because it had rejected him, and not simply a nonconformist sometimes represented as a great sinner. Unlike Coleridge's ancient mariner or the guilty outcasts in Wordsworth's *Guilt and Sorrow* and *Peter Bell*, Byron's violators of conventional laws and limits remain proudly unrepentant. The title character of Byron's *Manfred*, for example — guilty and proud yet anything but repentant — successfully defies the demons who have come to drag his soul to hell:

> Thou has no power upon me, *that* I feel;
> Thou never shalt possess me, *that* I know:
> What I have done is done; I bear within
> A torture which could nothing gain from thing:
> The mind which is immortal makes itself
> Requital for its good or evil thoughts —
> Is its own origin of ill and end —
> And its own place and time...
> .... .
> [I] was my own destroyer, and will be
> My own hereafter.— Back, ye baffled fiends!" [3.4.125–112, 139–40].

Tannhäuser is an alienated artist, at odds with his society, but he is not a Byronic hero. The Landgrave refers to the minstrel's former "haughty pride" ("Hochmut stolz"), but Wolfram quickly corrects this perception: "Is this the demeanour of pride?"

For a brief but useful discussion of *Weltschmertz* and a related tone, *morbidzetta*, as they appear in music, see Longyear 4–5.

9. Like Dahlhaus and Holland, Berthold Hoeckner bases much of his article about *Lohengrin* on Wagner's equation of "human being" with "absolute artist." He also builds part of his article on Wagner's contention, in *Opera and Drama*, that music is woman and poetry is man.

10. One of the most astute analysts of English Romanticism, Northrop Frye, includes an insightful discussion of this point in *A Study of English Romanticism*. He believes that the Romantic writers were rejecting the social reality of the earlier period and that the social ideals that writers took from the medieval world could be disparate as the writers themselves. The conservative Sir Walter Scott and the radical William Morris, for instance, each found something of purpose in the Middle Ages.

11. In contrast with Furness, Stewart maintains that Lehrs "awakened" Wagner's interest in the German Middle Ages. Both essays occur in the same volume, *The Wagner Compendium*, and Furness refers readers to Stewart's article "for an alternative perspective" (56). Furness's interpretation — that Wagner's interest in the German Middle Ages came first through the influence of his uncle — is persuasive. The difference between the two writers' interpretations simply demonstrates Spencer's point that "it is often difficult to disentangle the strands of literary, political and philosophical influence" ("Literary Tastes" 149).

12. Stewart Spencer points out that although Wagner "later displayed a typically ungenerous attitude" to Romantic writers, including Hoffmann and Tieck, one cannot deny the "seminal importance" of these writers to "the whole of his later oeuvre in terms of subject-matter and themes, from fairytale motifs to the supernatural and the world of dreams, from the mood of world-weariness to the artist's role in society" ("Literary Tastes" 149).

13. Certainly, any Romantic would have been attracted by the Renaissance worldview, with its celebration of the limitless potentialities of humans, the high value it placed on intensity, and its imaginative expansion into new and strange worlds. Between the worldviews of the Renaissance and of the Romantics came the Neoclassic worldview, and although this series of reactions is not exactly like the movement of a pendulum, one cannot ignore the many similarities between Renaissance and Romantic thinking.

14. Berthold Hoeckner writes of the influence of this idea of Feuerbach on *Tannhäuser*. He hears Feuerbach's "collapse [of] the difference between God and human beings, between the metaphysical and the physical" echoed in Wagner's statement that "The essence of love is the *desire for full physical reality*" (Wagner's *A Communication to My Friends*," qtd. p. 119).

15. In "Wagner's Middle Ages," Stewart Spencer discusses the varieties of medieval views of love, including the notion of love as "destructive and demonic." This dark view does not characterize *Tannhäuser* though it is important to Wagner's later works (*The Wagner Compendium*, 164–67).

Bibliography

Abrams, M.H., and Stephen Greenblatt. "The Romantic Period: 1785–1830." *The Norton Anthology of English Literature*. 7th ed. Vol. 2A: *The Romantic Period*. New York: Norton, 2000.

Auerbach, Alan David. *The Ideas of Richard Wagner: An Examination and Analysis*. 2nd ed. Lanham: University Press of America, 2003.

Beethoven, Ludwig van. *Beethoven's Letters: A Critical Edition with Explanatory Notes*. Trans. J. S. Shedlock. Ed. A. C. Kalischer. Vol. 1. London: Dent, 1909.

Bone, Drummond. "The Question of a European Romanticism." *Questioning Romanticism*. Ed. John Beer. Baltimore: Johns Hopkins University Press, 1995.

Bowra, C. M. *The Romantic Imagination*. New York: Oxford University Press, 1961.

[Byron] George Gordon, Lord Byron. *The Poetical Works of Lord Byron*. London: Oxford University Press, 1961.

Coleridge, Samuel Taylor. *Poetical Works*. 1834. Ed. Ernest Hartley Coleridge. Oxford, UK: Oxford University Press, 1969.

Dahlhaus, Carl. *Nineteenth-Century Music*. Trans. J. Bradford Robinson. Berkeley: University of California Press, 1989.

_____. *Richard Wagner's Music Dramas*. Trans. Mary Whittall. Cambridge, UK: Cambridge University Press, 1971.

Danto, Arthur C. "Hegel's End-of-Art Thesis." *A New History of German Literature*. Ed. David E. Wellbery et al. Cambridge, MA: Harvard University Press, 2004.

Deathridge, John. "Germany: the 'Special Path.'" *The Late Romantic Era*. Ed. Jim Samson. London: MacMillan, 1991.

_____, and Carl Dahlhaus. *The New Grove Wagner*. London: Macmillan, 1984.

DiGaetani, John Louis. *Richard Wagner and the Modern British Novel*. Cranbury, NJ: Associated University Presses, 1978.

Frye, Northrop. *A Study of English Romanticism*. New York: Random House, 1968.

Furness, Raymond. "Literature." *The Wagner Compendium: A Guide to Wagner's Life and Music.* Ed. Barry Millington. New York: Schirmer, 1992.
Goethe, Johann Wolfgang von. *The Sorrows of Young Werther* and *Novella*. 1774; 1886. Trans. Elizabeth Mayer and Louise Bogan. New York: Random House, 1971.
Heine, Heinrich. "The Romantic School." Trans. Helen Mustard. *The Romantic School and Other Essays.* Ed. Jost Hermand and Robert C. Holub. New York: Continuum, 1985.
Hoeckner, Berthold. "Elsa Screams, or the Birth of Music Drama." *Cambridge Opera Journal* 9.2 (1997): 97–132.
Holland, Dietmar. "Lohengrin's Tragic Dialectic." Trans. Chris Wood. [CD booklet.] Decca, 1987. 17–22.
Hollinrake, Roger. "Philosophical Outlook." *The Wagner Compendium: A Guide to Wagner's Life and Music.* Ed. Barry Millington. New York: Schirmer, 1992.
_____. "Philosophy." *The Wagner Compendium: A Guide to Wagner's Life and Music.* Ed. Barry Millington. New York: Schirmer, 1992.
_____. " Social and Political Attitudes." *The Wagner Compendium: A Guide to Wagner's Life and Music.* Ed. Barry Millington. New York: Schirmer, 1992.
Horton, Rod. W,. and Vincent F. Hopper. *Backgrounds of European Literature: The Political, Social, and Intellectual Development behind the Great Books of Western Civilization.* New York: Appleton, 1954.
Hugo, Howard E. "Masterpieces of Romanticism." Introduction. *The Continental Edition of World Masterpieces.* Ed. Maynard Mack. Vol. 2. New York: Norton, 1966.
_____. *The Portable Romantic Reader.* New York: Viking, 1957.
Keats, John. *The Poetical Works of John Keats.* Ed. H.W.Garrod. London: Oxford University Press, 1961.
Kester, Sally. "The Relativity of Good and Evil in 'Lohengrin.'" *Conspectus Carminis: Essays for David Galliver.* Vol. 15 of *Miscellanea Musicologica: Adelaide Studies in Musicology.* 56.15 (1988). 133–42.
Kestner, Joseph. "Romantic Rebel." *Opera News* 8 (1 January 1983). 16–19.
Longyear, Ray M. *Nineteenth-Century Romanticism in Music.* 2d ed. Englewood Cliffs, NJ: Prentice-Hall, 1973.
Magee, Bryan. *Wagner and Philosophy.* London: Penguin, 2000.
Mann, William. "The Creation of *Lohengrin*. Trans Chris Wood. [CD booklet.] Decca, 1987. 14–16.
Marchand, Leslie A. *Byron's Poetry: A Critical Introduction.* Boston: Houghton, 1965.
Millington, Barry. "An Introduction to the Paris 'Tannhäuser.'" [CD booklet.] Hamburg: DGD, 1989. 25–33.
_____, ed. *The Wagner Compendium: A Guide to Wagner's Life and Music.* New York: Schirmer, 1992.
Moshinsky, Elijah. "'Tannhäuser' and the Unity of Opposites." *Opera* 35 (1984): 963– 69.
Pavlovič, Mirka. "Romanticism as a Period." *Colloquia on the History and Theory of Music at the International Music Festival in Brno.* Ed. Petr Macek. Vol. 22 [1987]. Brno, 1992.
Plantinga, Leon. *Romantic Music: A History of Musical Style in Nineteenth-Century Europe.* New York: Norton, 1984.
Plaskitt, James. "'The Language of Passion'— Wagner and Romanticism." *Wagner 1976: A Celebration of the Bayreuth Festival.* [Ed. Stewart Spencer] London: Wagner Society, 1976.
Prawer, S .S. *Frankenstein's Island: England and the English in the Writings of Heinrich Heine.* Cambridge, UK: Cambridge University Press, 1986.
Shelley, Percy Bysshe. *Shelley: Poetical Works.* Ed. Thomas Hutchinson, rev. G. M. Matthews. Oxford, UK: Oxford University Press, 1970.
Simpson, David. "Romanticism, Criticism and Theory." *The Cambridge Companion to British Romanticism.* Ed. Stuart Curran. Cambridge, UK: Cambridge University Press, 1993.
Spencer, Stewart. "Literary Tastes." *The Wagner Compendium: A Guide to Wagner's Life and Music.* Ed. Barry Millington. New York: Schirmer, 1992.
_____. "Wagner's Middle Ages." *The Wagner Compendium: A Guide to Wagner's Life and Music.* Ed. Barry Millington. New York: Schirmer, 1992.
Thorslev, Peter. "German Romantic Idealism." *The Cambridge Companion to British Romanticism.* Ed. Stuart Curran. Cambridge, MA: Cambridge University Press, 1993.
Wagner, Richard. *Lohengrin.* Trans. Chris Wood. [CD booklet.] Decca, 1987. 66–240.
_____. *Opera and Drama.* Trans. William Ashton Ellis. Vol. 2. New York: Broude, 1966.
_____. *Tannhäuser.* Trans. Lionel Salter. [CD booklet.] Hamburg: DGG, 1989. 68–169.
Watanabe-O'Kelly, Helen. *The Cambridge History of German Literature.* Cambridge, UK: Cambridge University Press, 1997.
Whittall, Arnold. *Romantic Music: A Concise History from Schubert to Sibelius.* London: Thames, 1987.
Wordsworth, William. *Poetical Works.* 1849–50. Ed. Thomas Hutchinson, rev. Ernest de Selincourt. Oxford, UK: Oxford University Press, 1969.

6

Don't Ask: Faith, Magic, Knowledge, and Sources in *Lohengrin*

Lisa Feurzeig

> Nie sollst du mich befragen, noch Wissens Sorge tragen
> Woher ich kam der Fahrt, noch wie mein Nam' und Art.
>
> Elsa, the Woman ... — made me a Revolutionary at one blow. [Wagner/Ellis 347]

It is here that we find a situation which has been observed both to foster sorcery accusations and to offer scope for resort to sorcery. This is when *two systems of power* are sensed to clash within the one society. On the one hand, there is *articulate* power, power defined and agreed upon by everyone (and especially by its holders!): authority vested in precise persons; admiration and success gained by recognized channels. Running counter to this there may be other forms of influence less easy to pin down — *inarticulate* power: the disturbing intangibles of social life; the imponderable advantages of certain groups; personal skills that succeed in a way that is unacceptable or difficult to understand. Where these two systems overlap, we may expect to find the sorcerer [Brown 124].

Wagner's *Lohengrin* presents the complex social world of a medieval court that is plagued by a royal disappearance, conflicting claims to the succession, and a tangled legal case combining political, filial, and erotic elements. One might expect that this messy situation would lead to a whole range of interpretations of the opera, readings that attempt to discover the facts of the case and the best ways of understanding the characters and their actions. In fact, the opposite is true: there is one generally accepted reading of the story, which views it as a myth about the struggle between pure Christian faith and small-minded reason. According to this reading, the story ends tragically, with the departure of godlike hero Lohengrin and the failure of his marriage to Elsa, all because she could not maintain her pure trust in him. Ortrud, an evil woman governed by paganism and personal ambition, manages to arouse Elsa's suspicions, transforming her from a religious visionary into a fearful, doubting woman who ruins everything by asking the fateful question she has vowed to avoid, bringing about the end of her own life and of Lohengrin's residence on earth. Even critical readings tend to assume that Wagner himself held this view at the time that he composed the work, but then quickly turned against it in the following years (Deathridge). In other words, modern scholars may reject certain aspects of the traditional reading, but they do so from outside the work, rather than considering the possibility that the critique is already contained within it.

In this essay, I will treat the standard view outlined above as a sort of straw man, and I will present an alternate interpretation. I hope to show that Wagner was aware (whether on a conscious or subconscious level) of the questions and unresolved issues in the story, and that he built these issues into his text: both the words sung by the characters and at times the stage directions as well. This reading may seem less satisfying than the standard view. It is less clear-cut; it arrives at no clear moral; and it opens the work to the accusation of untidiness because of the sheer volume of loose ends. These qualities may be viewed as points against the interpretation; or, alternately, they may show that Wagner was writing a very modern work. In support of this interpretation, it could be pointed out that it shows ways in which *Lohengrin* prefigures elements in Wagner's thinking in his later operas, particularly the *Ring* cycle, long noted for its ambiguities—and it helps account for Wagner's comment quoted above. After all, he really did become a revolutionary within the next few years of composing *Lohengrin*. If we read this opera as one that ultimately challenges the validity of authority and critiques human judgement, it may help us understand what spurred Wagner to man the Dresden barricades in 1849.

To begin the process of unraveling, let us consider the role of magic in *Lohengrin*. While it will eventually be learned that the first relevant magical event, Gottfried's transformation into a swan, occurred before the opera began, the first apparent magic is Lohengrin's arrival on a boat pulled by a swan. This arrival, despite its strangeness, seems to arouse no suspicion of evil magic in the onlookers. Medieval Latin made a distinction between *mira* (wonder) and *miracula* (miracle) (Peters xvi). The German word *Wunder*, sung by the chorus, seems to encompass both concepts, and thus avoids the issue of whether suspicion is appropriate. This plays very well into the standard view that the people of Brabant represent a simple and pure Christian faith; but as we shall see below, this is actually a historically inaccurate perspective on what a good medieval Christian ought to think when confronted with such a wondrous event.

If we do accept the notion that the Brabantians are confident and pure in their faith, then it should disturb us that the herald, before the trial by combat, pronounces a prohibition of evil magic to subvert the result of the ordeal: "Durch bösen Zaubers List und Trug stört nicht des Urteils Eigenschaft" (Through evil magic's trick and deception disturb not the quality of the ordeal) (126–27). This warning suggests a lack of confidence in God's ability to regulate the outcome, even though the whole concept of a trial by combat is that God is in control.

How can these anomalies be explained? When suspicion of evil magic might be expected, the people of Brabant have no concern, yet when suspicion is inappropriate, they voice it. Before we explore these questions further, let us compare Wagner's libretto with two actual medieval stories from the twelfth century: the "Lay of Yonec" by Marie de France, and "The Story of the Grail" by Chrétien de Troyes, each of which presents an interesting foil for certain events in the opera.

The unnamed heroine of the "Lay of Yonec" (whom I will refer to simply as "the lady") has been wed to a much older man. He is so jealous of her beauty that he keeps her locked in a tower, and she prays for a lover. Both here and in *Lohengrin*, young women in distress appeal to a higher power for help, using a private and intense form of communication. Elsa's sorrow brings her a dream of a champion, and the lady's prayer for a lover is granted. Each woman is helped by someone who comes in the form of a bird: Elsa by Lohengrin, whose boat is drawn by a swan, and the lady by a knight who flies through her window in the form of a hawk and then regains his human form.

These stories also have similar endings. In the lay, the knight, after a passionate romance with the lady, is killed by her husband. As he is dying, he gives her a ring and a sword to pass on to their son, with whom she is pregnant. Years later, when her son has grown to manhood, she travels with him and her husband to the place where the body of her lover — a king, as we discover — is embalmed. She then recounts the whole story to her son, revealing his true father and thus enabling him to claim his rightful rank and inheritance. Having fulfilled this duty, she "fell senseless across the tomb, neither did she speak any further word until the soul had gone from her body" (136). Similarly, Lohengrin, as he departs, gives Elsa the three gifts of a horn, sword, and ring to be passed on to her brother, the rightful heir; at the moment of Lohengrin's departure, Elsa collapses "entseelt." The stories are like two different arrangements of the colored fragments in a kaleidoscope. The bird-transformation may affect either lover or brother; the heir may be son or brother; the marriage in one story is legal but never consummated, whereas in the other it is illicit and produces a son. These parallels could be spun out in many directions — but it is a key difference between the stories that is more important to my argument.

The difference is that in the "Lay of Yonec," the lady immediately suspects the man who has entered her chamber in the shape of a bird. She refuses to trust him until she has some proof that his transformation does not result from evil magic. Also crucial is that he does not take umbrage at this demand. Instead, he understands it, and volunteers to undergo a generally-accepted test to prove that he is a good Christian: he arranges a subterfuge through which it is possible for her to observe him taking communion at mass. Her knight's words are the direct opposite of Lohengrin's: "Lady, you ask rightly. For nothing that man can give would I have you doubt my faith and affiance" (128). Lohengrin, by contrast, not only fails to acknowledge that Elsa may reasonably have doubts about him, but directly forbids her to ask him any of the standard questions — or even to be troubled by them. He wishes to exercise control not only over her words, but over her thoughts as well. Furthermore, he sets up this control as a condition before he will marry her.

These demands are all the more striking in the light of Elsa's dynastic responsibilities. In Gottfried's absence, she is the heiress to an important land; her husband will become duke of Brabant. The *Saxon Mirror*, a German law code from the thirteenth century, includes two statements that shed light on how great a risk Elsa may be taking in trusting Lohengrin and agreeing to marry him. First, we read that "Paid champions and their children ... are all without legal rights." (It is interesting that the other groups treated this way are illegitimate children, robbers and thieves, and minstrels) (Dobozy 80). One might protest that Lohengrin is not an ordinary hired champion, but consider the circumstances. He appears out of nowhere, agrees to fight for Elsa's honor, and then specifies harsh conditions which she must accept before he will marry her. Elsa is heiress to a significant fortune and fief; her husband will have much wealth and power. Even if Lohengrin does not present himself as a champion for hire, he is performing an assigned task for a price agreed on in advance. Is Elsa endangering the succession of her children by agreeing to marry someone of such dubious social position?

Second, we read that "when someone eligible to be a *Schöffe* [this is a legal status approximately equivalent to "juror"] challenges someone of equal rank to a trial by combat, he needs to know accurately his four ancestors and his family estate and *must name them*; otherwise the defendant can by rights refuse him the duel" (Dobozy 83, 196–97). (The italics are mine.) In the opera, Telramund has accused Elsa, so he, not Lohengrin, is in the role of challenger.

Nevertheless, this requirement reveals how greatly rank and family influenced the legal standing, and even the possibility, of a combat. By refusing to divulge basic information about himself, Lohengrin undermines the basic legal structures of medieval Saxon society; Elsa, as the heiress responsible for her realm, might be viewed as criminally irresponsible if she continued to ignore these issues.

As we shall see below, attitudes toward magic shifted over the centuries; they also varied regionally. It is possible that attitudes toward hired champions were also different in the time of Henry the Fowler, or in Brabant, than in the society represented by the *Saxon Mirror*. These issues, nonetheless, are worth considering before we unthinkingly accept the notion that Elsa's virtue stands or falls with her complete and unquestioning trust of the peculiar individual who has turned up to rescue her.

In the first scene of Chrétien's "Story of the Grail," young Perceval encounters a party of knights riding through the forest. Perceval is ignorant of almost everything worldly, since his mother is trying to protect him from the dangers of knightly life. All that he has been taught is a very simple religious outlook in which there exist God, angels, and devils. When he hears the riders clattering through the forest, his first thought is that they must be devils, so he decides to throw his javelin at them. He quickly changes his mind, though, upon seeing them:

> When he did see them in the open without the woods concealing them, and noticed the jingling hauberks and the bright shining helmets, and beheld the green and the scarlet and the gold and the azure and the silver gleaming in the sun, he found everything most noble and beautiful. "Ah, Lord God, have mercy!" he then exclaimed. "These are angels I behold here..." [340–41].

He then quickly inflates his estimate, concluding that the most handsome of the knights must be not an angel, but God himself. His reasoning is very much like the collective assumption of the Brabantian nobles that Lohengrin, the beautiful knight pulled by a swan, must be a messenger from God: "Ein Wunder ist gekommen, ein unerhörtes Wunder! Dank, du Herr und Gott, der die Schwache beschirmet! Gegrüsst, du gottgesandter Held!" (A wonder is come, an unheard-of wonder! Thanks, you Lord and God, who protects the weak one! Greetings, you godsent hero!) (88–92) The key point here is that the young Perceval (who, incidentally, will eventually father Lohengrin in Wolfram von Eschenbach's version) is the classic medieval model of a fool. From a twelfth-century perspective, the Brabantians' assumption that Lohengrin comes from God would be evidence, not of their pure faith, but of their foolish naiveté.

A Brief History of Attitudes Toward Magic

The following summary is drawn from the work of historians Peter Brown, Edward Peters, and Richard Kieckhefer, who have all worked intensively with primary sources concerning magic. My goal here is to trace the shifting attitudes towards magic, particularly its relation to Christianity, from late antiquity through the late Middle Ages, and thus to give a chronological estimate of what types of attitudes are represented in *Lohengrin*. As we shall find, Wagner chose well (following one of his sources, the late thirteenth-century poem *Lohengrin*) when he placed this opera in the early tenth century (Mertens 242). Henry the Fowler's nine-year tribute agreement with the Magyars began in 926; thus the opera is set in the 930s, at the end of that agreement. The attitudes portrayed in the opera — particularly the lack of clarity about magic and its possible strength — match this period well.

Placido Domingo as Lohengrin in the Metropolitan Opera production (photograph by Winnie Klotz).

While magic was generally deplored in antiquity, the picture was somewhat mixed, in that it was believed that both good magic (*mageia*) and evil magic (*goeteia*) were possible, depending on whether the magician communicated with good or evil spirits (*daimones*). Nevertheless, "hostility more often than not characterized the Greek and later the Roman attitude toward magical practices and practitioners" (Peters 2). Early Christianity strongly opposed magic, but viewed divine intervention as something entirely different. When a Christian was victorious in a confrontation with a non–Christian — for example, when Paul brought temporary blindness upon the Jewish magician Elymas, or when Peter caused the downfall (literally) of Simon Magus — non–Christians might well view the incident as evidence that the new god was acting in a magical way to prove his strength (Peters 3–4, 8; Kieckhefer 33–34).

In Brown's view, "late Roman society was dominated by the problem of the conflict between change and stability in a traditional society" (123–24). The old hierarchy was still formally in place, yet had been largely displaced by new kinds of power and particularly by Christian ideas, which had "seeped triumphantly upwards, at just this time, from the lower middle classes into a court aristocracy of *parvenus*" (123). This complex situation in the fourth to sixth centuries led Brown to formulate his theory that a society characterized by conflict between articulate and inarticulate power is prone to suspicions of sorcery. (See the opening quotation of this essay.) The Christian *parvenus* had become the new elite that held articulate power, while the old aristocracy, losing its influence, fell into the role of the inarticulate power, possessing less formal authority, yet still able to call on old networks, loyal servants, etc.

Peters then applied this theory to later times. Since "Brown ... suggests that sorcery is best understood as a function of explaining misfortune on the part of those who consider themselves victims," it makes sense that there were fewer accusations after Christianity stopped facing significant rivalry from paganism. "Brown's model may help indeed to explain the relative fearlessness of Christians between the seventh and eleventh centuries when faced with sorcery. ... [but] that certainty and security of a completely Christianized world began to slip during the late tenth and eleventh centuries." Peters then moves to consider parallels between the late Roman Empire and Western European courts in the thirteenth and fourteenth centuries (117–19).

I follow partially in Peters' footsteps here, since I also extend Brown's ideas into later centuries. By considering political circumstances rather than the documents concerning magic in particular, however, I arrive at a somewhat different conclusion about which periods should be considered transitional and which more stable. Peters places the tenth century in the middle of the period of relative stability for Christianity, but this is debatable. In the words of Polish historian O. Halecki,

> the tenth century ... was an epoch of profound transformation for the whole of Europe.... Up to this date only the southern and western part of Europe was well known to history. Henceforth, the historic community, so long limited to the ancient territories of the Roman Empire and to its sphere of influence, was gradually extended towards the north-east, to the entire Slavonic world, and to the Scandinavian countries [3–4].

During the time of Henry the Fowler, from the late ninth into the tenth century, there was an ongoing power struggle between the Holy Roman Empire and the lands surrounding it, along with tension between Christianity and paganism. Wagner's framing historical narrative accurately represents Henry's main aims as king of Saxony and emperor:

Henry spent the first few years of his reign forcing the dukes of Lorraine, Bavaria, and Swabia to recognize his kingship. He then concentrated on strengthening his own duchy of Saxony.... He repulsed the northern Slavs and began a deliberate policy of eastern expansion called the *Drang nach Osten* (push to the east). The essence of this policy was the colonization of frontier regions from which the Slavs and other peoples were pushed back.... Henry also built fortifications against the Magyars and raised a cavalry force that inflicted the first defeat on the fast-moving Magyar raiders in 933 [Hoyt and Chodorow 196–97].

In the realm of religion, too, the ninth and tenth centuries were a conflicted time. In the East, the Byzantine and Roman churches vied for conversions (Hoyt & Chodorow 311–13). On both the Eastern and Western borders of Central Europe, several nations — including Poland, Bohemia, Hungary, Denmark, and Iceland — made the conversion to Christianity in or close to the year 1000. Thus the time just before that was characterized by tension between old and new religions.

These historical circumstances are portrayed quite directly in *Lohengrin*. Brabant and Frisia were part of the western border area; hence Henry's satisfaction at finding that the Brabantian nobles are supporting him in his struggle against the Hungarians at the eastern border. While that particular region had been Christian for some time, it is certainly plausible that someone like Ortrud, who still worships the Norse gods, might still be found on the fringes of Christian society. On the whole, one might expect the people of Brabant to feel somewhat insecure both about their government and their religion, and to be aware of living in a borderland where it was still a real possibility that the existing institutions would be swept away by new changes. To heighten the insecurity, Wagner presents a situation of dynastic conflict. After Gottfried's disappearance, and with Elsa under suspicion, there is a significant possibility that the succession will pass to the descendants of Radbod, who are next in line to the dukedom. Thus, the Brabantians might in the near future be ruled by someone who would forcibly convert them all back to paganism.

In several ways, then, *Lohengrin* presents a situation of conflicting claims to power. Articulate power is vested in the king, the ducal family, and the Christian faith. Inarticulate power is represented doubly by Ortrud, since she is both Radbod's descendant (thus linked to the old aristocracy) and an adherent of the old pagan faith. Furthermore, Ortrud possesses to a high degree what Brown describes as "personal skills that succeed in a way that is unacceptable or difficult to understand": she successfully uses her acting ability and claims of prophetic knowledge to manipulate Elsa and Telramund so that they help her carry out her plans. Altogether, then, *Lohengrin* perfectly demonstrates the type of situation in which "we may expect to find the sorcerer." Christianity is new and tenuous enough so that it is still, to a degree, viewed as a stronger magic than paganism. This accounts both for the uncritical attitude of Elsa and the Brabantians toward Lohengrin and for their acceptance of the possibility that evil magic might prevail in a trial by combat.

The standard view of the opera, by contrast with the interpretation sketched out above, uncritically mixes elements from the two sides of the divide. It assumes that Christianity is paramount and dominant, and Ortrud a mere vestige of the distant past. At the same time, it equates an unquestioning acceptance of Lohengrin with pure Christian faith. The contradiction here is that when Christianity *does* reach that level of supremacy (for example, in the twelfth century) the type of faith that goes with that includes skepticism about apparent miracles. We saw that in the "Lay of Yonec": the lady did not uncritically accept an apparent miracle, but tested it. Similarly, the Catholic Church in our own day tests claims of miracles before being willing to confer sainthood.

At the stage when a faith is still tenuous and in competition with other belief systems, it is normal and accepted to present evidence from one's personal experience as confirmation of the religion's validity. (Once again, the encounter between Simon Magus and the apostle Peter, described in the apocryphal Acts of Peter, clearly illustrates this.) By the time that the religion is firmly established, faith becomes non-empirical and should not depend on outside circumstances in this way. With this distinction in mind, let us examine the opera from the beginning, paying close attention to the various and sundry types of claims to knowledge. Even if there is some retracing of points already made above, it will be helpful to consider events in the order that they occur onstage.

Claims to Knowledge

Opening of Elsa's Trial

As the prelude comes to an end, we see the nobles of Brabant, gathered to welcome the visiting king. After the nobles greet him and pledge their allegiance, King Henry opens with a summary of recent historical events: the nine-year ceasefire with Hungary is about to end, and he is calling the entire German nation to arms. To his dismay, though, he finds Brabant without a leader and plunged into conflict. With that, he invites Friedrich von Telramund to present his case, and we hear the first direct claim to knowledge in the work: "ich kenne dich als aller Tugend Preis" (I know you as the prize of all virtue).[1] Henry's first approach to the case, then, is to trust Telramund's word because of his past behavior: what we might call a character-reference type of knowledge.

Telramund now comes forward, and like the king, begins by reviewing recent history. He explains that upon the death of the previous duke of Brabant, he was appointed guardian of the duke's two children, Elsa and Gottfried. Recently, Elsa and Gottfried had gone walking together in the forest; when Elsa returned alone, she could not explain what had happened to her brother. Telramund's response to this frightening news was to threaten Elsa, and her reaction persuaded him that she was guilty of her brother's death: "als ich mit Drohen nun in Elsa zwang, da ließ in bleichem Zagen und Erbeben der gräßlichen Schuld Bekenntnis sie uns sehn" (when I now pressured Elsa with threats, then she, through pale hesitation and trembling, allowed us to see confession of the most horrible guilt) (27). We hear little about the investigation outside of his threats: only that "fruchtlos war all Bemühn um den Verlornen" (fruitless were all efforts for the lost one) (26). Telramund could have approached Elsa gently, attempting to plumb her memory for evidence that might help the search for Gottfried; instead, he questioned her roughly, frightening her, and chose to interpret her fear as evidence of guilt. Elsa's hand had been promised him, but he now renounced it, horrified by the crime he believed her to have committed. In her place, he then married Ortrud, descendant of Radbod—and in consequence, he now claims for himself the rulership of Brabant.

Telramund's exposition of the situation, while brief, is rich in nuance and implication. To put it bluntly, by quickly jumping to a conclusion and then interpreting the evidence so as to confirm his theory, he seems to have botched the investigation. Elsa, meanwhile, has been put in the position of having to prove a negative—that she has not harmed her brother—and since no Gottfried can be found alive or dead, she has no basis to support her claim of innocence.

Telramund is embroiled in a conflict of interest: since he has married into the family which claims the right of succession, he now has a personal interest in having Elsa's family deposed from the dukedom. As will be revealed in due course, one central reason for his belief in Elsa's guilt is that Ortrud has borne false witness against Elsa, claiming that she saw Elsa drown Gottfried. Telramund's choice of wife strongly affects his perception of the two women's trustworthiness and guilt or innocence. When he later accuses Elsa of having a lover, we may well wonder whether one of Telramund's underlying motives throughout the episode of Gottfried's disappearance was jealousy. While no formal claim of knowledge is made here, we can see that Wagner suggests that what someone believes may be based on his personal ties more than on the objective evidence.

After Telramund's narration, Elsa approaches, summoned to answer the charges. The chorus of noblemen responds like any audience in a courtroom drama: based on her lovely appearance, they imagine her to be innocent, but then reason that Telramund must have very strong evidence if he is willing to accuse such a pure-looking young woman: "Ha! wie erscheint sie so licht und rein! Der sie so schwer zu zeihen wagte, wie sicher muß der Schuld er sein!" (Ha! how light and pure she appears! He who dared to accuse her so heaviliy, how sure he must be of [her] guilt!) (40–42). They thus combine intuition (she looks like a good person) with a kind of psychological logic (he must be really certain of her guilt, since she looks so innocent).

We can understand the thought process of the chorus; that is, we follow the reason for each step of the argument. This is not the same, though, as approving of it or being convinced by this type of reasoning ourselves. By using a separate criterion for each step of this argument, the chorus brings out the lack of a coherent societal model for determining truth. It would be problematic enough if different members of society used different models; but the chorus, through this confused response, makes it clear that even within one character (in this case a collective one that represents society as a whole), very different types of claims are persuasive. We do not have a situation in which two characters have different approaches to judging a case, but a situation in which everyone is pulled in multiple directions.

Further complicating matters, Elsa behaves most inappropriately for the situation. Whereas we expect that someone accused in a court of law will address the court and reply to the accusation, Elsa first responds to the king's direct questions only with mute gestures and then launches unprovoked into the narrative of her dream, which is clearly out of place in a trial. When the king interrupts and admonishes her to answer the accusations, she once again veers off course, describing the knight she believes will come to defend her honor. The chorus expresses understandable confusion about the whole situation: "Bewahre uns des Himmels Huld, daß klar wir sehen, wer hier Schuld!" (may Heaven's grace preserve us, so that we may clearly see who here is guilty!) (56–58).

The king, though, is sufficiently moved by Elsa's dreamy persuasiveness (we might wonder whether he thinks she is too good to have harmed Gottfried, or simply too incompetent) that he warns Telramund, asking him to reconsider. Telramund rejects this suggestion, claiming that her dreaminess only demonstrates that she has a secret lover; he has evidence of Elsa's guilt, but is not willing to share it: "Glaubwürdig ward ihr Frevel mir bezeugt; doch eurem Zweifel durch ein Zeugnis wehren, das stünde wahrlich übel meinem Stolz." (Her blasphemy was credibly proven to me, but to answer your doubt with a witness/testimony would truly wound my pride) (59–60).

Thus far, the two adversaries are working in completely different realms. Telramund presents facts and conjectures, while Elsa talks of her dreams and visions. Telramund's model of a trial is an essentially modern one of evidence and proof; but his practice of this model is flawed, since (1) he has approached one witness with threats; (2) he refuses to share information he received from another witness; and (3) he appeals to his past record as much as the facts of the case as reason to believe him. Elsa's model is more traditionally medieval: she invites a trial by combat, thus commending her case to divine judgement. It could be argued that she has no alternative, since she is unable to produce any positive evidence in her favor, but her confidence in dreams seems deeper than that. She is essentially a person whose experience does not correspond to the visible factual world most people live in; it is not hard to believe that she could simply lose track of her brother in the forest.

Lohengrin's Arrival

In the action thus far, we can discern many types of claims to knowledge. Henry and Telramund give weight to a character reference based on someone's past behavior. The chorus is moved by Elsa's innocent appearance. Telramund appears to value physical evidence, though he has not gathered it very well. He also accepts hearsay as evidence, if the statement is made by someone close to him. Elsa attributes truth to visions and dreams. As Lohengrin arrives on the River Scheldt, riding on a boat drawn by a swan, we see that the chorus also appreciates physical evidence. Wagner's stage directions for this arrival are very explicit; they show him using the space on stage in a conscious way so as to demonstrate how the crowd seeks out and responds to direct visual evidence.

For this part of Act I Scene 2, he divides the male chorus into two parts, based on where they are standing. Because of their significance, I reproduce his stage directions here.

> Den ersten Chor bilden die dem Ufer des Flusses zunächst stehenden Männer:— sie gewahren zuerst die Ankunft Lohengrins, welcher auf einem Nachen von einem Schwan gezogen auf dem Flusse in der Ferne sichtbar wird. Den zweiten Chor bilden die dem Ufer entfernter stehenden Männer im Vordergrunde, welche, ohne zunächst ihren Platz zu verlassen, mit immerer regerer Neugier sich fragend an die dem Ufer näher Stehenden wenden; sodann verlassen sie in einzelnen Haufen den Vordergrund, um selbst am Ufer nachzusehen.
>
> (The first chorus consists of the men standing next to the riverbank; they are first to perceive the arrival of Lohengrin, who becomes visible in the distance, in a boat pulled by a swan on the river. The second chorus consists of the men standing farther from the riverbank in the foreground, who, without at first leaving their places, turn with ever livelier curiosity to question those standing close to the bank; then they leave the foreground in small groups so they can look themselves from the shore) [79].

Within the first chorus, first the tenor 1 section, then the tenor 2 section, and finally the bass section sees the swan, as we gather from their staggered entrances on the text "Seht! Welch ein seltsam Wunder! Wie? Ein Schwan! ..." (See! What a strange wonder! What? A swan! ...) Next, as the members of Chorus 1 begin to describe the sight more specifically, Chorus 2 enters with questions: "Wie? Was ist? Ein Schwan? Wo? ..." (What? What is it? A swan? Where? ...) The stage directions specify the moment at which each vocal section within Chorus 2 approaches the bank, and the texts switch correspondingly from questions to assertions about the approaching swan, boat, and knight (79–88).

Wagner continues to describe the scene in terms of who can see Lohengrin; at one point, for example, the boat is behind the trees, so that the public cannot see him but the performers can (83). Remaining in the foreground are the female chorus, the king, Elsa, Telramund, and Ortrud. At m. 644, as the two male choruses reunite on the text "Ein Wunder ist gekommen" (A wonder has come), all the principal characters except Elsa react to Lohengrin's arrival. She keeps her gaze cast downward until the climactic moment when she sees him and cries out, marking the beginning of Scene 3.

This carefully timed spectacle demonstrates that Wagner was already working here with

Gesamtkunstwerk. By carefully designing many elements of the scene, he achieved a desired dramatic effect. Similar staging details occur in other parts of the opera; for example, at the beginning of Act III scene 3, Wagner specifies when each nobleman and his soldiers appear, and from which side of the stage. The scene of Lohengrin's arrival, though, is particularly well suited for such painstaking staging, for here the specific instructions bring out a central issue of the drama: the question of what constitutes knowledge. Each section of the chorus moves from questioning to belief at the moment when it sees Lohengrin's approach — and, as we saw above, that sight leads instantly to the conclusion that he must be a divine messenger, as the chorus sings "Gegrüßt, du gottgesandter Held!"

Trial by Combat

At first reading, the various characters' attitudes toward Elsa's trial by combat (which is to be fought by Telramund, her accuser, against Lohengrin, her champion) appear to fit neatly into a division between faith and materialism. All the characters except Ortrud express their belief that the trial will be determined by God's judgement.

Trial by combat, as we know, was one of the possible ordeals an accused person could undergo as a test of guilt or innocence. In Jacob Grimm's study of medieval German law, *Deutsche Rechtsaltertümer* — a work which according to Dahlhaus was consulted by Wagner as he wrote the libretto (Dahlhaus 37) — the role of these ordeals is described as follows:

> War eine that dunkel, ein recht zweifelhaft, so konnten prüfungen angestellt werden, durch deren untrügenden ausgang die aufgerufne gottheit selbst, als höchster richter, das wahre u. rechte verkündete. Sie ruhten auf dem festen glauben, daß jedesmal der schuldlose siegen, der schuldige unterliegen werde.
>
> If a deed were mysterious, or a claim doubtful, then tests could be appointed through whose undeceiving outcome the appealed-to godhead itself, as highest judge, made known the true and right. They rested on the secure faith that every time the guiltless would win and the guilty would be defeated [II: 563].

The *Saxon Mirror* also refers to God's role in the judgement: "Both should step fully armed before the judge and swear — the one that the accusation made against the defendant has been truthfully made, and the other that he is not guilty — so that God may stand by them in combat" (Dobozy 88).

King Henry's prayer before the combat seems to echo this understanding:

> Mein Herr und Gott, nun ruf' ich dich!
> Daß du dem Kampf zugegen seist!
> Durch Schwertes Sieg ein Urteil sprich,[2]
> Das Trug und Weisheit klar erweist!
> Des Reinen Arm gib Heldenkraft,
> Des Falschen Stärke sei erschlafft.
> So hilf uns, Gott, zu dieser Frist,
> Weil unsre Weisheit Einfalt ist.
>
> My Lord and God, now I call upon thee!
> May you be present during the combat!
> Through the sword's victory speak a judgement,
> Distinguish clearly between deception and wisdom.
> To the arm of the pure one give heroic strength,
> May the strength of the false one be slackened.
> So help us, God, at this time,
> For our wisdom is foolishness [129–32].

In the quintet that follows, four singers echo these sentiments, expressing confidence in God's fair judgement (132–38). Telramund is among them, since he believes his accusation to be true. (This circumstance subtly points out that medieval justice did not allow for the case of someone who is himself honest but has been deceived into fighting.) Ortrud's words, by contrast, reflect her non–Christian perspective: "Ich baue fest auf seine Kraft, die, wo er kämpft, ihm Sieg verschafft." (I rely firmly on his strength, which, wherever he fights, brings him victory.) As a non-believer in the Christian god, Ortrud has no reason to believe that this combat will be determined by right and wrong; nor does she seem to expect her Norse deities to take direct action. Therefore, she bases her expectation of the outcome purely on her husband's strength.

This first reading of the scene preceding the combat accounts for most of the evidence, and also supports the idea that Wagner's story conforms closely to historical information on the basic circumstances of medieval justice. If we move one stage earlier in the scene, however, we find the sentence quoted earlier that sows doubt about God's full power — a doubt that corresponds quite directly to the suspicion Ortrud will arouse in Act 2 in both Telramund and Elsa. After the customary instruction that no one may interfere with the fight,[3] the Herald warns: "Durch bösen Zauber List und Trug stört nicht des Urteils Eigenschaft" (may Heaven's grace preserve us, so that we may clearly see who here is guilty!) (56–58).

This statement is made here as if it were a standard part of the ritual of the trial by combat, but I cannot find any evidence to support this in sources on medieval law or magic. Historian D. Jonathan Boulton, an authority on heraldry, also finds this statement peculiar, and has not encountered it in his readings of primary heraldic sources (personal communication). Wagner's insertion of the phrase, then, appears to be his own idea. Its presence in the scene suggests that Christian faith, rather than being strongly shared by the community of Brabant, is still tenuous and shadowed by doubt. As we have seen, that is a very reasonable view of circumstances in the tenth century.

Could one of the fighters be using magical forces to deceive humans and subvert God's will? Ortrud will arouse that suspicion about Lohengrin in Act 2. According to the standard view of the opera, Elsa's downfall starts when she begins to succumb to Ortrud's insinuations — and yet, as we have seen, due caution about strange events would be a sign of proper Christian belief a mere two centuries later. These complex issues suggest that it may be time to move away from centering the opera on Elsa's guilt or innocence or on the purity of Christian faith. Instead, let us consider it as a work that presents a time of conflict between two world-views.

Interesting support for this possible reading is found in a remark from Cosima Wagner's diary on 21 July 1871:

> We come to talk about so-called cultural matters, and R. agrees with me when I tell him that I feel no trace of sympathy for the imposition of Christianity on others (Charlemagne and the Saxons) and that I would give the whole of discovered America in exchange for the poor natives' not having been burned or persecuted. He tells of Radbod, the Prince of Frisia, who, with one foot already in the font, leaped back when he heard that he would not meet his heathen father in Heaven (Siegmund!); that was why he had made his Ortrud, an inadequately converted heathen, a descendant of Radbod. The Roman conquest of countries being much more humane, they did not impose their religion [I: 393–94].

This account suggests that when he wrote the *Lohengrin* libretto, Wagner already felt some sympathy for the pagan religion that would take center stage in the Ring cycle, and that he viewed the earlier opera more as a conflict between old and new than as a tale promoting the clear superiority of Christianity. This is not to claim that Wagner liked or appreciated Ortrud — he identified her in a letter to Liszt as a "reactionary" (Borchmeyer 155) — but to point out that he did have some appreciation for the tradition she represented and some aspects of its humanity.

What if Wagner's main purpose in *Lohengrin* were not to tell a simple story culminating in Elsa's loss of faith, but instead to present the messy situation of a society in transition? He does this very persuasively. We have seen that the characters base their views on a motley assortment of claims; that there is no generally accepted basis for knowledge; that even a hero apparently sent by God could lose the trial as a result of trickery, or might win it by using evil magic. While procedures are in place to decide legal cases, they are fluid — the verbal trial shifts quickly to a physical one — and subject to question. As the staging of Lohengrin's arrival demonstrates, each individual is more satisfied to believe something when he has seen it with his own eyes, not fully trusting his neighbors to give an accurate account. Yet once Lohengrin is seen, what people believe about him goes far beyond anything that can be discerned by physical sight: thus suspicion and credulity are mixed in bizarre ways.

Wagner's main concern here, I claim, is not to help us figure out what really happened, or who is innocent or guilty. Rather, he is presenting the chaos that occurs in situations devoid of clarity, and at times when a society does not have a stable and shared set of ideas about what constitutes truth and how it can be determined.

And indeed, by the time the opera ends, a great deal has been accepted on faith and without clear evidence. Lohengrin kills Telramund in self-defense; the audience sees this, but the king and chorus accept it on his word alone, and state that he was justified.

> LOH: Da dieser Mann zur Nacht mich überfallen, sagt, ob ich ihn mit Recht erschlug?
> KÖNIG & CHOR: Wie deine Hand ihn schlug auf Erden, soll dort ihm Gottes Strafe werden!
> LOH: Since this man fell upon me by night, say whether I justly struck him down?
> KING & CHORUS: Just as your hand struck him on earth, so shall be God's punishment [in the next world] [593–94].

Gottfried is released from his enchantment into a swan. It turns out that Ortrud had not seen Elsa kill him, but rather had transformed him herself. We never figure out, though, what really happened in the forest. Did Elsa wander off or start daydreaming, leaving her brother all the more vulnerable to Ortrud's attack? It is also never addressed how it happened that Gottfried then came into the service of the Grail and ended up pulling Lohengrin's boat.[4] This peculiar linkage at least suggests that Lohengrin is somehow implicated in Ortrud's evil magic. The lady of the "Lay of Yonec" would have been rightfully suspicious to see her knight drawn by a magic swan — and perhaps if Elsa had questioned earlier (as the lady did immediately, and as Perceval/Parsifal failed to do in another Grail story), Gottfried would have been released much sooner.

Of course, the Lohengrin story is what it is; what I am suggesting would make it another story altogether. My purpose here is not to rewrite, but simply to point out that the story, as it stands, is inherently unresolved. It leaves us unsatisfied not only in the obvious direct way, through Elsa's death and Lohengrin's departure, but also in an even more fundamental way: because it does not fully answer any of the questions that are posed in Act 1.

In the end, the opera seems to tell us, history is written by the victors. Lohengrin has won over public opinion; thus his killing of Telramund is accepted as lawful and right. Elsa has broken her unwisely-given promise. Even though it might have been more responsible for her to refuse Lohengrin's demand for silence and unthinking acceptance, she is punished

6. Don't Ask: Faith, Magic, Knowledge, and Sources in *Lohengrin* (Feurzeig)

Act 1 of the August Everding production of *Lohengrin* at the Metropolitan Opera (photograph by Winnie Klotz).

for her defiance—first by separation from her husband, then by death. Ortrud is discredited and Gottfried left holding the emblems of rulership. Thus Christianity has triumphed; and Christian chroniclers have written the version of the story we have before us, in which it is clear that the ancient gods are both evil and impotent, and that the Christian god, if not fully benevolent, at least possesses the stronger magic This is a very tenth-century perspective, as has been demonstrated. Had Ortrud's side won, then the Brabantians would have reverted to paganism, and the story would have been written by someone else, with a different apparent moral.

This story, as Wagner tells it, is about *Realpolitik*, not simple Christian faith—and thus it prefigures the *Ring* cycle, in which a central question is whether principles or raw power rule the world. The ring carries raw power; Wotan's spear seems to represent principles, but— one might argue—he eventually comes to wonder whether even those principles prevail of their own strength or because he has external power to impose his authority.

In *Lohengrin*, spiritual and intellectual confusion lead to political and social disorder; neither reason nor faith can prevail and create a satisfying solution. By rewriting his medieval stories in ways that bring out these issues, Wagner took part in the nineteenth-century critique of Enlightenment optimism. The eighteenth-century view that the world was characterized by clarity and reason began to crumble in the face of new explorations of psychological and material factors. The non-rational and irrational elements of our nature, for better or worse, were seen to determine much of what goes on in the world. As we shall see below, Wagner may have used literary models from the turn of the nineteenth century—many of them originating in his native Saxony—to help shape this part of his Romantic outlook.

A Literary Context from the Turn of the Nineteenth Century

In the second half of the nineteenth century, the popular novel skyrocketed to a prominent place in the German literary cosmos. Both the number of novels published and their share in the total number of works increased exponentially. By 1800 over half the books sold at the annual Leipzig book fair were novels. See the chart below.

Decade	Published Novels
1750–60	73
1761–70	189
1771–80	413
1781–90	907
1791–1800	1623

[Dahnke 73].

Much of this literary activity took place in Saxony. This kingdom had an interest in the publishing industry, since that industry was centered in the city of Leipzig, and therefore the censorship laws were much looser in Saxony than elsewhere in Germany or Austria.

The significance of these novels is to some degree underplayed by scholars, since they are considered low art. Literary histories written in East Germany tend to accord them more attention, since they are valued as literature of the masses. In any case, whether or not they are accurately categorized as low art, the sheer magnitude of their popular success makes them significant as social history.

The new novels were read by a wide cross-section of society. Various contemporary documents characterized the readership of Carl Gottlob Cramer (1758–1817), for example.

> "Mr. Cramer can, among others, boast of being read in all watchrooms and spinning rooms," it said in 1802 in the *Neuen allgemeinen deutschen Bibliothek*. Other authorities speak of "grisettes and shopkeepers," "soldiers, servingmaids, and apprentices" as his predominant public. But also "educated" women and girls belonged to it, and men like E. T. A. Hoffmann, Fouqué, and the Brothers Grimm read Cramer's novels as borrowers from lending libraries [Dahnke 81].

The young Wagner is very likely to have been among the young intellectuals who did just that, particularly since there is evidence that Cramer's popularity continued for several decades. In an undated essay, "Die Bücher und die Lesewelt," the writer Wilhelm Hauff (1802–27) satirized the reading world of his time. We can presume that it describes the situation in the 1820s, and thus reflects the continued popularity of the works of Cramer and his contemporaries. The scenario: Hauff is observing the choices of readers at a lending library. The cynical librarian asks him whether he knows a certain young woman of the upper class, and Hauff describes her as "eine Dame von feinstem Geschmack und sehr belesen" (a lady of the finest taste, and very well read). He guesses that she will want to check out literature specifically written for ladies, or perhaps a historical novel by the upper-class Austrian Karoline Pichler. To his shock, after her maid has placed the order, he finds that she has requested Cramer's novel *Leben und Meinungen Erasmus Schleichers* (on which more below). His reaction:

> "Wie! Dieses, um wenig zu sagen, gemeine Buch darf Fräulein Rosa, die liebenswürdige Einfalt, lesen? ... Welche Heuchlerin ist dieses Mädchen? Das ist ihre Lektüre, und ich glaubte, sie werde nur die Stunden der Andacht lesen."

(What! This, to say the least, common book Miss Rosa, the adorable simplicity, may read? ... What kind of a hypocrite is this girl? That is her reading, and I thought she would only read prayerbooks [lit. trans: books of hours] [329–31].

To fully understand Hauff's shock at Fräulein Rosa's reading, we need to explore the content of these widely-read novels. As we shall see through the examples discussed below, they strongly criticized political and social institutions. In addition, certain writers challenged the optimistic Enlightenment view of human nature by chronicling various types of insanity and other aberrations. As a result, the articulate powers that be became quite alarmed about the fashion for novel-reading. Martha Woodmansee explores the social ramifications of these novels in her article "Toward a Genealogy of the Aesthetic: The German Reading Debate of the 1790s."

To the conservative majority, extensive reading represented a threat to the established moral and social order. It was not just that readers shirked their responsibilities in the home and in the work place, we are told; their passions and their minds filled with the half-truths generated by the books they read, avid readers even began to question the justice of the order that dictated such responsibilities [208].

Beyer is afraid that readers who have glimpsed an other, better world in books will rise up and forcibly attempt to impose their vision on the real world. His fears were widely shared. So alarming was the spectre of revolutionary France that, much as in England at this time, many one-time advocates of literacy had begun to have second thoughts [209].

We might characterize this new reading public as partaking in Brown's concept of inarticulate power.

Popular literature of the 1780s and 1790s was often set in the medieval past, which was sometimes used as a cloak to disguise a more contemporary social critique.

The complex of medieval subjects (mittelalterliche Sujetkomplex) from which, around 1790, novels of knights, bandits, and ghosts (Ritter-, Räuber, und Geisterromane) emerged, often in close proximity, proved itself well-suited for a narrative encounter with two stirring political phenomena of the time: clerical obscurantism and the existence of secret societies.... [These motives] stand as a commentary against superstition and religious intolerance, linked particularly to the ideological battles of the Berlin Enlightenment against the feudal-clerical reaction [Dahnke 84].

Notable here are the historical novels of Christiane Benedikte Naubert (1756–1819) and the seven volumes of tales entitled *Sagen der Vorzeit* (Tales of Long Ago; 1787–98) by Veit Weber (pseudonym for Leonhard Wächter, 1762–1837).

One strand of the popular literature portrayed the exciting adventures and unconventional lifestyle of bandits. While the high-art writers Johann Wolfgang von Goethe and Friedrich von Schiller set early examples with the plays *Claudine von Villa Bella* (Goethe, 1776) and *Die Räuber* (Schiller, 1781), the novel that cornered the bandit market was *Rinaldo Rinaldini, der Räuberhauptmann* (1798/1800) by Christian August Vulpius (1762–1827), another Weimar resident who became Goethe's brother-in-law many years later. Rinaldo, a noble-spirited outlaw, tries to enforce civil behavior among his followers, and abhors random violence, yet is often drawn into it through circumstance. He frequently rescues females in distress, and thus becomes haplessly involved with several women at once, until the superfluous ones conveniently die. This novel criticizes conventional society by making it clear that good and bad people may be found on either side of the law. Rinaldo also encounters the dilemma of trying to decide whether to trust a mysterious character whose motives and allegiance are unclear; Vulpius was probably borrowing this suspenseful device from the novel *Das Petermännchen*, discussed below.

Since folk and fairy tales are set either long ago or in an indeterminate time, the retelling of such stories fit neatly into this tendency. It was also appealing because of the broader interest in folk literature which was beginning in the late eighteenth century and continued into the nineteenth. Notable here were the *Volksmärchen der Deutschen* of Johann Karl August Musäus (1735–87), published in 1782–86. Musäus was not from Saxony; he was a government official and later a *Gymnasium* instructor in Weimar, and thus part of the intense cultural climate of that city, where Johann Gottfried Herder (1744–1803) had already begun publishing folk poetry in the 1770s. Naubert, the only female among the popular novelists — it is probably no coincidence that she hailed from Leipzig, the publishing capital — began, just after Musäus' death, a set of tales just after whose title suggests a deliberate continuation or homage: the *Neue Volksmährchen der Deutschen* (1789–93).

Naubert wrote many of her novels anonymously — they were often identified by the name of one of the earlier novels, as in "von dem Verfasser der *Thekla von Thurn*" (by the author of *Thekla von Thurn*) — and her identity was not revealed until just before her death. Naturally, readers speculated on who the author might be, and Cramer's name came up as one of the candidates; but it is hard to believe that it was not obvious, after a few of her novels, that this anonymous author was probably female. Her title characters were often strong heroines, such as Thekla von Thurn, who makes her way through the male-dominated world by disguising herself as her brother after he is killed.

One final strand should be mentioned here to round out the collection of tendencies in late eighteenth-century popular literature: a new interest in abnormal human psychology, irrational perspectives, and superstition. These concerns reflect a shift away from the Enlightenment view that humans are essentially governed by reason, and that the world can be understood as the ordered creation of a rational god. The psychological angle may certainly be linked to the influence of Mesmer, whose treatments of illness by inducing trance, which he began in Vienna and Paris during the 1770s, had made a sensation. By the 1820s, the control had passed out of the hands of doctors, and untrained Mesmerists were attempting to treat serious mental illness all over Europe, with little or no legal constraint to prevent them (Feurzeig 225–26).

The German author most associated with these explorations was Christian Heinrich Spieß (1755–99); this tendency is particularly evident in his two series, *Biographien der Selbstmörder* (Biographies of Suicides, 4 vols., 1786–89) and *Biographien der Wahnsinnigen* (Biographies of the Insane, 4 vols., 1795–96). While the sensational appeal of these topics is self-evident, Spiess approaches his case histories less for their shock value than as opportunities to consider what people might do differently to avoid tragic consequences for others. Without stating a moral, his stories have didactic implications about the value of community, the danger of inflexible moral codes, and so on.

The themes and tendencies discussed thus far — attraction to the Middle Ages, retelling of old tales, stories of bandits and ghosts, a new awareness of women's issues, and fascination with abnormal psychology — support a claim that the popular literature of the late eighteenth century pushed society forward into the Romantic era. In other words, this literature reflects a time of transition from one world-view to another, a situation somewhat parallel to the claim I am making about the tenth century. Before looking at the implications of these thoughts, let us consider four specific examples from the popular literature I have discussed above in its broad outline. Each of these is linked conceptually with at least one issue or topic in *Lohengrin*.

Erasmus Schleicher

The title character of the Cramer novel mentioned above — its full title is *Leben und Meinungen, auch seltsamliche Abentheuer Erasmus Schleichers, eines reisenden Mechanikus* (Life and Opinions, also Strange Adventures of Erasmus Schleicher, a Traveling Mechanic, 4 vols., 1789/91) — is a mechanic, or perhaps we would call him an engineer, who arrives at a small German court and makes himself useful by repairing clocks, putting on a fireworks show, designing a water system that makes a mechanical fountain possible in the reigning prince's garden, and so forth. He endears himself to many people, and by keeping his eyes open eventually notices that the lavish lifestyle of the prince and his courtiers is creating significant economic problems for the people of the area. Schleicher solves this problem by bringing it very dramatically to the prince's attention. I quote this passage at length; it presents not only the social message, but also Cramer's wonderfully ironic humor.

> Directly at the door is a large esplanade, from the middle of which one can look out over the entire expanse of the garden, up the hill. It is true, the fountains, and how the water from them tumbled over the natural rocks, created a splendid prospect; especially when the sun shined through it all as even now; but because of this the miller had no bread, and his children would have been no less hungry if they could have gazed at this wonder steadily from dawn to dusk. Schleicher scanned the horizon worriedly, since it was earlier than planned; aha! there are a couple of worms wriggling around in the sand....
>
> The prince stood, just as if Providence had decreed that stand here he must, exactly on the spot that Schleicher had foreseen, and looked out over the garden. "But isn't it true, Engineer!" said he, "isn't it true, it looks magnificent? And when it's all finished as it should be; isn't it true?" —
>
> SCHLEICHER: Beautiful! Magnificent! Excellent! (as if lost in the view) Isn't it as if God's great sun multiplies itself to millions in these rainbows!
>
> THE PRINCE: O, but it has not yet risen high enough: then it reflects all the colors there are.
>
> SCHLEICHER (as before): As if entire kingdoms of diamonds and rubies, with the Lord God as their shepherd, were bubbling up from the earth unto his heaven!—And when the great Neptune finally reawakens—then it must look none other than as if the whole of Nature were rebelling against his laws.
>
> THE PRINCE: O, it's truly a spectacle!
>
> SCHLEICHER (repeating coldly): Truly a spectacle! But—(with an intimate glance to the Prince, and then toward the miller, who now approaches with his children) but, now if only the bread of this poor man and his eight children would bubble up to our Lord God in these magnificent bows of diamonds, along with their cries of hunger.
>
> THE PRINCE (stricken): What?— So who is this man?
>
> The chamberlain Zedro tugged at Schleicher's sleeve, others threw him glances; but he appeared not to notice.
>
> SCHLEICHER: (in a storytelling tone) He owns the mill down there on the brook, on a hereditary lease. In the winter the brook is frozen most of the time, and in the summer his water bubbles here, when can he do any milling?
>
> THE PRINCE: (most upset) That's just awful! I can't remember having heard anything about it? (to his people) What kind of business has been done with that mill?—(and before anyone can answer, to the miller) Have you not come to me about this?
>
> THE MILLER: Oh, I came right away, when all this here was about to be built ten years ago, to ask you not to take the water from the mill; but it was no help at all! Since that time, I have come to you just about every year, to petition only for release from my hereditary lease; but I have never received even an answer, to say nothing of any relief.
>
> THE PRINCE: (with a grim searching look at his people) Why do I know nothing of this!
>
> SCHLEICHER: O, Your Majesty may well know nothing about so many things! (he gives him a sealed document)

The Prince stared at him; Schleicher stared back, unwavering. "You believe your land to be happy," he added, "because all these people who surround you make such zealous efforts to satisfy your every wish, and this is your most noble and fervent wish — for which God bless you! But —"

The Prince quickly ripped open the seal and read. The courtiers, taken aback, stuck their heads together, and whispered into each other's ears; Schleicher alone observed calmly this Hercules facing him, who looked to be cutting off the last head of the dying Hydra. The Prince colored more than once while reading; every eye stole glances at him, like the eye of the goose at the lightning, and every ear listened, like the ear of the goose to the thunder. "Tear out the pipes," he cried decisively, "and you, miller, go home and start up your mill! (to the Master of the Horse) We will proceed immediately! (to an Officer of the Guard) Send a rider in advance, to Councillor Hammer; he will be in his garden. Invite him to come to my chamber, forthwith. (to those remaining) And you, gentlemen, we will find, when the time comes, in your houses!" [I: 299–303].

The East German literary historians view this type of scene with a certain skepticism:

> Always emphasizing the goodness and cleverness of princes, he saw in the transfer of evil courtiers and punishment of overweening nobles the guarantee of a fortunate nation. When the kingship was eliminated and eventually Louis XVI was executed, Cramer published a bloodcurdling appeal for participation in the counter-revolutionary war of coalition [Dahnke 81].

Yes, Cramer probably remained a royalist, but he certainly saw the dangerous potential for abuse of royal power. It should be noted that one of the worst offenders in *Erasmus Schleicher* is the prince's son. This novel combines two elements found in *Lohengrin*: a critique of court life and a kind of sorcery. Schleicher's technical abilities are perceived rather similarly to what was called "natural magic" in the Middle Ages and Renaissance. Schleicher achieves a position of influence over the prince not because of his moral nature and concern for others, but because he can use science and technology to command natural forces that others in the novel do not comprehend. Only because he can build the almost-magical fountains does he gain the power to persuade the prince to disconnect them.

Das Petermännchen

Erasmus Schleicher presents a rationalistic world in which the clever, thinking people win; Spieß's novel *Das Petermännchen* (1791f), by contrast, brings us right into the world of the *Geisterroman*. The protagonist, young nobleman Rudolph von Westerburg, is aided in making his way through the world by a spirit-dwarf named Peter who has long been viewed as his family's ancestral friendly ghost. Peter seems to be working to further Rudolph's goals, particularly various romantic intrigues — and yet, somehow, they always seem to come out very wrong. (Peter is the character I suggested above was probably the model for the mysterious character in *Rinaldo Rinaldini*.) Rudolph, not being too bright, does not notice this contradiction until long after the reader has become suspicious. When Peter reveals, though, that there is a counterforce working against him — the spirit of his estranged wife — the watchful reader is soon as unsure as Rudolph about how to interpret the situation. Is Peter a benevolent spirit whose plans are always thwarted by his evil wife, or is she the good one who is desperately trying to rescue Rudolph from her husband's evil schemes?

This question does eventually get resolved in the novel's second volume, and by the end of the novel it is quite clear which spirit is good and which is evil. However, Spieß is evidently less concerned about the resolution than about the problem itself. The sheer ambiguity of a situation in which there are two strong opposed authority figures, and an individual has to decide based on very little evidence which one to obey, is what makes this novel remark-

6. Don't Ask: Faith, Magic, Knowledge, and Sources in *Lohengrin* (Feurzeig)   99

able. For example, what about the time that Peter's wife has told Rudolph to keep wearing a hat she gave him, *no matter what*, and it then turns out that if he keeps the hat on, he will be castrated by the Turkish sultan? It does seem clear that Peter is the one who has the continuation of the Westerburg family at heart.

That association with sexuality is actually quite central to Peter's identity and purpose. He tends to encourage Rudolph's erotic impulses, while his wife is always advising restraint and self-discipline. The lewd implications of Peter's name become quite evident in the second volume, when the erstwhile dwarf suddenly reappears as a giant.

This novel's links to *Lohengrin* are quite obvious. The opera is full of situations in which two characters make believable claims. The Brabantians must determine whether to believe Telramund, because of his previous record, or Elsa, because she looks so pure. Elsa must decide whether to trust the swan-knight or the reasonable doubts raised by Ortrud. Both Ortrud and Elsa have claims on the dukedom of Brabant. And so forth.

Glaubensmuth

The short story *Glaubensmuth* (Courage in Faith) comes from the seventh volume of Veit Weber's *Sagen der Vorzeit*, which appeared in 1798. Like other stories by both Weber and Naubert, it is extremely well-researched; indeed, Weber includes footnotes with quotations from primary historical sources. Set on the border of Prussia and Lithuania, the story tells of young Landshort, a Christian nobleman from Germany serving with the Teutonic Knights. Landshort falls in love with the daughter of a pagan Lithuanian prince and eventually engages in a contest in order to win both her hand and her father's conversion. Though set in the thirteenth century, this story is in a contested border area, so the naive Landshort speaks of the powers of his god in words reminiscent of much earlier times when gods proved their strength through their magical powers.

> LANDSHORT: If you had faith and confidence in the man-become-God, you could through this faith, while working to spread it, move mountains, still hurricanes, direct lightning bolts, and bring the dead back to life.
> KOSSISKO: I do not mock a crazy man [217–18].

The story is notable for its honest, unsanitized account of the bitter cruelties that have been committed in the name of Christianity. Weber never fully condemns the religion — he leaves open the possibility that these evils were aberrations from its true essence — but the amount of brutal unvarnished truth in the story is startling. The two passages presented here do not repreent this historical writing, but rather the story's even-handed approach to the two clashing religions. These passages make a natural pair: in the first, Kossisko describes his view of Christian practices, and in the second, from earlier in the story, Landshort's old retainer Kernhart presents his thoughts on a Lithuanian religious ceremony he has witnessed by chance.

> One person, among the thousands whom your people believe have the ability to multiply your god in flour and water as often as he can strike the cross and repeat magic formulas, who then worships the lifeless work of his hand and voice ... desires that the original inhabitants of Prussia, Liefland, and Lithuania no longer worship as divine blocks of stone or wood shaped by the chisel, but rather slices of dough kneaded from flour and water; no longer dance around an evergreen tree, but rather fall down before an uprooted trunk [210].
>
> "The fools!"— repeated Kernhart aloud, when distance had turned the green of the forest to blue.—"Why should no Christian look on when they hold their devotions? Truly they ought not

to be ashamed of what they offer their gods or ask from them, and, in fairness, they shouldn't keep it a secret from us how they stand with the supernatural. They drink to them; we don't dare to do that. They are merry, dance and leap beneath the eyes of their gods like young antelopes coming into the open; we lie before ours like livestock in a slaughterhouse whose legs have been tied together, and show our broadest surface to heaven as if we lay there to be whipped. They clap their hands, with the highest of pleasure; we beat our breasts, sighing, as if such a bass-drum tone would please a good being. They cry out that they feel themselves capable of bravery; we soul-bathe in our badness and uselessness, as if a father would be pleased that his children call themselves rascals and villains. And how their priests act! Our pastors scold, threaten, and curse, excommunicate all who won't go down before the holy cross, demand from the heavenly King that he should heap his rage upon non–Christians; their priests pray to the Lord God that he should, although these things must happen sometime, not allow thunderstorms, hurricanes, and hailstorms to flash, roar, and rage anywhere where people would be scared, or might become poor and miserable, but instead to let their chastising rods fall only upon uncultivated forests, barren heaths, and swamps. Had the Lithuanians known we would now be riding through this swamp, they would have asked that it be spared. O, they are real Christians, even if they have polluted no baptismal water!" [201–2].

This very positive representation of a pagan religion bears comparison with Cosima's comment about Radbod in her diary. While Weber certainly takes a much more even-handed stance in *Glaubensmuth* than Wagner in *Lohengrin*, the awareness that such literary models existed supports the possibility that Wagner's opera was not intended to be read from a purely Christian perspective.

Elisabeth von Toggenburg

In Naubert's 1789 novel *Elisabeth Erbin von Toggenburg, oder Geschichte der Frauen von Sargans in der Schweiz* (Elisabeth, Heiress of Toggenburg, or the History of the Women of Sargans in Switzerland), there are several important female characters, some of whom accomplish heroic feats of the type usually assigned to men. Elisabeth's heroism is more of the mind than the body; the story traces her coming of age as a thinking person. She has been deliberately raised in a very sheltered environment, uninformed of important aspects of family history that, as it turns out, she really needs to know in order to make reasonable decisions. Early in the novel, a bishop writes to the abbot who is in direct contact with Elizabeth and her family, counseling him that it is best to keep her in ignorance:

> Your idea, to bring the whole history of the two dispossessed Toggenburg heiresses before Elisabeth's eyes, and thereby justify your opinion of them, is good, but what shall I say to the thought of making her acquainted with the secret annals of Sargans? My imprudent, rash friend! Don't you know what kind of a role our cloister plays in these memorials of antiquity? And is it advisable to reveal to the laity too much about the offenses of the clergy? Let it be enough for us that we walk the path of virtue. We do not need to use the vices of our predecessors as a foil for our brilliance.
>
> But my Konrad is free from such bad intentions, he errs only from a lack of thinking it over!— I will do my utmost to correct your error, my letters thereupon to the Abbess have already been sent, and I hope Elisabeth will obtain nothing.
>
> These papers were once for a short time in my hands, and I assure you, if you, as I must infer, are ignorant of their contents, that they contain things which, to preserve the honor of the cloister of Churwald, and unfortunately also that of some of my predecessors, should remain hidden for ever [14–16].

In the above passage, Naubert takes aim simultaneously at corruption of the church and the notion that ignorance can be beneficial. Earlier in the letter, it is made clear that Elisabeth's proper role is to submit herself to the authority of men: not only the abbot, but also certain civil authorities in Zurich. What she actually does, instead, is to investigate her family archive. Like Elsa, Elisabeth is expected to respect religion and submit to male authority. Unlike Elsa, she breaks away from this model of female virtue.

Conclusion

There is little direct evidence that Wagner encountered these authors and their works. The one exception is Musäus, whose *Volksmärchen* were in Wagner's library at Wahnfried (Wahnfried-Bibliothek). Cosima also mentioned this author in her second diary entry, 2 January 1869, writing "He goes for his walk, I to sleep with Musäus in my hand." (I:29) The absence of the other authors in Wagner's collections is not surprising, given the prominent role of lending libraries in the dissemination of popular literature. The fact that he does not mention those authors is also consistent with the image of himself that he strove to present.

Wagner preferred to be associated with literature classified as high art and with primary sources from the Middle Ages, not contemporary retellings of medieval stories. Dieter Borchmeyer makes this clear in the case of *Tannhäuser*: he demonstrates that the elusive primary source Wagner claimed to have used does not exist, and that the opera actually benefitted from the influence of works written during Wagner's lifetime by Heine, Tieck, and E. T. A. Hoffman (102–10). Thus it is quite credible that Wagner knew some popular literature of the previous generation, but did not wish to have it in his library or acknowledge his awareness. Not only were these works considered of low literary value, but some of them, particularly

The Metropolitan Opera's *Lohengrin* (photograph by Winnie Klotz).

the works of Cramer, were viewed as crude and coarse — recall Hauff's reaction to the idea of a lady reading *Erasmus Schleicher*— because they addressed sexuality and bodily functions more directly than polite literature. It is hard to imagine that the semi-rebellious schoolboy with literary tendencies did not read some of these stories, even if he later abandoned them for other types of reading (Köhler 43–44).

The popular literature of the late eighteenth century, though often dismissed as *Trivialliteratur*, offered a number of significant ideas and perspectives that show the European world's transition from the Enlightenment to Romanticism. These writings not only questioned basic European institutions, but also began to transfer attention from society as a whole to individual characters in their full psychological complexity. Works in this tradition criticized court life; exposed Church corruption and brutality committed in the name of Christianity; explored psychology and the role of irrational forces in human decision-making; and challenged prevailing views on women's education. In some cases — *Das Petermännchen* and *Glaubensmuth* do this in different ways — these works featured situations in which someone must choose between two opposite worldviews, each of which presents strong and credible arguments.

Does Wagner's *Lohengrin* simply display medieval life, with uncritical appreciation for its ceremony, pageantry, and piety? Or does the opera at the same time, like these literary works, critique medieval institutions, with some implications for contemporary European institutions, while using characters from medieval legend to showcase larger issues that apply to Wagner's nineteenth-century compatriots? The standard view of the opera has persisted for a long time without considering this second possibility, so that view evidently possesses qualities that make it satisfying for many opera lovers. I have no particular desire to replace that interpretation for those who find it sufficient; and yet I find the reading suggested here to be more complete for three reasons. First, it brings *Lohengrin* into closer connection with Wagner's later works. Second, it takes Wagner's libretto more seriously, regarding its complexities and contradictions as part of the intended effect rather than unconsidered side effects or simple inconsistencies. Finally, this reading places Wagner directly into the cultural milieu of his time in all its complexity, revealing *Lohengrin* to be a very modern work rather than an anachronistic one.

I will move now to some broad historical claims which I cannot fully support here, since they go beyond the central topic of this article. There was unquestionably a strand of Romanticism — represented, for example, by the novels of Walter Scott, Novalis' essay *Die Christenheit oder Europa*, and the poems of Eichendorff— that tended to idealize the Middle Ages, setting that era up as a foil to the drab nineteenth century that was both purer and more exciting. Because that strand exists, is easy to understand, and appeals to a broad audience, characterizations of the Romantic movement often over-emphasize it. It can even happen that idealization is set up as a normative expectation for certain kinds of literature, as witness the following comment on Naubert, from a survey of German literature as recent as 1970:

> She is perhaps the best informed and the most ambitious historical novelist of her generation but her insight into past cultures is limited by her rationalistic education and essentially middle-class common-sense: affairs of state tend to be seen in terms of minor commercial transactions, momentous movements like the Crusades regarded as irresponsible follies [Stahl and Yuill 178].

One might conclude that the authors of that study have generic expectations of a book depending on its subject matter. A book set in the Middle Ages is supposed to be an idealization à la Walter Scott, not a practical, hard-headed look at some real problems of that time period. The fact that Naubert's perspective is actually closely linked to some very current historical approaches to the period, and to the Crusades in particular, does not affect their judgement.

The standard view of *Lohengrin* is based on the assumption (perhaps also a normative expectation) that the opera partakes in the idealizing tendency, while my interpretation associates it more with other aspects of the Romantic era. One of these is an awareness of the irrational and psychological elements of human decision-making, as represented by the work of Mesmer, carried through by Freud, and exemplified by numerous heroes and heroines of Romantic novels. A second is the presence of social criticism, particularly noticeable from the 1840s onward, as found in the work of Marx and others. In the nineteenth century, this criticism was often focused on issues of industrialization and exploitation; Wagner addressed these concerns very directly in the *Ring*. *Lohengrin* is not concerned with economics, but instead raises more general issues about the nature of authority. It also partakes in a practice that was very common in the nineteenth century: the setting of literary works in past eras as a way of disguising, or perhaps veiling, direct criticism of the present. This practice, as found in many operas of Meyerbeer, Verdi, and others, was very helpful in avoiding problems during an age of censorship. Finally, this view associates *Lohengrin* with a perspective that perceives the world not as a rationally constructed system directed by the divine, but rather as the result of a series of power struggles. This view was expressed and developed throughout the nineteenth century by thinkers such as Schopenhauer, Büchner (whose play *Woyzeck* became Berg's opera *Wozzeck*), Darwin, and Nietzsche.

Central to the Lohengrin story is the legend of a man who tells a woman that she may not ask questions. Whatever psychological or archetypal meaning this story, and the numerous related folk legends, may have had in their original setting, by the 1840s this story had to be read as a story about absolute authority and thought control. In my view, Wagner could not but react against this. Even if his original approach tried to work within the bounds of the story and its assumptions, the final version, through its exposition of the ambiguities and arbitrary assumptions of medieval society, ultimately reflected his own free-thinking nature. Elsa indeed made Wagner into a revolutionary.

This essay would not exist in this form without John Sienicki; I owe him thanks for help of many kinds. Thanks are also due to D. Jonathan Boulton for information on heraldry and to Susan Youens and David McGee for reading the essay at various stages.

Notes

1. Like many languages, German has two verbs concerning knowledge: "wissen," with connotations of knowing objective facts, and "kennen," which has to do with familiarity and is thus more subjective. In this case, Henry uses "kennen" because he is speaking of his own past experience with Telramund, or awareness of Telramund's reputation.

2. This line brings out an interesting etymological relationship.. "The word 'ordeal' (OE *ordâl*) originally meant like G *Urteil* a 'judicial decision' or 'verdict'" (Dobozy 22).

3. "Order shall be maintained in the enclosed combat ring on pain of death so that no one may interfere with their duel" (Dobozy 88).

4. Joachim Köhler points out that in earlier drafts, Lohengrin's Grail Narration did address this, stating that at the Castle of the Grail, a swan had "turned up on the riverbank, together with a boat. Lohengrin's father immediately recognized in it a bewitched soul that would be redeemed only if it spent a year providing a ferry service for the Grail" (204). While this convenient explanation may have remained present in Wagner's mind, its omission from the actual opera nevertheless leaves significant ambiguity.

Bibliography

Borchmeyer, Dieter. *Drama and the World of Richard Wagner*. Trans. Daphne Ellis. Princeton, NJ: Princeton University Press, 2003.

Boulton, D. Jonathan. Personal communication regarding heraldry and magic. January 2008.
Brown, Peter. "Sorcery, Demons, and the Rise of Christianity: From Late Antiquity into the Middle Ages." *Witchcraft Confessions and Accusations*: Association of Social Anthropologists Monograph 9 (1970): 17–45. Rpt. in *Religion and Society in the Age of Saint Augustine*. New York: Harper & Row, 1972.
Chrétien de Troyes. *The Complete Romances of Chrétien de Troyes*. Trans. David Staines. Bloomington: University of Indiana Press, 1990.
Colman, Rebecca V. "Reason and Unreason in Medieval Law." *Journal of Interdisciplinary Law* 4 (1974): 571–91.
Cramer, Carl Gottlob. *Leben und Meinungen, auch seltsamliche Abentheuer Erasmus Schleichers, eines reisenden Mechanikus*. 4 vols. New ed. Frankfurt and Leipzig: n.p., 1794.
Dahlhaus, Carl. *Richard Wagner's Music Dramas*. Trans. Mary Whittall. Cambridge, UK: Cambridge University Press, 1979.
Dahnke, Hans-Dietrich, Thomas Höhle, and Hans-Georg Werner. *Geschichte der deutschen Literatur: 1789 bis 1830*. Berlin: Volk und Wissen Volkseigener Verlag, 1978.
Deathridge, John. "Wagner the Progressive: Another Look at Lohengrin." From *Wagner Beyond Good and Evil*. Berkeley: University of California Press, 2008.
Dobozy, Maria, trans. *The Saxon Mirror: A Sachsenspiegel of the Fourteenth Century*. Philadelphia: University of Pennsylvania Press, 1999.
Ellis, William Ashton, trans. *Richard Wagner's Prose Works*. Vol. 1. New York: Broude Brothers, 1966.
Feurzeig, Lisa. "Heroines in Perversity: Marie Schmith, Animal Magnetism, and the Schubert Circle." *19th-Century Music* 21 (1997): 223–43.
Grimm, Jacob. *Deutsche Rechtsalterthum*. 2 vols. 4th ed. Leipzig: Dieterich'sche Verlagsbuchhandlung Theodor Weicher, 1899.
Halecki, O. *A History of Poland*. 9th ed. New York: David McKay, 1976.
Hauff, Wilhelm. "Die Bücher und die Lesewelt." *Wilhelm Hauff's Werke* II: 1. Ed. Felix Bobertag. Stuttgart: J. Cotta, 1961.
Hoyt, Robert S., and Stanley Chodorow. *Europe in the Middle Ages*. 3rd ed. New York: Harcourt Brace Jovanovich, 1976.
Kester, Sally. "The Relativity of Good and Evil in *Lohengrin*." *Miscellanea musicologica: Adelaide Studies in Musicology* 15 (1988): 133–42.
Kieckhefer, Richard. *Magic in the Middle Ages*. Cambridge, UK: Cambridge University Press, 1989.
Köhler, Joachim. *Richard Wagner: The Last of the Titans*. Trans. Stewart Spencer. New Haven, CT: Yale University Press, 2004.
Marie de France. *Lays of Marie de France*. Trans. Eugene Mason. London: Dent, 1911.
Mertens, Volker. "Wagner's Middle Ages." *The Wagner Handbook*. Ed. Ulrich Müller and Peter Wapnewski. Trans. ed. John Deathridge. Cambridge, MA: Harvard University Press, 1992. 236–68.
[Naubert, Christiane Benedikte.] *Elisabeth Erbin von Toggenburg, oder Geschichte der Frauen von Sargans in der Schweiz*. New ed. Leipzig: Kleefeld, 1799.
Peters, Edward. *The Magician, the Witch, and the Law*. [Philadelphia]: University of Pennsylvania Press, 1978.
Rank, Otto. "Die Lohengrinsage: Ein Beitrag zu ihrer Motivgestaltung und Deutung." *Schriften zur angewandten Seelenkunde*. Ed. Sigmund Freud. Leipzig & Vienna, 1911. Rpt. Nendeln: Kraus, 1970.
Spieß, Ch[ristian] H[einrich]. *Das Petermännchen*. Frankfurt und Leipzig: n. p. 1795. Reprint: Frankfurt am Main Minerva, 1971.
Stahl, E. L., and W. E. Yuill. *German Literature of the Eighteenth and Nineteenth Centuries*. New York: Barnes and Noble, 1970.
Sweeney, Michelle. *Magic in Medieval Romance from Chrétien de Troyes to Geoffrey Chaucer*. Dublin: Four Courts Press, 2000.
Wagner, Cosima. *Cosima Wagner's Diaries*. 2 vols. Ed. Martin Gregor-Dellin and Dietrich Mack. Trans. Geoffrey Skelton. New York: Harcourt Brace Jovanovich, 1976, 1977.
Wagner, Richard. *Lohengrin*. Ed. John Deathridge and Klaus Döge. London: Eulenburg, 2007.
Wahnfried-Bibliothek. A catalog of Wagner's books at Wahnfried, available as a pdf from the Bayreuth website. http://www.wahnfried.de/_engl/aktuelles/index.html.
Weber, Veit. [Leonhard Wächter.] *Glaubensmuth. Sagen der Vorzeit*, vol. 7. Zofingen: n.p., 1798.
Woodmansee, Martha. "Toward a Genealogy of the Aesthetic: The German Reading Debate of the 1790s." *Cultural Critique* 11 (1988–89): 203–21.

7

Tristan and Ecstasy

HANS RUDOLF VAGET

One of the most common symptoms of Wagnermania has been the psychological phenomenon of ecstasy, or transport, and no work has caused the outbreak of such symptoms more frequently or reliably than *Tristan und Isolde*. Among the many varieties of Wagnermania that the world has witnessed ever since the sensational success of *Rienzi* in 1842, the one caused by *Tristan* appears to be more resistant to cure than any other. The primary cause of such a painfully blissful condition is, of course, the music that Wagner imagined for this work—music of an infinite variety of colors and textures, of mystifying harmonic progressions, of overwhelmingly grand architectural design. To a greater extent than has usually been suggested, however, an ecstatic reaction to *Tristan und Isolde* is triggered by the ecstasy that is enacted before us, on the stage and in the orchestra, as we become inexorably drawn into the drama of a spiritual journey which, from the outset, points toward an ecstasy of the ultimate sort.

Before turning to a close reading of that ultimate ecstasy, enacted in the so-called "Liebestod" at the end of the work, I should like to retrace the steps both in the music drama itself and in its genesis that will eventually lead us to that, in a literal sense, out-of-this-world experience that marks the most extraordinary moment not only in all of Wagner and, perhaps, in all of opera. The evidence we have regarding the origins of *Tristan und Isolde* is so copious that it lends itself to different models for the reconstruction of its genesis—a biographical, an economic, and an aesthetic model. In the final analysis these three views of how *Tristan* came into existence become inseparable. But for the purpose of clarity, I shall here consider them separately.

Let us first look at the biographical evidence and turn to the alluring but enigmatic figure of Mathilde Wesendonck.[1] The chief reason that Mathilde remains an enigma is that almost all of her letters to Wagner have disappeared. The fourteen letters that have survived date from a later period of their relationship and are of little interest.[2] We can only guess how many written communications they actually exchanged. Nor do we know how many communications the correspondents themselves destroyed, or who destroyed Mathilde's letters from the crucial years of the relationship. (We do know that they were preserved for publication.) Was it Cosima, motivated by jealousy, or rather by fidelity to Wagner's own wishes? Was it Mathilde herself, as Cosima at one point suggested?[3] As John Deathridge has recently observed, "the history of this correspondence is shrouded in mystery, lending it an air of perceived erotic tension that for the most part disguises its essential formal qualities." From what we can tell on the basis of the surviving documents, "the correspondence has many of the hallmarks of an exchange of letters between late 18th-century figures"; it appears to have been a "serious formal engagement, a pact even, with responsibilities on each side."[4] Indeed, the serious and formal nature of their engagement can be glimpsed from Wagner's letters alone, which contain more, and more revealing, comments about aesthetic matters and about some of his works than any other correspondence of his from those years.

The story of Richard Wagner and Mathilde Wesendonck is dear to the hearts of all romantically inclined Wagnerians. But how far does their romantic involvement really go in illuminating the origins of *Tristan und Isolde*? Let us consider the biographical setting of their romance. At the end of April 1857, Wagner and his wife, Minna, accepted the offer from Otto Wesendonck to live in the comfortable little cottage next to the Wesendonck's own newly built villa on their spacious property in Zürich. Otto Wesendonck, who hailed from Wuppertal, an industrial town near Düsseldorf, had been a partner in a New York silk trading company and, at thirty-six, had made enough money to be able to retire and to devote himself to the pleasant task of supporting the arts. Together with Mathilde, his attractive and talented German wife, Otto's junior by thirteen years, Wesendonck decided to settle in Zürich, where he and Mathilde soon made the acquaintance of Wagner.

Mathilde first met the composer in 1852, after a concert that he conducted. At the time she was twenty-four, he thirty-nine. Some five years later their friendship, according to the *Wagner Compendium*, "developed into a sexual relationship which may or may not have been consummated."[5] This sounds puzzling and leads you to wonder what precisely is meant here by "sexual relationship." In fact, indications are that, contrary to what is often assumed or insinuated, Wagner did not have sexual relations with that woman. John Deathridge is undoubtedly right to say that "The supposed sexual shenanigans between Wagner and Mathilde Wesendonck have been so grossly exaggerated that it has become all the harder to trace the underlying seriousness of their relationship."[6] Both seem to have understood that, if not for Otto's sake, then for the sake of the new work struggling to be born, they ought not to go that far. Once the decision to write an opera on the subject of Tristan and Isolde was taken, Wagner needed a muse — and only a muse — to get his creative juices flowing. In the event they gushed — thanks to Mathilde, who very clearly understood her role as an unattainable object of intense desire. For his part, and true to form, Wagner instinctively knew that he needed to be in love in order to make the new work a "monument to love," as he described his project to Franz Liszt, and that the object of his love should in fact be unattainable.[7]

One year after the Wagners had moved into the cottage they dubbed "Asyl" (refuge), Minna intercepted one of the countless messages that went back and forth between the "Asyl" and the Wesendonck villa. This happened to be a lengthy and weighty epistle, which Wagner described as a "Morgenbeichte" — an early morning confession. What was he confessing? The previous evening had not gone well. Wagner was having dinner with Mathilde while Otto was away on business — with operatic opportuneness, as Shaw would say. There was, however, another dinner guest, Francesco De Sanctis, a professor of Aesthetics and Italian literature at the Technical University of Zürich, and a brilliant and good-looking man, whom Mathilde had hired as her private tutor in Italian. De Sanctis, like Wagner, was a political radical; he later served as the Italian Minister of Education and became an eminent literary historian.[8] Wagner did not like what he saw; the Italian academic, his junior by four years, was openly acting like a serious contender for Mathilde's affections. What made things

Johanna Meier as Isolde in the Metropolitan Opera's Tristan und Isolde *(photograph by Winnie Klotz).*

even more uncomfortable was the fact that Francesco was holding forth on Schopenhauer and on Goethe's *Faust*—two subjects in which Wagner, too, could claim some expertise. The discussions must have been lively, and since Wagner felt that he had not gotten his points across with the customary forcefulness he wrote a long letter first thing next morning—"just out of bed." This, then, was his "Morgenbeichte."

In large part, his letter may be described as an incisive critique of Goethe's Faust, who, in Wagner's eyes, does not deserve redemption because his love of Gretchen lacks compassion. But the letter also contains—perhaps to fend off his Italian competition—an unambiguous declaration of love for Mathilde, who is referred to as "the well-spring of my redemption."[9] The letter concludes with an urgent request for an assignation later that day. Minna is not known to have had an interest in the question of Faust's redemption, but she had become convinced that the two of them were having an affair and that she could no longer ignore what was going on. Even though her marriage to Richard had for all intents and purposes been dead for some time, Minna thought that now was the time to break up the idyll. In the aftermath of the storm, the continuation of the near-cohabitation of the Wesendoncks and the Wagners became impossible. Wagner thus took off for Venice, where he completed the score of Act II of *Tristan und Isolde*—a score in which messy personal relationships are transformed, miraculously, into exquisite musical symbolism.

Those who like biographical and romantic notions about the origin of works of art will want to cling to the story just summarized, and will want to view *Tristan und Isolde* as the dramatization of Wagner's personal situation—with King Marke as a portrait of Otto Wesendonck. There is, however, enough evidence to support quite a different and decidedly more prosaic narrative about the origin of this extraordinary work. In 1856, the music publishers Breitkopf & Härtel declined to give Wagner a contract for *The Ring of the Nibelung*, which at that time was, of course, far from completion. This meant that for the foreseeable future Wagner could expect no royalties and no advances. He thus had to think of a work that theaters would be able to produce expeditiously. What he had in mind was a potboiler that would quickly generate a lot of royalties. With a considerable measure of self-delusion that we now find touching, Wagner assured his publishers that his new opera would make no great demands in terms of sets and choral forces; that all that was needed was a pair of good singers.[10] This, of course, did not quite work out as expected. Several theaters, among them the Vienna Court Opera, sampled *Tristan* and gave up on it. In Vienna it had gone through no less than seventy-seven rehearsals. Even after the very successful Munich premiere of the work in 1865, it took a while before other theaters would even touch it. It is a sign of Wagner's desperate financial situation that he asked Breitkopf & Härtel to pay him for *Tristan* in three installments, one after the completion of Act I, one after the completion of Act II, and one after the completion of Act III. This arrangement was advantageous to the publishers because they could begin setting the score in print even before Wagner had completed the work in its entirety. It also meant that composing the later parts coincided with the proofreading of the earlier ones. This made for a compositional procedure that is unique in all of Wagner and leads one to one wonder to what extent such exceptional circumstances were a contributing factor to the exceptional character of the work.

The truly decisive factor in the genesis of *Tristan und Isolde* was, as one might well expect with an artist such as Wagner, an aesthetic one. In a sense, this work demanded to be written, which is another way of saying that the dynamics of Wagner's development as a composer compelled him to set down this score at this time. In the famous letter to Franz Liszt to which I earlier alluded, Wagner declared that he wished to erect a monument to "the most beautiful dream of all," the dream of love, not, as one might think, because he was overflowing with happiness and joy but because he himself had never really tasted these emotions. Psychologically more plausible than any biographical explanation, the letter to Liszt in fact precludes the actual experience of sexual fulfillment with Mathilde as a contributing factor to the central creative impulse. The idea of love to which Wagner wanted to erect a monument was the fruit not of an experience but of a dream — a dream that would take him above and beyond the realm of ordinary human experience.

By the time Wagner turned to the subject of Tristan, Mathilde had already been on his mind for some time. She was slowly becoming a factor in the husbanding of Wagner's creative energies. In June of 1853 he wrote a little "Sonata for Mathilde Wesendonck." As an epigraph he used a rather suggestive, even ominous, line from *Götterdämmerung*: "Wißt Ihr wie das wird?" — Do you know what will become of this? A year later, in the compositional sketch for Act I of *Die Walküre* he wrote "G. S. M.," meaning: Gott segne Mathilde — Blessed be Mathilde. Whatever was brewing here, it came into focus only after Wagner's dramatic discovery of the writings of Arthur Schopenhauer. In Schopenhauer's philosophy the composer found clarification and confirmation of much of what he had been thinking about life and the world except on one crucial point: the question of sexual love. To Schopenhauer, sex was the ultimate cause for the ceaseless perpetuation of life's suffering. To Wagner, sex was and remained a "Heilsweg" — a road to salvation. Wagner's reservations about Schopenhauer's metaphysics of sexual love arose, inconveniently, when he was at work on *Die Walküre*, where the die, so to speak, had already been cast. To engage with Schopenhauer required the clean slate of a separate work. Reading Schopenhauer, he writes in *Mein Leben*, had put him in a serious frame of mind and in a philosophically contentious "mood" that became so intense that it sought "ecstatic expression."[11] Much later, in conversations with Cosima, he admitted that composing *Tristan* had in fact been an ecstatic experience. He had felt an irrepressible desire, "sich auszurasen"—to give it his all and, for once, completely to let himself go, symphonically speaking.[12] When Wagner decided to take leave of his Siegfried, he did so as someone who had exhausted all the possibilities of the essentially diatonic style that dominates the first two parts of *The Ring*, as someone who in Act II of *Siegfried* had tasted the artistic possibilities of overwhelming chromaticism, and who now wanted to give this new road his full attention, thereby to move beyond the boundaries of what was then thought possible and acceptable. Tellingly, Wagner became aware of the ground-breaking nature of *Tristan und Isolde* when he had to divide his attention between the second and third acts. As he wrote in *Mein Leben*: "The process of correcting the proofs of the second act, while I was simultaneously in the throes of composing the ecstasies of the third act, had the strangest, even uncanny, effect on me; for it was in just those first scenes of this act that I realized with complete clarity that I had written the most audacious and original work of my life."[13] Just how audacious he felt he had been emerges from a letter to Mathilde written just as he was composing those "ecstasies" in Act III: "This *Tristan* is turning into something *terrible*! This last act!!!—I fear the opera will be banned—unless the whole thing is parodied by bad performances—: only mediocre performances can save me. Perfectly *good* ones are bound to drive people mad [...] That's just how far I've had to go."[14]

Thus, what had originally been conceived as a potboiler was turning under Wagner's own eyes into a music drama that would stretch to the breaking point the capacities of the leading opera houses. And what had been intended as a monument to "the most beautiful dream of all"—the common dream of love—was leading him to probe the outer limit of human experience where love slides into ecstasy or into madness.

Here then lies Mathilde's true significance in the genesis of *Tristan und Isolde*—she played the role of Wagner's partner, balancing her powers to awaken sexual desire and, by withholding gratification, leading him to transform desire into music—music that revels in the excess of pain. Unique among the women in his life, Mathilde became part of an aesthetic project; she was instrumental to his achieving

Hildegard Behrens as Isolde and Richard Cassilly as Tristan in Act 2 of *Tristan und Isolde*, the Everding production at the Metropolitan Opera (photograph by Winnie Klotz).

that quantum leap from the largely diatonic loveliness of the "Forest Murmurs" in *Siegfried* to the chromatic hell of desire and suffering in the Prelude to *Tristan*. A perfect illustration of Mathilde's role as muse, or rather, partner, may be found in the set of five songs "for female voice and piano" known as the "Wesendonck-Lieder." From what we know of her, Mathilde was a good listener, this being an obvious and paramount requirement of a muse to Richard Wagner. She also had literary ambitions of her own, which Wagner apparently encouraged her to pursue. In fact, after the Wagner affair, Mathilde Wesendonck made a name for herself as a writer. She published poetry and wrote plays, including one on the subject of Siegfried. As Chris Walton observes, all of her writings, in one way or other, echo Wagner.[15] It was her talent, then, more than anything else, that qualified her to become Wagner's partner not only in love but also in some small yet significant measure in the creative process — in the ecstasy of Richard Wagner, the composer.

As we have seen, Wagner began drawing Mathilde towards him and into the still shadowy world of *Tristan* by dedicating the piano sonata to her. He made a more explicit move when, on 18 September 1857, he offered her the autograph manuscript of Act III of the libretto of *Tristan und Isolde*. Wagner himself presented the manuscript to Mathilde, who, as he described a year later, led him to a chair in front of the sofa, embraced him, and said: "Now I can wish for nothing more."[16] A few days later he began the compositional sketch for Act I. When this sketch was completed, he presented it, too, to Mathilde, complete with an ecstatic dedicatory poem. Now it was Mathilde's turn. Having read the libretto she responded by writing a number of poems reflecting her reaction to *Tristan*. Wagner set some of these to music as soon as they came off Mathilde's desk — an extraordinary and in fact unique occurrence in his creative life. Two of these settings — "Träume" and "Im Treibhaus" — he later designated as "studies for *Tristan und Isolde*."[17] "Träume," the best-known song of the group, clearly foreshadows the incipient ecstasy of the love duet in Act II: "O sink hernieder, Nacht der Liebe." There is a certain opaqueness to Mathilde's poem, but we can easily see that Wagner read it as a veiled declaration of love, which in turn inspired him to the grand loving gesture of setting Mathilde's poems to music. Of his setting of *Träume* Wagner later wrote to Mathilde: "God knows, I liked this lied better than the proud scene [the love scene of Act II]. Heaven, this is more beautiful than anything I have done. When I listen to it, my innermost nerves are stirring."[18]

Träume

Sag,' welch wunderbare Träume
halten meinen Sinn umfangen,
daß sie nicht wie leere Schäume
sind in ödes Nichts vergangen?
Träume, die in jeder Stunde,
jedem Tage schöner blüh'n,
und mit ihrer Himmelskunde
selig durch's Gemüte ziehn!
Träume, die wie hehre Strahlen
in die Seele sich versenken,
dort ein ewig Bild zu malen:
Allvergessen, Eingedenken!
Träume, wie wenn Frühlingssonne
aus dem Schnee die Blüten küßt,
daß zu nie geahnter Wonne
sie der neue Tag begrüßt,

Act 2 of *Tristan und Isolde* (Robert Dean Smith, Irene Theorin) at the Bayreuth Festival (courtesy Bayreuth Festival).

> dass sie wachsen, dass sie blühen,
> träumend spenden ihren Duft,
> sanft an deiner Brust verglühen,
> und dann sinken in die Gruft.[19]

Mathilde's poem speaks of dreams which, like the sun in spring, melt and, with a kiss, draw flowers from the ice. To summarize the miraculous effect of that dream of love she cites two characteristically Tristanesque words from Wagner's text: "Allvergessen, Eingedenken!"—total oblivion, [total] remembering. Mathilde's poem concludes with the wish that her dreams might grow and bloom and impart their scent upon "your breast"—Wagner's breast, that is. "Träume" is Mathilde's response to the text of *Tristan*; by setting it to music, Wagner allowed Mathilde's poem to feed back into the love music of Act II. In fact, Wagner was moved to make an extraordinary gesture: he gave his muse a voice in the creation of *Tristan*.

Strangely, Mathilde's authorship of these five poem was for a long time obscured. The *Wesendonck Lieder* appeared in 1862 and were designated as "Five Poems for Woman's Voice Set to Music by Richard Wagner." Mathilde's name was not printed in the publication. It was thus assumed that Wagner himself had penned the poems, for they contain many verbal echoes of *Tristan und Isolde* and they capture much of the opera's unmistakable mood of passion and gloom. Actually Wagner had wanted to advertise the fact that these were settings of someone else's poems when he proposed to add the subtitle, "Fünf Dilettanten-Gedichte," meaning five poems by a dilettante, the term "dilettante" taken in the positive sense of lover of poetry.[20] But Schott, the publishers, rejected Wagner's subtitle.

* * *

The three acts of *Tristan*, although written in the same new musical idiom, display a variety of moods. In the literature, Act I has perhaps been less appreciated than the others, which is a pity, because there is no finer example in all of Wagner of the composer's prowess as a dramatist. We are on board a ship sailing from Ireland to Cornwall. After the prelude, the action begins in complete silence. It is broken by the voice of a young sailor singing without accompaniment his haunting and taunting song to his Irish love. When the orchestra finally enters, we are slowly transported on an ocean of sound, unfolding gradually and with increasing forward momentum to the tumultuous arrival of the ship at Cornwall, marked by a blinding blast of solid C-Major that washes away the harmonic uncertainties to which we have been treated since the beginning and drowns, though not for long, the distinctly troubled and conflicted sentiments of the two ill-fated passengers. They have agreed to die to-

Katharina Dalayman as Brangaene in the Metropolitan Opera production of *Tristan und Isolde* (photograph by Winnie Klotz).

gether and have finally confessed their love, which instantly makes them forget where they are. They are lost to the world. They are literally "beside themselves"—which is precisely the meaning of ecstasy.

Act I is above all a model of dramatic economy. Wagner had to condense vast stretches of narrative from his primary source, Gottfried von Strassburg's courtly epic, *Tristan*, into one dramatic situation, and he had to present from the lovers' lives the key moments that would make plausible the turn of events while at sea — the irruption of hatred and despair into open passion. Furthermore, he had to define the nature of their love. Consider how much we learn during the claustrophobic action on board ship that leads to their common desire to die together. The lovers' history, embedded as it is in the political history of English-Irish relations, is long, complicated, and fraught with deception and betrayal. In earlier times, England had been obligated to pay taxes to Ireland until young Tristan, King Marke's nephew, killed in battle the Irish emissary, Morold, betrothed to the Irish princess Isolde, thereby ending

Hildegard Behrens as Isolde, seated, and Tatiana Troyanos as Brangaene in *Tristan und Isolde* at the Metropolitan Opera (photograph by Winnie Klotz).

England's subservience to Ireland. In a nasty gesture of schadenfreude, the English sent Morold's severed head back to Ireland. However, Tristan's triumph was severely diminished when it became apparent that the wound he had received in the battle with Morold was incurable. Aware of the medical wizardry of princess Isolde, and of that of her mother, Tristan sails to Ireland and appears before Isolde under the false name of Tantris. Isolde heals Tantris and allows him to return to England, but at a terrible emotional price—for as she performs her healing rites she discovers that the splinter she had earlier found in Morold's skull is in fact missing from Tantris' sword. However, as she is about to do what honor and loyalty demand—namely killing the killer of her betrothed—her eyes meet the eyes of the wounded Tantris, who lies prostate before her. She is unable to proceed and drops the sword. Since England wishes to seal the peace with Ireland, Tristan, denying his love for Isolde out of loyalty to his uncle, is again sent back to Ireland, this time under his real name, not in order to woo Isolde for himself but rather to woo her for his uncle, King Marke, whom she is now, as they approach Cornwall, about to meet for the first time. The prospect of being given in marriage to an aging king—Marke is said to be a "tired" man—while the most desirable man is going to be ever present, despite his fragile denial of love out of loyalty to Marke—this prospect is simply too much for her to contemplate. In despair, she thus decides to demand penance of Tristan for his "betrayal" of their as yet unannounced love. He agrees to die with her. Having drunk what they believed was a death potion and thus firmly expecting to die before they reach shore, Tristan and Isolde finally feel released from the bonds of custom and morality and openly acknowledge their feelings. In the symbolic language of Act II, they have left behind the world of the "day" and entered the realm of the "night." The musical gestures Wagner invented to signify the lovers' emotional turmoil and its magical transformation into desire, with reminiscences of the motifs from the prelude punctuated by silences of extraordinary expressivity, are thrilling and justly celebrated.

Of even greater importance for the understanding of the inner action is that moment in Isolde's great retrospective narration when she recalls the fatal glance, the meeting of her eyes with Tristan's. This signifies the birth of love from compassion. It is a scene nearly identical to that seminal scene in Act I of *Die Walküre*, where Sieglinde's and Siegmund's eyes meet in similar embrace. In *Tristan*, instead of a cello, it is a solo viola that intones

Hildegard Behrens as Isolde in the third act of *Tristan und Isolde* at the Metropolitan Opera (photograph by Winnie Klotz).

the melody of desire. Wagner even marks the dropping of the sword with a pluck of the strings. And while in *Die Walküre* the birth of love from compassion, embodied in the glance, is acted out before our eyes, in *Tristan* it occurs as a recollection from the distant past.

Acts I and II end with the expression of the lovers' desire forever to thwart the forces of the "day" in order to enter forever the realm of the "night." When Tristan and Isolde finally die — separately, not together — they do indeed enter the realm of "eternal night" through a mystical experience, which in the case of Isolde is commonly referred to as "Liebestod," literally "love-death" but more appropriately as transfiguration. While many have analyzed the music of the concluding "Liebestod," few have attempted to understand and to interpret the words. And yet if we really wish to comprehend this mystical experience we must understand what the words of the "Liebestod" mean, what they signify, and how in poetic terms this culminating point of the opera is designed.

Analysis of the text requires us, first and foremost, to throw overboard most of the familiar and apparently ineradicable notions about the poetic quality, or rather lack thereof, of Wagner's librettos. While few now contest his excellence as a composer, many continue to dispute or to deny his talent as a poet. Jacques Barzun was surely speaking for many when in his 1941 book on Marx, Darwin, and Wagner he opined: "Whether in translation or in the original, the lines [of Wagner's librettos] fail to strike us as remarkable for anything but dullness." For good measure Barzun added that there are only a few "living Wagnerians who could face a performance or a reading of the librettos as plays."[21] This widespread perception was put to the test in January 2005 when the eminent Wagnerian Dieter Borchmeyer organized a purely "literary" reading of *The Ring* without the music. That reading, carried out by professional actors and singers, filled Munich's Residenztheater on two consecutive evenings and proved to be a surprising success.

In marked contrast to Barzun, Patrick Smith, to whom we owe the most authoritative history of the libretto, *The Tenth Muse*, flatly asserts that Wagner's achievement as a librettist was "the greatest the form has produced."[22] To substantiate this claim, Smith underlines three outstanding characteristics of the Wagnerian libretto. First, "for the first time in its history the libretto itself served as reflection of the range of a man's mind and his deepest thoughts." In other words, Wagner appropriated and applied to the text of the opera the modern, Romantic concept of authorship as the medium for the most authentic realization of the self. Second, Wagner's "organizational genius," as evidenced in *The Ring of the Nibelung*, is "by far the greatest structural achievement ever carried to fruition by a librettist." Third, Wagner's "command of the stage, from both the point of view of technical knowledge and that of intuitive sense of the dramatic," is said to have been "greater" than that of "any other librettist."[23]

There is one issue on which Patrick Smith sounds hesitant and tentative and that is the poetic dimension of Wagner's operatic texts. Considering the experimental character of much of Wagner's poetic language, especially in *The Ring* and in *Tristan*, such hesitation is understandable. Wagner deliberately strove for a new poetic language that would maximize the effect of the new music he was devising — a music that dissolved the set numbers and the traditional periodic structures of the classical style and transformed them into a seamless symphonic web. He found such a poetic idiom suited to his new musical language when he turned to the famous medieval "Stabreim" — a short-line alliterative verse of irregular length. The Wagnerian "Stabreim" is designed to sound archaic. But on close inspection it turns out to be, at least in the art of the libretto, a decidedly avant-garde idiom and a highly effective vehicle that is ideally suited to Wagner's purposes in *The Ring*. Practical-minded and undogmatic as he was in all artistic matters, Wagner, in *Tristan*, modified and augmented the alliterative verse technique he had invented for another purpose.

Thomas Mann was on target — as he usually was with respect to Wagner — when he remarked: "It has always seemed to me absurd to question Wagner's poetic gifts."[24] From the Dutchman's great monologue in Act I of *The Flying Dutchman* to the monologues of Amfortas in *Parsifal*, Wagner lends his voice above all to the expression of pain and suffering. Usually the suffering is related to sexual desire, particularly in *Tristan* and in *Parsifal*. Wagner is at his most innovative and subtle when he explores his characters' interiority, when he brings into focus their hidden motivation. In these cases — think of Siegfried and Brünnhilde, or of Parsifal and Kundry — Wagner proceeds very much in the manner of a psychoanalyst, using musical motifs to lay bare hidden connections. It was as an explorer of interiority, of course, that Wagner served as a model and inspiration for countless later poets and writers who wished to refine the literary means of rendering subconscious thoughts and feelings. It is not by accident that some of the pioneers and leading practitioners of literary modernism were Wagnerians, among them Edouard Dujardin, Arthur Schnitzler, Thomas Mann, James Joyce, and Marcel Proust.

This brings us back to *Tristan und Isolde* and to the remarkable manner both musically and poetically in which Wagner brings his drama of desire to the devastating conclusion of Isolde's "Liebestod." Given the popularity of this music today and the often cliché-ridden program notes that usually accompany it, the temptation to deflate the metaphysical hype of the commentators and to remind readers of the sexual foundation of it all is almost irresistible. One recent commentator, for instance, has described the climactic conclusion of *Tristan und Isolde* as "Isolde's musical orgasm" and "a thoroughly masculine cliché." This music, he explains, "is essentially a voyeuristic male depiction of a woman's onanistic fantasy: it is Wagner imagining how his lover [Mathilde] fantasizes about him while he watches from afar."[25] Such wild iconoclasm, imaginative though it may be, fails to do justice to the undeniably spiritual dimension of this supreme moment.

Tristan und Isolde, Act 1, the August Everding production at the Metropolitan Opera (photograph by Winnie Klotz).

Act 1 of *Tristan und Isolde*, the Christoph Marthaler production at the Bayreuth Festival (courtesy Bayreuth Festival).

In order to grasp the spiritual dimension a close reading of Wagner's poetry must be the first order of business for any commentator or interpreter. Just as the music of the "Liebestod" can be performed as a separate concert item, or as a sequel to the prelude to Act I, as it often is, so, too, can the end of *Tristan* be read as a poem in its own right. It was the great philologist, Leo Spitzer, who, in a comparative study of John Donne, St. John of the Cross, and Wagner, established that the conclusion of *Tristan und Isolde* harks back to the tradition of "ecstatic" religious poetry. The proper subject of such poetry, wrote Spitzer, is "the ecstatic union of a human ego with a non-ego."[26] In pre-romantic religious poetry that non-ego is god. Wagner deviates from tradition in making the non-ego something other than god and something clearly non–Christian — the "Welt-Atem," the World Spirit. In the universe of *Tristan und Isolde*, there is no personal god. So it does not seem appropriate, despite the claims of so excellent a commentator as Joseph Kerman, to speak of *Tristan und Isolde* as a "religious drama," if we take religion to involve some kind of personal god.[27] As a follower of Ludwig Feuerbach, Wagner had discarded all notions of a personal god long before he conceived this music drama. Wagner deviates from tradition in another way, too, for in traditional religious poetry the ecstatic union with god is a temporary trance, while in Wagner, Isolde's transfiguration is terminal.

Generally, an ecstatic union is to be achieved by only exceptional individuals such as saints and mystics. Ecstatic union is a spiritual occurrence on the outer edges of human experience. Ecstasy, according to the OED, is, as we have seen, "the state of being 'beside oneself.'" In late Greek antiquity the word denoted "the withdrawal of the soul from the body." All of this is very much to the point as concerns Wagner's "Liebestod," as one realizes as soon as one disentangles the syntactical design of the text, which at first may appear to be a bit woolly but which turns out to be highly sophisticated indeed.

Isolde's ecstasy is preceded by the ecstasies of the ailing and dying Tristan — those ecstasies which, if properly performed, should drive listeners insane, as Wagner believed. As Tristan predicted in Act II, he has preceded her to the land from which there is no return. The first twenty-one lines of the "Liebestod," each one notably short, are composed of a series of three questions addressed to King Marke and Brangäne, Isolde's "friends," who are called upon to witness the miraculous transfiguration of Tristan's body. Isolde poses three pairs of rhetorical questions, the second challenging the negative answer implied in the first, as in "Can you see it, friends? — How can you not see it?" Here then is a close rendering of the first 21 lines, starting from "Mild und leise."

> How gently and softly he smiles; how sweetly his eyes open: do you know see this, friends? How could you not see it?
> How he glows, ever brighter, how he raises himself, stars sparkling around him! Do you not see it?
> How his heart is bravely swelling, how, full and noble, it fills his breast; and how sweet breath drifts softly from his gentle, blissful lips! See friends — do you not feel and see it?

It is clear from these rhetorical questions that only Isolde perceives Tristan's transfiguration — a transfiguration, like her incipient ecstasy, that is confined to her own sensibility and consciousness. The phenomena that her "friends" are unable to perceive — that the deceased Tristan is actually smiling; that he is opening his eyes; that his heart is swelling; that a sweet fragrance is flowing from his lips — are familiar items of ecstatic religious poetry.

The next several questions are directed to Isolde herself. The first, running from lines 22 to 33, is extraordinarily involved. It is a question — beginning with "Höre ich nur diese Weise?" — raised by an aural sensation. Isolde — and only she — hears a melody issuing from Tristan's transfigured body, as though his essence had been distilled from him and transubstantiated into music. It is the same "Weise" that has dominated Tristan's entire life, except that now, in Isolde's inner ear, it is transformed from a tune of sadness into a melody of bliss. A cluster of three verbs and seven adverbs is marshaled to describe the miraculous music emanating from Tristan's body. This inaudible "Weise," then, is the catalyst of the traditional mystical climax, as Isolde, in a quasi-sexual ecstasy, is penetrated by the musical embodiment of Tristan.

> Am I the only one to hear this melody, which, so wondrous and tender in its blissful lament, revealing everything and gently soothing, emanates from him, penetrates me, sweetly echoing about me?

There follow, with increasing urgency, seven more questions, again addressed to herself. The text now shifts from the realm of hearing to the sphere of touch and smell, as Isolde rapidly loses her sense of identity. Unable to make out whether she is feeling waves of gentle breezes, or clouds of delicious fragrances, she is unsure of her response. "Shall I breathe them; shall I listen to them? Shall I sip them, dive into them, and expire in these perfumes?" Sliding from one sense perception to another she is moved to breathe her last and become one with the enveloping clouds of perfume. She does so sweetly, reconciled to her fate. In the remaining eight lines all syntactical order is abandoned. Three participial phrases — the surging flood, the ringing sound, the World Spirit's wafting breath — are followed by two infinitives — "ertrinken, versinken"; to drown, to sink. The last two elements are an adjective — "unbewusst"; unconscious — and a distantly audible exclamation — "höchste Lust"; bliss supreme! The last two lines are ambiguous as to what precisely is happening to Isolde. To "drown" and to "sink" denote downward movements, as though she were falling below the ocean of sound that is a manifestation of the World Spirit. "Bliss supreme," on the other hand, points upward, as does the vocal line at this climactic point of ecstasy by the upward leap of an octave. It is supremely fitting, then, that a poem of ecstasy — the so-called "Liebestod" — should provide the capstone to a musical architecture that thematizes ecstasy in various forms and that has given the composer the much-desired opportunity for an ecstatic experience in an emphatically musical and artistic sense.

The purely poetic excellence of Wagner's "Liebestod" may now be perceived more clearly. It rests on the sophistication with which the structure of the poem is made to reflect the mystical experience of ecstasy. All of the elements are of a piece. In concert, they admirably fulfill the chief function that Wagner's theory assigns to the word: it makes distinct — "verdeutlichen" — and comprehensible the "deeds of the music."[28] The poetic text proceeds from alliterative verse to alternate rhymes and to pairs of rhymes enhanced by assonance. In the process a kind of synthesis of sensation is achieved, the one blending with the other and leading up to the most spiritual — "verhauchen," to expire. Most tellingly, the convoluted syntax of the first set of questions gives way, gradually, via simpler but more agitated questions, to a complete dissolution of syntax — mirroring exactly Isolde's loss of self and loss, ultimately, of individual identity.

Wagner makes it quite clear that the goal of Isolde's ecstasy is a mystical union not with Tristan but with the "Welt-Atem" — the World Spirit. Tristan is her partner in this transition,

Act 1 of *Tristan und Isolde* at the Bayreuth Festival (courtesy Bayreuth Festival).

just as Mathilde had been Wagner's partner in achieving his ecstasy as a composer. This can hardly be called ecstasy in the traditional religious sense. Isolde's ecstasy is terminal, as we have said, and associated not with a personal god but with the essence of a pantheistic universe. Thus the "Liebestod"—Isolde's going out of this world—does bring to fruition Wagner's stunning and disturbing project of creating a monument to love. Wagner makes the point with what is, at last, irrefutable certainty, by having the seemingly endless harmonic tension, deception, and ambiguity that we have experienced throughout this miraculous music drama finally climax in an overwhelming, ecstatic B major chord that leaves no room for further argument and no room for doubt as to the ecstatic nature of this supreme moment.

*For my translation of the "Liebestod" poem, I gratefully acknowledge the expert help I have received from my friend and colleague Peter Bloom.

Notes

1. See Martha Schad and Horst Schad, *"Meine erste und einzige Liebe." Richard Wagner und Mathilde Wesendonck* (München: Langen/Müller, 2002). Cf. also the recent documentary novel by Jörg Aufenanger, *Richard Wagner und Mathilde Wesendonck* (Düsseldorf: Patmos, 2007).

2. These were published as an appendix to the edition of Wagner's letters to Mathilde; cf. *Richard Wagner an Mathilde Wesendon[c]k: Tagebuchblätter und Briefe 1853—1871*, edited with an introduction by Wolfgang Golther (Berlin: Breitkopf & Härtel, 1904), 341—362.

3. See John Deathridge, "Public and Private Life: Scenes and Episodes from the Composition of *Tristan und Isolde*," *The Wagner Journal*, vol. 2, Number 1 (2008), 20—32. Deathridge (p. 31) cites an unpublished letter of 28 December 1903 from Cosima to Fritz von Bissing, Mathilde's grandson: "Die Briefe Ihrer theuren Grossmutter wurden ihr Alle zurückgestattet u. sie hat sie zerstört."

4. Deathridge (see n. 3), 31.

5. *The Wagner Compendium. A Guide to Wagner's Life and Music*, ed. Barry Millington (London: Thames & Hudson, 1992), 33; cf. also 120.

6. Deathridge (n. 3), 28.

7. See the letter to Franz Liszt, 16 December 1854 in *Selected Letters of Richard Wagner*, tr. and ed. Stewart Spencer and Barry Millington (New York: W. W. Norton & Co, 1988), 323; Richard Wagner, *Sämtliche Briefe*, vol. VI, ed. Hans Joachim Bauer and Johannes Forner (Leipzig: VEB Deutscher Verlag für Musik, 1986), 299 (henceforth: SB).

8. See Chris Walton, "Voicing Mathilde: Wagner's Controlling Muse," *The Wagner Journal*, vol.1, no. 2 (2007), 3—18. Walton's comments, pp. 11—16, represent the most detailed treatment we have of the Mathilde—De Sanctis relationship.

9. Letter to Mathilde Wesendonck, 7 April 1858, *Selected Letters* (n. 7), 381: "[...] In the morning I regained my senses, and was able to pray to my angel from the very depths of my heart; and this prayer is love! Love! My soul rejoices in this love, which is the well-spring of my redemption."

10. Letter to Breitkopf & Härtel, 30 September 1857. SB, vol. IX, ed. by Klaus Burmeister and Johannes Forner, 46f.

11. Richard Wagner, *My Life*, tr. Andrew Gray, ed. Mary Whittal (New York: Da Capo, 1992), 510. Cf. *Mein Leben*, complete, annotated text, ed. Martin Gregor-Dellin (München List, 1976), 523f: "Es war wohl zum Teil die ernste Stimmung, in welche mich Schopenhauer versetzt hatte und die nach einem ekstatischen Ausdrucke ihrer Grundzüge drängte, was mir die Konzeption eines, 'Tristan und Isolde' eingab."

12. *Cosima Wagner's Diaries*, tr. Geoffrey Skelton (New Haven, CT: Yale University Press, 1997), 1 October, 11 December 1878.

13. *My Life* (n. 11), 588.

14. Letter to Mathilde Wesendonck, undated (April 1859), SB XI, 58.

15. See Walton (n. 8), 17.

16. Diary for Mathilde Wesendonck, 18 September 1858, in *Richard Wagner an Mathilde Wesendon[c]k* (n. 2), 44f.

17. John Deathridge and Carl Dahlhaus, *The New Grove Wagner* (New York: W. W. Norton, 1984), 184.

18. Egon Voss, "'Besseres, als diese Lieder, hab ich nie gemacht ...' Zu den Wesendonck-Liedern," in Voss, *"Wagner und kein Ende." Betrachtungen und Studien* (Zürich, Mainz: Atlantis Musikbuch-Verlag, 1996), 105—109.

19. For a fine translation by William Mann see the booklet accompanying the EMI CD (7243-5-56165-2-4) featuring Marjana Lipousek, Wolfgang Sawallisch, and the Philadelphia Orchestra.
20. Voss (n. 18), 108.
21. Jacques Barzun, *Darwin, Marx, Wagner: Critique of a Heritage* (New York: Little, Brown, 1958), 261. Cf. John D. Heyl, "Der Fall Barzun: Wagner and the 19th Century," *Wagner in Retrospect: A Centennial Reappraisal*, ed. Leroy R. Shaw et al. (Amsterdam: Rodopi, 1987), 224—234.
22. Patrick J. Smith, *The Tenth Muse: A Historical Study of the Opera Libretto* (New York: A. A. Knopf, 1970), 287.
23. Ibid., 229, 260, 279, 289.
24. "Richard Wagner and 'Der Ring des Nibelungen,'" Thomas Mann, *Pro and Contra Wagner*, tr. Allan Blunden, with an introduction by Erich Heller (Chicago: University of Chicago Press, 1985), 190.
25. Walton (n. 8), 7f.
26. Leo Spitzer, "Three Poems on Ecstasy (John Donne, St. John of the Cross, Richard Wagner)," L. Spitzer, *A Method of Interpreting Literature* (Northampton, Mass.: Smith College, 1945), 5.
27. Joseph Kerman, *Opera as Drama* (New York: Vintage, 1956), 194—197.
28. See "Über die Benennung 'Musikdrama,'" Richard Wagner, *Dichtungen und Schriften*. Jubiläumsausgabe in zehn Bänden, ed. Dieter Borchmeyer (Frankfurt/Main: Insel Verlag, 1983), vol. IX, 276.

Bibliography

Aufenanger, Jörg. *Richard Wagner und Mathilde Wesendonck*. Düsseldorf: Patmos, 2007.
Barzun, Jacques. *Darwin, Marx, Wagner: Critique of a Heritage*. New York: Little, Brown, 1958.
Deathridge, John. "Public and Private Life: Scenes and Episodes from the Composition of *Tristan und Isolde*." *The Wagner Journal* 2 (2008): 20—32.
_____, and Carl Dahlhaus. *The New Grove Wagner*. New York: W. W. Norton, 1984.
Heyl, John D. "Der Fall Barzun: Wagner and the 19th Century." *Wagner in Retrospect: A Centennial Reappraisal*, ed. Leroy R. Shaw. Amsterdam: Rodopi, 1987.
Kerman, Joseph. *Opera as Drama*. New York: Vintage 1956.
Mann, Thomas. *Pro and Contra Wagner*, tr. Allan Blunden, with an introduction by Erich Heller. Chicago: University of Chicago Press, 1985.
Millington, Barry, ed. *The Wagner Compenium. A Guide to Wagner's Life and Music*. London: Thames and Hudson, 1992.
Schad, Martha, and Horst Schad. *"Meine erste und einzige Liebe." Richard Wagner und Mathilde Wesendonck*. München: Langen und Müller, 2002.
Smith, Patrick J. *The Tenth Muse: A Historical Study of the Opera Libretto*. New York: Alfred A. Knopf, 1970.
Spitzer, Leo. "Three Poems of Ecstasy (John Donne, St. John of the Cross, Richard Wagner." *A Method of Interpreting Literature*. Northampton, MA: Smith College, 1945.
Voss, Egon. *"Wagner und kein Ende." Betrachtungen und Studien*. Zürich, Mainz: Atlantis Musikbuch-Verlag, 1996.
Wagner, Cosima. *Die Tagebücher 1869—1883*, ed. Martin Gregor-Dellin and Dietrich Mack. München, Zürich: Piper, 1976; tr. and ed. Geoffrey Skelton. New Haven, CT: Yale University Press, 1997.
Wagner, Richard. *Dichtungen und Schriften*. Jubiläumsausgabe in zehn Bänden, ed. Dieter Borchmeyer. Frankfurt/Main: Insel Verlag, 1983.
_____. *Mein Leben*, ed. Martin Gregor-Dellin. München: List, 1992; tr. Andrew Gray, ed. Mary Whittal New York: Da Capo, 1992.
_____. *Richard Wagner an Mathilde Wesendon[c]k: Tagebuchblätter und Briefe,1853—1871*, ed. Wolfgang Golther. Berlin: Breitkopf & Härtel, 1904.
_____. *Sämtliche Briefe*. Vol. VI, ed. Hans Joachim Bauer and Johannes Forner. Leipzig: VEB Deutscher Verlag für Musik, 1986.
_____. *Sämtliche Briefe*. Vol. IX, ed. Klaus Burmeister and Johannes Forner. Leipzig: Deutscher Verlag für Musik, 2000.
_____. *Sämtliche Briefe*. Vol. XI, ed. Martin Dürrer and Isabel Kraft. Wiesbaden: Breitkopf & Härtel, 1999.
_____. *Selected Letters of Richard Wagner*, tr. and ed. Stewart Spencer and Barry Millington. New York: W.W. Norton, 1988.
Walton, Chris. "Voicing Mathilde: Wagner's Controlling Muse." *The Wagner Journal* I (2007): 3—18.

8

Infomercial in Three Acts:
Die Meistersinger von Nürnberg

Nicholas Vazsonyi

Keiner wie du so hold zu werben weiß
Eva to Walther; Act III, *Die Meistersinger*[1]

Roughly translated, Eva Pogner's declaration to Walther von Stolzing at the sublime conclusion to the Prize Song in act three of *Die Meistersinger von Nürnberg* means "no one woos as beautifully as you" (Keiner wie du so hold zu werben weiß). "Werben" means to "woo" or to "court." But it also means "to try to acquire" and "to advertise."

Within the context of the drama, there would seem to be no question that Eva is referring to Walther's ability to "court" her. Eva's father, Veit Pogner, has quite astonishingly proposed that her hand in marriage be the prize for the victor of the upcoming mastersong competition. True, he gives her the right to refuse, but then she may marry no one else. Either way, the stakes for her are high, but Walther must still win both the competition and her heart in order to get the entire prize package. However, our interpretation of the way "werben" is used in this closing scene of the opera becomes more complicated, given that it is actually not Eva who first uses this word. Instead, she merely repeats the line voiced by the entire Volk of Nürnberg immediately before. Since the Volk is surely not referring to Walther's abilities at amorous courtship leading to marriage, what are they thinking when they unanimously choose this word, rather than saying that he "sang" beautifully, or that he should obviously "win" the contest.[2] Why do they say "werben" instead of "singen" or "gewinnen"?

Many interpreters of Wagner's *Die Meistersinger* have noted that the work constitutes an elaborate aestheticized defense of the composer's approach to and style of composition, that "Wagner conceptualized *Die Meistersinger* ... as an accompaniment to the composition of his other works, partially ... to serve as their justification."[3] In this reading of the opera as an exposition of aesthetic difference and choice, Walther represents unbridled inspiration and talent with no awareness of formal structures, Sixtus Beckmesser stands for closed-minded, rule-bound pedantry, and Hans Sachs wisely mediates between the two, giving talent and creativity its due, though tempered by established, time-honored principles of poetic convention.[4]

But are "defense" or "justification" the most suitable terms to describe the opera? The triumphant tone which so overwhelms from start to finish suggests that, far from a defensive justification, *Die Meistersinger* quite aggressively and proactively promotes Wagner's aesthetic direction by disparaging, distorting, and ultimately silencing the competition. Consumption of the Wagnerian aesthetic becomes irresistibly seductive and is, ultimately, the only choice.

Lydia Goehr has argued recently that *Die Meistersinger* should be read as a calculated aesthetic failure, showing the dangers of a "too-easy satisfaction," thus preparing the way for Wagner's aesthetically more difficult but ultimately more "Wagnerian" works, especially *Tristan*.[5] Goehr's line of thinking is both stunning and clever, but in the following I suggest the exact opposite is taking place. In order to sustain her point, Goehr is forced to ignore the chronological sequence of composition and presentation to the public. *Tristan* came before *Meistersinger*, so the latter cannot function as a preparation for the first.[6] But this is minor. More problematically, according to Goehr, Wagner wanted audiences to reject the pleasure of the Prize Song in order to enjoy *Tristan*. Her argument is as counterintuitive (one should reject or at least be suspicious of an artwork that one enjoys) as it is elitist (an aesthetically more challenging work is more genuine than one that is more immediately digestible).

By contrast, I suggest that the intentional satisfaction elicited by *Die Meistersinger* models the satisfaction that should have been experienced in *Tristan*, but often was not. *Meistersinger* thematizes the issue of innovation — the innovation which in praxis is more difficult to accept in *Tristan* — so that we can more easily understand and enjoy *Tristan*. The public euphoria at the conclusion of the festival meadow scene echoes the intensely private orgasm of the *Liebestod*: we surely have permission to enjoy both!

Die Meistersinger is the aesthetic gateway to Wagner's mature operas. It is a marketing vehicle constructed in a manner similar to the so-called "infomercial," a television advertisement that runs the length of a normal program while employing devices to conceal its promotional agenda. Infomercials sometimes use the format of a talk show. An actor plays moderator (actually the salesperson) who "interviews" the product's designer. A pseudo-technical conversation imparts important "information" about the product and how it differs from previous designs or the competition. A guest star will play the "ideal" consumer, or a paid studio audience (representing the "average" consumer) samples the product at the conclusion of the program.

It is not new to suggest that Wagner operas are also about Wagnerian opera. That Wagner weaves his aesthetic theories into the dramatic fabric of the work itself, that his works serve to thematize his aesthetic theories. Already during the first run of the *Ring* cycle in 1876, Wilhelm Mohr answered critics, who accused Wagner of destroying operatic form, by describing Wagner's innovative approach in these terms: "The old forms have not been shattered in these beautiful sections but rather, just as Siegfried does with the sword Nothung, filed, smelted, recast and newly forged."[7] In other words: Siegfried's forging of Nothung out of the fragments of the old sword is a metaphor for the *Gesamtkunstwerk*.

It would of course be wrong to overdraw the parallels between the normally 30- or 60-minute highly forgettable and transitory infomercial on the one hand, and Richard Wagner's five-hour masterpiece — certainly among the greatest operas ever written — that continues to provide deep and lasting aesthetic nourishment to audiences around the world on the other hand. Nevertheless, it is intriguing to what extent Wagner perhaps instinctively incorporates promotional techniques that have more recently become so familiar.

This reading of *Die Meistersinger* is part of a larger project, introduced in the previous volume of this series as well as in other articles, which argues that Wagner's extravagant behaviors, activities and pronouncements — previously considered simply the expression of a self-absorbed megalomaniac — actually constitute an imaginative and highly effective exercise in all the various forms of marketing: image making, advertising, public relations, and product branding.[8] Wagner's "enterprise" (his term) responds to the economic turn precipitated by the spread in Europe of the industrial revolution, its transformation of the consumer market, and its resonance in the art world. My project explores the self-marketing and entrepreneurial dimensions of Wagner's theoretical and compositional work. I resist speculating on the degree to which Wagner "intentionally" or "instinctively" engaged in self-marketing, though much speaks for instinct and proclivity. There is also a good deal of irony, if not hypocrisy, in the self-marketing aspects of Wagner's career, given his own insistent critique of modernity, industrialization, consumerism, the debilitating role of newspapers and the critics (paid taste-makers) who published in them, and the commodification especially of music. However, the case of Wagner is instructive because, as Andreas Huyssen so aptly points out, "in the vortex of commodification there was never an outside."[9]

Act One

As if to prove Huyssen's observation, while *Die Meistersinger* appears to be a hymn to the priceless autonomy of art; its structure and devices reveal to what extent Wagner is engaged in a fight to stake his claim in the world of opera. *Die Meistersinger* stands out as the work in which Wagner sets out not just to write an easy success — as he himself admitted — but to make the case for his aesthetic direction. So it seems ironic that this case should be wrapped in what was Wagner's formally most conservative work. With the possible exception of the opening of *Tannhäuser*, no opera by the mature Wagner begins with as marked a gesture of conventionality as the prelude to *Die Meistersinger*, with its characteristic descending fourth (C-G) which launches a rather simple if not simplistic exploration of a basic C–major triad and C–major scale (*Tannhäuser* opens with a rising and descending fourth). Into this diatonic world of conventionality bursts the chromatic love theme in E major, and in so doing suggests the contrasting reference points — product A and product B — that will be pitted against one another as the work unfolds.

This polarity is repeated musically and enacted dramatically when the curtain rises at the beginning of act one: the traditional chorale sung by solid church-going burgers begins with a descending fourth (C-G) and a rising C–major scale. Between the fermatas which normally mark the division between the chorale's phrases, the chromatic love theme again bursts in as musical commentary to the equally audacious glances being exchanged on the stage by Walther and Eva, who pay attention to their feelings and each other rather than to God and the religious service. As if to steal space, Wagner extends these "natural" gaps to the breaking point. For a while, the two worlds co-exist, though occupying separate spheres. As the chorale ends, however, tradition and resistance mix, with the chromatic love theme providing counterpoint to the chorale melody: the two worlds are, it seems, not mutually exclusive. After all, both are about devotion. This opening scene functions structurally as a metaphor of the whole, and anticipates the opera's concluding gesture: the ever-problematic closing monolog of Hans Sachs which, I will argue contrary to the prevailing academic opinion sadly still so burdened by the perversions of history, is not at all a foreign or forced element in the work.

The binary opposition finds its next variation in the figure of David, who is both a stage

The Katharina Wagner production of *Die Meistersinger*, Act 1, at the Bayreuth Festival (courtesy Bayreuth Festival).

character as well as a referent in the opera. The confusion between character and image is thematized when Eva exuberantly remarks to Magdalene that Walther looks just like David. "Are you mad, like David?" (Bist du toll? Wie David?) asks Magdalene, thinking of her boyfriend David, Sachs's apprentice. "No, like David in the picture," (wie David im Bild) responds Eva. But this only causes yet another misunderstanding. Magdalene now thinks Eva is referring to the image of the old King David, with long beard, playing the harp, who functions as the symbol for the Mastersinger guild. "No," says Eva, she means the dashing young David with the sling-shot who felled Goliath, so handsomely painted by Albrecht Dürer. Of course, these two Davids are one and the same person at different stages of their lives. Eva is thinking of the upstart who fights and wins against the entrenched Philistines. Young David heroically fights the establishment, while King David becomes its symbol. It is significant that the most significant artist of German history until that point, Albrecht Dürer, would choose to paint the younger version. So much for the image. Hearing his name called, David, the apprentice, enters. The real David is neither a Goliath-killer nor a King but rather a "blank sheet of paper waiting to be written on."[10] His lengthy aria that follows recounts in great detail a catalog of Master tunes and their appellations, proving that he has been a good student. Critics, starting with Eduard Hanslick, who suggest that the aria is "horribly boring," miss the point.[11] The product of rote learning, this aria needs to be annoying, even boring, because it sets up the conditions for standard mastersong against which Walther will stand as the counter-example at the conclusion of the act: i.e. the unthinking memorization and application of rules and tradition versus unbridled intuitive talent. Depending on his development,

David runs the risk of becoming another Beckmesser. At the conclusion of the opera, this question remains open.

The dichotomy between the regurgitation of tradition (old product) and innovation (new product) reaches its initial tension-filled climax at the meeting of the mastersinger guild which concludes the first act. The mastersingers are introduced as a body of older men dedicated to preserving tradition for its own sake, having lost sight of the fact that the tradition itself came about as a result of change and progress. Enter Hans Sachs: the prodigious poet-cobbler and most respected of the mastersingers present who ends up playing the role of moderator. In Wagner's words, the historical Sachs, who lived from 1494 to 1576, was "the last example of the artistically-productive folk spirit."[12] This description is crucial, because the "Volk" will assume a critical (in both senses of the word) role at the conclusion of the drama. Their significance is already addressed in the first act meeting when Sachs, true to his designation, suggests that "das Volk" be the final judges of the upcoming song contest so as to test the effectiveness of the criteria the mastersingers use to evaluate new works. The rest of the masters reject Sachs's apparently demagogic proposal, which serves not only to confirm their isolation from the people, but the degree to which consumer satisfaction is not a valid criterion in their view.

The thesis of art's deterioration, its potential for reinvigoration only possible through the "Volk," is not Wagner's idea. Johann Gottfried Herder, the eighteenth-century pioneer of cultural anthropology, lamented that "our pedants patch together and memorize everything ahead of time only to stammer really methodically." As a corrective, he argued, the "best speakers of our time [are] uncorrupted children, woman, people with good common sense — educated more through activity than contemplation." Herder praises the "poets of old" like Homer who "improvised because back then one knew of nothing but improvised speech ... until finally art came and extinguished nature. In foreign tongues one then had to torture oneself ... trying to learn syllable quantities which ear and nature no longer let us feel, and to work according to rules which a genius would least of all recognize as rules of nature."[13]

The degree to which *Die Meistersinger* dramatizes this passage from Herder is stunning. Herder's distinction between pedants who "memorize" and "stammer" on the one hand, and the natural poetic creativity of older masters which now can only be found amongst the "uncorrupted" (i.e. women, the people) is emphasized in the opera. Beyond Herder's attention to the cultural significance of the Volk, the eighteenth-century saw a broader debate concerning the degree to which ancient Greek drama was written according to rules Aristotle had formalized in his poetics, or whether Aristotle had derived rules from those works he considered exemplary. Herder's contemporary, Gotthold Ephraim Lessing, argued that true "rules," rules that work, are descriptive, not normative because they reflect the logic, the pattern of successful art.

Sachs's proposal that the people, with Eva as their representative, be the judges at the upcoming song contest seems to be a direct paraphrase of Herder and is in keeping with the spirit of Lessing's argument. I quote Sachs at length:

Sachs:

Verzeiht,	Forgive me!
Vielleicht schon ginget ihr zu weit.	Perhaps you have already gone too far.
Ein Mädchenherz und Meisterkunst	A girl's heart and the Master's Art
Erglühn nicht stets von gleicher Brunst:	do not always glow with equal ardor;
Der Frauen Sinn, gar unbelehrt,	a woman's opinion, quite untutored,
Dünkt mich dem Sinn des Volks gleich wert.	I think is equally valid with popular opinion.

Wollt ihr nun vor dem Volke zeigen,	If now you want to show the people
Wie hoch die Kunst ihr ehrt,	How highly you honor Art;
Und laßt ihr dem Kind die Wahl zu eigen,	and if you leave the child to her own choice,
Wollt nicht, daß dem Spruch es wehrt, —	you don't want her to oppose the verdict:
So laßt das Volk auch Richter sein;	so let the people be judges too;
Mit dem Kinde sicher stimmt's überein.	they will assuredly agree with the child.
...	
Doch einmal im Jahre fänd' ich's weise,	But once a year I should find it wise
Daß man die Regel selbst probir',	to test the rules themselves,
Ob in der Gewohnheit trägem Gleise	to see whether in the dull course of habit
Ihr' Kraft und Leben nicht sich verlier'.	their strength and life doesn't get lost:
Und ob ihr der Natur	and whether you are still
Noch seid auf rechter Spur,	on the right track of Nature
Das sagt euch nur,	will only be told you by someone
Wer nichts weiß von der Tabulatur.	who knows nothing of the table of rules.
...	
Drum mocht's es euch nie gereuen,	For that reason you might never regret
Daß jährlich am Sankt Johannisfest,	that each year on St. John's Day,
Statt daß das Volk man kommen läßt,	instead of letting the people come to you,
Herab aus hoher Meisterwolk'	from your high Masters' clouds
Ihr selbst euch wendet zu dem Volk.	you yourselves turn to the people.
...	
Daß Volk und Kunst gleich blüh' und wachs',	That people and Art bloom & thrive equally
Bestellt ihr so, mein' ich, Hans Sachs!"	do it in this way, say I, Hans Sachs!

The Masters of course reject Sachs's proposal. Kothner's response is exemplary:

Kothner:

Nein, Sachs! Gewiß, das hat keinen Sinn!	No Sachs! Certainly there's no sense in that!
Gebt ihr dem Volk die Regeln hin?[14]	Would you abandon the rules to the people?
...	
Der Kunst droht allweil Fall uind Schmach,	Art is threatened with downfall and disgrace
Läuft sie der Gunst des Volkes nach.	if it runs after the favors of the people.

But Kothner and Sachs are talking about two different audiences. Kothner is thinking of the contemporary "masses," the mindless body manipulated by critics and the press, blindly consuming wares peddled by the entertainment industry. Sachs has a different Volk in mind. Like Wagner, he imagines an uncorrupted pre-modern body responding intuitively and naturally to great art.[15] Sachs trusts the innate aesthetic good taste of the "Volk;" Kothner, ever the elitist, is suspicious and disdainful of the "masses" and wants to protect his art from them.

Given the different paradigms, there can be no fruitful exchange between Sachs and the others, so it is time to introduce the special guest. Enter Walther von Stolzing. Since this is an infomercial, we need to know a bit about this newcomer, so he is interviewed. Apparently, he has left his aristocratic estate, declared his intent to settle in Nürnberg, and become one of its residents. Walther embodies the transition from the rural feudal middle ages to a new town-centered modernity, while also turning his back on the aristocracy (coded French) in favor of a German-national bourgeois Volk. He comes from the establishment (though it is different from that of the mastersingers), but has demonstrated independence of spirit.

Walther seems to be the opposite of the masters: he doesn't belong, is young, good-looking, and totally ignorant of the mastersinger rules and tradition. But is this really the case? When asked about his qualifications, he mentions that he has learned from a book of poetry by Walther von der Vogelweide. Walther von der Vogelweide (known simply as "Walther") may well be "long since dead" (doch lang' schon tot) as Beckmesser sneeringly remarks, but he is one of the so-called Twelve Old Masters ("Zwölf alte Meister") whose memory the mastersingers are themselves dedicated to preserving.[16] In other words, Walther von Stolzing (literally "proud to be Walther") is grounded in the same poetic tradition as the mastersingers themselves. In many ways, Walther von der Vogelweide relates to the mastersingers as Bach does to the mid-nineteenth century (Wagner). Beckmesser's remark thus lacks aesthetic legitimacy and is motivated out of jealousy for the prospective rival that Walther von Stolzing turns out to be. Beckmesser's comment also marks him as an aesthetic outsider, since Kunz Vogelgesang points out that Walther has just sung "two nice verses" (zwei artige Stollen) i.e. that even when he is speaking informally Walther naturally communicates in traditional forms.

Musically, Wagner emphasizes this deep connection between Walther and the mastersingers. The motif used to signify the mastersinger's meeting — first heard at the very beginning of the scene when the masters enter the Church — comprises a stepwise downward major third followed by a leap of a fifth (A-[G]-F-C) outlining an F-major triad. This theme is repeated in the same key when Kothner subsequently calls the roll. His roll call and explanation of the Tabulatur — both set to a faux-Baroque rich contrupunctal accompaniment in the orchestra — reek of pomposity and a marked datedness. In performance these are often interpreted with a smug cynicism, especially the richly melismatic rendition of the Tabulatur, to which I will return later. But such readings, I argue, miss the fact that, musically, Wagner in these passages presents the compositional foundation of the Western (German) art music tradition of which he too was a product. Kothner may not represent the *terminus ad quem* of Wagner's efforts, but he does embody the *terminus a quo*. So it should come as no surprise that Walther's first aria, "Am stillen Herd" in which he talks about the influences on his writing and singing style, though in D major, begins with exactly the same melodic line in terms of interval relationships: F#-D-A. There can be no doubt: even if they don't realize it just yet, the mastersingers and Walther come from the same place: Walther von der Vogelweide. However, the way they honor that heritage differs. The common origin and different path is stressed even more forcefully in Walther's so-called Trial Song ("Fanget an") which follows. After his emphatically uncertain introduction that echoes Beckmesser's instruction to begin, Walther outlines the *identical* melody line from the mastersinger meeting and even in the same key, F major: A-[G]-F-C.[17] Only then does he stray from the path. While the F-major tonic triad of the meeting/roll-call motif has been repeated over and over and over turning in on itself, suggesting a blinkered self-absorption, trapped in an endless loop, unable to move forward or change, Walther breaks free. Carried by rising chromatic waves in the strings, he moves rapidly up the F-major scale, ending on a massive dominant seventh chord that sets up the roller-coaster ride to follow. Walther's song has a kind of pulsating momentum and an undulating harmonic freedom not yet heard in the opera, so the rejection by the masters is quite understandable: they are literally shaken to the core.

Led by Beckmesser, the masters criticize the incomprehensibility of Walther's song, seemingly unaware that his beginning was identical to the tone and melody of their own meeting. When Sachs offers an alternative reading of Walther's song, ("Halt, Meister! Nicht so geeilt!") a starkly chromatic figure plays in the orchestra that is reminiscent of a motif from the first act of *Tristan*. Walther's song may be "new," but it was not confused. He may have "left our path," says Sachs, but he strode with confidence.[18] Sachs's metaphor is both instructive and precise. He is alone in realizing that Walther was initially on the same path, but has taken a different route.

At the behest of Sachs, but over the screaming and chaotic objections of Beckmesser and his supporters, Walther continues his aria, comparing himself to a bird with golden wings, soaring above the miserable scavenger birds (ravens, crows, magpies) who stay closer to the ground and feast on the remains of the day. He flies bravely away from the town and back to the meadows (grünen Vogelweid) where he can once again commune directly with "Master Walther."[19] Walther von Stolzing has an unmediated connection to the old master whose very name stands for nature. Still, staying with the ornithological analogy, even though his particular species of bird may move with greater freedom than its more land-bound relations, it is nonetheless subject to the same universal laws of gravity.

Act Two

The bird analogy continues. Alone in his workshop, Hans Sachs broods over the events of the day. As the warm evening breeze spreads sweet scents, the horns play a haunting version of Walther's aria accompanied by an ever-so-gentle shimmer in the strings. Removed from the noisy chaos that sought to drown out Walther at the end of the previous act, the essence of his song is now presented much slower and drawn out, its constituent parts separated like ingredients which Sachs can savor with gastronomic delight. He tries to grasp the elusiveness of inspiration: "it sounded so old, but was so new: like birdsong in sweet May."[20] Sachs has grasped the essence of Walther's art: its novelty is grounded in fundamental and tested aesthetic principles of composition, a song inspired but not fettered by tradition.

It is not—as Katharina Wagner would have us believe in her well-intentioned but fundamentally misguided 2007 Bayreuth staging of the opera—that the originally rebellious Walther "sells out" in order to win his prize. Walther never sought nor stood for the destruction of the aesthetic system, because he was (unbeknownst to himself) rooted in it.

The centerpiece of act two—Beckmesser's serenade—relates retrospectively to the preceding act and prospectively to the workshop scene in the third act. Both structurally and aesthetically, Beckmesser's song (as opposed to the mastersingers *per se*) is the competition against which Walther's is being judged.

Retrospectively, the circumstances of the act one "Trial Song" scene are replayed, but this time Beckmesser performs and Sachs is the marker. The structural repetition is underscored both musically and textually with exact references back to the first act. Prospectively, however, Beckmesser offers a test performance of what he expects to be the prize-winning song. Sachs offers aesthetic insights and critical commentary which transcend his job as marker, and prefigure the role he will play in the lengthy duet with Walther during the third act.

The chaotic—indeed riotous—ending of the second act provides a form of sociological commentary on the aesthetic stakes of the opera, and serves as an exponential intensification of the discord (literally) which concluded the first. There, too, chaos had served to reflect the aesthetic turmoil evident in the theoretical rift between the masters and Walther. At the conclusion of the second act, this aesthetic discord becomes social, triggered by Beckmesser's song which quite literally drives people mad. If, in William Congreve's often misquoted words: "Musick has Charms to sooth a savage Breast," Beckmesser's offering has the opposite effect: it transforms people into savages.

I will not address the issue of whether Beckmesser's song does or does not mimic the Jewish cantorial style—as Marc Weiner has argued in his substantial and thought-provoking book.[21] If Weiner is correct, then the issue of Beckmesser as a caricature of the Jew is settled already at this stage of the work. However, without addressing the specificity of Jewishness

The Katharina Wagner production of *Die Meistersinger,* Act 2, at the Bayreuth Festival (courtesy Bayreuth Festival).

which can only be determined on the subtextual level, the composition does communicate openly that Beckmesser does not belong. Weiner emphasizes the melismatic qualities of Beckmesser's serenade, which for him is a marker for the cantorial style. However, Kothner's rendition of the Tabulatur in the first act had already used this musical-vocal device. Melisma *per se* stands for outdatedness and, to quote Herbert Schneider, was considered "unsuitable for the presentation of serious, noble or deep feelings," by Wagner and the so-called "New German School."[22] The difference between Kothner and Beckmesser is that the reading of the Tabulatur is supported by a rich orchestral accompaniment, while the town clerk is left to stand sonically naked with nothing but the grating twang of the lute. It is not the melismas (i.e. the vocal line), but presence or absence of the orchestra which delivers the crucial commentary. Kothner may be pompous and outdated, but he represents core values of the tradition that the opera never disparages, as opposed to Beckmesser, who is left all but cast out.

Act Three

If the first act served to introduce the basic set of product possibilities (conventional works produced in a routine manner adhering to a rigid regimen of rules, versus a naïve free-flowing creativity in harmony with nature), it also granted an insider look at a guild meeting, and offered the theater audience an opportunity to witness first hand the extent to which the body

Donald McIntyre as Hans Sachs and Karita Mattila as Eva in *Die Meistersinger,* Act 2, at the the Metropolitan Opera (photograph by Winnie Klotz).

controlling the production of art was not interested in the consumer — so often the negative consequence of a monopoly. The second act centered around a public demonstration of the competing product. Normally, given the experience, status, and reputation of its maker, such a product should have received good consumer ratings. However, Beckmesser's song fails at every level.

The Otto Schenk production of *Die Meistersinger,* Act 2, at the Metropolitan Opera (photograph by Winnie Klotz).

The third act introduces the advertised new product and at some length. Approximately the duration of acts one and two combined, the proportions of act three are nonetheless fitting, if *Die Meistersinger* is to succeed as an infomercial. The first scene again grants the theater audience a behind-the-scenes look. This time in the workshop itself, the creative act is revealed with explanatory narration from Sachs.

The first *Bar* of Walther's song is presented in its discrete segments: *Stollen, Stollen, Abgesang,* thus apparently laying bare its internal structure. We hear the second *Bar* without interruption. The third and final *Bar* is delayed — to increase the suspense — only to be "improvised" later when Walther sees Eva. This will be Eva's first meeting with the song and, although Sachs whispers to her that this is a "mastersong," she clearly already senses this (intuitively). The suspense is ours (will Walther manage to come up with the required third *Bar*?), not hers. Like the Volk in the festival scene that follows, Eva "knows it when she hears it." For the theater audience, this third hearing of the song represents a musical-emotional release that anticipates the major cathartic "pay off" at the fourth and final performance in the Festival scene. It is a consumer satisfaction, achieved through what Adorno would later describe as the new mode of listening to music, characteristic of the age of mechanical reproduction.[23]

Modern listeners hardly know anymore what it means to hear music for the first time, because it is omnipresent. Relationships with music are based on repeated listening. Knowing "how it goes" replicates a feeling of coming home — a sense of familiarity confirmed, and expectation satisfied. A half century before recording technology would begin to offer consumers this possibility, Wagner creates its conditions in *Die Meistersinger,* a condition that also lies at the heart of Wagner's so-called "leitmotiv" technique, which creates a subtle interplay between what Wagner called memory and presentiment (*Erinnerung* und *Ahnung*).

Top and Above: The Otto Schenk production of *Die Meistersinger,* Act 3, at the Metropolitan Opera (photograph by Winnie Klotz).

Was Wagner's technique based on the intuition that the modern audience is no longer open to that with which it is not already familiar? The constant replaying of the prize-song-to-be in *Die Meistersinger* anticipates the age of mechanical reproduction which, like a form of brain washing, lends music a sense of inevitability.

The theater audience is not only privy to the creative act, but also simultaneously exposed to its explication. Sachs provides pseudo-technical information seemingly to Walther, but actually delivers a short course in song appreciation to the theater audience. This serves to amplify the sense of familiarity with the product. But it is only the appearance of technical information. The theater audience understands as little about the art of composition at the conclusion of the scene as today's ordinary consumer really understands how "High Definition" or "Bluetooth" or "fuel cells" work. In both cases, however, technical terms and buzzwords are dispensed with a modicum of explanation sufficient to make the consumer feel empowered.

Walther launches the epic "technical" conversation on aesthetics by asking Sachs naïvely: "how shall I begin according to the rules?" (Wie fang' ich nach der Regel an?). Sachs's much-quoted answer: "You set them yourself and then follow them" (Ihr stellt sie selbst, und folgt ihr dann) has often been interpreted as Wagner's self-justification to ignore rules, as a mandate to be original for its own sake. This reading turns Wagner into an aesthetic anarchist, architect of a poetics that grant license to create at will with no regard to anything other than personal inclination. This is not, however, Wagner's theoretical position, nor is it the aesthetic agenda of either *Die Meistersinger* or even the more adventurous *Tristan und Isolde*. The musical cues discussed in the first act already make this clear. Wagner actually suggests the opposite of aesthetic anarchy: that true creativity, while based on inspiration, nevertheless adheres to forms that are (feel) natural.

"Inspiration" defines Walther's song. Following Herder, Walther narrates his dream as a "spontaneous" combination of poetry and melody, born together in perfect symbiotic harmony. He follows the *Bar* form of the mastersingers, suggesting that this structure is *per se* not at all the object of Wagner's aesthetic attack. This common heritage is depicted melodically in each *Stollen* which begins with a fourth drop (E-B), an echo of the mastersinger motif that begins the entire opera also with a drop of a fourth: (C-G). Walther begins on the same path, but, as in the first act "Trial Song," he strays.

The composition of the two *Stollen* represent the most serious deviation from tradition, which stipulates that they must end identically. While the first *Stollen* begins and ends solidly in C major, confirming the basic key, Walther fills the second half of the second *Stollen* with F#s, setting up a move to the dominant G where it ends. The increased tension makes the release into the *Abgesang* much more "irresistible" and thus "satisfying." The *Abgesang* then begins not with the conservative drop of a fourth, but with a drop of a fifth (G-C) followed immediately with a drop of a sixth (E-G). Walther takes the tradition "a couple of steps further": quite literally so. Following Lessing, Sachs takes this example of "successful" art and derives rules from it.

Walther's "organic" creation supposedly reflects Wagner's own creative approach. Actually, Wagner did not compose this way, but it is how he would have us believe he composed. His theoretical works, his supposedly factual autobiographies, even the artwork itself, all press home this claim of spontaneous composition which Walther embodies on stage. Wagner's art is thus genuine, not "artifice" like the competition, or what Wagner would call "nur eine Schale ohne Kern" (only surface and no substance).[24] What he meant by "der organische eines wirklichen Kunstwerkes" (the organic nature of a real artwork)[25] is perhaps most famously recounted in the famous "vision of La Spezia" when he describes how the beginning of *Das*

The Katharina Wagner production of *Die Meistersinger*, Act 3, at the Bayreuth Festival (courtesy Bayreuth Festival).

Rheingold came to him in a half-sleep. Wagner's (and Walther's) art comes directly from the subconscious world of dreams, uncorrupted by calculated reason. It is superior because it is more natural, a favorite advertising tag of contemporary companies, accompanied by the claim that the average person, the people — the consumer — will be able to judge correctly the difference in product quality and do so uncoached. Walther's "naturalness" and hence proximity to the "purer" (Homeric) oral tradition is underscored by the fact that he does not even write down the song he sings. Instead, Sachs takes dictation, and thus — true to Wagner's description of him — represents "the last example of the artistically-productive folk spirit" as it transitions to the less intuitive, written, logocentric modern culture.

But, before this new product gets its final push, Wagner dispatches the competition one last time, and devastatingly so. Re-enter Beckmesser, who finds and steals the text of Walther's song. Because of the handwriting, Beckmesser wrongly concludes that it is Sachs's, an assumption Sachs slyly does nothing to rectify. Even though Sachs lets Beckmesser keep the poem, Beckmesser's forthcoming performance originates in a criminal act. This is crucial, because it foreshadows the aesthetic crime he is about to commit. Sachs even warns him of this:

Doch Freund, ich führ's Euch zu Gemüte,	But friend, I draw to your attention,
und rat' es auch in aller Güte:	and advise you with all kindness:
studiert mir recht das Lied;	study the song properly!
sein Vortrag ist nicht leicht;	Its performance is not easy
ob euch die Weise geriet',	even if you find the right melody
und ihr den Ton errieicht.	and get the proper tone.

But Beckmesser pays no attention. He will take what he thinks are Sachs's words and marry them to his own pre-existing melody already heard in act two, saying:

Freund Sachs, ihr seid ein guter Poet;	Friend Sachs, you are a good poet
doch was Ton und Weise betrifft, gesteht,	But where tone and melody are concerned, admit,
da tut's mir keiner vor	no one surpasses me!

In this moment, Beckmesser perpetrates the greatest crime of all. He abandons the time-honored aesthetics of the mastersingers who composed both text and music, and moves over to the "dark side" (to borrow a term from popular culture). Articulating, even advocating, the divorce between music and word characteristic of modernity, Beckmesser has transformed himself into the sole outsider of the drama, the foreign element in the work. By a quirk of the dramatic action, his song will replicate the aesthetic constitution of French and Italian opera because text and music originate from two different creators. Saved from being a common thief by Sachs's "generosity," Beckmesser ends up worse: an aesthetic fraud.

As if to embody Herder's disdainful comments about "pedants," Beckmesser scurries off to "memorize" his lines, a hopeless task. He next appears on the Festival meadow, his efforts at memorization so far without success. Unaware of his fundamentally erroneous aesthetic judgment, Beckmesser blames the text, but consoles himself with the following remark to Sachs: "I'm sure no one will understand the song, but I'll rely on your popularity" (Das Lied, bin's sicher, zwar niemand versteht; / Doch bau' ich auf eure Popularität).

Like Kothner before him, Beckmesser has not understood the special nature of the Nürnberg "Volk" and so misjudges the significance of Sachs's "popularity." Beckmesser is thinking of modern consumer culture — controlled by a well-oiled conspiracy of critics, the media, and successful advertising — that more readily accepts new products from established sources with a familiar and trusted brand name. Perhaps the Volk won't understand the song, he thinks, but because of Sachs's reputation, that won't matter. The quality of the artwork is less important than the PR it receives: appearance over substance (Schale ohne Kern). The public (as opposed to the Volk) is conditioned not to trust its own aesthetic judgment but, instead, to follow the transitory whims of the opinion makers.

But the Volk of Nürnberg behaves quite differently, and apparently undermines this logic of the entertainment industry by spontaneously rejecting an artwork that is clearly ludicrous, even if it is performed by a leading member of the community. Beckmesser's debacle may be overdrawn — as is Walther's success which will follow shortly — but Wagner's point is that bad art should be self-evidently so, only the senses and good judgment of the modern consumer have been numbed by the forces of commodification. Of course this is a ruse, because the Volk of Nürnberg is in fact no premodern body reacting spontaneously, but a professional studio audience following a closely scripted and carefully choreographed scenario: could Wagner have been any more "modern" than this?

Carefully prepped with repeated hearings of the prize song, the theater audience watches the "spontaneous" reaction of the Volk with a sense of approving superiority which causes its own tremendous emotional satisfaction.

The Festival meadow scene packs yet more tactics now common to advertisers. For instance, the competing product is presented in a poor light, while the advertised product is shown under the most favorable conditions. Nowhere is this stacking of the deck more deliberate than in the difference between the grating twang of the lute that visibly accompanies Beckmesser, and the ethereally expansive tones from the full orchestra that magically and invisibly accompany Walther. In 1860, Wagner had used the term "monstrous guitar" to belittle the role played by the orchestra in Italian opera,[26] an almost shocking description realized with wounding comical effect at Beckmesser's expense, only for Walther to be supported by a seeming anticipation of the yet-to-be-built Bayreuth festival theater with the unparalleled acoustics of its hidden orchestra.

How could the Volk not once again react spontaneously? Walther may be unknown to them, but what he sings is "self-evidently beautiful"—no pre-publicity necessary. More significantly still, the Volk reacts not as passive consumers, but actively as a community of feeling. They model Wagner's imagined "audience of the future,"[27] functioning as co-creators[28] singing along "like the congregation in the church."[29] Just as Walther had inserted himself musically and dramatically into the pauses between the chorale phrases at the very beginning of the opera, now, in a structural analogy, the Volk of Nürnberg inserts itself into the pauses between the discrete sections of Walther's song. They extend the duration of the dominant seventh that ends the second *Stollen* by delaying its resolution. In wave upon wave of self-generated euphoria, the Volk sits on the dominant, not only increasing the tension but literally propelling Walther into the *Abgesang*, exponentially magnifying the "satisfaction" of the release.

Conclusion

The antagonism suggested throughout the opera between tradition and innovation, between old and new, turns out to have been a false dichotomy. This is the crux of Sachs's closing monolog ("Verachtet mir die Meister nicht" / "Don't disdain the masters"), so misappropriated first by the German nationalists in the early part of the twentieth century, and more recently by Wagner critics who, tragically, have simply accepted and adopted the Nazi reading of Wagner, using it as the noose to hang around his neck. Instead, Sachs's monolog is about honoring the old German masters who have provided the bedrock upon which the new can flourish. The gesture is clear: the new must respect the old, but does so by taking the tradition one step further. Nowhere is this message more deliberate than in the orchestral response to Sachs's exhortation: "So I say unto you: Honor your German Masters" (D'rum sag ich euch: / ehrt eure deutschen Meister). At this moment, the violins play the melody of Walther's *Abgesang* (with its downward leaps of a fifth and sixth) while in the basses, the Mastersinger motif sounds with its characteristic drop of a fourth: innovation supported by tradition (quite literally), sounding magnificent together in perfect contrupunctal harmony.[30]

The choice is thus not between old and new but between home-grown and foreign products. Sachs's closing paean to the glories of "German" art is an explication and summation of the preceding dramatic action. The lesson of the opera is certainly neither to invade Europe nor to exterminate the Jews, but rather to "buy German" which in this case means "buy Wagner."

"Nobody advertises as well as you do." Eva and the Volk both play consumers: one of Walther's body and person, the other of his artistic product: Walther commodified. But the relationship is reciprocal: Walther wants to acquire Eva too. This transaction may take place independently from the world of money—indeed the premodern setting is indispensable to the drama's subterfuge—but it is nevertheless a commercial transaction, which Wagner spends the better part of the opera trying to mask with the argument that the great artwork, like Eva's "love," is "priceless." Such is the conundrum the opera presents. Pogner's gesture to offer his daughter as the prize may be wholly immoral in its premodern disrespect for the dignity of the human being, but it is frighteningly modern in its brutal recognition of the prostitution embedded in the practice of commodification which traffics as much in the human body as it does in inanimate material wares. The opera works hard to shield us from this truth.

"No one woos as beautifully as you." Just as Sachs had predicted, Eva, naïve child, embodies the voice of the people[31] by echoing their words and musical line: to be sure, a love between Walther and Eva, but also a love affair between artist of the future and audience of the future. The potential inherent in art can only be realized and unleashed if both artist and audience are spontaneous and active, if the separation between them melts away. This is surely the vision *Die Meistersinger* is supposed to convey, modeled by the audience of the future to transform the audience of the present. The Volk of Nurnberg: the ideal consumer, responding "naturally" to the *Gesamtkunstwerk*, which has healed the wounds of the riot and restored both aesthetic and social order: the greatest happy ending of all.

When you buy Wagner, you get everything: aesthetic pleasure and satisfaction, and social harmony as well.

But does Wagner believe he has transformed us, the modern audience of the present, into exercising our own aesthetic judgment spontaneously, intuitively, now liberated from the forces of marketing, PR and advertising, able once again to appreciate the authentic work of art, i.e. Wagner?

We would surely like to think so. But Wagner doesn't leave much to chance. He understands the modern consumer only too well. Just as the on-stage audience is NOT the Volk of Nürnberg, but paid actors, so too is our response to the rousing final moments anything but "natural" and "spontaneous." Instead it has been musically and dramatically prepared for over five hours, and modeled for us by the on-stage audience.

I can think of no better metaphor for the paradoxical nature of the Wagner industry. Engineered by Wagner himself, his aesthetic enterprise disavows all association with the commercialized commodified world, yet he employs the most sophisticated marketing techniques to commodify his own products and create nothing short of a Wagnerian brand name and accompanying customer loyalty. In the music world, there is no one as devoted and loyal as a Wagnerite.

Notes

1. All quotations from *Die Meistersinger von Nürnberg*, Klavierauszug mit Text von G. Kogel (Leipzig: Edition Peters, 1914).

2. Volk: Keiner wie er so hold zu werben weiß.

3. Lydia Goehr, *The Quest for Voice: On Music, Politics, and the Limits of Philosophy*. The 1997 Ernest Bloch Lectures (Oxford, UK: Clarendon, 1998; New York: Oxford University Press, 1998), 50.

4. For an excellent introduction to the work as well as its genesis, see John Warrack, ed., *Richard Wagner, Die Meistersinger von Nürnberg. Cambridge Opera Handbooks* (Cambridge: Cambridge University Press, 1994); see also my "Introduction" to *Wagner's* Meistersinger: *Performance, History, Representation*. Ed. Nicholas Vazsonyi. (Rochester, NY: University of Rochester Press, 2003).

5. See Lydia Goehr, "The Dangers of Satisfaction: On Songs, Rehearsals, and Repetition in *Die Meistersinger*," *Wagner's* Meistersinger: *Performance, History, Representation*, ed. Nicholas Vazsonyi (Rochester, NY: University of Rochester Press, 2003): 56–70.

6. Goehr, "Dangers of Satisfaction," 67.

7. Wilhelm Mohr "Brief eines baireuther Patronatsherrn" VIII, *Kölnische Zeitung* Nr. 238, 23 August 1876 (qtd. in Großmann-Vendrey, *Bayreuth in der deutschen Presse*, 110): "Nicht zertrümmert ist in diesen schönen Partieen die alte Form, sondern genau wie es Siegfried mit dem Schwerte Nothung macht, zerfeilt, geschmolzen, umgegossen und blank geschmiedet." Unless otherwise noted, all translations are mine.

8. Nicholas Vazsonyi, "Selling the *Ring*: Wagner's 'Enterprise,'" *Inside the* Ring, *Essays on Wagner's Opera Cycle*, Ed. John Louis DiGaetani (Jefferson, NC: McFarland, 2006): 51–68.

9. Andreas Huyssen, *After the Great Divide: Modernism, Mass Culture, Postmodernism* (Bloomington: Indiana University Press, 1986), 42.

10. Originally the phrase Mathilde Wesendonck used to describe how she related to Wagner, though, in this case also an apt description for David.

11. Eduard Hanslick, "*Die Meistersinger* von Richard Wagner," *Die moderne Oper: Kritiken und Studien* (Berlin: A. Hoffmann, 1875), 292–305, here 294.

12. Richard Wagner, "Mitteilung an meine Freunde," *Sämtliche Schriften und Dichtungen*, 16 Vols. (Leipzig: Breitkopf & Härtel, [1911]), 4: 284 [Hereafter *SSD* Vol: Page]: "die letzte Erscheinung des künstlerisch produktiven Volksgeistes."

13. Johann Gottfried Herder, "Auszug aus einem Briefwechsel über Ossian und die Lieder alter Völker," *Von deutscher Art und Kunst. Einige fliegende Blätter*, in: *Werke* in 10 Bänden, hrsg. Gunter Grimm (Frankfurt/M: Deutscher Klassiker Verlag, 1993): "Unsre Pedanten, die alles vorher zusammen stoppeln, und auswendig lernen müssen, um alsdenn recht methodisch zu stammeln ... — Wer noch bei uns Spuren von dieser Festigkeit finden will, der suche sie ja nicht bei solchen:— unverdorbne Kinder, Frauenzimmer, Leute von gutem Naturverstande, mehr durch Tätigkeit, als Spekulation gebildet, die sind ... alsdenn die Einzigen und besten Redner unsrer Zeit. In der alten Zeit aber waren es Dichter ... die eben diese Sicherheit und Festigkeit des Ausdrucks am meisten mit Würde, mit Wohlklang, mit Schönheit zu paaren wußten.... Homers Rhapsodien und Ossians Lieder waren gleichsam Impromptus, weil man damals noch von Nichts als impromptus der Rede wußte ... bis endlich die Kunst kam und die Natur auslöschte. In fremden Sprachen quälte man sich von Jugend auf Quantitäten von Silben kennenzulernen, die uns nicht mehr Ohr und Natur zu fühlen gibt; nach Regeln zu arbeiten, deren wenigste, ein Genie als Naturregeln anerkennet" (2:473–74).

14. In the *Sämtliche Schriften und Dichtungen*, as well as editions based on that version, Nachtigall sings these two lines, not Kothner.

15. Wagner talks of his ideal that the public respond with feeling, not reason to his works ("zu wirklichen Gefühls- [nicht kritischem] Verständnisse") "Mitteilung an meine Freunde" *SSD* 4: 343. Michael Karbaum hails this as Wagner's vision of "Publikum der Zukunft," see his *Studien zur Geschichte der Bayreuther Festspiele (1876–1976)* (Regensburg: Bosse, 1976): 11.

16. The original twelve are Walther von der Vogelweide, Wolfram von Eschenbach (author of *Parzival*), Reinmar von Hagenau, Frauenlob (d.i. Heinrich von Meißen), Konrad von Würzburg, Der Marner, Hartmann von Aue, Heinrich von Mügeln, Reinmar von Zweter, Bruder Wernher, Friedrich von Suonenburg, Meister Boppe.

17. To the words: So rief der Lenz in den Wald.

18. Sachs: verließ er uns're G'leise, / schritt er doch fest und unbeirrt.

19. Walther: dahin zur grünen Vogelweid,' / wo Meister Walther einst mich freit.'

20. Sachs: "Es klang so alt, und war doch so neu,—/ wie Vogelsang im süßen Mai."

21. Marc Weiner, *Richard Wagner and the Anti-Semitic Imagination* (Lincoln: University of Nebraska Press, 1995): esp. 117–27.

22. Herbert Schneider, "Wagner, Berlioz und die Zukunftsmusik," *Liszt und die Neudeutsche Schule* (Laaber: Laaber, 2006), 77–96, here 85. I disagree with Weiner's argument that symptomatically links Kothner's coloratura with Beckmesser's melisma, marking both as foreign (126–35). True, Wagner ultimately rejects both in favor of the Walther-Sachs alternative, but while Beckmesser is banished, Kothner (and what he represents) is retained as essential to German art.

23. Theodor W. Adorno, "Über den Fetischcharakter in der Musik und die Regression des Hörens (1938)," in: *Dissonanzen: Muisk in der verwalteten Welt, Gesammelte Schriften* Bd. 14 , hrsg. Rolf Tiedemann (Frankfurt/Main: Suhrkamp, 1980), 14–50.

24. Wagner, "Ein Theater in Zürich," *SSD* 5:31.

25. Wagner, "Ein Theater in Zürich" *SSD* 5:32.

26. "Daß er dieses hierzu in einem ganz anderen Sinne verwenden wird, als der italienische Opernkomponist, in dessen Händen das Orchester nichts Anderes als eine monströse Guitarre zum Akkompagnement der Arie war, brauche ich Ihnen nicht näher hervorzuheben," Wagner, "Zukunftsmusik," *SSD* 7: 130.

27. "Mein publikum der zukunft," undated Letter to Ferdinand Heine, presumably September 1849, Richard Wagner: *Sämtliche Briefe: Briefe der Jahre 1849 bis 1851*, hrsg. Gertrud Strobel und Werner Wolf (Leipzig: VEB Deutscher Verlag für Musik, 1983), 3: 131.

28. "Mitschöpfer des Kunstwerkes," Richard Wagner, *Oper und Drama*, *SSD* 4: 186.

29. "Das Publikum (wie in der Kirche die Gemeinde) mit singen soll," Letter dated 7 April 1872 to Friedrich Feustel and Theodor Muncker; *Bayreuther Briefe (1871–1883)*, 2nd ed. (Leipzig: Breitkopf & Härtel, [1907] 1912): 71.

30. In his biography of Cosima Wagner, Richard Graf du Moulin Eckart quotes a letter (albeit without date or source) from Cosima to King Ludwig II in which she claims that, shortly before completion of the composition in 1867, Wagner had considered dropping Sachs's closing monolog and ending instead with Walther's prize song. According to Cosima, she disapproved and "made a face" ("ich machte ein so jämmerliches Gesicht dazu") so he reconsidered. This letter of 31 January 1867 has been repeated off and on in the Wagner literature, usually without attribution (e.g. Warrack 30–31) as a way of exculpating Wagner from what many consider a misjudgement and a nationalistic stain on the opera, laying the blame on Cosima. However, Sachs's closing monolog was always integral to the drama from its inception in 1845, though the gravity of the sentiments expressed certainly grew in time. Any heistation Wagner may have had was surely momentary at the threshhold of completion. It is neither to Cosima's credit nor is it her fault that the monolog was retained. See Richard Graf du Moulin Eckart, *Cosima Wagner: Ein Lebens- und Charakterbild* (München: Drei Masken, 1929), here 333–34; and Cosima Wagner und Ludwig II. von Bayern, *Briefe: Eine erstaunliche Korrespondenz*, hrsg. Martha Schad unter Mitarbeit von H.H. Schad (Bergisch Gladbach: Gustav Lübbe, 1996): 348–49.

31. In his discussion of *Lohengrin* in "Eine Mitteilung an meine Freunde," Wagner describes Elsa as the "spirit of the people" which, it strikes me, bears similarities to Eva's role in *Meistersinger*: "Elsa, das Weib ... diese nothwendigste Wesenäußerung der reinsten sinnlichen Unwillkür.... Sie war der Geist des Volkes" (*SSD* 4: 302).

Bibliography

Adorno, Theodor W. "Über den Fetischcharakter in der Musik und die Regression des Hörens (1938). In *Dissonanzen: Muisk in der verwalteten Welt. Gesammelte Schriften* Bd. 14. Hrsg. Rolf Tiedemann. Frankfurt/Main: Suhrkamp, 1980.

du Moulin Eckart, Richard Graf. *Cosima Wagner: Ein Lebens- und Charakterbild*. München: Drei Masken, 1929.

Goehr, Lydia. "The Dangers of Satisfaction: On Songs, Rehearsals, and Repetition in *Die Meistersinger*." *Wagner's* Meistersinger: *Performance, History, Representation*. Ed. Nicholas Vazsonyi. Rochester, NY: University of Rochester Press, 2003.

_____. *The Quest for Voice: On Music, Politics, and the Limits of Philosophy*. The 1997 Ernest Bloch Lectures. Oxford, UK: Clarendon, 1998; New York: Oxford University Press, 1998.

Großmann-Vendrey, Susanna. *Bayreuth in der deutschen Presse: Beiträge zur Rezeptions-geschichte Richard Wagners und seiner Festspiele*, Dokumentband 1: *Die Grundstein-legung und die ersten Festspiele (1872–1876)*. Regensburg: Bosse, 1977.

Hanslick, Eduard. "*Die Meistersinger* von Richard Wagner." *Die moderne Oper: Kritiken und Studien*. Berlin: A. Hoffmann, 1875.

Herder, Johann Gottfried. "Auszug aus einem Briefwechsel über Ossian und die Lieder alter Völker." *Von deutscher Art und Kunst. Einige fliegende Blätter*. In: *Werke* in 10 Bänden. Hrsg. Gunter Grimm. Frankfurt/M: Deutscher Klassiker Verlag, 1993.

Huyssen, Andreas. *After the Great Divide: Modernism, Mass Culture, Postmodernism*. Bloomington, Indiana University Press, 1986.

Karbaum, Michael. *Studien zur Geschichte der Bayreuther Festspiele (1876–1976)*. Regensburg: Bosse, 1976.

Schneider, Herbert. "Wagner, Berlioz und die Zukunftsmusik." *Liszt und die Neudeutsche Schule*. Laaber: Laaber, 2006.

Vazsonyi, Nicholas. "Selling the *Ring*: Wagner's 'Enterprise.'" In *Inside the Ring, Essays on Wagner's Opera Cycle*. Ed. John Louis DiGaetani. Jefferson, NC: McFarland, 2006.

_____, ed. *Wagner's* Meistersinger: *Performance, History, Representation*. Rochester, NY: University of Rochester Press, 2003.

Wagner, Cosima, und Ludwig II von Bayern. *Briefe: Eine erstaunliche Korrespondenz*. Hrsg. Martha Schad unter Mitarbeit von H.H. Schad. Bergisch Gladbach: Gustav Lübbe, 1996.

Wagner, Richard. *Bayreuther Briefe* (1871–1883). 2nd ed. Leipzig: Breitkopf & Härtel, 1912.

_____. *Die Meistersinger von Nürnberg*. Klavierauszug mit Text von G. Kogel. Leipzig: Edition Peters, 1914.

_____. *Sämtliche Briefe: Briefe der Jahre 1849 bis 1851*. Hrsg. Gertrud Strobel und Werner Wolf. Leipzig: VEB Deutscher Verlag für Musik, 1983.

_____. *Sämtliche Schriften und Dichtungen*. 16 Vols. Leipzig: Breitkopf & Härtel, [1911].

Warrack, John Hamilton, ed. *Richard Wagner*, Die Meistersinger von Nürnberg. *Cambridge Opera Handbooks*. Cambridge, UK: Cambridge University Press, 1994.

Weiner, Marc. *Richard Wagner and the Anti-Semitic Imagination*. Lincoln: University of Nebraska Press, 1995.

9

Relativities: Einstein, Wagner, and *Die Meistersinger*

James K. Holman

Decade Mirabilis 1

Einstein, musically gifted as a violinist, loved Mozart. In fact, he thought Mozart one of the perfections of this world. Given a fiddle early on, and despite having lessons piled on, Einstein emerged in love with music, which remained one of the two or three central passions and rewards of his long life. "Mozart's music," he once said, "is so pure and beautiful that I see it as a reflection of the inner beauty of the universe itself," and added in a remark that reflected his view of mathematics and physics as well as of Mozart, "like all great beauty, his music was pure simplicity."[1]

For the last hundred years, physicists have been equally rapturous about the pure and Mozart-like beauty of Einstein, his mind and achievement — the radical innovation of his ideas; his uniquely conceptual approach to big problems; and the mathematical proofs which confirmed his stunning solutions to them. The adulation is not just for the General Theory of Relativity of 1915. Einstein won his only Nobel Prize, in 1922, not for the General Theory (politically, because the academy was still divided over the Theory), but for the discovery of the photoelectric effect. That dated from 1905, when the unknown patent clerk in Zurich published five papers: on the photoelectric effect, on light quanta, on the size of atoms (which helped prove their existence), on Brownian motion, and on "the electrodynamics of moving bodies which employs a modification of the theory of space and time," the last becoming known as the Special Theory of Relativity.

A few months later he added another paper arguing that "mass (is) a direct measure of the energy contained in a body" ($e = mc^2$). These papers astonished any physicist who bothered to read them, or who could understand them, and constitute the most creative outburst in the history of physics.[2]

Decade Mirabilis 2

Richard Wagner had a miracle decade, too. In 1857, Wagner abandoned work on *Der Ring des Nibelungen*, even though he had completed nearly three-fourths of the cycle, and did not go back to it until 1869. There were many reasons for his long abandonment: he felt his work was stale, and he doubted the *Ring* would ever be staged. In addition, he needed to write something that would make money quickly, and he experienced an artistic and emotional compulsion to get to the composition of *Tristan*. In this period, he produced only two music dramas: *Tristan und Isolde*, and its antipode, the colossal *Die Meistersinger von Nürnburg*, two works which, taken together, form an achievement in music parallel to Einstein's miracle period 1905–1915.

Tristan was written feverishly, the whole thing in less than two years. Everything about it seemed new and perplexing, not least the effect of "continuous music" and, even more, the celebrated chromaticism and ambiguous harmonies. The work stretches the diatonic style to a maximum — it takes five hours, from the opening "Tristan Chord" to the final bars, to reward us with harmonic resolution. It took a long time before the architectural structure of the piece would be widely understood; it has come to be cherished as a surpassing masterpiece in the development of musical form. For his *Tristan* achievement, Wagner was rewarded with an entirely new set of frustrations, beginning with the unfortunate fact that, after seventy-seven rehearsals at the first attempt to stage it, in Vienna in 1859, most of the performers could not sing or play it, and the production was cancelled. King Ludwig would not rescue Wagner for another five years, and *Tristan* would not be premiered until 1865. In the meantime, Wagner needed money, and so he turned back to a work he had begun to plan (like all of his seven music dramas after *Lohengrin*) in the mid–1840s: a comedy of the Nuremburg guilds — a short, light piece, with a small cast, and staged in the Greek tradition, as a sort of tag-end, a satyr-play to the center-piece tragedy (in this case, *Tannhäuser*).

As with *Tristan*, Wagner got to work quickly. The massive libretto was written in thirty days, in January 1862. The Prelude, still among the most performed of all orchestral pieces, was completed by mid–April, and was at once given in concert. But composition of the opera itself became an arduous and tortured process, often interrupted by financial or other necessities, and also by Wagner's repeated if "temporary loss of heart for it."[3] But Ludwig did appear, in 1864, and problems were solved. The work was finished in October 1867, and performed, under von Bülow, in June of the following year. The little "afterwork" had become the longest work in all opera.

Over the past 150 years there has been much attention, and speculation, about the polarities in *Tristan* and *Meistersinger*, about the way *Tristan*'s shocking modernism, its push against the edge of the harmonic limits, contrasts with *Meistersinger*'s relentless tonality and archaic forms. These differences, true as they are, can be misleading, because we know now that *Tristan*'s tonal structures are rigidly "logical," while there is much in *Meistersinger* that is chromatic and daring. But few would quarrel with Georg Solti's description of *Meistersinger* as "a diatonic miracle."[4]

It may well be, after the failure of *Tristan* to be understood, that Wagner wanted an approachable, melodic piece that would be widely accepted, both artistically and in the marketplace. Or, as the analyst Saul Lilienstein has suggested, writing the sunny *Meistersinger* was Wagner's way of getting *Tristan*'s chromatic irresolution and unending tension out of his system.

Another appealing notion[5] is that Wagner needed to throw a pie in the face of those *Tris-*

The Katharina Wagner production of *Die Meistersinger,* Act 3, at the Bayreuth Festival (courtesy Bayreuth Festival).

tan critics who believed he was not capable of composing classical music. And so in titanic defiance, after the assertive and sturdy Prelude, he gives us Lutheran chorales, folk dances, an (only semi-satirical) lesson in Renaissance "Tones and Modes," instructions on melodic construction, a "Tabulatur" of the rules of song-making, a parody of Handelian ornamentation, a handful of choral masterworks, a rousing tympanic march, and even a polyphonic brawl — not to mention an old-fashioned quintet, one of the glories of German music.

Cosmic Structures 1

Einstein had little interest in the musical works of either Beethoven ("I feel uncomfortable listening to Beethoven. I think he is too personal, almost naked") or Wagner, which had a "lack of architectural structure I see as decadent."[6] This is not surprising; throughout his life Einstein was absorbed with the physical structure and behavior of *things*, and steadfastly avoided emotional engagement and intimate commitment in his personal relationships. For those closest to him, his considerable charm could not cover the essential aloofness that allowed Einstein to *be* Einstein, and there were casualties. This is surely part of the attraction for him of the austere Mozart *chamber* pieces, and not the complex and subversive Mozart operas.

In fact, *Meistersinger* may be one of the most elaborately "structured" works in opera, or any other musical form. For starters, the eminent analyst Owen Lee has pointed out that the *dramatis personae* adhere precisely to traditional Greek and Roman comedic structures: the *adolescens* (hero pursuing girl); the *mulier* (girl who is to be given away); the *servus* (lecturing slave who gets into his own trouble); the *nutrix* (girl's confidante); the *senex* (philosophizing wise man); the *leno* (who gives the girl away); and the *miles gloriosus* (braggart who also pursues the girl).[7]

Einstein's work suggested a new structure of the cosmos, and the same might be said of Wagner's structures in music. It has been argued, initially by Alfred Lorenz,[8] that the whole of *Die Meistersinger* is constructed in an over-arching Bar form, simply described as A-A-B: two repeated parts (*stollen*) contrasted against a concluding third part (*abgesang*). The first two acts of the opera follow similar patterns of musical and dramatic action: opening chorus; intimate inter-action of main characters; a song "test" resulting in chaos. The third act resolves the drama in very different ways, built on the development of musical material laid down in the first two acts.

Underneath this broad canopy, long sections within the acts are also structured in Bar form as well, most obviously in the several versions of Stolzing's prize songs. The Tabulator itself, recited by Kothner in Act 1, explicitly demands invention within the Bar form. In Act 2, the third of the three "Jerum!" stanzas is subtly differentiated by an orchestral descant, or under-theme, of the motive that will describe Sachs's anguish at the beginning of Act 3. Beckmesser makes three attempts at his wooing song in Act 2; the first two are interrupted, and the third leads to the brawl. It is easy to miss this kind of over-arching architecture in the Wagner operas—if it exists, for there is disagreement about this—just as it is difficult to comprehend the scope of an expanding universe. One of Wagner's more skeptical biographers, Robert Gutman, is correct in saying that the Wagnerian edifice is constructed brick by brick, but he is also correct in acknowledging that a crucial mark of the Wagner genius, as opposed to that of Chopin or Schumann, was "keeping his over-all plan in view," with the result that, the operas achieve "coherent unity."[9]

Cosmic Structures 2

The General Theory was an attempt by Einstein to describe a "coherent unity" in the physical world. His non-traditional equations reconciling gravity, light, motion and time necessarily caused revisions in seemingly immutable Newtonian laws. In measurements of sunlight taken at the Cape Verde Islands from a solar eclipse in 1919, the British physicist, Arthur Eddington, confirmed that the gravity of the earth could bend light, almost exactly the way Einstein had predicted it would, so that even time must be measured relatively, that there is no such thing as "absolute time." Eddington's observations proved, at least to a preponderance of the best physicists, that the General Theory was right. Among the encomia from fellow scientists, it is enough here to cite just Paul Dirac, who would win the Nobel Prize in 1933 for pioneering work in quantum mechanics: it was (said Dirac) "probably the greatest scientific discovery ever made."[10]

Eddington's announcement did more than confirm the General Theory, because the resulting publicity immediately launched its author into a stratosphere of popular stardom unprecedented for any scientist before or since. Einstein became, in a post–War world desperate for heroic achievement, the poster boy not only of science (to the mystification, even revulsion, of many in the academy, for whom public attention was inconsistent with scientific inquiry), but also as the great man of the age. Simply put, Einstein was to become one of the most famous, admired and recognizable figure of the twentieth century.

Wagner also became the overwhelming man in his field — the art world of the third quarter of the nineteenth century. He emerged as the first super-star composer, not overnight, nor through the sly self-deprecation that Einstein calculated so well, but over a painfully long period of disappointment, exile, rejection, and through a fearsome and insistent will power. But like Einstein *cum* Eddington, Wagner succeeded by a spectacular intervention: the unexpected patronage of Ludwig II. The initial performances in Munich of *Tristan* (1865) and *Meistersinger* (1868), underwritten by the Bavarian king, confirmed the Wagner ascendency.

The Genius of Youth: Stolzing and Einstein

Walther von Stolzing occupies a very big space in *Meistersinger*. He is, after all, the hero of the piece, at least in conventional terms. Yet Stolzing remains something of an empty shell, and it is difficult to imagine anybody leaving the theater thinking much about him. Wagner never bothers to tell us a lot about him, and his "dramatic motivation" seems one dimensional: to win the girl.

He sings because it is necessary to win. He dreams, and that becomes his song, but it is Sachs, rather, who interprets the dream, and Stolzing stands like a statue, mute and ignored, at the climax of the opera — Sachs's and Eva's mutual relinquishment in Act 3 Scene 3. Why the "secondariness" of Stolzing? For most tenors, Stolzing's vocal territory is uncomfortably

Klaus Florian Vogt as Walther, standing, in the Katharina Wagner production of *Die Meistersinger*, Act 1, at the Bayreuth Festival (courtesy Bayreuth Festival).

high. Like Siegfried, he must sing at his best, literally on a stage *on* the stage, five hours after the opening curtain. The opera is infrequently staged, so it is not a role that tenors are ambitious to take on.

All of this is unfortunate, because Stolzing's aesthetic announces a central theme of the opera itself: that "the inspiration of genius must be regulated by form."[11] Even before his first attempt at a mastersong, near the end of Act 1, he has demonstrated (in "Am stillen Herd") not just a poetic and musical imagination of astonishing agility; he has already worked this account of his "training by Nature" into the Bar form, the structure required by both the Guild and the opera.

Stolzing's artistic genius, for innovation with structure, might bring to mind the young Einstein. Out of the blue, a presumptuous outsider to big-time physics, Einstein publishes five papers of (ultimately) massive importance, recognized at first by only a few. The approval of the masters of the physics guild comes slowly, but the laurel wreath of victory will come.

Stolzing and Einstein create in parallel. The knight dreams, and learns to interpret and ultimately to articulate his dreams in musical form. He changes the rules. The contest ends in victory, and even during the Prize Song he is still innovating upon the written text, and indulging in musical elaboration. After 1905, Einstein has ten years to think, to argue, to dream — and to improve his mathematics!— until he, too, reaches the vast German meadow, and publishes his mastersong, the General Theory.

A Universe in Micrososm

Wagner's achievement was as much "sub-molecular" as it was "cosmic"; at its heart are short musical ideas, the harmonic elaboration of these ideas, and their connectedness, by transition, from measure to measure. There is no more telling display of the artist in total control of his craftsmanship than in the way Wagner makes mountains of music out of the most atomistic elements. *Meistersinger* offers a wealth of examples, but only Act 2 Scene 3 will be considered here.

At its beginning, Sachs sits alone at his workbench, in the golden glow of the Midsummer evening, pondering the inexplicable attraction of Stolzing's melody from Act 1.[12] Sachs and the orchestra, in a way that makes complete textual sense, play with an eight-note "Mode" from Stolzing's song as if it were a piece of clay, re-shaping, re-harmonizing it. The novelty of it plagues him: "nothing is clear; cannot forget it,— nor can I enfold it: e'en when I hold it! ... I found no rule that would fit it, and yet was no fault therein. It sounded old, yet was newborn."[13] This little eight-note phrase begins (like Beethoven's First Symphony) with a strong dominant pull — the musical condition of "penultimate-ness" that wants to be resolved into its tonic mode. Rather, the Stolzing motive ends on the same, unresolved dominant chord!

This is nothing less than a kind of "Tristan Chord," ambiguous and tense, and at the passage "Yet what could gauge its greatness? A measure no mortal hath seen," the music *blossoms*— for just half a measure — into an *exact* quotation from *Tristan*,[14] until each opera moves back into its own sound world. Though the *Meistersinger* chords are traditional and the *Tristan* chords "defy analysis," the

Musical excerpt A.

Top: **Musical excerpt B.** *Middle:* **Musical excerpt C.** *Bottom:* **Musical excerpt D.**

"sense of infinitely delayed resolution is highly analogous."[15] On and on Sachs puzzles through the little phrase, for pages (Wagner moving through the keys of C, F, A-flat, B and E), until he realizes — as Stolzing had claimed in Act 1— that he sings from Nature, that what is new is not to be feared, and that innovation can be reconciled with the rules. And so the matter is solved by means of a new module of heartwarming comprehension: "then sang he as nature bade; and to his need the power was granted from her dower."[16]

This leads directly into the first Sachs/Eva encounter, the subtlest (both erotic and heartbreaking) love encounter in opera, built upon two tiny modules, each consisting — impossibly! — of just three notes.[17] Wagner weaves through this conversation in such a way that the orchestral music and the emotional context become superficially *divorced* from the dialogue. Wagner's orchestra tells us what the characters dare not. It is a scene of banter and mild flirtation. But the music — ah! the music! — builds and dips and weaves, relentlessly chromaticizing these atomic particles in an upward arc of rising tension, and it finally dawns on us that this encounter is about a last chance, an impossible love that has grown, and been repressed, even before the death of his wife and children, when Sachs had taken into his arms the little

Top: Musical excerpt E. *Above:* Musical excerpt F.

girl Eva, now grown to womanhood. And we realize that we are seeing something so human, so momentously human, that we are no longer in the realm of comedy.

Or perhaps it is that comedy has the capacity to move us more than tragedy, for the softness and gentleness in it, and the bittersweet. Alone in Wagner's great operas, there is here no mythology, no stern gods or overt metaphysical symbols. Just two people, Sachs and Eva, naked in their humanity, whose longing is every bit as unquenchable as Tristan's or Isolde's, desire that is barely acknowledged by either, but which will be denied (in Act 3) not in favor of death, but as concession to the right of youthful passion, and doing the right thing, and the wisdom of inevitable relinquishment. This is no passage of simple C Major brightness; it is among the most delicate, and wrenching, music that we know.

But is it funny? *Meistersinger* is filled with abundant charm and amusements. The libretto alone, the longest in opera, the whole thing in rhymed couplets, is filled with tricks, puns, *double entendres*, scarcely disguised vulgarisms, and references to people and events now long forgotten. The musical score, among a score of witticisms, includes an homage to Martin Luther at the beginning, and to Rossini at the entry of the tailors in Act 3, a reference to the popular "Di tanti palpiti" in *Tancredi*. All three acts are filled with stage actions meant to make us laugh. But is *Die Meistersinger* funny? As noted, Wagner conceived *Meistersinger* as a comic vehicle. The original idea was to offer a short piece after the tragedy of *Tannhäuser*, a practice taken directly from the Greek stage. The Greek theater was a passion and constant companion all of Wagner's life, from the 1820s until the evening of his death in 1883.

Wagner thought he could rely on two sure-fire jokes. The first stemmed from a street brawl he helped provoke in Nuremburg late one night in 1835 "by cruelly baiting a local simpleton who fancied himself absurdly as a singer."[18] The second was the parallel situation of the pedantic marker (Beckmesser) tormenting Stolzing in Act 1, and Sachs the cobbler/marker tormenting the awkward wooer (Beckmesser) in Act 2. But neither joke works well: they are sabotaged by Wagner himself. A convivial man, who found much humor in life, Wagner was nevertheless incapable of injecting into his artwork much that was empty-headed, lighthearted, or without deep intention. In *Meistersinger* he seems almost deliberately to subvert both big comic scenes.

Any fun we might have been tempted to have at the end of Act 2 is obliterated by the Prelude to Act 3, a stunning and sudden plunge into the bitter heart of a wise man (and, by the way, among the finest pages of polyphonic composition since Bach). When the curtain rises, Sachs seethes with a seering contemplation of violence, the urge to violence as part of our irrational nature, and our inability to prevent it.

And later at Beckmesser's limping (and over-long) entrance into Sachs's workshop, we wonder, after all, whether the mob (and Wagner) has dealt with the clerk cruelly. Never mind his unprincipled theft of the Stolzing prize song; Sachs (and Wagner) have set up the pedantic clerk for a fall which, when it comes, leaves us uneasy. Beackmesser's humiliation is not funny.

James Morris as Hans Sachs in the Metropolitan Opera's *Die Meistersinger,* Act 2 (photograph by Winnie Klotz).

Ambiguity 1

The General Theory of Relativity was the apex of the Einstein contribution, and its influence, along with its author's super-stardom, spread throughout the culture. But at the height of his triumph, and because of it, the cutting edge of physics began to move away from Albert Einstein. Having advanced the notion in 1905 that light might consist not of waves, but particles, or quanta, Einstein opened the door to the discoveries that very small things do not behave the way big things do, or the way they "should"—for example, that nuclear particles emit radiation randomly and unpredictably, if not chaotically. Quantum mechanics, as this field of physics came to be known after 1925, and which has dominated physics ever since, embraced uncertainty as a fundamental premise, and astonishingly allowed for effects to occur without discernible cause. Probability, rather than predictability, was the best the new physics could offer. Observation itself became relative, for position and motion now formed mutually incompatible aspects of reality.

Relativity and quantum mechanics were largely concerned with the weird behavior of atomic particles, but the supposed implications were not long confined to the handful of physicists who actually understood them. Within a week of Eddington's confirmation of the General Theory, *The Times* headlined a "Revolution in Science," adding that "the scientific concept of the fabric of the universe must be changed." A few days later *The New York Times* was speculating that "it may well be that the physical aspects of the unrest, the war, the strikes, the Bolshevist uprisings, are in reality the visible objects of some underlying deeper disturbance, worldwide in character. This same spirit has invaded science," and that "the foundations of human thought have been undermined."[19]

There are wonderful ironies at work here, among them that the Theory itself was incomprehensible to almost everybody outside physics, but was nevertheless embraced or loathed—often hysterically—by psychiatrists, politicians, priests, behaviorists, poets, atheists, evolutionists, cosmologists, evangelicals and dramaturgs to confirm or deny their own speculations about Einstein's apparent proof of chaos—in the cosmos, and also in ourselves. It is one of the great spectacles of the century that so many became so aroused while understanding so little.

An equal irony is that Einstein himself was increasingly troubled by the direction in physics to which he had contributed so much. He distrusted the quirky and counter-intuitive mathematics underlying the quantum theories. In fact, Einstein's theories of relativity, both the Special and the General, were first entitled theories of *Invariance* (italics mine). In other words, from the first Einstein, though breaking with Newton, was seeking a new *order* in the cosmos, to describe iconoclastic, but nevertheless rational and knowable laws governing the behavior of gravity, light, time, space and mass.

But the champions of quantum mechanics were having none of it. Always respectful of Einstein and in awe of the achievements of his decade *mirabilis*, they continuously urged him to join them down this path. But he could not. He responded that "I still cannot believe that the good Lord plays dice,"[20] and for more than thirty years he kept looking for a new "field theory," for a mathematical proof that there is an underlying harmony in nature, consistent, one is tempted to suppose, with the "simple harmony" Einstein relished in Mozart—in short, to prove, out of a belief that he called "religious"[21] that the physical world can be accurately described, that *things make sense*.

Ambiguity 2

The tonal structure of music — the most comprehensive and sustained achievement in Western art — defined the character of music for three centuries after the Renaissance, and, despite the twentieth century's concerted effort to do without formality, still dominates our intuitive understanding of music. Until the beginning of the nineteenth century, the "laws" of tonal music were adhered to as happily as those Newtonian laws which, over the same period, provided an amazing and supposedly harmonious certainty in our understanding of the physical world.

Three figures rise up as the preeminent disturbers of this peace: the first was Beethoven and the third Wagner.[22] Beethoven, the titan of classicism, initiated the revolution; it is impossible to imagine the mystifying effect the Third Symphony (let alone the late string quartets and piano sonatas) must have had on audiences inevitably attuned to comprehensible, generally impersonal order in music, both in form and content. In *Tristan* and *Meistersinger*, Wagner delivered the final blows, the former a leap into the future, the latter an apparent, if subversive and ironic, homage to the past. In between, and the most deliberate innovator among the three, is Berlioz. Berlioz's standing has fallen, it seems, irretrievably into the second class, and his few masterpieces are admired most by professional musicians rather than a large public, but there can be no doubt about his historical impact. In fact, Barzun's restorative biography, *Berlioz and His Century* makes it clear that Berlioz's ideas and intentions can be read as precursor to Wagner's, and as such are more original and revolutionary.

"Extinction redeemed by heroism ... that music was one of the necessities of existence, not a decoration or an artificial pleasure ... non-repeating length of line ... balance by asymmetry ... a sense of scale which achieves the heroic and grandiose without giantism ... the revelation of the orchestra as an instrument of dramatic music ... the relation between dramatic and orchestral thought ... a strong daemonic impulse ... the possibility of creating drama in music by treating the orchestra as a collection of independent groups of timbres ... applying his dramatic instinct to the musical problem."[23] Just these random quotations make clear how Berlioz decisively cleared a path for Wagner. The consonance of their intentions also illuminates the troubled relationship between the two men, alternatively attracted and repelled, admiring and competitive.

What was occurring was the relentless dislocation of music from its tonal certainties, resulting, as Leonard Bernstein has elegantly described it, in ambiguity: harmonies that are implied rather than explicit; the use of the deceptive cadence "violating our expectaton" (a fundamental of Wagnerian transition); the prevalence of the diminished seventh, with its uncertainty as to key. Here is Bernstein's description of Berlioz's *Romeo et Juliet*: the juxtaposition of "two musics together ... a clear case of contrapuntal syntax ... the contradiction of bright diatonic sound against the chromaticism of Romeo's yearning ... a triumph of ambiguities, a brilliant illustration of the deliberate exploitation of ambiguity for increased expressive power."[24]

Increased expressive power: that is the great gain, and harmonic dislocation was the price paid. The Wagner miracle was a quantum jump in musical vocabulary, capable of unprecedentedly nuanced and explicit expressions of human emotion, conflict and drama. Wagner's works, and especially the *Tristan* and *Meistersinger* of his decade *mirabilis*, are the apex, the mountain top from which music reaches its most expressive tonal height, and from which the descent from the diatonic style becomes irreversible. Or in Bernstein's words: "*Tristan* is the very crux of ambiguity — the turning point after which music could never be the same; it points musical history directly toward the upcoming crisis of the twentieth century."[25]

This is why *Tristan* and *Meistersinger*, taken together, are mutually illuminating: the former so direct an assault on the status quo; the latter so seemingly stable, its ambiguity, in form and content, indirect, subtle, and, the more one embraces it, wonderfully disconcerting.

Meanings

None of Wagner's operas is so patent, and yet as multi-layered as *Meistersinger*. The story is set in a certain time and specific place. As noted, there is no mythological basis to it, with its universal symbols. We are not coerced into a complex psychological fabric — no proto-Jungianisms here, no explicit exploration of the Wagner psyche. Nor do we venture, as *Tristan* so boldly does, into outright metaphysics. Scratch the surface, however, and one might find all of these things.

Any catalogue of *Meistersinger* interpretations must begin with the way the work illuminates, one might reasonably say *advocates*, and at great length, the position of the artist in society, the qualities of good art, the nature of the creative process, and the tensions between innovation and tradition. The amount of words and music devoted to these subjects is, to say the least, unprecedented in opera.

In addition, *Meistersinger* is Wagner's only work that openly explores the social fabric of real life, and we are exposed to the broad sweep of it. The burgher class takes center stage — it is vaguely odd that Wagner, the artistic egoist, showers so much good-humored affection on it. Stolzing comes from the aristocracy, if only of the *petit* and out-of-luck variety, but he provides genuine class tension. There are playful boys, flirtatious girls, and a night watchman.

The Otto Schenk production of *Die Meistersinger*, Act 2, at the Metropolitan Opera (photograph by Winnie Klotz).

And we see the ordinary folk — in church, brawling, and finally discerning — at their worst and best. This is not just sixteenth century Bavaria, but anywhere, any time. And Sach's reflection on it all is filled with disappointment, but never contempt.

Owen Lee argues, convincingly, that the scriptural references running throughout the piece define a deliberate intention.[26] The first act takes place in a church, and opens at the conclusion of a Sunday service. There is an Eva, a David, and a Magdalena, and innumerable references to St. John's Day. David sings about crossing the Jordan. Most strikingly, there is a formal baptism — of the Prize Song, as well as a consecration of it. There are different interpretations of this: the way that the Christian experience and tradition, entwined in the fabric of the society of the sixteenth century, does or does not relate to the state of the mid-nineteenth, or that it is Art, even Nature, that will one day replace them.

The subject of dreams is also of fundamental importance in *Meistersinger*, as it is in other Wagner operas, especially *Lohengrin* and *Der Fliegende Holländer*. The startling depth of Stolzing's revelation of his dream, and Sachs's interpretation of it (and the significance of dreams in general), is Wagner at his most proto–Freudian.

The "Wahn" monologue exposes *Meistersinger* as one of Wagner's most Schopenhauerian works. It is an expression of resignation and regret toward the vanity and folly of human intention, that all is illusion, that what we love will be lost. Eva and Sachs must renounce the object of their longing. Eva, in particular, concedes that she cannot *will* her desires, that she has no choice but to follow Stolzing. For Sachs, there is "an extraordinarily powerful ... life-assertion within the very renunciation, an acceptance that life is, after all, worth living even on these terms."[27]

Aftermath

Einstein, as we have seen, faced the same kind of problem after 1915 that composers faced after Wagner: his and Wagner's accomplishments were so potent that they required a vast reconsideration of both physics and music. The breakdowns were caused by the subversion of the foundations of classical physics, on the one hand, leading to a new paradigm, quantum mechanics, and the expansion of tonal harmony, on the other, leading to "ambiguity" in music and, later, to the abandonment of tonalism as the pathway of twentieth century music.

Luckily for him, Wagner never had to be challenged or aggrieved by the future course of music; as long as he was alive, he *was* the future of music, at least in his own mind, but also by a large consensus, whether it was for or against him. And unlike Einstein, he continued to create and dominate and succeed for twenty years after his decade *mirabilis*, until his death in 1883: the completion of *Der Ring des Nibelungen*, the construction of the Festspielhaus, the establishment of the first music festival, and the composition of *Parsifal*.

Einstein was not spared, however, because he never was able to accept quantum mechanics as the "right" answer to the questions his own contributions had posed. Between 1915 and 1927, he made a few significant contributions to physics, but none after that, and for the rest of his life, for almost thirty years, he continued to argue, to attempt to fashion an antidote to ambiguity in the physical world, to find a field theory and re-establish a mathematical proof of harmony in Nature.

Wagner's lifelong search extends the parallels with Einstein. It was a central function of Wagner's artistic momentum to explore the cosmic and eternal questions, each of which wrestles with the possibility of harmony in life, with the possibility of redemption. As a man,

Wagner's need to dominate was a central and crucial element of his psyche, but as artist Wagner never imposed answers to these questions of redemption. Rather, he explored options, and challenged us to be caught up in them.

That is why it is useless to try to summarize Wagner's "philosophy," even beyond the ineffability of the music itself, or the often tortured and self-justifying arguments in his essays. Wagner was intellectually curious, a voracious reader, open to new ideas, and profoundly philosophical — but he was no philosopher; unlike science, it is not in the nature of high art to *prove*. Rather, Wagner walks us through dilemma after human dilemma — bringing us face to face with "our lonely and intolerable awareness of our place in an indifferent universe of unexhausted suffering (aware not only) of our own unhappiness but that of others."[28]

Each opera offers, not a mathematical solution, but a musical possibility. Every one of them ends in a major key, a tonic resolution, and it is always musically magnificent, even triumphant (only the conclusion of *Rheingold* is substantially ironic). The possibilities that Wagner offers may include redemption through death-union and wholeness, by the destruction of a corrupt order, the bliss of sexual liberation, or the primacy of compassion.

In *Meistersinger*, we are offered the virtue of social harmony. This is not a banal triumph. Sachs succeeds where Wotan fails. Wotan abandons love for power, and catastrophically loses his way. He does achieve self-awareness, and tries (bitterly, failing at the last) to make way, to achieve the final, telling monument to a successful life: relinquishment. Sachs abandons love out of self-sacrifice, and does the right thing. It is a victory filled with pain, but a victory nonetheless.

Act 1 of *Meistersinger* has sometimes been pushed to the side as exposition, the stage setting for the initial *Stollen*. But there is an extended passage in it which carries one of Wagner's most powerful messages: the beginning of Scene 3, from the trivial dialogue of Beckmesser and Pogner, through the reading of the roll of the Masters. The content is in the orchestra, without much regard for what the characters are saying. It begins in an unassuming manner growing, like so many extended passages in this opera, from a single, non-descript musical kernel.[29] The orchestral tapestry gradually becomes insistent, and the little theme is developed as a polyphonic crescendo. There is an almost inexplicable excitement at the arrival of the Masters. We smile at their good nature, their little puns, the charming exchange when the page tells them that Niklaus Vogel is sick. By the time Kothner pronounces the quorum is met, and we move on to Pogner's monologue, we have experienced yet another miracle of Wagnerian structure and orchestration.

This music bears an unmistakable message, as if from *West Side Story*, that "Something's Coming, Something Good." So powerful is this feeling that it is tempting to hear in this passage from *Meistersinger*, if not a philosophy, then at least a point of view, even if it is subliminal: that there is hope. God may be alive or dead. We may be driven by unquenchable longing. We may be hurtling through an unfathomable and random cosmos. And it all will come to an end.

But in 1874, Wagner looked back on his comic opera and saw in it not pathos, not ecstasy, "but emotional depth, good humor; I like to think that there is hope on this foundation." It is because that hope is so authentic and so potent that *The Mastersingers* continues to warm the hearts of all who come into contact with what has been described as the "the longest smile in the German langauge."[30]

Einstein did not need Wagner. He did just fine without him, and Mozart helped. But *Meistersinger* is one of our most profoundly comforting possessions, coming to grips in music with the issues of redemptive value that Einstein, always with good humor, never stopped seeking. One likes to suppose, had he probed Wagner's comedy, that his great heart, too, would have been warmed by that "longest smile."

NOTES

1. Walter Isaacson, *Einstein: His Life and Universe*, p. 38.
2. For a review of Einstein's decade *mirabilis*, see Isaacson, pp. 90–107. Although Einstein is still the only universally famous physicist, he was always happy to credit others in a long roster of physicists who made important contributions between 1895 and 1925, including Planck, Bohr, Born, Bose, Heisenberg, Schrödinger, Diroc, Broglie, Ehrenfest, Poincaré, Rutherford, Lorentz, and Sommerfield, to name a few.
3. Ernest Newman, *The Wagner Operas*, p. 292.
4. Georg Solti, *Memoirs*, p. 112.
5. See Michael Tanner's excellent commentary "The Glory of Art" in the Royal Opera Company *Meistersinger* program, May 2000.
6. Isaacson, p. 38.
7. See Father Lee's superlative essay, "Songbirds and Saints," in *First Intermissions*.
8. See Millington, *Wagner*, pp. 135–137.
9. Gutman, *Richard Wagner: The Man, His Mind, and His Music*, pp. 408–413. One of the advantages of Gutman's analysis is its strict lack of sentiment in favor of Wagner. Throughout this underestimated biography is the sense of Gutman's suspicions about Wagner, making his praise all the more credible. For example, he observes that Nietzsche's late criticisms, that Wagner worked in a "patchwork manner," is true, but ultimately results in music well beyond the achievements of Chopin or Schumann.
10. Isaacson, p. 223.
11. Millington, p. 245.
12. Schirmer, p. 213, Staff 1, Measures 1–2. See musical excerpt A.
13. Schirmer, pp. 214–215.
14. Compare Schirmer, p. 215, Staff 2, Measure 1 with *Tristan and Isolda*, Schirmer, p. 162, Staff 1, Measure 5. See musical excerpts B and C.
15. I am indebted to the concert pianist and Wagner expert Jeffrey Swann for his innumerable insights into Wagner's music and for his efforts to correct and restrain my tendency toward musicological error.
16. Schirmer, p. 217. See musical excerpt D.
17. Schirmer, p. 291, Staff 3, Measure 1, and p. 226, Staff 2, Measures 2–3. See musical excerpts E and F.
18. Newman, *The Life of Richard Wagner*, Volume 1, p. 193.
19. Isaacson, p. 278.
20. Isaacson, p. 515.
21. When asked what ramifications relativity had for religion, Einstein answered: "None. Relativity is purely a scientific matter and has nothing to do with religion." Isaacson, p. 279. For a discussion of Einstein's religious views, see Isaacson, pp. 384–393.
22. There were of course others, notably both Chopin and Schumann.
23. See Barzun, pp. 23–64.
24. See Bernstein, "The Delights and Dangers of Ambiguity," in *The Unanswered Question*.
25. See Bernstein, p. 231.
26. See Lee, "Songbirds and Saints."
27. Bryan Magee, *Wagner and Philosophy*, pp. 251–5. One might add that is absurd to see Wagner's works as literally political, or Wagner himself as political. Through the course of their lives, Wagner found politics as increasingly irrelevant to his work as Einstein delved ever deeper into political issues outside of physics.
28. See Magee, pp. 183.
29. Schirmer, p. 75, Staff 1, Measures 2–3. See musical notation.
30. See Roland Matthews, "My Most Genial Creation," *The Mastersingers of Nuremburg*, Nicholas John, ed., p. 14.

BIBLIOGRAPHY

Gutman, Robert. *Richard Wagner: The Man, His Mind, and His Music*. New York: Harcourt Brace Jovanovich, 1968.

Isaacson, Walter. *Einstein: His Life and Universe*. New York: Simon & Schuster, 2007.
John, Nicholas, ed. *The Mastersingers of Nuremburg*. London: John Calder, 1983.
Kleinmichel, Richard. *Tristan and Isolde*. New York: G. Schirmer, 1906.
Klindworth, Karl. *The Mastersingers of Nuremburg*. New York: G. Schirmer, 1903.
Magee, Bran. *Wagner and Philosophy*. London: Penguin, 2000.
Newman, Ernest. *The Life of Richard Wagner*, Vol. 1. Cambridge, UK: Cambridge University Press, 1976.
_____. *The Wagner Operas*. Princeton, NJ: Princeton University Press, 1991.
Pais, Abraham. *The Genius of Science*. Oxford, UK: Oxford University Press, 2000.
Smith, Patrick J. *The Tenth Muse*. New York: Alfred A. Knopf, 1970.

10

Musical Characterization in *Parsifal*: A Study of Parsifal and Kundry

John J.H. Muller

An examination of last works suggests that there are certain characteristics in the late style periods of some composers, and that their final compositions exhibit qualities of "lateness." For instance, a composer might explore a specific compositional technique, as Beethoven did exhaustively with the fugue. In other cases, the issues of lateness could be philosophical and psychological and relate to a confrontation with death. In this regard, the late period of Mahler springs to mind. In addition, a final work could be seen as a musical last will and testament, the summation of a composer's style, the distillation of a musical language. Bach's final works certainly demonstrate this desire for summary, especially *The Art of the Fugue*. Wagner's *Parsifal* is clearly a work informed by lateness. In so many ways, it represents a final statement on matters, both musical and extra-musical, which occupied the composer throughout his career. On one level, *Parsifal* demonstrates the possibilities and refinement of his harmonic language and leitmotif technique. It is also his final step towards the union of the arts and music drama. *Parsifal* may also contain Wagner's last ideas on racial thinking.[1] Beyond these features, in *Parsifal* Wagner continues to show his masterly ability to create flesh and blood characters out of music, and to probe the inner lives of the characters. In a sense, *Parsifal* is the end of a journey, not just of Wagner's musical development, but of his psychological development as well. As a work composed at the end of the common practice era, *Parsifal* is also a late work of a late period.[2]

Wagner's works lend themselves to a great variety of interpretations and approaches of study, and this is especially true of *Parsifal*.[3] The present essay is concerned specifically with the musical characterization of Parsifal and Kundry, and will demonstrate how Wagner utilizes many elements of music — theme, harmony, rhythm, register, timbre, even structure — to embody his drama and characters. Before embarking on this musical study, it is vital to review the long gestation of the work and to consider the forces that shaped Wagner's own personality. Only then can one fully appreciate the totality of Wagner's accomplishment.

Although it was Wagner's last completed opera, his first thoughts concerning a work based on the Parzival legend date back to the mid–1840s. Thus, the initial conception of *Parsifal* was contemporary with *Tannhäuser* and *Lohengrin*, even if the musical realization followed the mature stage of *Tristan und Isolde* and the *Ring* cycle. One often marvels at the twenty six-year time span that Wagner devoted to the *Ring*, yet *Parsifal* was developing, with many interruptions, over a period of thirty seven years! A brief summary of the gestation of this final work, therefore, is in order.

In July of 1845, Wagner visited Marienbad to benefit from the curative effects of the waters. The books he took for light summer reading included Wolfram von Eschenbach's medieval epics *Parzival* and *Titurel*. He saw operatic possibility in this subject, but plans for *Lohengrin* attracted his immediate attention. Over the next thirty years, Wagner intermittently returned to *Parsifal* , and as he did, the work evolved in many ways he could never have envisioned in 1845. His study of Schopenhauer in the 1850s certainly influenced the direction that the project was to take, as did his plans (never realized) for dramatic works on the life of Christ (*Jesus von Nazareth*) and on a Buddhist theme (*Die Sieger*). (The former, from 1849, exists as a prose scenario, and the later, from 1856, as a prose sketch.) During the early planning of *Tristan*, Wagner actually contemplated introducing the wandering Parsifal into Act III, and even penned a fore square eight-measure sketch of music. By 1857, Wagner had written his first prose sketch for *Parsifal* (now lost). Letters of the 1860s show that the composer was contemplating the subject, and a prose draft, quite similar to the final version, dates from 1865. The final prose draft and actual libretto followed one another closely in 1877. Work on the music, from drafting to finished orchestration, occupied the composer from 1877 to 1882. During this time, Wagner's health was in decline and there were long interruptions on the work.[4]

Obviously, had Wagner composed *Parsifal* in the first flush of enthusiasm, it would have had the musical style of *Tannhäuser* and would have lacked the extraordinary richness of the work we know. It was hardly coincidental that Wagner set *Parsifal* aside in the 1840s and allowed his conception of the work to mature over the decades. He clearly sensed that he was not ready to do justice to the project. For instance, a letter to Mathilde Wesendonck dating from 1860 contains the following passage. "*Parzival* is again very much coming to life in me; all the time I see it more and more clearly; when one day it is all finally ripe in me, the bringing of this poem into the world will be for me an extreme pleasure. But between now and then a good few years may yet have to pass" (Quoted in Beckett 2). Later in the 1860s, he went even further and indicated to several friends that it would be his final composition (Beckett 13). A work such as *Parsifal* required a composer who had undergone his own life's journey. In other words, *Parsifal* had to be a last work.

There is a strong correlation between Wagner's life and the subject matter of his operas, and they are often viewed as being "autobiographical" in nature. Stewart Spencer offers a more nuanced view when he writes, "Wagner's music dramas might be regarded, therefore, not as slices of life but as the composer's attempt to propose a solution to the problems which beset him and, in particular, to the problem why his relations with other people so frequently ended in failure" (Millington *Compendium* 404). It is fitting to review some details of his early life in order to understand how Wagner, in his last work, continued the process of exploring his own psychological needs through his characters.

Any number of biographers have discussed the emotional difficulties of Wagner's early years, but in Joachim Köhler's treatment, Wagner's childhood emerges as positively traumatic. Two major factors concern the question of Wagner's paternity and the emotional and physical distance of his mother. The paternity issue is well known and can be summarized briefly. Friedrich Wagner died when Richard was three months old, and although he had many older siblings, Wagner never learned very much about him. Ludwig Geyer, a family friend, married Johanna in August of 1814 and they had a daughter. It simply is not known which man was actually Wagner's father; compelling arguments can be made in favor of either man. All that matters is Wagner's view, and he believed, at least for a time, that Geyer was actually his father. In fact, he used his stepfather's last name up to the age of fourteen. Geyer died when Wagner was eight; he had now lost a second father figure before leaving childhood. Most biographers present a positive portrait of the relationship between Geyer and Richard,[5] but Köhler offers a different view. Whatever positive statements Wagner may have made about Geyer publicly, it appears that time spent in the Geyer household was far from pleasant. Wagner did not get the attention he needed and had to compete with his sisters for Geyer's attention. Köhler believes that Wagner actually came to fear and hate his stepfather (15–16 and 23).

Wagner's relationship with his mother had an even greater impact on his development. He was desperate for his mother's affection, but she withheld any sense of maternal warmth, and Wagner suffered from "emotional deprivation" (Millington *Wagner* 4). Martin Gregor-Dellin emphasizes Wagner's mother fixation, quoting a letter of 1835. "Only to you, dearest Mother, does my mind return with the sincerest love and deepest emotion. See, Mother, now that we are apart, I am so overwhelmed with feelings of gratitude for your glorious love for your child, which you lately showed again with such warmth and affection, that I should dearly like to write and talk of it to you in the fondest tones of a lover to his beloved. Ah, but far more than that, for is not the love of one's mother far more — far more unsullied than any other?" (Gregor-Dellin 23). As we will see, such feelings are clearly played out in the Parsifal/Kundry relationship.[6] It appears that neither his mother nor stepfather welcomed Richard's presence in the household. Both before and after Geyer death, Wagner was sent away periodically to live with other families and suffered from inconsolable homesickness (Köhler 18).

Devoid of the qualities a young boy seeks in his mother, Wagner turned to his oldest sister Rosalie, who functioned in effect as a substitute mother. An actress herself, it was she who encouraged Wagner's musical ambitions (Köhler 26–27). He sought her approval in the way a boy would ordinarily seek the approval of his mother.

As a child, Wagner was beset by terrible fears. He was frightened by ghosts, and in his youthful imagination, inanimate objects — furniture, paintings, even beer bottles — came to life and terrified young Wagner. Köhler interprets Wagner's fears as stemming from his fear of Geyer. Even into adulthood, he was haunted in his dreams by Geyer (Köhler 20–22). Wagner's frail health completes the image of a very bleak childhood. The difficulties of his early years contributed to "probably more serious and far-reaching psychological disorders as well" (Millington *Wagner* 4).

Even a cursory view of the pre–*Parsifal* works reveals how the formative events of Wagner's childhood often play a central role in an opera. From the writing of *Leubald*, his unfinished drama of 1828, a search for identify is a leitmotif in Wagner's works (Gregor-Dellin 21). The theme of the absent father figures prominently in *Die Walküre* and *Siegfried*. (Siegmund's impassioned cries of "Wälse!" could well be Wagner's own.) One encounters malignant father figures in Alberich and Mime.[7] (And has there even been a father/son scene such as that between Alberich and Hagen at the start of Act II of *Götterdämmerung*? The fact that this may be a dream only strengthens its psychological power.) In Wotan's famous monologue from Act II of *Die Walküre*, the god poignantly contrasts his paternal feelings to those of Alberich.' Referring to the woman Alberich has bought with his gold, Wotan laments "and she will bear Alberich's son; the seed of spite stirs in her womb; this wonder befell the loveless Niblung; while I, who loved so truly, my free son I never could win" (Porter's translation 111).

Even more notable are the examples of Wagner's mother fixation. In a very tender passage, Siegfried attempts to imagine what his mother was like in Act II of the opera. Later in Act III, when confronted with fear for the first time (in the form of Brünnhilde), he calls out to his mother, and shortly thereafter, believes that Brünnhilde might actually *be* his mother! We learn in Act III of *Tristan* that the hero lost both parents in childhood, his mother during childbirth. One should also consider the idealization of womanhood in the characters of Senta and Elisabeth, and the brother/sister love of *Die Walküre*. (On this latter relationship, it is worth noting that Rosalie died in childbirth [Köhler 27].) Wagner continues to work with some of these themes in *Parsifal*, as the aging composer seeks a resolution to the conflicts of his childhood. Gamuret died before Parsifal's birth, but the theme of the absent father is not explored to any great degree.[8] It is worth noting that Parsifal, like Wagner, knows very little about his father (Gregor-Dellin 23). However, *Parsifal* represents the composer's final attempt to work through his mother fixation, and that will be examined in detail later in this essay.

Before dealing specifically with Wagner's musical characterization, some general observations on Parsifal and Kundry are in order. Parsifal is a very different kind of hero from the one generally encountered in opera, and a comparison to Siegfried is instructive. Siegfried is an active hero; he slays a dragon, defeats Wotan, and then walks through a wall of flame to claim his bride. Later, he goes on numerous adventures, musically narrated in the famous Rhine Journey interlude. His exploits are known far and wide. Parsifal, on the other hand, is a passive hero; he attains his goal by resisting the temptation of Kundry. Yet they are not total opposites: "Siegfried, the naïve man of action, recurs in Parsifal, the naïve man of faith" (Gregor-Dellin 447).

One side of Wagner's genius was his ability to take a discursive medieval epic and transform it into a workable drama. This is true of characters as well as plot. Kundry is Wagner's most fascinating and complex figure, and she is very much his own idea. She embodies aspects of any number of different figures in Wolfram's *Parzival* (including one called Cundrie), and her creation in the 1860s proved to be the dramatic key for the work. In Wagner's hands, she links Amfortas and Parsifal (Beckett 8–9). She has been wandering for centuries, and during the course of the opera, we learn of her earlier incarnations. When Klingsor summons her in Act II, he refers to her at first in general terms: "*Urteufelin! Höllenrose!*" ("primaeval witch! rose of hell!")[9] He then becomes more specific, connecting her to Herodias, who brought about John the Baptist's end, and Gundryggia, a Valkyrie-like figure of Norse mythology. Later, she identifies herself with Ahasuerus, the wandering Jew of medieval legend who mocked Christ on the cross. In Acts I and III, she appears as an almost feral creature, serving the knights of the grail, while in Act II, she is transformed into a beautiful seductress, bent on destroying the knighthood.[10]

Kundry and Parsifal are therefore two very different characters, presented in the opera at different stages of development, and Wagner's musical treatment conveys this. Kundry's progress towards redemption is depicted through a reduction of her music. Parsifal, on the other hand, is on a journey of growth, and his themes reflect this.

Act I

Fittingly, more than four different motifs are associated with Kundry at various times in the opera, and her dual nature is already suggested musically in Act I. As the esquires see her approach, a propulsive dotted figure suggests her desperate ride bringing balsam from Arabia.[11] Her entrance is marked by the shocking Kundry motif, the musical embodiment of a scream or hideous laugh. Its two main components are a dissonant chord and a rapid descent through three and a half octaves. (Robert Gutman has very aptly likened the contour of this motif to the "whiplash" of Jugendstil, 438.) The "Kundry chord" colors much of the work,

Tatiana Troyanos as Kundry in *Parsifal*, Act 1, at the Metropolitan Opera (photograph by Winnie Klotz).

and is similar to a chord associated with Hagen in *Götterdämmerung* which casts a lurid pallor over much of that opera. Throughout Act I, her vocal line has a wild quality, angular and broken up with rests. Notice her barely verbal opening exclamations: "*Hier! Nimm du!—Balsam....*" ("Here! Take this!—Balsam ...") As Gurnemanz begins to explain to the esquires what he knows of her background, another motif is introduced, that of magic. The sinuous chromatic movement of the theme conveys another side of Kundry, that of temptress. (This theme outlines the same diminished seventh chord heard in the Kundry motif.) Gurnemanz's narrative "*Titurel, der fromme Held*" ("Titurel, the godly hero") includes a motif associated with Klingsor, who holds power over Kundry. The lilting Flower Maidens' motif, especially prominent in Act II, is heard during this scene as well, and is associated with Kundry's sensual side. She is, after all, the *Überblumenmädchen*.

Parsifal does not possess as great a range of character as Kundry, but he also is depicted by several themes, and two are stated one right after another. At the conclusion of his narrative, Gurnemanz sings the guileless fool motif in its complete form for the first time.[12] "'*Durch Mitleid wissend, der reine Tor; harre sein, den ich erkor.*'" ("'Enlightened through compassion, the innocent fool; wait for him, the appointed one.'") The prophecy is then echoed by the four Esquires, only to be cut off (perhaps too conveniently) by Parsifal's main motif as he is spotted off stage. With its diatonic quality and fanfare-like character, this theme embodies the hero-to-be and differs greatly from Kundry's more chromatic music. Since the opera ultimately is about Parsifal's growth and inner journey, the full potential of this motif is not realized until Act III, when Parsifal is anointed as king. In the immediate scene, as he is questioned

Parsifal, Act 1, the Stefan Herheim production at the Bayreuth Festival (courtesy Bayreuth Festival).

about killing the swan and his background, fragments of the motif are heard, usually scored for horns and woodwinds.

Prodded by Gurnemanz, Parsifal attempts to relate his history, but it is clear there is much he does not know. With appropriate motifs, Kundry fills in important details of his life. When she informs Parsifal of his mother's death and offers his mother's greeting, this provokes a violent response on the part of Parsifal. Kundry relates this in the recitative-like style of her Act I character, as if objectively reporting facts. (When she takes Parsifal through his early life in Act II, it is emotionally charged. In particular, the simple greeting in Act II becomes a kiss, and Parsifal has an even more violent reaction. This parallel passage will be explored in detail later in the essay.) Kundry's struggle against sleep is clear from the fragmented vocal line and low register, and the themes of magic and Klingsor indicate that this sleep will lead to her transformation as a seductress. Kundry is not encountered again in the act.

Although the attention now shifts to Amfortas and the knighthood, the grail scene which Parsifal witnesses is of great importance to his development. He may not be able to articulate his feelings, but as we will learn in Act II, Amfortas's suffering makes a deep impression upon him. At the close of Act I, the contrast between Parsifal's apparent insensitivity and his very real empathy is made clear by the handling of motifs. As Gurnemanz tries to get a reaction from Parsifal, the alto oboe, with its lamenting quality, intones the guileless fool motif, followed by the motif of sorrow. Gurnemanz mistakes his mute thoughtfulness for stupidity, and dismisses Parsifal as a mere fool. At this point, the motif is trivialized in the violas with trills, staccato, and frag-

Wolfgang Brendel as Amfortas in the Metropolitan Opera's *Parsifal* (photograph by Winnie Klotz).

mentation, but a disembodied voice, singing in the same register as the oboe, confirms Parsifal as the pure fool. The statement of the Parsifal motif as Gurnemanz gruffly throws him out is not simply a musical nametag. The scoring for muted horns implies the hero he will become. As we will see, when Parsifal is actually recognized as the prophesied savior of the knighthood and anointed as king in Act III, the mutes come off.

Act II

The difference between the Flower Maidens' coy, frivolous, and rather humorous attempt at enticing Parsifal and Kundry's far more serious approach is clear from the music. Their embellished line, with its arabesque-like figures and small notes values give way to Kundry's sustained intoning of "Parsifal." As she suggestively drapes her voice over his name, she both banishes the Flower Maidens and entices the hero. One senses a suspension of time. (These three notes of "Parsifal" are also the opening pitches of the wound motif, heard first in the Prelude to Act I. Perhaps Kundry had begun her seduction of Amfortas with the sensuous sound of her voice as well.)

The psychological impact of this moment can not be over emphasized. Parsifal is hearing his name for the first time since he left his mother. (Indeed, it is the first time *anyone* hears his name in the opera.) Kundry's strategy is very clear: she will take him back to his most vulnerable state, and playing the role of his mother, bring back forgotten memories. Appropriately, the motif of his mother, Herzeleide, is heard in the orchestra. Kundry's knowledge of Parsifal's past gives her tremendous power over him. As she dismisses the Flower Maidens, there is a foreshadowing of the melody that will make up the lullaby "*Ich sah das Kind an seiner Mutter Brust*" ("I saw the child on its mother's breast"). Kundry goes on to play with his name, calling him "Falparsi," in the way that a mother might toy with her child's name.[13] She even brings up the subject of his father Gamuret, who gave him the name

Jessye Norman as Kundry and Placido Domingo as Parsifal in the Metropolitan Opera's *Parsifal* (photograph by Winnie Klotz).

Parsifal while dying on a distant battlefield. Kundry knows exactly how to put him in a weak position.

Over the next thirty minutes, Kundry will employ all of her powers — seduction, appeal for pity, and blatant sexual advance — to ensnare Parsifal. Yet, the more she presses the seduction, the closer Parsifal comes to self-understanding. Ultimately, this will lead to her own redemption. Wagner's abilities to express every nuance of character were never more telling than in this scene. As examples of penetrating insight into the psychology of his characters, only the Act III monologues from *Tristan* can compare. In the first half of the scene, Kundry is in control, and the musical form conveys this. After the kiss, however, the formal structure begins to break down as she starts losing control over Parsifal. This pivotal scene demands close scrutiny.

In the first section, Kundry attempts to break Parsifal down by returning him to infancy, his weakest state. Although she describes a scene of Herzeleide's maternal love, clearly she herself is taking on the role of Parsifal's mother. Two ideas emerge as she recounts his early years: Herzeleide's tenderness, and her desire to keep her son ignorant of the world which drew her husband Gamuret away. The gentle rocking motion of Wagner's 6/8 meter clearly evokes a lullaby, and Kundry's melodic contour outlines this motion as well. For the most part, her line moves by step, with few leaps, suggesting the intimate way a mother would speak to a child. Kundry's melodic material, often doubled in the orchestra, is derived from Herzeleide's motif. (None of the thematic material associated with Kundry is used in this section. Musically, she has become Parsifal's mother.) The scene is an excellent example of Wagner's symphonic approach to opera. The scoring also emphasizes Kundry's role as mother; Wagner largely employs the warmth of the strings, with an occasional woodwind coloration.

The climax of this section, based on an ongoing development of Herzeleide's motif, describes her surge of emotion upon finding the lost Parsifal. Almost as an aside, Kundry suggestively asks, *"ward dir es wohl gar dein Küssen bang?"* ("Did you perhaps fear her kisses?") Gregor-Dellin states, "Nowhere else in pre–Freudian literature can one find such an overt reference to sexuality in early childhood." (24) Parsifal will soon learn that it is Kundry's kiss that he should fear. As she describes Herzeleide's sorrow and death there is a reduction of motion and texture, and Wagner introduces a new motif, one associated with Herzeleide's anguish. This stabbing 16th-note figure conveys her sense of loss. As she relates Herzeleide's death, Kundry's vocal line is fragmented. Her sense of confidence and control is reflected in the very clear phrase structure of this lullaby. Indeed, it is essentially a self-contained musical number.

Kundry is trying to weaken Parsifal by making him feel responsible for his mother's death. Guilt he certainly feels, as he rebukes himself with the words "*O Thor! Blöder, taumelnder Thor!*" ("Fool! Blind, blundering fool!") However, his feelings are soon linked to his guilt over forgetting Amfortas's plight. Although he is not yet able consciously to recognize this, the orchestra indicates what he senses. As Parsifal asks, "*Was Alles vergass ich wohl noch?*" ("What else have I forgotten"), the spear motif is stated three times, first with the plaintive coloring of English horn. As it smoothly shifts into Kundry's motif, it is evident that Parsifal is starting to sense a link between Amfortas's suffering and Kundry.

Inadvertently, Kundry has pushed him towards the understanding he seeks. In the next section, she must redirect Parsifal's reaction to his mother's death to suit her own purpose. To accomplish this, Kundry delves farther into Parsifal's past, before he was born, to describe the love of Herzeleide and Gamuret. She seeks to inflame in Parsifal the passion Gamuret had for his mother, the very passion that produced Parsifal. Kundry is more overt about her seduction, and now her motif and that of magic appear frequently. At the climax of this scene, Kundry offers Parsifal a farewell kiss from his mother, the kiss alluded to earlier. This kiss, which was to bring about Parsifal's downfall, instead proves to be the turning point in the development of both characters, and indeed, the turning point in the opera. The kiss leads Parsifal to understand the source of Amfortas's pain; at the same time, Parsifal's resistance to Kundry's kiss ultimately opens the way to her redemption in Act III. Such a potent kiss requires further discussion.

Wagner is able to depict musically Parsifal's physical and emotional reaction to Kundry through leitmotifs. Initially, the kiss is a very drawn-out statement of magic, which is gradually transformed into the wound motif. Parsifal feels Amfortas's pain, and expresses this with sudden declamatory outbursts ("*Amfortas!— Die Wunde*"—) interspersed with Kundry's motif. Full orchestra recapitulates themes associated with Amfortas.

Kundry's kiss has given Parsifal great insight, yet a conflict rages within him. He doesn't just feel Amfortas's pain; he himself experiences a sexual awakening, and his torment is expressed with turbulent harmonies in the orchestra. (During the kiss, could the gradual rise of the magic motif through several octaves have been a musical erection?) He is in danger of succumbing to Kundry's allure. To counteract these new and unfamiliar feelings, he focuses on the grail, and in doing so, gains greater understanding of his mission. With an extensive restatement of thematic material from the Act I Prelude, he hears Christ calling for a grail savior. Parsifal ends his scene of self-lacerating torment with the question, "*Wie büss ich, Sünder, meine Schuld?*" ("How can I, a sinner, purge my guilt?")

Kundry attempts to resume her advances, but once again, they have the opposite effect on Parsifal. In contrast to the previous heavy scoring, Wagner writes a scene with intimate, chamber-like sonorities. Parsifal now has a clearer image of Amfortas's fate (and the fate he must resist) and imagines in graphic language Kundry's seduction of the grail king. A solo violin states Kundry's motive over and over, but it is no longer a wild howl, but rather an alluring, slithering, caressing phrase. Parsifal's enlightenment is complete — be reliving Amfortas's downfall in his mind, he recognizes the power of the kiss and rejects Kundry.

For Kundry, seduction, whether veiled with maternal love or overtly sexual in nature, has not succeeded. Seeing the compassion that Parsifal has expressed towards Amfortas, she decides to appeal to Parsifal's sympathy in order to destroy him. To this end, Kundry, who earlier had recounted Parsifal's background, now reveals her own. Yet the narration of her prior incarnation as Ahasuerus is disingenuous. She is not truly seeking redemption at this point; still in the thrall of Klingsor, such a goal is impossible. In one of the most striking (and forward-looking) passages in the opera, she describes how she mocked Christ on the cross. The texture of the scene is quite stark as the orchestra plays a minor variant of the opening Last Supper motive. Kundry's words are halting and broken up by rests —"*Ich sah ... Ihm ... Ihm ... und ... lachte...!*" ("I saw ... Him ... Him ... and ... mocked...!") — as if the memory of this event is too difficult to relate. The climax of this passage, a precipitous downward leap of almost two octaves on the word "lachte," would not be out of place in a 20th-century expressionistic work such as *Erwartung* or *Wozzeck*. Significantly, the interval of this leap covers the outer pitches of Kundry's motive. The origin of Kundry's scream is now revealed — it arose out of her mocking laugh, and she is condemned to repeat it for eternity.

As she describes her accursed state, capable only of laughing, shouting, and raging, her vocal line becomes a series of outbursts, with large, dissonant intervals over the Klingsor motif in the orchestra. She implores that one hour with Parsifal can give her peace, even if she is spurned by God. He points out (with the guileless fool motif in the orchestra) that he must

Leonie Rysanek as Kundry in *Parsifal* at the Metropolitan Opera (photograph by Winnie Klotz).

not lose sight of his mission. It is not only to save Amfortas and the knighthood, but to offer her salvation as well, if she will only turn from her sinful ways. Yet Parsifal is still tormented within; the kiss that gave him understanding of Amfortas's suffering also draws him towards Kundry. This conflict is depicted musically as motifs associated with Monsalvat (faith, for instance) alternate with those of Kundry and her destructive power. He asks, "*Doch wer erkennt ihn klar und hell, des einz'gen Heiles wahren Quell? O Elend, aller Rettung Flucht! O, Weltenwahn's Umnachten, in höchsten Heiles heisser Sucht nach der Verdammniss Quell zu schmachten!*" ("But who can know aright and clear the only true source of salvation? O misery that banishes all deliverance! O blackness of earthly error, that while feverishly pursuing supreme salvation yet thirsts for the fount of perdition!") This passage reaches a climax with a sustained high note on "*Verdammniss*" for the tenor, while the orchestra intensifies his turmoil with the motifs of Kundry and magic.

Kundry senses his vacillation and abandons any pretense of subtlety. The Flower Maidens' motif has a new insistence, as she points out that if a kiss could give him such a vision, he could attain Godhood from her all-embracing love. Kundry declaims her anticipated triumph with a phrase covering over two octaves in the voice. (From here to the end of the act, there is a gradual rise in tessitura reflecting her increasing desperation.) For the first time since the Flower Maidens' scene earlier in the act, Parsifal's hero motif is heard, expressing his resolve. Such resistance brings about a greater frenzy from Kundry, with her motif and that of riding prominent. Her vocal line is more and more declamatory, and the extensive use of the upper register conveys her extreme emotional state. Calling upon help from Klingsor, she curses Parsifal to stray and never find the way to Amfortas.[14] Having withstood Kundry, Parsifal is able to regain the sacred spear from Klingsor. The magic garden withers to uncharacteristic fortissimo statements of the Flower Maiden's plaint. With the curse broken, Kundry moves closer to finding redemption. Parsifal, however, still in search of inner knowledge, will wander for many years before restoring the spear to the knighthood.

Act III

The Prelude to Act III is a supreme example of Wagner's fully mature style, with its juxtaposing of themes, both new and previously heard, and striking harmonic language. Indeed, although *Tristan* is the work usually cited when discussing Wagner's extension of tonality, this Prelude takes an even closer step towards twentieth-century harmonic practice. Wagner applies these techniques in a penetrating musical study of Parsifal's ongoing development. The Prelude presents him in the midst of an arduous journey, both physical and psychological. He is no longer the naïve fool of Act I, but he has not achieved full understanding either. The music embodies both his past struggle with Kundry and his ongoing search. The opening motif of desolation or bereavement is a new one, and its strongly chromatic character, including the dissonant tritone, expresses the weakened state of the knighthood. The theme of straying, which follows, could be viewed as a subtle transformation of two motifs associated with Kundry. The two-note ascent capped by a triplet has the same contour as riding, and the two-note phrase itself could be a subtle reference to the Flower Maidens (although no longer in a waltz rhythm). Moreover, the straying motif is also a highly chromatic version of the grail theme. (These multiple references contained within an ostensibly new motif offer testimony to the highly refined late-period leitmotif technique.) Underneath this motif magic is stated in several forms. Up to this point, only the strings have been scored, but now Wagner employs the full ensemble. Twice the orchestra strives upward with the grail motif, only to be thwarted by Kundry and the spear. The guileless fool is presented in a richer harmonic context and denser texture than previously in the opera, conveying Parsifal's process of development. The musical character of the Prelude may also express Wagner's own long struggle with this work (Beckett 4).

By the end of Act II, Kundry was placed in the passive position; she must await her redemption, but she cannot bring it about. Parsifal now takes on the more active role. The opening of the act is concerned with Kundry's awakening, and many motifs associated with her former self are worked into Wagner's orchestral fabric. As the curtain opens, the Flower Maidens' plaint is heard, but played very slowly. The spare texture of the scene, with a sustained quality interrupted by periodic fitful gestures in the orchestra, conveys a character gradually coming out of a deep sleep. A lengthy pantomime depicts Gurnemanz's attempt to warm Kundry back to life.[15] She finally awakens with a scream, the only time in Act III that this motif is heard from her. Kundry's only word in the act is "*Dienen*" ("Service"), sung twice in the halting manner of her Act I character. Although she will remain on stage for the entire act, she never utters another sound.

The presentation of Parsifal's motifs makes clear the growth and greater complexity of the character. When he first appears, his face is hidden by a visor, and so his motif is "disguised" in the minor mode. The pianissimo scoring of horns, trumpet, and trombones faintly foreshadows the heroic orchestration to come at his anointing, but the motif trails off with a chromatic descent. Combined with this motif is the tritone figure of bereavement. At first, Gurnemanz can not understand how this mysterious figure could be ignorant of Good Friday. His recognition of Parsifal comes during a return of the Last Supper motif, with both major and minor statements. The guileless fool is placed in the context of this recapitulation, and is especially tied to the Spear. During Parsifal's narration of his wanderings and his protection of the spear, the orchestra extends the material of the Prelude, for the most part. News of Titurel's death brings about the same agonized, self-recrimination that was Parsifal's response to learning of his mother's death in Act II. "*Und ich, ich bin's, der all diess Elend schuf.*" ("And it is I, I, who caused all this woe.") Before Parsifal can move on and accomplish his task, two steps remain; he must be baptized and anointed king. Both these scenes afford Gurnemanz his most lyrical music in the opera. The baptism introduces a new motif, blessing, and during the anointing, the Parsifal theme attains its apotheosis. The naïve Parsifal of Act I, armed with a home-made weapon, was illustrated with a motif of heroic potential. Now that Parsifal bears the spear and is about to become king, his theme reached its full potential. Initially, it is given out forte and, for the first time, with a large compliment of full brass. After an extension of the motif, Parsifal's compassionate side is conveyed with a brief development on the guileless fool motif, which yields to a closing full orchestra statement of the Parsifal theme with the rising Grail motif. By bringing both these themes together, Wagner makes it very clear that Parsifal is closer to restoring the knighthood.

In his first official act, Parsifal baptizes Kundry, preparing her for eventual redemption. Parsifal is not yet ready to take his place in Monsalvat; he has more to learn from Gurnemanz. During the famous Good Friday music, the character of this nature music contrasts greatly from that of the seductive flower maidens of Act II. As Parsifal asks if even the flowers seek redemption, the use of the Flower Maidens' plaint suggests Kundry's own redemption.

The scene now shifts to the grail temple and Amfortas's anguished scene before the knighthood, but once Parsifal enters and returns the spear, no other voice is heard (with the exception of the chorus). The focus is on the new king, who returns the lance and presides

Placido Domingo as Parsifal and Jessye Norman as Kundry in *Parsifal* at the Metropolitan Opera (photograph by Winnie Klotz).

over the grail ceremony. Amfortas's wound is healed, the knighthood's strength is restored, and Kundry, after years of wandering, sinks lifeless, on the most distantly-related chord in the increasingly ethereal final moments of the work. Wagner's directions are clear. He indicates, "*Kundry sinkt, mit dem Blicke zu ihm auf, langsam vor Parsifal entseelt zu Boden.*" ("Kundry slowly sinks lifeless — "*entseelt*"— to the ground in front of Parsifal, her eyes uplifted to him." No Isolde-like "she sinks as if transfigured" ambiguity here.) On one level, we see the story of Kundry and Parsifal brought to a completion. Beyond this, the scene depicts the end of Wagner's own long journey, a journey both musical and personal. Referring to Wagner's mother fixation, Gregor-Dellin writes "The son has come of age: no longer in need of redemption, he dispenses it himself. Wagner's own cure is not complete until the close of this final act" (*Richard Wagner* 24). Wagner had spent his artistic career working out conflicts in his own life, in particular, seeking "a cure" for his mother fixation, and in the closing moments of his final work, Wagner resolves, at least artistically, this conflict from his childhood.

Notes

1. See Gutman and Rose, for instance.
2. Gutman has linked elements of *Parsifal*, such as necromancy, to fin-de-siècle traits in general (*Richard Wagner* 438–439).
3. To cite several, Gutman views *Parsifal* as a decidedly anti–Christian work, whereas Beckett suggests it offers a very positive Christian message. Kinderman and Syer also treat the religious side of the work. Schofield has recently stressed elements of Buddhist thought in the opera. In the purely musical realm, Lorenz subjects *Parsifal* to a minute structural analysis in his monumental series of studies on the music dramas.
4. For more information on the genesis of the work, see Newman, Beckett, and Kinderman and Syer.
5. See, for instance, Gregor-Dellin 10 and 17 and Gutman 4–9.
6. Wagner's well-known love of feminine fabrics has been treated with humorous ridicule (Gutman 395) but Gregor-Dellin proposes a different view. "All his security fantasies were centered on the mother whose protection he instinctively sought at crucial moments in his childhood, just as everything suggests that his desire to take refuge in soft, caressing fabrics — in silk, satin, and velvet — should be construed as an unconscious and instinctive urge to reproduce that all-encompassing maternal warmth" (12).
7. Köhler suggests that Mime loathsome character may reflect Wagner's feelings towards his stepfather. Geyer was an actor, and the German word for "*Mime*" means "mime" (363–363).
8. There is, of course, another father/son relationship in the work, that of Titurel and Amfortas, but it falls outside the scope of this essay.
9. All translations of the *Parsifal* libretto are by Lionel Salter.
10. Wagner designated Kundry as a soprano, and although mezzo sopranos do essay the role, they sometimes do so at their own peril. The close of Act II is very demanding on the upper register.
11. This is not the place to engage in a detailed discussion on the suitability of labeling leitmotifs. Although it is true that Wagner rarely assigned an actual name to a motif, he obviously did associate these themes with characters, objects, and ideas, and it is useful to have a convenient method of referring to them. One would hardly ignore the thematic material of a Beethoven symphony. Nevertheless, an overly literal approach to the leitmotifs is a danger. Their significance is not in their mere presence in the opera, but in the ways they embody, depict, and enact the drama musically. Wagner's ability to develop and transform motifs, to combine them and subtly "morph" from one to another, is remarkable. In this essay, I am using the leitmotif names commonly encountered in the English language literature, but I do not claim fidelity to any one study.
12. It had been foreshadowed earlier in the act. When Gurnemanz explains Amfortas's suffering to the esquires, the motif is hinted at in the orchestra. Amfortas himself sings the first half on his way to his bath. Clearly, Wagner wanted to gradually reveal this all-important motif.
13. In different circumstances, this name inversion is reminiscent of Tantris/Tristan from in Act I of *Tristan und Isolde*.
14. As if Wagner's two cries of "*Irre! Irre!*" ("Stray and be lost"), fairly high in the voice, are not enough, some sopranos sing the exclamation up a third, with a climactic high a and b-flat.

Jon Vickers as Parsifal at the Metropolitan Opera (photograph by Winnie Klotz).

15. This passage, with its suggestions of both physical and emotional stirrings, is reminiscent of scenes in earlier operas. There are several such passages between Siegmund and Sieglinde in Act I of *Die Walküre*. A similar approach is found after the drinking of the love potion in the first act of *Tristan*, and Tristan's awakening in Act III.

Bibliography

Beckett, Lucy. *Parsifal*. Cambridge, UK: Cambridge University Press, 1981.

Gregor-Dellin, Martin. *Richard Wagner: His Life, His Work, His Century*. Trans. J. Maxwell Brownjohn. London: Collins, 1983.

Gutman, Robert W. *Richard Wagner: The Man, His Mind, and His Music*. New York: Harcourt Brace Jovanovich, 1968.

Kinderman, William, and Katherine R. Syer, eds. *A Companion to Wagner's "Parsifal."* Rochester, NY: Camden House, 2005.

Köhler, Joachim. *Richard Wagner: The Last of the Titans*. Trans. Stewart Spencer. New Haven, CT: Yale University Press, 2004.

Lorenz, Alfred. *Das Geheimis der Form bei Richard Wagner*, vol. IV. Tutzing: Hans Schneider, 1966.

Millington, Barry. *Wagner*, rev. ed. Princeton, NJ: Princeton University Press, 1992.

_____, ed. *The Wagner Compendium: A Guide to Wagner's Life and Music*. New York: Schirmer, 1992.

Newman, Ernest. *The Wagner Operas*. New York: Knopf, 1949.

Rose, Paul Lawrence. *Wagner: Race and Revolution*. New Haven, CT: Yale University Press, 1992.

Schofield, Paul. *The Redeemer Reborn: "Parsifal" as the Fifth Opera of Wagner's "Ring."* New York: Amadeus, 2007.

Wagner, Richard. *Parsifal*. Trans. Lionel Salter. 1970.

_____. *The Ring of the Nibelung*. Trans. Andrew Porter. New York: W. W. Norton, 1976.

II. Wagnerian Opera and the Other Arts

11

Wagner and Dance: *Tannhäuser* and Beyond

MARY CARGILL

Richard Wagner's travails regarding the 1861 Paris Opéra's production of *Tannhäuser* are certainly the image brought up when the words "Wagner" and "dance" are combined. Certainly the anti–German and pro-ballet girl politics behind the 160 rehearsals and the three performances are endlessly fascinating. The "handful of hooligans" described by Baudelaire (quoted by von Westernhagen 291) have become legendary. But it is harder to find descriptions of what the ballet they hooted was really like, and I have tried to find descriptions or impressions of the 1861 ballet, and some others choreographed by famous or unexpected choreographers. In looking for information about Wagner and dance, I also found that his influence extended far beyond the *Tannhäuser* Bacchanal or the few, mainly undistinguished or overblown, pieces choreographed to his music; Wagner's ideas as well as his music found an enthusiastic audience in a group of young Russian aesthetes, one of whom, Sergei Diaghilev, established the brilliant and monumentally influential Ballets Russes, many of whose ballets were influenced, at least indirectly, by the overarching idea of the *Gesamtkunstwerk*.

Though Wagner certainly was encouraged to add a ballet to the Paris production, the fact that it was in the artistically more suitable first act rather than the more convenient to the Jockey Club second act was not the only reason for the anti–*Tannhäuser* furor. An article by Edward House in the June 1891 *New England Magazine* has a lengthy description of the anti–Wagner atmosphere in Paris during the rehearsals, as remembered by a sympathetic American observer who saw several rehearsals and the first performance. Long before that first performance, House was aware of the hostility. "The Parisians may not cherish long hatreds against individuals, but they are eminently capable of sudden gusts of spite, and of meeting the elaborate and systematic attacks of a censor like Wagner with a sharp guerrilla onslaught of merciless ridicule, more deadly, perhaps, than the more serious process of logical warfare. The name of the innovator was already a byword of derision" (413). Unfortunately for those wanting details of the production, he writes "It is not my purpose to speak too minutely of the performance" (419), but he does give a sense of the atmosphere.

> The adverse element was undoubtedly in force from the beginning. The box habitually retained by the young furies of the Jockey Club, close upon the stage, at the left of the spectators, was

crowded. In the earlier years it had been knows as "*la loge infernale*," and on this evening it proudly sustained the ancient character. The overture was passed by in silence, or at least with so few manifestations of disfavor as to cause no interruption. Before it was finished, the vacant spaces were all occupied, and the assemblage was ready for its work. The curtain rose, and, almost simultaneously with the first notes that followed, the assault began. Before the introductory scene was half through, the uproar had reached such a height that the actors upon the stage and the orchestra in front were alike inaudible except to those who sat nearest the proscenium. There was not even a pretense of waiting to form an opinion [House 425].

It is much harder to determine what exactly the audience saw in the opening scenes. The choreographer was Lucien Petipa, the brother of the more famous Marius, who was then beginning his career in St. Petersburg—*Swan Lake* and *The Sleeping Beauty* were far in the future; Wagner's autobiography refers to him only as Petipas [sic], and there have been some, including the Cambridge University Press edition of *My Life*, who have confused the two. But Lucien Petipa was the ballet master of the Opéra from 1860 to 1868. As a sop to convention, the Opéra had actually scheduled an independent ballet between Acts 1 and 2; entitled *Graziosa*, it had a libretto by one Count Roger de Sainte-Marie, a member of the Jockey Club, and music by a Théodore Labarre, the foster brother of Napoleon III. Wagner's reaction, if he was aware of the plan, is not recorded. In any event, Petipa didn't finish it before the third and last performance of *Tannhäuser*, though when it was performed, the Jockey Club was most appreciative. Gutman describes Wagner's original intentions. Wagner, he wrote,

> thought much in terms of Nordic mythology. As a mob of bacchantes drove in a menagerie of animal monster, the Strömkarl was to emerge from whirling waters (into which maenads would perhaps throw the head of the murdered Orpheus) and accompany the frenzied dancing on his marvelous violin.... Although centaurs, nymphs, fauns, amoretti, the Graces, and the dismembered Orpheus formed a part of the original scheme of the Paris Bacchanal, the Mediterranean element grew steadily stronger and ousted the *Strömkarl* [a Nordic storm god], who had so pleased Wagner in the beginning [he would be back at a later Bayreuth production], and the stage was filled with Nereids, Tritons, and elaborate visions of Europa, Leda and their lover Jupiter in his disguises as bull and swan [Gutman 196–197].

According to Dale Harris "the received opinion is that Petipa's dances for the Venusberg scene were undistinguished, though it would hardly have affected the work's reception if he had delivered himself of an immortal masterpiece. In any case, Petipa cannot be blamed for failing to achieve outstanding results, if such indeed was the case. Not only was his attention divided between the two commissions, but he couldn't begin to work on *Tannhäuser* until the last minute, since Wagner was late in finishing the new ballet sequence" (Harris 11).

Wagner himself had a somewhat different recollection.

> I threw myself enthusiastically into the task of setting up the huge and unconventional dance scenes in the first act, for which I now tried to win the sympathy of the ballet-master Petipas [sic]; what I demanded was unheard-of and departed radically from traditional choreographic practices. I drew attention to the dances of the Maenads and the Bacchantes, but only astounded Petipas [sic] by my assumption that such things, which he well comprehended, could only be done by his little dancing pupils; for, as he revealed to me, by placing my ballet in the first act, I had in effect renounced the services of the main *corps de ballet*.... While I was quite content to be spared the need to have anything to do with the prima ballerinas, I was all the more determined to have the *corps de ballet* itself execute some significant movements. I wanted the male component brought up to a respectable strength, but was told that, apart from a few skinny youths who, for fifty francs a month, hovered uselessly round the edge of the stage during the performances of the solo dancers, nothing could be done [Wagner 629–630].

Since the dancers of the Paris Opéra refused to dance in the first act (they were apparently second act girls) and Petipa "with effort found near the Porte St Martin three Hungarian ladies, known for their fairy pantomimes, who consented to mime the Three Graces.... There seemed no way around the tradition of starched gauze, and the Hungarian Graces were outfitted in pink *tutus*" (Gutman 196). Harris quotes from the most detailed description of the actual choreography, by the critic Pier Angelo Fiorentino which, for all its sarcasm, is quite evocative.

> Twenty-four bacchants walk from right to left and raise their arms above their heads in a slow, gentle movement. Then twenty-four fauns walk from left to right, raising their arms like the bacchants. Sixteen nymphs follow the fauns, raising their arms in the same manner. Then sixteen youths, who were asleep on the rocks, wake up suddenly and raise their arms as though stretching. Finally, twelve cupids, not to be different, raise their little arms in the air, without knowing why. All these raised arms undoubtedly make a charming scene, but it lasts too long. There remain the three Graces — Mlles. Rousseau, Stoïkoff and Troisvallets. One hopes for a moment that they will be excepted from the routine and do what they like with their arms; but one soon sees that they, no less than the fauns, the bacchants, the youths and the nymphs, will not be allowed to lower them, and that they will end by catching cramp. Apparently the dance of the future only permits arms in the air. I admit this simultaneous elevation of all those assembled arms gives an impression of mysticism and devotion [Harris 11].

Another unexpected choreographer got a chance at the bacchanal in 1891 when Cosima Wagner staged the first production of *Tannhäuser* in Bayreuth; she wanted to produce the ballet as she believed her husband would have wanted, "in a way that would be both original and free from balletic convention" (Guest, *Divine Virginia* 147). She invited the famous Italian dramatic ballerina Virginia Zucchi to choreograph the ballet. Zucchi was born in 1849 and studied under various teachers in Italy. She had danced with many companies, but her greatest success came in Russia, where her realistic mime had an enormous impact on the ballet of the time. Cosima felt that the 1861 choreography of Petipa had failed in part because of the old-fashioned approach and she wanted "someone with a broader understanding of movement than a ballet-master in the traditional mould and decided that this quality was most likely to be possessed by an experienced mime" (147).

Zucchi, whose dancing days were winding down, was excited about the prospect, and traveled to Bayreuth in August 1890. Cosima wrote about the meeting to her son-in-law, Houston Chamberlain, describing Zucchi as someone "through whom we came to experience that Italian spontaneity which shines through her constant amiability. Whether she will be equal to the enormous task which is to be given to her I do not know. I do know, however, that this human experience was heartwarming, and that this woman, with her sensitiveness, her simplicity and her perseverance, has enriched our little group" (Pretzsch 183, quoting a letter dated August 1890, translated by Ivor Guest).

Again, detailed descriptions of the dancing are few, but the critic of the *Times of London*, felt that the scenery cramped the dancing, but wrote that though

> the complete realization of the composer's intentions with regard to the Bacchanalian orgy, which plays so important a part in this scene is obviously impossible, it could not be more fully accomplished than was done by the very excellent body of male and female dancers who had been trained for the occasion by Signora Zucchi. Unfortunately the effect was much spoilt by the very clumsy and conventional dresses of the female members of the corps de ballet, in which an unsuccessful attempt had been made to reproduce classical draperies. On the other hand, the representations of the Three Graces [one of whom was Zucchi herself] were excellent, and the tableaux representing the Rape of Europa and Leda and the Swan were extremely beautiful in colour and grouping ["The Bayreuth Festival"].

An anonymous reviewer from the *Chicago Daily* also left an impression of the opening scene of the 1891 production.

> When the well-known overture merged into the bacchanal and the curtains were parted, a scene of magical beauty was revealed. The pictures which stir the imagination on reading Wagner's minute and poetic directions in the text-book were variously presented and the most ravishing dreams realized. The deep blue of the grotto, stretching into indefinite space, the murmuring of waterfalls, the merry feasting and dancing of nymphs and youths, the seductive chorus of sirens, the procession of semi-delirious bacchantes, the lovely pacifying graces, the amorettes shooting their arrows, all combined to form a vision out of the most beautiful elements of Greek mythology ["Tannhäuser the Card"].

According to Frederic Spotts "the opening Venusberg scene was a bit of Victoriana at its frilliest. These settings must have been tremendously admired since they became the international norm for many years" (108).

Zucchi repeated her appearance as a Grace in 1894 and in 1895, at Cosima's insistence, was asked by the Paris Opéra to set her version of the Bacchanal and to appear as one of the Graces for their new production of *Tannhäuser*. The dancers of the Paris Opéra did appear this time, but were apparently still not enthusiastic. Alfred Ernst, in the June 1, 1895, *Revue Encyclopédique* wrote, as quoted by Ivor Guest

> The bacchanal of the first act is much too cold. It was mimed without passion, ardour or excitement by a group that was not large enough and whose routine style Mlle. Zucchi's efforts were unable to overcome. The celebrated Italian dancer tried in vain to obtain the violence, the fury, the frantic gyration of the movement that Wagner's scenario and music demands. At Bayreuth Mlle. Zucchi had been guided by the personality of Frau Wagner that effectively impressed itself on everyone, down to the last important supernumerary [*Divine Virginia* 158].

There is a vivid account of the Paris Bacchanal by Richard O'Monroy in the May 13 issue of *Gil Blas*, which was in all probability very similar to Zucchi's choreography at Bayreuth.

> "Groups of bacchantes invade the stage with head-dresses of vine leaves and tunics trimmed with fur. They are followed by fauns, and soon the dancing takes on a wilder character; the crotales, cymbals and tambourines sound as the bacchantes shake their beribboned thyrses. Then, at a sign from Venus, the cupids nestling in the trees loose their arrows at the dancers. Overcome by a sudden languor, the bacchantes and the fauns retire, and the Graces, portrayed by Mms. Zucchi, Robin and Carré in pink peplum, return hand in hand to announce to Venus that calm has been restored," after which a series of tableaux was seen at the back of the stage. "Europa passes on her bull, and then a swan advances friskily on Leda, who is lying on a bank. She stretches out her arms and — But then a cloud descends from the flies and conceals everything from view. A pity! The old *abonnés* [some of whom may possibly have been part of the Jockey Club cabal of 1861] were preparing themselves for a spectacle reserved for the gods" [Guest, *Divine Virginia* 157–158].

But no matter how daring the choreography was, the dancers still wore pointe shoes. It was only in the 1904 Bayreuth revival of *Tannhäuser* that point shoes were discarded, and that was only one dancer — Isadora Duncan danced one of the Graces. Zucchi had retired from dancing in 1989 and Siegfried Wagner, who had seen Duncan perform in Munich in 1903, suggested her as Zucchi's replacement. Since the choreography otherwise was not changed "this meant an absurd combination of Isadora's dance with that of the regular ballet" (Cameron 281). She also appeared barefoot during the intermissions, which caused a bit of a scandal, but not as large a one as her telling Cosima over dinner at Wahnfried that Wagner's errors were as great as his genius.

Cosima's *Tannhäuser*, with its to our eyes kitchy Victorian Graces, was replaced in 1930 by Siegfried Wagner's starker version. He possibly remembered the more modern effect of the 1904 Duncan and he asked Rudolf von Laban, the Hungarian-born, German-based modern dancer and dance theorist, to choreograph the Venusberg scene. At the time, he was the director of ballet at the Staatsoper in Berlin, but was far from a traditional ballet director; in fact he was feuding with the ballet dancers, and fired many of them, replacing them with modern dancers. He was an influential exponent of *Ausdruckstanz*, the German expressionist dance movement, and he was influenced by a number of different ideas — from Gurdjieff to the Dada movement, to the early twentieth-century enthusiasm for gymnastics. He worked with groups, rather than the more formal hierarchies of the older ballet forms, and, though his early dances were not overtly political, did believe in some sort of mythical Volk, and the ideas of Wagner had been an early inspiration.

> He used the parallel of the warm relationship between the political leadership of the German Empire and Richard Wagner's opera house in Bayreuth, to illustrate how his dance theater followed in the great tradition of German national art. The Master, Richard Wagner, provided the tested model for the future of German dance [Karina 109].

He, and several other German modern dancers, thought that the Hitler regime would support their dreams of regenerative dance, and Laban joined Goebbels Propaganda Ministry in 1934, and put together the Deutsche Tanzfestspiele, whose program read in part "We Germans often are considered coarse and graceless, and yet the vigor of the German temperament and the depth of the German soul often have conquered the world, not only through music and poetry but also through the art of dance" (Manning 175). (Despite his loyalty, Goebbels condemned him in 1936 for a variety of crimes, from Freemasonry to being too intellectual, and he fled to England.)

Laban had choreographed the *Tannhäuser* Bacchanal in Mannheim in 1921; there, according to his autobiography, he retrieved Wagner's earlier sketches that were 'Nordic fantasies, and had nothing to do with the classical Roman dance-poem that Wagner later created expressly for Paris'" (Karina 109–110). He resurrected Wagner's idea of the Strömkarl, and tried to "recreate this Romantic vision in terms of contemporary dance" (Cameron 283). Some writers, including Borchmeyer, actually see a connection between Wagner and *Austruckstanz*, seeing a connection through Heinrich Heine. "It is remarkable that [Wagner's] Venusberg ballet is not only profoundly influenced by the same ideas as those found in Heine's writings, but that [those writings] too inspired leading figures of the *Ausdruckstanz* movement, which saw itself as a radical alternative to traditional ballet. Dance historians have repeatedly stressed that Wagner anticipated many of the new movement's main ideas with his demand — first formulated in *The Artwork of the Future* in 1849 — that dance should be the basis of drama and that, following the classical model, it should be an elemental form of mimed expression diametrically opposed to the aesthetics of classical ballet" (Borchmeyer 142).

His choreography for the Siegfried Wagner production of *Tannhäuser*, with 70 of his modern-trained dancers, was based on his Mannheim concept and was a complete break from the Zucchi/Cosima model. Laban amplified his approach in his autobiography. "There were no Bacchantes or fauns, no images of Leda and Jupiter or any other figures of the Graeco–Roman world of gods. It was a witches-sabbath with Nordic sacrificial rites and with Strömkarl, the demon of music, as the inciter dominating the whole scene ... the passions were not stirred up by beautiful goddesses, but were represented as innate drives" (Laban 172–3).

There is a silent 6 minute film of the Bacchanal made in 1930 at the Dance Collection at Lincoln Center, and it is fascinating to see the nearly naked cavortings of the groups of dancers leaping gymnastically and massively from rock to rock. There is a certain "Me Tarzan" feel to the choreography, but apart from the dancers' unfashionable chunkiness, it looks surprisingly modern. (Had Wagner been able to see them, it might have compensated for the "skinny youths" of the Paris production.) Despite Laban's description, there appear to be three graces in vaguely Grecian style draperies, who appear to calm the restless hordes, and who move with a stately and grounded calm.

The next production of the Bacchanal at Bayreuth was for the 1954 *Tannhäuser*, which was choreographed by Wieland Wagner's wife, Gertrude, a modern dancer who had studied with Maja Lex, one of the many post–Laban German dancers. Her theory of *Elementere Tanz* "drew inspiration from single elements, or themes which were then explored in rhythmical, gestural and expressive movement. Likewise the 1954 Bacchanal abolished all extraneous components from Wagner's scenario.... Within this concept, mythological pictures were rendered obsolete" (Cameron 286). The trend towards abstraction continued in the 1965 production, choreographed by Birgit Cullberg, whose Bacchanal was "interpreted symbolically, rather than in mythological fashion" (289). It is impossible to speculate on Wagner's reaction to the increasingly abstract and gymnastic productions of his Bacchanal, though certainly the contemporary versions have none of the eerie terror that Wagner's original scenario described.

But possibly the most interesting intersection of Wagner and dance has to do with his ideas, which more so than his music, had a long-range, though somewhat indirect, effect on the dance world, through Sergei Diaghilev's Ballets Russes, that basically ad hoc collection of geniuses that Diaghilev managed from 1909 to 1929. It is impossible to overestimate the importance of Diaghilev to twentieth-century ballet; every major company, except ironically the Russian ones, were founded or at one time headed by someone associated with or artistically related to Diaghilev; Serge Lifar in Paris; Ninette de Valois, founder of the Royal Ballet; and George Balanchine of the New York City Ballet are just a few of his progeny.

The incredible story of the Ballet Russes has been well-documented — the hand-to-mouth existence, the feuds, the triumphs, the basically impromptu artistic decisions. But long before the Ballets Russes began its incredible journey, there was a salon of young, artistically omnivorous Russian intellectuals who were enthralled by Wagner's music and ideas. Alexandre Benois, one of the leaders of the artistic group, first saw Wagner's *Ring* in a German production which was performed in St. Petersburg in 1889. His autobiography recalls

> I cannot however remain silent about Neumann's enterprise of bringing the *Ring of the Nibelungs* to St. Petersburg in March of 1889, because these performances played a decisive part in developing and educating my taste in music. I was already acquainted with Wagner's text and, as soon as the *Ring* was announced, I became deeply interested in the dramatic side of the production.... It seemed to me, under the spell of the musical sounds, that I had become regenerated and had gained an entirely new perspective and understanding in life.... In those years we were all (actually we had just become) Wagnerians. We demanded from operatic music neither arias, fiorituri nor virtuosity, but moods, imagery, dramatic effects, and a close relationship between music and action [112–113].

The friends became known as the World of Art (*mir iskusstva*) group, and were joined by Sergei Diaghilev, the provincial cousin of one of the members, who had moved to St. Petersburg ostensibly to study law. Diaghilev also knew and loved Wagner's music; he and his cousin had traveled to Europe in 1890, where they saw *Lohengrin* in Vienna, and he visited Bayreuth regularly. Wagner's music remained important to Diaghilev, and Boris Kochno, Diaghilev's long-time secretary, shared his memories with Richard Buckle, who was writing a biography of Diaghilev. Buckle quotes from his letter: "During our last stay in Monte Carlo D[iaghilev] took me several times to hear *Parsifal*.... On the eve of his death in Venice, D. spoke to me again of Wagner's genius" (*Diaghilev* 334).

It wasn't the music alone, though, that inspired the group. It was the approach to art itself. As Rosamund Bartlett writes, the *mir iskusstva* group "in their determined anti-realist stance, in their interest in individual and inner experience, and in their refusal to sub-divide the 'work of art' into its constituent parts, embodied much that was characteristic of the artistic aspirations of late nineteenth-century and early twentieth-century European culture ... all these factors made it inevitable that Wagner would prove to be an attractive figure to them.... Wagner was of towering importance to both Diaghilev and Alexandre Benois" (66). And Boult adds, in "the quest for artistic synthecism undertaken by so many of the World of Art painters and writers was particularly evident from their discovery and support of Wagner and the operatic drama" (77). And later "the primary reason why Diaghilev, Benois, and their colleagues shared a passion for Wagner was because, for them, he had been the first artist in modern times to integrate the disparate art forms into that grand *Gesamtkunstwerk* of which they all dreamed (192).

In 1898 Diaghilev founded the journal *Mir Iskusstva* (which he, along with Benois, edited until 1904), a journal devoted to the world of art, as understood by their group; there were many articles on various new, old, and emerging artists, as well as discussions of various wide-ranging artistic trends, including Wagnerian operas and artistic opinions. Diaghilev himself wrote a long review in 1899 on the first Russian production of *Tristan und Isolde*, which "showed how knowledgeable he already was about Wagner throughout Europe" (Buckle, *Diaghilev* 53). In that same year, the journal published a Russian translation of extracts from Henri Lichtenberger's literary and philosophical study of Wagner's music and ideas. "This was the first time in Russia that an article about Wagner appeared in a non-musical journal as part of a particular artistic credo, and *Mir Iskusstva* continued to publish other materials concerning Wagner until its closing. With the emergence of the 'World of Art' movement, then, it can be said that Russian Wagnerism had truly begun" (67).

Diaghilev was profoundly influenced by Wagner's idea of the unity of arts and when he, almost accidentally, put together his pick-up group of dancers to go to Paris in 1909 (he had originally wanted to present both opera and ballet, with ballet playing second fiddle), he worked with a group of musicians, designers, and choreographers to create works emphasizing atmosphere, mood, and drama over the purely technical tricks. As he wrote later

> The more I thought of that problem of the composition of ballet, the more plainly I understood that perfect ballet can only be created by the very closest fusion of three elements — dancing, painting and music. When I mount a ballet, I always keep these three elements in mind. That is why almost daily I go into the artists' studios, watch their work and the actual execution of the costumes, examine the scores and listen to the orchestra with close attention, and then visit the practice rooms where all the dancers practice and rehearse daily [Sorell 163–164].

The first collaborative ballet presented by the Ballets Russes, *Le Pavillon d'Armide*, "was a true collaboration between the choreographer [Michel Fokine], the composer (Tcherepnine) and the designer (Benois), and this notion too was a complete novelty: it was also the first appearance of the balletic aesthetic that was to dominate all Diaghilev's work for the stage—the Wagnerian idea of the *Gesamtkunstwerk*" (Shead 22).

This is a long way from the hooligans of the Jockey Club, or even from the often less-then-successful Bacchanals of *Tannhäuser*. But Wagner and dance have a distinguished and honorable relationship.

Robert Lloyd as Guernamanz, left, Placido Domingo as Parsifal, and Jessye Norman as Kundry in the Otto Schenk production of *Parsifal* at the Metropolitan Opera (photograph by Winnie Klotz).

Bibliography

Bartlett, Rosamund. *Wagner in Russia*. Cambridge Studies in Russian Literature. Cambridge, UK: Cambridge University Press, 1995.
"Bayreuth Festival." *Times* 29 July 1891: 3.
Benois, Alexandre. *Reminiscences of the Russian Ballet*. London: Putnam, 1945.
Borchmeyer, Dieter. *Drama and the World of Richard Wagner*. Princeton, NJ: Princeton University Press, 2003.
Bowlt, John E. *The Silver Age: Russian Art of the Early Twentieth Century and the "World of Art" Group*. ORP Studies in Russian Art History. Newtonville, MA: Oriental Research Partners, 1982.
Buckle, Richard. *Diaghilev*. New York: Atheneum, 1979.
_____. *In the Wake of Diaghilev*. New York: Holt, Rinehart and Winston, 1982.
Cameron, Theresa. "The Tannhäuser Bacchanale in Bayreuth: Realizations of Wagner's Vision through Qualities of Ausdruckstanz." In *Austruckstanz*. Ed. Gunhild Oberzaucher-Schüller. Wilhelmshaven: F. Noetzel, 1992.
Carnegy, Patrick. *Wagner and the Art of the Theatre*. New Haven, CT: Yale University Press, 2006.
Garafola, Lynn. *Diaghilev's Ballets Russes*. New York: Oxford University Press, 1989.
Guest, Ivor. *The Ballet of the Second Empire*. London: Pitman, 1974.
_____. *The Divine Virginia: A Biography of Virginia Zucchi*. New York: Marcel Dekker, 1977.
Gutman, Robert W. *Richard Wagner: The Man, His Mind and His Music*. New York: Harcourt Brace Jovanovich, 1990.
Harris, Dale. "Against the Rules." *Opera News* 15 April 1992: 8–11.
House, Edward H. "Wagner and Tannhäuser in Paris, 1861." *The New England Magazine* n.s. 4 (June 1891): 411–427.
Karina, Lilian. *Hitler's Dancers: German Modern Dance and the Third Reich*. New York: Berghahn, 2003.
Kennedy, Janet. *The "Mir Iskusstva" Group and Russian Art, 1898–1912*. New York: Columbia University, 1976.
Laban, Rudolf von. *A Life for Dance: Reminiscences*. London: Macdonald & Evans, 1975.
Manning, Susan. *Ecstasy and the Demon: Feminism and Nationalism in the Dances of Mary Wigman*. Berkeley: University of California Press, 1993.
Pretzsch, Paul, ed. *Cosima Wagner und Houston S. Chamberlain im Briefwechsel*. Leipzig: P. Reclam, 1934.
Shead, Richard. *Ballets Russes*. Secaucus, NJ: Wellfleet, 1989.
Sorrel, Walter. *The Dance Through the Ages*. New York: Grosset & Dunlap, 1967.
Spotts, Frederic. *Bayreuth: A History of the Wagner Festival*. New Haven, CT: Yale University Press, 1994.
"Tannhäuser The Card." *Chicago Daily* 23 July 1891: 1.
Wagner, Richard. *My Life*. Cambridge, UK: Cambridge University Press, 1983.
Westernhagen, Curt von. *Wagner: a Biography. Volume 1, 1813–64*. Cambridge, UK: Cambridge University Press, 1978.

12

"The Dream Organ": Wagner as a Proto-Filmmaker

Hilan Warshaw

When Richard Wagner died in February 1883, the cinematographic pioneer Eadweard Muybridge was in the midst of an American lecture tour, presenting screenings of moving images to enthusiastic acclaim.[1] The previous year in France, Étienne-Jules Marey had invented an important predecessor of the film camera, and the Lumière family founded their photographic company.[2]

That Wagner's lifetime overlapped with the birth of cinema is a telling fact. In many ways, Wagner's art is profoundly analogous to the art of film, and his work was to exert a deep influence on the new medium as it developed. One might argue, in fact, that Wagner is best understood as a proto-filmmaker: a Romantic artist whose ideal art was an intricate fusion of musical, dramatic, and visual information, capable of communicating a narrative with enormous visceral power. The first part of this essay draws on Wagner's music dramas and theoretical writings to gain perspective on his proto-cinematic qualities — or the fact that, as Wolfgang Wagner once put it, his grandfather would want to work in Hollywood if he were alive.[3] This discussion relates not only to specific techniques in Wagner's craft, but to ideological themes in his work that underscore his broader context in Romantic art and philosophy.

The second part addresses the historical impact of Wagner on the film industry, particularly in Germany and in America — where Wagnerian traditions were an artistic bequest of the composers, writers, and filmmakers who fled the Nazis and settled in Hollywood. Through this cultural transference, Wagner's art attained a new kind of influence — one with important implications for both his legacy and the powerful medium that fulfills many of his ideals.

"Co-creative sympathy"

The most obvious parallel between Wagner's work and film is the sheer force with which Wagner hoped to impact his audience. From the electrifying orchestral gale that opens his first mature opera, *The Flying Dutchman,* we are placed on alert that this is a theater that means to surround us on all sides — to fling us into the heart of the action. Wagner's operatic innovations — the elimination of discrete musical "numbers" and applause, the bypassing of conventional pleasures such as ballet, the length of his works — were all developed with an eye towards keeping the audience absorbed in the darkly dramatic world onstage. The effect is furthered through the use of musical motifs, through which the characters' thoughts and responses become perceptible to us. In such ways, we become deeply involved in the protagonists' struggles and invested in seeing the story through to its conclusion. Wagner writes in his book-length essay *Opera and Drama*:

> Such a presentiment as this has the poet to wake within us, *in order, through its longing, to make us necessary sharers in the creation of his artwork*.[4] [The emphasis is Wagner's.]

He uses similar language in explaining a use of motifs in *Lohengrin*:

> The poet wishes ... to attune our feeling that we ourselves may frame the necessity of a further, an altered development of the situation, through our co-creative sympathy.[5]

"Co-creative sympathy": it is difficult to summon a better phrase for the effect of watching a well-made film. Through its ability to play on the audience's sensory instincts, film has powerful tools to make spectators instinctively identify with the characters onscreen. In film, not only can we see a character in dire dramatic straits, as we can see onstage; through subjective camerawork, we can see *what the character sees*. Editing, music, acting and visual design work together to convey the character's inner responses, until those responses become ours as well. Film thus provides a vivid realization of the effect that Richard Wagner worked to achieve.

Wagner's concern for audience engagement is equally reflected in the theater he designed at Bayreuth. Here was a chamber for total immersion. The hall's décor is radically sparse by the standards of opera theaters of the time; the seating is designed to detract attention from the spectacle of other patrons; the house lights were dimmed during the performance, a first for opera; the orchestra is kept hidden, leaving spectators to concentrate on the single luminous image of the stage. The similarities with the interior of a movie theater have often been pointed out. Indeed, in explaining the design, Wagner made an explicit reference to early projection technologies such as Eadweard Muybridge's:

> With a dramatic representation ... it is a matter of focusing the eye itself upon a picture; and that can be done only by leading it away from any sight of bodies lying in between, such as is done with a technical apparatus for projecting a picture.[6]

If Wagner's creative priorities and modes of presentation have obvious similarities with those of film, I would argue that a more specific parallel exists in his music. For that, we will turn to his music dramas themselves, and the extraordinary manner in which they were composed.

Inspirations and Montages

Wagner always emphasized that his music did not stem from "absolute" inspirations, as they might for a composer who worked with customarily abstract forms such as the symphony or sonata. For Wagner, music emerged to address the needs of specific dramatic inspirations. Quite unusual for a composer of his stature, he had no serious musical education until his mid-teens, when he sought out lessons with the express intention of becoming an opera composer. According to his account, what prompted him to it was his love of theater; the experience of writing youthful plays convinced him that music was necessary in order to reach the heightened effect that he desired. Speaking of a drama he wrote at fifteen, he recalled, "I'm no composer. I wanted to learn only enough to set *Leubald and Adelaide* to music."[7] The remark was tongue-in-cheek, but its point is borne out by his artistic career.

Accordingly, the musical materials in Wagner's operas were intimately connected with the contents of the story being dramatized. The antecedents for his musical ideas could be dramatic characters or concepts; hence the well-known technique that Hans von Wolzogen dubbed "*leitmotif.*" Just as often, though, the cell of inspiration could be a purely visual moment. Witness Wagner's guidelines on the performance of *The Flying Dutchman*, in which he directs the actors, and explicates his score, with extraordinary precision:

> During the deep trumpet notes (B-minor) at quite the close of the introductory scene, [the Dutchman] has come off board ... his rolling gait, proper to seafolk on first treading dry land after a long voyage, is accompanied by a wavelike figure for violins and "tenors" ... his third and fourth steps coincide with the notes of the eighth and tenth bars.[8]

He discusses a later scene in a similar vein:

> Throughout the lengthy first fermata [the Dutchman] stays motionless beside the door; at the commencement of the drum solo he slowly strides towards the front ... The two bars *accelerando* for the strings relate to the gestures of Daland, who still stands wonderingly in the doorway awaiting Senta's welcome.... The recurrence of the figure for the strings relates to the emphatic repetition of Daland's gesture.[9]

This fascinating document reveals a composer who approached a dramatic scene in utterly specific and moment-to-moment ways — whose scores are woven together from responses to the individual images and situations in a dramatic narrative. It is evident here why the mature Wagner decided to reject the dominant tendencies of French and Italian opera, in which arias were largely composed within standard operatic structures — ternary or couplet song forms that closely resembled their counterparts in other operas. Such methods were incomprehensible to Wagner; he was dealing with the bricks before he dealt with the final architecture. It was the stimuli in the stories themselves that mandated musical structure. Wagner's music was imitative of content, not of form.

Another way of saying this is that Wagner was, in essence, working as a film composer. The specificity and brevity of the moments that he delineated with his score in *The Flying Dutchman* strongly resemble shots — the basic building-blocks of cinematic storytelling, the visual fragments which are filmed and edited together to depict a scene. Here, Wagner's compositional skills are roused to action in order to evoke adequately each successive image — each step in the shot-sequence that he himself devised, as the author of the libretto. He is not only dramatically inspired by the pathos of a scene; he is viscerally responding to its *fragments*.

This radical aspect of Wagner's work directly presages one of the basic elements of film technique: montage. In the early days of film, narrative films often resembled stage productions filmed from the back of the theater; entire scenes took place within one lengthy shot, filmed with a stationary camera. With montage — whose most enthusiastic pioneers were Sergei Eisenstein and other early Soviet filmmakers — film craft evolved onto an entirely different plane. Sequences were now edited together from numerous shots, intricately planned out to maximize the story's dramatic, psychological, and intellectual impact. The transition into visual fragmentation was the defining leap that allowed cinema to tell stories in ways that it, as opposed to any other medium, could fully utilize. This same logic is evident in the way that Wagner approached dramatic composition.

When the continuum between Wagner and film is discussed, commentators often mention the operas' epic settings and fantastical action, which can be virtually impossible to render realistically onstage. On the level of technique, however, Wagner's kinship with film lies not in cinema's potential for visual grandeur, but conversely in the small-scale intimacy with which shots and editing communicate a scene in specific fragments, whether the setting is a mythic landscape or a simple room. In *The Art-Work of the Future*, he expresses how his need to communicate specific images in music led to his dissatisfaction with "absolute music":

> Absolute Music ... can never, of her own unaided powers, bring the physical and ethical man to distinct and plainly recognizable presentment. Even in her most infinite enhancement, she still is but *emotion* ... she can set moods and feelings side by side, but not evolve one mood from another by any dictate of her own necessity.[10]

But if the non-specificity of abstract music seems frustrating and arbitrary to Wagner, the orchestral tone poems of Mendelssohn and Berlioz — who depicted dramatic scenarios in sound — are equally unfulfilling:

> Not only can [orchestral music] be heightened beyond all measure, but its expression [can] be at the same time rid of its chillingness, if the tone painter may but address himself again to feeling, in place of fantasy. This opportunity is offered him when the subject of his mere describings to thought is revealed in actual presence to the senses.[11]

In other words, Wagner could never be satisfied with writing pieces such as Berlioz' *Symphonie Fantastique* because he needs to depict *visually* the specific images that give rise to musical ideas and gestures. In the latter passage, Wagner explains why he writes for the opera house; however, visual presentations there consist of lengthy, full-stage *tableaux*. Given how Wagner longed to visualize the antecedents of his musical inspirations, it is easy to imagine how he might have relished the film camera, which would have allowed him to present every individual stimulus and character, edited together in symphonic montage.

Wagner not only emerges as the prototype of a filmmaker, but of a highly sophisticated one — who uses his tools in psychologically complex ways, and understands that the relationship between sight and sound can be dialectical as well as correlative. An example of this can be found in Act II of *Lohengrin*, in which Friedrich and his wife, the scheming Ortrud, are reacting to the defeat of their plans by the mysterious Lohengrin. The two characters' words are scored quite differently. Friedrich's speeches are accompanied by anguished string *tremolos*, building to frequent rhetorical climaxes. The accompaniment for Ortrud is much more opaque, consisting largely of eerie harmonies sustained in the woodwind section. At first, the distinction between the two characters' "underscore" is watertight. As the scene becomes a confrontation, however, elements of her orchestral language seep into his own accompaniment, as though he is struggling with his awareness of her influence on him. Ultimately, when she wins back his allegiance with a plot to destroy Lohengrin ("The revelers are now fast asleep..." [measure 261]), her accompaniment, and the motif associated with her scheming, dominate the orchestral narrative.[12] When Friedrich speaks ("Then Elsa must be persuaded!" [measure 296]),[13] he is accompanied by *her* musical material. Our eyes see Friedrich speaking, but the score tells us that he has lost control of his tonality; he is following her drift. The audio-visual storytelling here is subtler than in the scene from *Flying Dutchman*, in which visual fragments prompt direct musical parallels. Here, one character is speaking, but Wagner's camera lingers on the other one.

And if Wagner was masterful at using music to heighten dramatic action, he knew when to work in quieter ways. He writes in *Opera and Drama*:

> Where gesture lapses into rest, and the melodic discourse of the actor hushes ... unspoken moods [may] be spoken by the orchestra in such a way that their utterance shall bear the character of a *foreboding* necessitated by the poet's aim.... What is offered our eye by a scene of nature or a still and silent human figure ... this same thing Music can present to our emotions in such a way that, starting from the "moment" of repose, she moves them to a state of strained expectancy.[14]

We have only to think of an early sequence from the film *Vertigo* (1958) — in which James Stewart's detective trails the mysterious Kim Novak through San Francisco for 14 nearly dialogue-free minutes, with nothing but mysterious events, Bernard Herrmann's music, and Stewart's haunted face to move us forward — to know precisely what Wagner is speaking about.

Wagner was pivotal to the development of modern music; the chromaticism and intensity of his scores made him an important influence for composers as diverse as Mahler, Schoenberg, and Bartók. Yet his musical innovations were often spurred by non-musical priorities. His uniquely fragmented dramatic approach — his inner cinema — helped make his scores furiously complex, teeming with brief musical cells that battle and combine as the drama soars towards its conclusion. His belief in heightened dramatic speech led him to compose vocal lines that bore little relation to melodic convention. His mindset as a man of the theater led him to be an adventurous orchestrator; committed to creating the most vivid effects for his dramas, Wagner mixed instrumental colors with extraordinary freedom. Wagner was the first to emphasize that these developments stemmed from dramatic concerns as opposed to musical ones, for there was nothing he loathed more in music than "effects without causes." Yet this same commitment to essentially non-musical priorities made him a highly important figure in purely musical terms. We can truly say that Wagner was a dramatist first and a composer second — although only if "second" refers to chronological sequence and not caliber. Music came for Richard Wagner from every gesture, thought, and vision in his operas — raising his words and ideas to the level of genius, and his work into the realm of proto-cinema.

The Dream Organ

If visual responses play an important role in Wagner's musical craft, it is striking how often they are at the center of his plots as well. On numerous occasions, his stories turn on a character's being transfixed at the sight of something or someone. Senta gazes spellbound at the portrait of the Dutchman; the revelation of the Grail leaves Parsifal wonder-struck; Lohengrin's gallant first appearance inspires the allegiance of an entire community. Love pairs such as Senta and the Dutchman, Elsa and Lohengrin, and Siegmund and Sieglinde feel an overwhelming sense of recognition when they first see each other. In all these dramatic moments, characters encounter powerful forces that alter their lives and turn them towards a higher purpose. They are, essentially, conversion experiences, and the primary impact is a visual one.

This reflects the deep seriousness with which Wagner, and other Romantic artists, approached sensory responses. For many Romantics, being moved by visual or aural phenomena was positive proof that the recipient had accessed a larger truth. Just as the beauty of nature, in Wordsworth's *The Prelude*, contains signals from "unknown modes of being";[15] just as, in Coleridge's "Rime of the Ancient Mariner," the Mariner's experience of the watersnakes' beauty begins his redemption and resurrects his victim; so Wagner's protagonists undergo their most profound spiritual transitions using their senses alone. There is no need for further questions. Lohengrin tells Elsa:

> Such is the magic that bound me to you
> since I first saw you, sweet one;
> I did not need to find out your origins,
> my eye saw you — and my heart understood you.[16]

Indeed, *Lohengrin* is largely about the mistaken judgment of Elsa, a character who refuses to share her compatriots' absolute faith in Lohengrin — faith that, in light of the near-total lack of information about him, comes down to an intense and favorable sensory response. Elsa allows herself to cling to the nagging questions of the rational mind, and the opera depicts this as tragic foolishness.

The Romantic faith in beauty is reflected in the aesthetic theory of Friedrich Schiller, whose philosophy Wagner considered a precursor to his own.[17] In "The Use of Chorus in Tragedy," Schiller uses the subject of the Greek chorus to inveigh against naturalism in theater, saying that writers should not feel obligated to present the world as they experience it everyday, and that "the artist can use no single element taken from reality as he finds it." If the resulting artwork is highly stylized, however, that does not mean that it is in any way unrealistic. Rather, for Schiller it is *hyper*-realistic, a reflection of the deepest truths in nature. What the artist has done is to "grasp the spirit of the All, and bind it in a corporeal form." The truths which are invisible to the eye are visible to the imagination; "it is thus that [art] becomes more true than all reality, and more real than all experience."[18]

In a sense, such idealizations reflect a central dilemma of the Romantics, which would persist long after Schiller. On one hand, they increasingly celebrated imagination, subjectivity, and sensory experience. On the other hand, they still felt the zeal of the Enlightenment for universal laws and higher truths. The way they reconciled these opposites was to interpret a sensory experience *as* a higher truth; the reason that aesthetic responses were so powerful was that they were reflections of a larger spiritual phenomenon. In this way, the Romantics regarded art with an essentially theological reverence, while remaining largely unable to celebrate it on its own terms. Enchantment had to *mean* something; they could not yet imagine sensations that were not signifiers.

This reasoning figures prominently with Wagner as well. In his theoretical writings, it is not sufficient for him to describe his works as the result of his own sensibility and craft; rather, they are the reflection of an organic human unity that has been buried by modernity. (Because of his nationalism, it is often described as a specifically German unity.) For Wagner, if audiences are transported by the power of his *Gesamtkunstwerke*, it is not because they are works of theatrical genius. It is because the spectators instinctively recognize the work of a national muse, a poet singing of and from the *Volk*. When Wagner used words such as "shared presentiment" and "instinctive sympathy" to describe audience response, he was using them in deadly political earnest.

These universalist tendencies of Romantic philosophy have not held up well to modern scrutiny. In practice, however, they help to explain the intense importance of visual responses in Wagner's work. Perhaps more than any other Romantic artist, Wagner embodies his generation's cult of sensory experience; because of the many tools that he has for communicating to our eyes and ears, Wagner is not only able to describe an experience of wonder, but to truly *present* one. Intense sensory response is both the substance and form of much of Wagnerian narrative. This, again, gives Wagner's approach a direct kinship with that of film, which makes use of sensory responses like no art form before it.[19]

In his late essay *Beethoven*, Wagner draws on the ideas of the philosopher Schopenhauer — whom he had long since adopted as his spiritual guide — to theorize about the origins of human musicality. He settles on Schopenhauer's theory of dreams, which the philosopher interpreted as a kind of revelatory light-show, transmitting images that elucidated the true nature of things. Wagner writes:

> As dreams must have brought to everyone's experience, beside the world envisaged by the functions of the waking brain there dwells a second ... and this form of the brain's perception Schopenhauer calls the dream organ.[20]

The visions of the dream organ strip away the veneer of appearances to reveal the truth — and the results are often frightening. According to Wagner, it is to these visions that music, indirectly, owes its existence:

> From the most terrifying of such dreams we wake with a scream, the immediate expression of the anguished will, which thus makes a definite entrance into the sound world.[21]

Wagner explains that this scream, presented in developed form by a composer, is the root of musical art, and audiences everywhere instinctively understand its emotional import. Musical expressions convey the deepest content of the composer's "will," which was first communicated in visual messages by the dream organ.

In this essay, Wagner describes music as a universal language, derived from the most essential truths in the human soul. What is striking is that Wagner chooses to describe music's origins not only in spiritual terms, but *visual* ones — the "dream organ" that projects overwhelming truths in the composer's subconscious. Scholars point to this essay as evidence of Wagner's shift from his earlier view of music as an obedient vassal of the libretto, to a greater reverence for music on its own terms. But in this essay, if music transcends the need for words, it still does not quite transcend the need for *sight*. The reason that we instinctively cherish music, according to Wagner, is that the visions of the dream organ itself are unavailable to us. In their absence, music is the best possible record of them.

We can only remark at how Wagner might have greeted the technological ability to record the "dream organ," in a sequence of paced images that re-ordered reality in the logic he intended. If this were to happen — if we as spectators were to share Wagner's dreams — then the music we hear would seem to flow from our own perceptions: the "co-creative sympathy" that was Wagner's highest ideal.

Myth and Nature

As an artist and a thinker, Wagner is relevant to film's physical craft: its techniques, its impact, its relationship with music. However, he also had a literary influence on film that persists, particularly in Hollywood: his treatment of myth. The influence stems in part from the impact on filmmakers of Wagner's narratives themselves, and of various works of epic literature that were influenced by Wagner. (J.R.R. Tolkien's The *Lord of the Rings* books are one obvious example.) It is also partly due to the prominence with which Wagner is discussed in the works of the mythologist Joseph Campbell. With the phenomenal success of the *Star Wars* trilogy, which was heavily influenced by Campbell, Hollywood became highly interested in Campbell's ideas. More recently, Christopher Vogler converted Campbell's work into a guide for screenwriters, *The Writer's Journey: Mythic Structure for Writers*, which has become something of a standard text in Hollywood. Vogler's chapter titles include "Return (Seizing the Sword)" and "Return with the Elixir."[22]

For Wagner the Romantic nationalist, stories from folk myth were the ultimate reflection of the natural human society that had been effaced by commerce, technology, and individual egoism. Many of Wagner's works express his yearning to restore this natural bond: in the *Ring* cycle it inspires an explicit historical parable, in *Tristan und Isolde* it becomes the desire to transcend reality and join in a cosmic unity. Such Romantic attitudes are highly apparent in the films that owe the most to epic myth: science-fiction and fantasy films, which tend to express suspicion of technology and longing for a natural community (even as the films, with their visually spectacular effects, are highly technological). Thematically speaking, *The Matrix* could be *Tristan und Isolde* with action sequences.

We will now consider the history of Wagner's influence on Hollywood more closely. It is ironic that, in large part, this influence was indirectly caused by the same development that indicts Wagner in many people's minds: the Nazis' insane attempt to create a Wagnerian political utopia.

From Bayreuth to Hollywood

It is unsurprising that Wagner should have figured prominently in the early German film industry. Ennio Simeon tallies nine short film versions of *Lohengrin* and seven *Tannhäusers* between 1907 and 1919 in Germany, in addition to adaptations of the other operas and the biographical *Richard Wagner* in 1913.[23] The impact of Wagner's brooding Romanticism on the cinema of Weimar Germany can be felt from the popular "mountain films" of Arnold Fanck to Expressionist horror films such as *Nosferatu* (1922). Wagner had long since become a German national obsession, whose works had entered the popular consciousness in countless ways; he was also more deeply associated with the search for a "total artwork" than any other canonical artist. As such, he was an unavoidable part of the world in which early German filmmakers worked. Many of those artists would flee to Hollywood with the rise of the Nazis, and their cultural legacies — such as Wagnerian opera and German Expressionism — would alter Hollywood filmmaking.

Even before the Europeans arrived, the American film world drew heavily on Wagner — or at least on his name. In the silent period, film periodicals published simplified versions of Wagner's method for the benefit of the theater pianists who provided live musical accompaniment; it was accepted as a given that Wagner was the chief musical influence. In 1911, W. Stephen Bush declared in *Motion Picture World*: "Every man or woman in charge of the music of a moving picture theatre is, consciously or unconsciously, a disciple of Richard Wagner."[24] What Wagner himself would have thought about some of these practices is, of course, debatable. Explaining his use of "*leitmotifs*," one pianist said, "I attach a certain theme to each person in the picture and work them out, in whatever form the occasion may call for, not forgetting to use popular strains if necessary."[25] In *The Classical Hollywood Cinema*, David Bordwell mentions a "motivic" moment from the 1928 sound film *The Wedding March*, which helpfully accompanied shots of the Danube with "The Blue Danube."[26]

With the rise of the Nazis, thousands of European writers, musicians and filmmakers settled in Los Angeles, attracted in large part by the promise of work in the film industry. Among their ranks were a staggering number of the twentieth century's most distinguished creators: Thomas and Heinrich Mann, Bertolt Brecht, Arnold Schoenberg, Ernst Toch, Fritz Lang, and many others. Many of them were gainfully employed by Hollywood; others, such as Brecht, worked fitfully but were unable to find their place in the system. Only the most well-established figures, such as Thomas Mann, could afford to stand entirely aside from the employment possibilities of film.

With this remarkable influx of refugees, film scoring and other aspects of film craft achieved a level of sophistication and intensity that was unprecedented in Hollywood. The most successful European film composers — Erich Wolfgang Korngold, Max Steiner, and Miklós Rósza among others — all openly acknowledged Wagner's influence, with Korngold, a prominent composer of through-composed operas, calling film "a textless opera."[27] In richly imagistic scores such as *The Adventures of Robin Hood* (1938) and *Deception* (1946), Korngold used Wagnerian techniques such as *leitmotifs* and *unendliche Melodie* [endless melody] to give a film tremendous sweep and unity. Asked for his advice to film composers, Samuel Goldwyn said simply, "Write music like Wagner, only louder."[28]

Scott D. Paulin argues that this reflexive citing of Wagner's legacy was partly a reflection of the film industry's desire to market its products as unified artworks, blessed with the imprimatur of European high culture. His point is compelling. But absent from his article is an examination of Wagner's operas themselves, and their parallels with the scores of the European Hollywood composers. Those parallels are real, and they utterly changed the way that American films were produced and watched.[29]

One European filmmaker who had a particularly profound Wagnerian encounter during the war — and who also found himself in Los Angeles — was Sergei Eisenstein, the preeminent Russian director and theorist of montage. Eisenstein was invited to stage *Die Walküre* at the Bolshoi Theater in 1940, and he employed cinematically inspired techniques, including fluidly moving scenery and a flashback pantomime, to picture Wagner's scenario as fully as possible. His work on the opera deeply influenced his thinking about the interaction of sound and picture in a film. While staging the opera, he wrote the *Vertical Montage* essays, in which he crystallized his thoughts about the function of music in film — both in retrospect, with regard to his film *Alexander Nevsky* (1938), and in preparation for filming *Ivan the Terrible* (1944–1946). He also discussed his work on *Die Walküre* in his essay "The Embodiment of Myth."[30]

In Germany, of course, the Nazis cloaked themselves in Wagner's cultural legacy, nationalism, and vicious anti–Semitism. The films of Leni Riefenstahl invite parallels with Wagner's operas in their epic feeling and immersive craft.[31] In at least one respect, Riefenstahl's films can seem profoundly un–Wagnerian: their near-total lack of dramatic conflict. In his operas, Wagner's characters struggle towards redemption or cataclysm; Riefenstahl's propaganda films argue that the political redemption has already happened, and the sheer amount of time that she spends on beaming faces and rapturous crowds in *The Triumph of the Will* (1935), her celebration of the 1934 Nazi Party Congress in Nuremberg, gives the film an oddly sterile tone. On the other hand, much of Riefenstahl's imagery recalls Wagner's political yearnings.

Hitler first appears in *The Triumph of the Will* in the form of an airborne plane that soars through the clouds towards Nuremberg, accompanied by Herbert Windt's Wagnerian score. Once Hitler emerges from the plane, his motorcade is greeted by boundlessly enthusiastic crowds as well as enraptured children, statues representing German folk archetypes, and even a curiously peering cat, all of whom appear to turn and greet him as he passes. After nearly eight minutes of this procession, he finally comes out on a balcony to greet his ecstatic followers face-to-face.

It is easy to recall another instance in German art in which a man making his entrance is instantly recognizable as a transcendent leader.

> *[The First Chorus] are the first to see Lohengrin arrive, as he comes into sight in the distance on the river in a skiff drawn by a swan.*

MEN

Look! Look! A mysterious wonder!
What? A swan?
A swan pulling a boat towards the shore!
A knight is there, he's standing in the boat!
His armor's glittering! My eyes are dazzled
by the light! Look! He is almost here! ...
A wonder! A wonder! A miracle has happened,
an overwhelming, strange, unheard-of wonder!

WOMEN

(sinking to their knees)
Thank you, Lord and God,
for protecting this woman!
All eyes are now turned expectantly upstage.

MEN AND WOMEN

We greet you, hero sent by God!

By now the swan-drawn skiff has reached the shore upstage center; in it stands Lohengrin in gleaming silver armor, helmet on head, a shield at his back and a small golden horn at his side; he is leaning on his sword.... All bare their heads in profound emotion. At this point Elsa turns round and cries out aloud on seeing Lohengrin. As Lohengrin makes a move to step out of the skiff, the most intense silence descends over the scene.[32]

In this scene—the first time the community has laid eyes on Lohengrin—emblems of sound and sight inform them, and us, that he is a peerless hero, using little else but our faith that aesthetic beauty does not lie. The visual *leitmotifs* surrounding Hitler's entrance in *Triumph of the Will* have precisely the same effect. The Romantics' universalist approach to the senses has returned, converted into political logic. The same can be said for the Nazi public sphere at large. The billowing, omnipresent flags; the armbands; the yellow badges worn by the Nazis' chosen victims—these visual signs created a total environment that reminded Germans of the truth of the Nazis' vision in unassailable, sensory terms. More than anything else, this reminds us of what can result when a government uses symbols and media enchantment to insidiously define public discourse. It speaks, too, to the distinctive quest of totalitarianism: to recreate society with a degree of control that is a hellish mirror of the formal order in an artwork. "We who shape modern German policy feel ourselves to be artists," said Josef Goebbels in 1933; "the task of art and the artist to form, to give shape, to remove the diseased and create freedom for the healthy."[33]

When the war ended, Wagner's creative approach was anathema to many in Europe and elsewhere. The notion of the *Gesamtkunstwerk*, which could sweep audiences away with its effects and narrative authority, was chillingly linked with memories of Nazi manipulation. German filmmakers increasingly turned to the model of Brecht, constantly reminding the audience that they were watching an illusion and refusing to provide the integrated pleasures of Wagnerism. One such filmmaker was Hans-Jürgen Syberberg, who repeatedly made the connection between Wagner and Hitler—whom he called "the greatest filmmaker in the world"[34]—in his epic film *Our Hitler: A Film from Germany* (1977). He addressed the same subject matter in *The Confessions of Winifred Wagner* (1975) and his fascinating, enigmatic film of *Parsifal* (1982). In other art forms, movements such as Brechtian theater and the Darmstadt School of composition emphasized the importance of creating works free of sentimentalism and manipulation. For many artists and critics, no figure more fully summarized what they were rebelling against than Richard Wagner.

In America, where the use of Wagnerian norms in film did not carry the same implications, Hollywood kept alive a sensibility that had become deeply discredited in Germany. When Wolfgang Wagner said in the 1970s that his grandfather would want to work in film, he specifically said *Hollywood* film. Wagner's tradition was by then firmly identified with American filmmaking. It is one historical paradox among many that this enduring Wagnerian legacy should have come about because of the mostly Jewish composers and filmmakers who fled the Third Reich.

The Wagnerian influence on Hollywood scores waned in the late 1960s and '70s. To some extent, this was due to the refreshing aesthetic influence of a new generation of filmmakers who scored their movies with newer sounds including rock and folk songs. From a dramatic vantage point, the great films of this era—*Bonnie and Clyde, The Graduate, The Godfather* among many others—often examined morally complex situations with a profoundly non-judgmental stance. No one can call Wagner's work non-judgmental; his music suggests answers and insights about everyone and everything in his narratives though these can be interpreted in various ways. American film of this period, then—whose tolerance for ambiguity was deeply linked to the politics of the time—had no room for the Wagnerian orchestra. Wagnerian scores made a grand return with the *Star Wars* films (1977, 1980, 1983) and other mythic fantasies. Indeed, to this day, the films that most often make use of the Wagnerian scoring model are science-fiction and fantasy films: narratives in which cosmic and earth-shaking forces are at play, fully meriting an emblem as definitive as a *leitmotif*.

But if Wagnerian harmonies no longer surged on film soundtracks in the '60s and '70s, that hardly meant that Wagner's influence on Hollywood had been lost. In the first place, the values which filmmakers like Eisenstein had associated with Wagner—about the integration of sight and sound, or about the nature of myth—went far beyond musical idiom. And Wagner's ideas about music and narrative—in passages such as the ones quoted in this article—did not relate to the *sound* of the music so much as they did the *role* that music played.

Francis Ford Coppola's *Apocalypse Now* (1979) is mostly scored with rock songs and ethereal electronic instruments. There is, however, one track that recalls the sound of symphonic Hollywood film scores: the "Ride of the Valkyries" from *Die Walküre*, the soundtrack for an unforgettable scene in which American bomber planes rain down destruction on a Vietnamese village. "I use Wagner!" shouts Robert Duvall as the war-crazed Lieutenant Kilgore. "...My boys love it." As the planes hurtle through the clouds, the soldiers nod and grin in time to the music, picking off fleeing Vietnamese as though they were target practice. The choice of music implicitly suggests both Nazi aggression and Hollywood action fantasies as the soldiers fight their senseless war. For the purposes of this discussion, though, it is equally important to note that the opening track of the film—"The End," by The Doors—eventually functions as a *leitmotif*.

In a recent interview with the *New York Times*, the Austrian filmmaker Michael Haneke described the emigration of artistic refugees to Hollywood.

> At the beginning of the 20th century, when film began in Europe, storytelling of the kind still popular in Hollywood was every bit as popular here. Then the Nazis came, and the intellectuals—a great number of whom were Jewish—were either murdered or managed to escape to America and elsewhere.... Those who escaped to America were able to continue the storytelling approach to film—really a 19th-century tradition—with a clear conscience, since it hadn't been tainted by fascism. But in the German-speaking world, and in most of the rest of Europe, that type of straightforward storytelling, which the Nazis had made such good use of, came to be viewed with distrust. The danger hidden in storytelling became clear—how easy it was to manipulate the crowd.[35]

Haneke does not mention Wagner by name here, but his comments about the dangerous nineteenth-century tradition perfectly reflect many Europeans' feelings about Wagner. Haneke's films use Brechtian methods to deliberately distance the audience and criticize the manipulations of classical film technique. For many German and Austrian artists of Haneke's generation, the Hollywood mode of "straightforward" narrative is fundamentally dishonest and "tainted by fascism." But the filmmakers who inherited Wagner did not inherit politics; they inherited craft. They could use it for a variety of purposes — even the Brechtian ideal of alienation. Consider two pieces of Wagnerian filmmaking.

The first is the aforementioned sequence from *Apocalypse Now*. Wagner's music soars on the soundtrack; the planes and ocean waves glitter sensuously in the sun. The camera perspectives and editing rhythm put us squarely in the helicopter, where we experience the bombing raid just as the soldiers do — including its euphoria and grandeur. This is not the model of Brechtian alienation; it is the model of Wagnerian co-creative sympathy. When it is over, the political commentary is even more jarring because we have *been* engaged; through the perceptual mirrors of film, we have ourselves felt the madness that drives these soldiers.

A second, non-political example is Alfred Hitchcock's *Vertigo* (1958). Here, Bernard Herrmann's score — his most overtly Wagnerian one, with its intricate *leitmotifs* and quotes from *Tristan und Isolde*— dramatizes the story largely from the perspective of the James Stewart character. Midway through the film, we realize that the elaborate scenario that he, and we, believed in was not quite what it seemed; the character is, in addition, arguably quite mad. But throughout the journey, the emotions and motivic reminders in Herrmann's score allowed us fully to inhabit his delusions. The resulting alienation is infinitely more powerful because the filmmakers have allowed us to view the character with co-creative sympathy. What film craft inherited from Wagner was the commitment to conveying intense human responses and perceptions, and techniques for doing so. Filmmakers can turn those tools on any subject they like — including the tools themselves.

Film: Wagner After Wagner

The Nazis loudly identified themselves with Wagner and his cultural prestige. They embraced the aspects of him that they could use and ignored what they could not, much as they did with all other information. One cannot read the history of the Nazis and their crimes backwards into the artworks that they exploited. But the process of misrepresenting Wagner began with Wagner himself.

In his prose writings, he repeatedly claimed to be what he was not. He said that his was an art that banished all illusion; in fact, his art is predicated on masterful illusion. He said that his music flowed from the soul of the German people; in fact, as Thomas Mann pointed out, Wagner was a fiercely individualistic composer who almost never quoted genuine German folk music.[36] He described his works as a Gospel whose message was the breakdown of individual differences; in fact, he was a lifelong narcissist who rarely tolerated compromise with his own will. At every turn, Wagner claimed to be universal and truth-telling, when in fact he was highly particular and above all a theater artist. His extremely effective public-relations work obscured the fact that his artistic priorities were nothing other than what creators have always tried to do: maximize the materials they are working with in order to create an artistic effect. If the twentieth century showed how impossible it was for Wagner to escape his own political shadow, it also unexpectedly showed, through the medium of film, that the impact of Wagner's art was ultimately apolitical. Film artists—whether in Nazi Germany, Soviet Russia, or America—drew closely from Wagner's work. They did this because they recognized the value of his example in bringing the film medium to life. What filmmakers did with Wagner's techniques differed from case to case. Their politics certainly did not always match his, much as the power of his works to stir us transcends his own views. With his cinematic legacy, Richard Wagner was, at last, the medium and not the message.

Notes

1. See Brian Clegg, *The Man Who Stopped Time: The Illuminating Story of Eadweard Muybridge—Pioneer Photographer, Father of the Motion Picture, Murderer* (Washington, DC: National Academies Press, 2007): 187–192.

2. See David A. Cook, *A History of Narrative Film* (New York: W.W. Norton, 1996): 4, and *Impossible Presence: Surface and Screen in the Photogenic Era*, ed. Terry Smith (Chicago: University of Chicago Press, 2001): 72–73.

3. Quoted in John C. Tibbetts, *Composers in the Movies: Studies in Musical Biography* (New Haven, CT: Yale University Press, 2005): 222. Wolfgang Wagner made the comment in 1977 to Tony Palmer, who directed the television miniseries *Richard Wagner*.

4. *Wagner on Music and Drama: A Selection from Richard Wagner's Prose Works,* ed. Albert Goldman and Evert Sprinchorn, trans. H. A. Ellis (London: Victor Gollancz, 1977): 224.

5. *Wagner on Music and Drama*, 227.

6. Quoted in Matthew Wilson Smith, *The Total Work of Art: From Bayreuth to Cyberspace* (London: Routledge, 2007): 37.

7. Quoted in Joachim Köhler, *Richard Wagner: The Last of the Titans*, trans. Stewart Spencer (New Haven, CT: Yale University Press, 2004): 50. Originally from Cosima Wagner's *Tagebücher*, January 31, 1870.

8. *Wagner on Music and Drama*, 330.

9. *Wagner on Music and Drama*, 333.

10. *Wagner on Music and Drama*, 157.

11. *Wagner on Music and Drama*, 225.

12. *Lohengrin*, orchestral score (New York: Dover, 1982): 126.

13. *Lohengrin*, orchestral score: 129.

14. *Wagner on Music and Drama*, 223–226.

15. William Wordsworth, *The Prelude*, Book I, line 420. *William Wordsworth: The Major Works,* ed. Stephen Gill (Oxford: Oxford University Press, 2000): 385.

16. Wagner's original German: "So ist der Zauber, der mich dir verbunden,/ da als ich zuerst, du Süsse, dich ersah;/ nicht deine Art ich brauchte zu erkunden,/ dich sah mein Aug,—mein Herz begriff dich da." The English translation here is mine, as Amanda Holden's translation (which I cite below) renders this passage in metered rhyme, and slightly differs from the literal meaning of Wagner's words.

17. For a discussion of Schiller's influence on Wagner, see *The Total Work of Art*, 11–21.

18. Friedrich Schiller, "The Use of the Chorus in Tragedy," ed. Nathan Haskell Dole (Boston: F. A. Nicolls, 1902): 227.

19. The observation about Wagner's art as a presentation of sensory experience was also made, highly critically, by German media theorist Friedrich Kittler. In "World-Breath: On Wagner's Media Technology" (*Opera Through Other Eyes,* ed. David J. Levin. Stanford, CA: Stanford University Press, 1994: 215–235), he writes, "Wagner invented the first artistic machine capable of reproducing sensuous data as such." (216) For Kittler, this aspect of Wagner overran the traditional values of Western art, which had always been guided by literacy and allusion: "Arts—to adopt an old word for an old institution—entertain only symbolic relations to the sensory fields they presuppose. Media, by contrast, correlate in the real itself to the materiality they deal with" (215). Elsewhere he writes, "Wagner's orchestra has the exact function of an amplifier" (224). When Isolde's invocations of a storm are echoed acoustically by the orchestra, it is a descent from the classical values of art into the sensationalism of mass media. Kittler's statements sometimes overreach; dramatic illustration in the orchestra had been a staple of both oratorio and opera technique since the Baroque period, and the article makes no reference to the field of visual arts, which customarily communicate meanings via "sensuous data." Nevertheless, he makes an important point in emphasizing the unprecedented sensory nature of Wagner's art.

20. *Wagner on Music and Drama*, 181.
21. *Wagner on Music and Drama*, 181–182.
22. Christopher Vogler, *The Writer's Journey: Mythic Structure for Writers*, 2nd ed. (Studio City, CA: Michael Wiese Productions, 1998).
23. Ennio Simeon, "Giuseppe Becce and *Richard Wagner*: Paradoxes of the First German Film Score," *A Second Life: German Cinema's First Decades*, ed. Thomas Elsaesser (Amsterdam: Amsterdam University Press, 1996): 219–225, endnote on p. 328.
24. Quoted in Scott D. Paulin, "Richard Wagner and the Fantasy of Cinematic Unity: The Idea of the *Gesamtkunstwerk* in the History and Theory of Film Music," *Music and Cinema*, ed. James Buhler, Caryl Flinn, and David Neumeyer (Wesleyan University Press, 2000): 58–84, here 58.
25. Quoted in David Bordwell, Janet Staiger, Kristin Thompson, *The Classical Hollywood Cinema: Film Style and Mode of Production to 1960* (New York: Columbia University Press, 1987): 33.
26. David Bordwell, *et al.*: 34.
27. Quoted in Bordwell, *et al.*: 34.
28. Quoted in Bordwell, *et al.*, 34.
29. See note 22 above.
30. For a detailed discussion of Eisenstein's *Die Walküre*, see Patrick Carnegy, *Wagner and the Art of the Theatre: The Operas in Stage Performance* (New Haven, CT: Yale University Press, 2006), 226–233. Among Eisenstein's many spectacular devices was the visualization of Wagner's "Magic Fire" music. Eisenstein wrote: "The blue flame swelled to the sound of the "Magic Fire" music ... sometimes echoing it, then colliding with it, then singling it out ... absorbing the red ... after first having turned its original silver into celestial azure — at the moment of the culminating scene of Wotan and Brunnhilde's farewell" (230). Eisenstein's synaesthetic use of color here parallels his discussion of color in the *Vertical Montage* essays, and his unrealized plans for Part III of *Ivan the Terrible*.
31. For a recent discussion of Riefenstahl and the *Gesamtkunstwerk* tradition, see Chapter 2 of Matthew Wilson Smith's *The Total Work of Art* (pp. 92–113).
32. Richard Wagner, *Lohengrin*, trans. Amanda Holden, in *Lohengrin: English National Opera Guide 47* (New York: Riverrun, 1993): 56–57. The stage directions were translated by Stewart Spencer.
33. Quoted in Susan Sontag, "Fascinating Fascism," *Movies and Methods: An Anthology*, ed. Bill Nichols (Berkeley: University of California Press, 1976): 31–43, here 41.
34. Quoted in Bert Cardullo, *Soundings on Cinema: Speaking to Film and Film Artists* (Albany, NY: SUNY Press, 2008), p. 258.
35. Interviewed in *The New York Times Magazine*, September 23, 2007. http://www.nytimes.com/2007/09/23/magazine/23haneke-t.html?scp=3&sq=michael%20haneke&st=cse
36. See Thomas Mann, "The Sorrows and Grandeur of Richard Wagner," *Pro and Contra Wagner*, trans. Alan Blunden (Chicago: University of Chicago Press, 1985): 91–148, here 144–148. Mann's comments here about Wagner's individualist and internationalist qualities — and his disdainful references to Nazi doctrines — led to the Nazis' pressuring him to leave Germany, which he did.

BIBLIOGRAPHY

Bordwell, David, Janet Staiger, and Kristin Thompson. *The Classical Hollywood Cinema: Film Style and Mode of Production to 1960.* New York: Columbia University Press, 1987.
Cardullo, Bert. *Soundings on Cinema: Speaking to Film and Film Artists.* Albany, NY: SUNY Press, 2008.
Carnegy, Patrick. *Wagner and the Art of the Theatre: The Operas in Stage Performance.* New Haven, CT: Yale University Press, 2006.
Clegg, Brian. *The Man Who Stopped Time: The Illuminating Story of Eadweard Muybridge — Pioneer Photographer, Father of the Motion Picture, Murderer.* Washington, DC: National Academies Press, 2007.
Cook, David A. *A History of Narrative Film*, 3rd ed. New York: W.W. Norton, 1996.
Kittler, Friedrich. "World-Breath: On Wagner's Media Technology." *Opera Through Other Eyes.* Ed. David J. Levin. Stanford, CA: Stanford University Press, 1994.
Köhler, Joachim. *Richard Wagner: The Last of the Titans.* Trans. Stewart Spencer. New Haven, CT: Yale University Press, 2004.
Mann, Thomas. *Pro and Contra Wagner.* Trans. Alan Blunden. Chicago: University of Chicago Press, 1985.
Paulin, Scott D. "Richard Wagner and the Fantasy of Cinematic Unity: The Idea of the *Gesamtkunstwerk* in the History and Theory of Film Music." *Music and Cinema.* Ed. James Buhler, Caryl Flinn, and David Neumeyer. Middletown, CT: Wesleyan University Press, 2000.

Schiller, Friedrich. "The Use of the Chorus in Tragedy," in *The Maid of Orleans, The Bride of Messina, Wilhelm Tell, Demetrius*. Ed. Nathan Haskell Dole. Boston: F. A. Nicolls, 1902.
Simeon, Ennio. "Giuseppe Becce and *Richard Wagner*: Paradoxes of the First German Film Score." *A Second Life: German Cinema's First Decades*. Ed. Thomas Elsaesser. Amsterdam: Amsterdam University Press, 1996.
Smith, Matthew Wilson. *The Total Work of Art: From Bayreuth to Cyberspace*. London: Routledge, 2007.
Smith, Terry, ed. *Impossible Presence: Surface and Screen in the Photogenic Era*. Chicago: University of Chicago Press, 2001.
Sontag, Susan. "Fascinating Fascism." *Movies and Methods: An Anthology*. Ed. Bill Nichols. University of California Press, 1976.
Tibbetts, John C. *Composers in the Movies: Studies in Musical Biography*. New Haven, CT: Yale University Press, 2005.
Vogler, Christopher. *The Writer's Journey: Mythic Structure for Writers*, 2nd ed. Studio City, CA: Michael Wiese Productions, 1998.
Wagner, Richard, *Lohengrin*. Trans. Amanda Holden. *Lohengrin: English National Opera Guide 47*. New York: Riverrun, 1993.
_____. *Lohengrin* (orchestral score). New York: Dover, 1982. Originally Leipzig: Breitkopf & Hartel, 1887.
_____. *Wagner on Music and Drama: A Selection from Richard Wagner's Prose Works*. Ed. Albert Goldman and Evert Sprinchorn. Trans. H. A. Ellis. London: Victor Gollancz, UK, 1977.
Wordsworth, William. *The Major Works*. Ed. Stephen Gill. Oxford: Oxford University Press, 2000.
Wray, John. "Minister of Fear." *The New York Times Magazine*, 23 September. 2007.

13

Wagnerian References in the Fiction of Willa Cather

RICHARD C. HARRIS

While references to the arts and artists have informed a multitude of literary works, one would be hard-pressed to find a writer more knowledgeable about and more inclined to refer to what F. R. Leavis called the "great tradition" than the American writer Willa Cather. As the notes to the University of Nebraska Press Scholarly Editions of her works have revealed, Cather comfortably—and knowledgably—made frequent reference to the arts—literature, painting, and music—throughout her work. Her major biographer, James Woodress, in fact, has declared her the most educated writer of her generation. Born in Virginia in 1873, Cather moved with her family to the Nebraska plains in 1883; enjoyed four years as a very precocious student and arts critic at the University of Nebraska in Lincoln; moved east, first to Pittsburgh and then to New York to become managing editor of *McClure's* magazine; and subsequently became a very highly respected and successful writer of fiction for the next four decades. At the time of her death in 1947, Cather had long been acknowledged as *la grande dame* of American letters.

No artistic area is more significant to her writing than music. A wide range of references to the classical repertoire includes Schubert's *Die schöne Müllerin* and *Die Wintereisse*, as well as a number of individual *Lieder*; Dvořák's "New World" Symphony; a number of works by Grieg, Massenet, Mendelssohn, Saint-Saëns, and Schumann; and approximately a dozen and a half operatic works by Bellini, Gluck, Gounod, Mascagni, Mozart, Rossini, and Wagner. The Wagnerian repertoire provided particularly important reference points, especially in Cather's earlier fiction, for in both novels and short stories allusions to Wagner's works are not merely tangential but rather are central to the thematic development of the works. In her fiction Cather mentions six non–Ring operas from *Der fliegende Holländer* to *Parsifal*, as well as refers to *Das Rheingold*, *Die Walküre*, and *Siegfried*.

Willa Cather was by no means an expert on musical theory or history. As Woodress notes, she had no formal education in music, and she did not learn to play a musical instrument, despite her mother's attempts to encourage her to learn to play the piano. According to Woodress, Cather "nearly drove her teacher mad when he tried to give her lessons" (54–55). The teacher, a German itinerant named Schindelmeisser, was retained, however, because young Willa so enjoyed listening to him play and delighted in hearing stories about his musical life in Europe. For Cather, as for Charlotte Waterford of her 1925 story "Uncle Valentine," music quite simply became "a way of living" (9). One of her long-time friends, Mrs. Charles Weisz of Chicago, remembered her saying, especially when she was anxious, unhappy, or simply tired, "I must have music" (Brown 301). Cather's long-time friend and companion Edith Lewis perhaps best described the relationship between Cather's attraction to music and her own art when she said, "Music, for Willa Cather, was hardly at all, I think, an intellectual interest. It was an emotional experience that had a potent influence on her own imaginative processes — quickening the flow of her ideas, suggesting new forms and associations, translating itself into parallel movements of thought and feeling" (47–48).

Cather thus might be referred to as a musical amateur, but as with so many of her interests, a love became a passion. For her in the 1890s and in the decade that followed, in particular, Wagner's music was a passion. The first printed mention of Wagner in Cather's works can be traced to a newspaper article that Cather, a junior at the University of Nebraska, wrote for the *Nebraska State Journal* in early 1894. Here she castigates those "drawing-room critics" [who] "sneer at the great and powerful, and adore the clever and the dainty" ("Parlor Critics" 186). "This race of critics," Cather says, "has declared Ruskin and Wagner and Turner, and Modjeska blasé and have taken unto themselves new gods in the very airy and fragile shapes of Whistler and Jerome K. Jerome and [Reginald] De Koven and Julia Marlowe" (186–87). In another piece, this one published in the *Lincoln Courier* in November of 1895, Cather again laments the current state of taste, asserting that "the Wagnerian flashes and thunders and tempests of Carlyle and the lofty repose and magnificent tranquility of Emerson seem to have gone out of the language" ("History in the Arts — Descent" 222).

In the spring of 1895, during her last semester of college, Cather went to Chicago and indulged herself by going to the opera every night for a week. (On the last night, she admitted, she fell asleep despite the music — Myerbeer's *Les Huguenots*, a lively piece marked by rousing passages for the percussion section.) While it is clear that Cather was at least somewhat familiar with Wagner while she was in college, it was after she moved to Pittsburgh in June of 1896 that she became really knowledgeable about his work. In his account of the friendship he and his wife developed with Cather, George Seibel notes that Cather, as editor of the *Home Monthly* magazine, was introduced to the Reverend Heinrich Baehr, who had previously been employed as a tutor by Wagner at Bayreuth. Cather was fascinated by his stories about the Wagner family (196). Fortunately, the new Carnegie Music Hall, which opened only months before she arrived in Pittsburgh, as well as other local sites, provided Cather with opportunities to see performances by some of the country's major orchestras, operatic ensembles, and individual performers. By the mid 1890s, for example, Walter Damrosch, conductor of the Metropolitan Opera Orchestra, was bringing an orchestra and operatic company to Pittsburgh once a year.

Several of Cather's reviews of these performances, published in the *Pittsburgh Leader*, provide a clear sense of both the confidence and the no-nonsense attitude of the twenty-four year old from Nebraska. In a 4 March 1897 article (*The World and the Parish*, I, 400–402), for example, she notes that *Lohengrin*, "probably the most popular of Wagner's operas in America," is "spiritual in theme" and "exalted in treatment"; "its melodies are among Wagner's most perfect," and the Grail idea "is in none of his other operas handled more beautifully and effectively." She finds Damrosch "the same vigorous, magnetic conductor as of old" and his orchestra "exceptionally good." Commenting on the performances of the singers, however, she is much less positive. While Mr. Ernest Kraus is "a most manly Lohengrin," his methods are "defective," and his voice, unfortunately, broke repeatedly, several times in the long recitative in the last act. "I suppose even knights of the Grail," Cather concedes, "are not exempt from colds, at least not in Pittsburgh." Johanna Gadski, who a year later would begin a long and very successful career with the Metropolitan Opera, is found "musically satisfactory and dramatically very insufficient ... conventional, traditional and quite spiritless" in the role of Elsa.

A 6 March review (*The World and the Parish*, I, 402–404) reveals more about Cather's knowledge of Wagner's work and her approach to reviewing performances. In this case the opera was *Tannhäuser*, in which, according to Cather, Wagner, having been carried away by "the tremendous dramatic possibilities of the theme" forgot his "cherished theories," thus creating not a "music-drama" but rather "an opera pure and simple; one of the most intense and direct of all operas." She continues,

> It has for its theme the conflict between human ideals and human weakness which is at the base of all great dramatic situations. Wagner himself said that Tannhäuser was young Germany, and so he is, the very essence of the German character, and of course German sentiment, though the person of Elizabeth at last prevails over him. The overture in the opera, the conflict between the Venus motif and the Pilgrim music, the Pilgrims' Chorus always gloriously triumphing, tells the whole story. The contrast is followed throughout the opera. It is repeated in the opposite characters of Venus and Elizabeth and in that sudden change of scenic atmosphere when Tannhäuser is transported from the sensuous splendor of Venusberg to the spring sunshine of the valley where the shepherd boy is singing his single melody and the pilgrims are passing on their way to Rome. The same idea is again repeated in the minstrels' ball at Wartburg, where Wolfram sings of ideal love and Tannhäuser responds with his exultant song of the heathen goddess.

Cather commends Paul Kalisch in the lead role, describing him as "peculiarly brilliant in it, both vocally and dramatically." Maria Brandis is "an exceedingly satisfactory Elizabeth," with a voice clearly strong enough to sing the "Dich, teure Halle" aria properly. Mme. Riza Eibenschuetz, whom Cather had praised for her performance in *Lohengrin* two nights before, here is seen to have too light a voice and to have been obviously nervous. Cather could not resist the opportunity to criticize one element of the production in particular: a paragraph-long diatribe begins, "The management of the drop curtain was as abominable as ever."

Both the substance and the spirit of Cather's reviews of these performances are summed up in a separate review that appeared in the *Nebraska State Journal* on 14 March 1897 (*The World and the Parish*, I, 404–408). She recalls Wagner's letter to Liszt in which he said that he felt like a priest while he was at work on *Lohengrin* and herself declares *Lohengrin*, "the most spiritual of Wagner's operas ... the incarnation of all the purest ideals of chivalry." She again notes that Mr. Damrosch's singers "were afflicted with most obtrusive colds of the sort which beset every singer who ventures into this foggy river atmosphere." She adds that she had not been able to hear Lili Lehmann because she had sung only once during the week as Brünnhilde in *Götterdämmerung*, perhaps because she too had a cold or because Damrosch could afford her $1000- a-performance fee only once a week. Apparently for the latter reason Damrosch "has engaged some very cheap people and his chorus is abominable." Cather adds that she has heard that Lehmann's voice has "gone off sadly" though her acting "is as superb as ever ... and really in Wagnerian operas acting counts for two-thirds."

Here Frau Gadski is said to have a powerful voice though she is judged to be "totally incompetent and unsatisfactory" dramatically. Cather describes her weight as "simply preposterous" and opines that "it must have been a very susceptible knight indeed who would descend from the gleaming heights of Mt. Monsalvat to get her out of her scrape." Cather's remarks about the performance of Herr Kraus are very similar to those that appeared in the Pittsburgh review. Again she mentions his physical stature — he is "a perfect giant, big and blonde and German as heart could wish" — but criticizes his "faulty methods": "After again singing 'Mein Lieber Schwan' — the most beautiful number in the whole opera — he leaves his plump Elsa as calmly as though she were a chance acquaintance and not his wife."

Cather's comments here again echo those of the previous reviews, but there are some significant additions, most of them in a humorous or rather sarcastic vein. Commenting on the performance of Riza Eibenschuetz in the role of Venus, Cather notes that she played the part not as a German Venus but as a "thoroughly pagan lady"; when she sang "Geliebter, Komm!" one "could very well understand why poor Heinrich had tarried in Venusberg so long." Maria Brandis as Elizabeth is once more cited for her apparent indifference, but Paul Kalisch is described as a "magnificent, faultless, tenor ... a most noble and knightly figure ... in the full vigor of his prime." Cather finds his work in the "Dir Göttin der Liebe" solo brilliant and concludes that his acting and singing in the long recitative when he returns from Rome in tattered pilgrim's clothing and staggers toward Venus's hill is full of "tragic power": "I never saw anything more pathetic than this poor wreck of a man staggering toward Venus. And then the glorious triumphant Pilgrim motif again, the final victory of good which we all hope for and believe in."

As excerpts from these reviews indicate, while Cather certainly was knowledgeable about Wagnerian opera, she generally focused more on the personalities of the performers of the music than on the music itself. From these and other early critical writings, Cather's interest in the artistic personality is clear. As Cather critic Mildred Bennett said in 1951, "She could not play any musical instrument, read music nor sing ...her apparent interest in music was really always confined to performers of music or to music connected with theatricals, as in the opera" (152). At the same time it is important to note that Cather was by no means interested in merely spreading gossip about the stars of stage and concert hall. As James Curtin says about this aspect of Cather's criticism, if Cather's reviews did touch upon the private lives of the performers, "her interest was manifestly not in gossip for its own sake, but a part of her concern with the personal element of their success" (*The World and the Parish*, I, 32). Her lengthiest exploration of the subject is found in her 1915 novel *The Song of the Lark*, the story of the development of the art and artistic personality of a young girl from the Midwest, who makes her career as an opera singer in Chicago and then on the stage of the Metropolitan Opera.

In the period from about 1900 to 1920, the period in which Cather was in the process of establishing her career, first as magazine editor and then as fiction writer, she was constantly exploring the causes and consequences of success. Particularly important were questions concerning the artistic personality, artistic sacrifice and integrity, and philistinism. The majority of stories in two collections titled *The Troll Garden* (1905) and *Youth and the Bright Medusa* (1920) focus on the subject. Two short stories from *The Troll Garden* employ references to Wagner in quite interesting ways. It is clear that Cather knew what she was talking about; however, it is important to note that Cather's method is allusive or suggestive. As with the literary allusions that fill her works, one should not attempt to see extended, point-by-point parallels between her sources and her fiction, and one should note that her references are often characterized by ironic juxtaposition.

In "The Garden Lodge" Cather presents Caroline Noble, a woman who gave up her early interest in the piano to marry well. Her father, a music teacher, had composed orchestral pieces "for which the world seemed to have no especial need" (188); her brother, a disappointed artist, had ended up committing suicide, devastating her mother both emotionally and physically.

Although most of her friends do not know about these "extenuating circumstances," Caroline's decision to leave behind "the shrine of idealism" and the "mystic worship of things distant, intangible, and unattainable" (189) is perhaps understandable. She married Howard Noble not only because his wealth would ensure a life of luxury but also because she wanted "the luxury of being like other people" (190), wealthy people, that is. For six years she has lived a very comfortable, conventional, stable life; she is "entirely safe" (190). She is known as a "paramountly cool-headed" if not coldly calculating woman. The stability is upset, however, by the appearance of tenor Raymond d'Esquerré, a man of great charm and "formidable power," who is making his way to New York for performances with the Met. He is invited to spend a month in the Nobles' garden lodge, an agreeable respite since "he, too, felt occasionally the need of getting out of Klingsor's garden, of dropping down somewhere for a time near a quiet nature, a cool head, a strong hand" (190). Caroline enjoys accompanying d'Esquerré on the piano but is determined not to allow the experience of knowing this dashing man or of enjoying playing music with him affect her.

In the two weeks after his departure, however, she finds herself returning to the garden lodge each day for "a quiet hour" in which she reflects on him and his stay. She is haunted by "an imploring little girlish ghost" (195) that demands that hour of reverie from her and, in particular, by the memory of d'Esquerré's singing the final duet from the first act of *Die Walküre*. The lines "Thou art the Spring for which I sighed in Winter's cold embraces" keep coming back to her, along with the memory of his putting his arm around her and lifting her right hand from the keys of the piano. As Richard Giannone notes, "The gesture transforms Caroline into Sieglinde. Willa Cather has not given us a woman whose destiny is linked with the vast affairs surrounding the strange gold ring, but she has given us Sieglinde, nonetheless — a woman who finds her spiritual twin, her namesake, Siegmund. It is this limited theme of *Die Walküre* which suits Cather's fictive purpose" (38).[1]

The shaking of Caroline Noble's "happy, useful, well-ordered life" is indicated by another allusion to Wagner's opera, this one involving seasonal symbolism. Raymond d'Esquerré had arrived in the spring, in the month of May; Caroline's experience with him makes her aware of the winter that, figuratively speaking, has existed in her heart for the previous six years. The storm in which Siegmund is lost in *Die Walküre* is echoed by a howling tempest that marks Caroline's final visit to the lodge and her attempt to deal with the sense of doubt or spiritual malaise that temporarily affects her. Storms rage both without and within as she reviews "the catalogue of her self-deprivations" (194) and reflects on the "relentless routine, unvarying as clockwork" (194) that has been her life for the last six years. Cather here brings an ironic turn to Wagner's story, for while Sieglinde *loses* Siegmund, Caroline Noble finally *rejects* d'Esquerré and the power, possibility, and enchantment that he represents.

There is yet another ironic parallel to Wagner's opera in the end of the story. Both Act I of *Die Walküre* and "The Garden Lodge" end with laughter, but whereas Sieglinde and Siegmund leave Hagan's house and laugh triumphantly "as they envision a house of spring," Caroline and Howard Noble sit at the breakfast table and, as the story ends, laugh at Caroline's inability to be even "a little bit foolish" (197). Whereas Caroline had earlier questioned her husband's suggestion that they might tear down the garden lodge and have a new summer house, "a big rustic affair," built in its place, she now has decided that she doesn't have "enough sentiment to forego a summer-house" (197). Thus in another nice ironic touch, Cather juxtaposes the heroic adventures of Siegmund and Sieglinde to the rather insignificant domestic affairs of the much less noble Nobles, who play out their little drama on the shore of the Long Island Sound.

As the title suggests, "A Wagner Matinée," originally published in 1904 and included in *The Troll Garden* (1905), also centers on Wagner's music, in this case referring to *Der fliegende Holländer*, *Tannhäuser*, *Tristan und Isolde*, and *Die Meistersinger*. As this story opens, the first-person narrator, Clark, has just received a letter from his uncle, announcing that his aunt will be arriving in Boston the next day and asking that he meet her train at the station and help get her settled for her visit there. For Clark the reunion with his Aunt Georgiana evokes a whole flood of memories, for as he reflects, "I owed to this woman most of the good that ever came my way in my boyhood, and had a reverential affection for her" (236).

His meeting with her is a sobering experience. Although decades before she had been a music teacher at the Boston Conservatory, infatuated with Howard Carpenter, she had eloped with him, moved west, and settled on the Nebraska frontier. The years and environment had taken a heavy toll:

> Originally stooped, her shoulders were now almost bent together over her sunken chest. She wore no stays, and her gown, which trailed unevenly behind, rose in a sort of peak over her abdomen. She wore ill-fitting false teeth, and her skin was as yellow as a Mongolian's from constant exposure to a pitiless wind and to the alkaline water which hardens the most transparent cuticle into a sort of flexible leather [236].

In addition, Clark realizes that in thirty years his aunt "had not been further than fifty miles" from that Nebraska homestead (236).

Clark decides that taking her to a matinée performance of Wagner's works by the Boston Symphony would be a fitting pleasure for the woman who had first taught him to appreciate literature and music. The next afternoon they enter the concert hall, a world "to which she had been dead for a quarter of a century" (238). Whereas Caroline Noble, the cold and calculating figure in "The Garden Lodge," had quickly dismissed the sense of loss she felt at having given up music and the emotions associated with it, Georgiana Carpenter is emotionally overwhelmed by her experience at the Wagner matinée.

The first number, the overture from *Tannhäuser*, "broke a silence of thirty years" (239). Clark watches with curiosity as his aunt sits silently, though her fingers "worked mechanically upon her black dress," through the playing of the prelude to *Tristan und Isolde* and a number from *Der fliegende Holländer*. The "Prize Song" from *Die Meistersinger* brought a gasp and then tears from her; "she wept so throughout the development and elaboration of the melody" (240). During the second half of the program, Georgiana Carpenter wept almost continuously through four pieces from the *Ring*, the last being Siegfried's funeral march. Unlike Caroline Noble whose fond remembrance of the role music had once played in her life is brief and rather easily ignored, Georgiana Carpenter, "who had heard nothing but the singing of Gospel Hymns at the Methodist services in the square frame school-house on Section Thirteen for so many years," is filled with a sense of loss (241). During the intermission she asks her nephew, "And you have been hearing this ever since you left me, Clark?" As they leave the concert hall, sobbing uncontrollably, she exclaims, "I don't want to go, Clark, I don't want to go!" (241).

Cather's use of Wagner's music is particularly well chosen in this short story. As noted previously, she does not attempt to establish exact parallels between Wagner's opera and her own story; rather references are suggestive, at times ironic, and are based upon the principle of juxtaposition.[2] Cather adopts Wagner's major thematic contrast between the sacred and the profane in contrasting the life of aesthetic endeavor and fulfillment through art to the harsh life Georgiana Carpenter has lived on the Midwestern plains. However, whereas

Tannhäuser ends by asserting the redemptive power of love, Cather's story ends with Georgiana's plaintive cry that comes out of the realization that there will be no positive outcome for her. Unlike Elizabeth and Tannhäuser who find salvation at the end of the opera, Clark's aunt foresees the continuing damnation that she will face upon her return to Nebraska. The story ends with the following words:

> For her, just outside the door of the concert hall, lay the black pond with the cattle-tracked bluffs; the tall, unpainted house, with the weather-curled boards; naked as a tower, the crook-backed ash seedlings where the dish-cloths hung to dry; the gaunt, moulting turkeys picking up refuse about the kitchen door [242].

Symbolically, no flowers will sprout from that landscape as they do from the staff in *Tannhäuser*. The chant of the pilgrims, which marks the beginning of the overture to *Tannhäuser*, and which returns in Act III, culminating with the redemption and salvation of Tannhäuser, at least suggests the possibility of salvation for those pilgrims; Georgiana Carpenter, who, in Cather's story, has made her own pilgrimage, can expect no such transformation. The enchantment of the Venusberg landscape momentarily lures Tannhäuser in Act III of Wagner's opera, but he finally rejects it. The prospect of returning to the landscape of the barren prairie overwhelms Georgiana Carpenter, but she has no choice but to return. As Giannone points out, the vulnerable pilgrim Georgiana stands no chance in the attempt to defeat "the powerful, ancient forces of such mysterious blackness and waste and aridity" (44).

The "awakening" that love brings to Elizabeth and Tannhäuser in Act II of the opera is paralleled by the aesthetic re-awakening that Georgiana experiences as she hears the first notes of the Pilgrim's Chorus. However, whereas the appeals of Elizabeth to the Virgin Mary and of Tännhauser to Elizabeth (and implicitly to God) are answered, Georgiana's religious belief has merely enabled her to survive. "She was a pious woman," Clark realizes, "she had the consolations of religion and, to her at least, her martyrdom was not wholly sordid" (237). The life of resignation that she has accepted for three decades does not end in the kind of spiritual triumph that characterizes the last act of *Tannhäuser*; rather, for Georgiana Carpenter, the future will be like the stage after the orchestra has left it, "empty as a winter cornfield" (241).

Several other specific references to Wagner add to the theme of defeat that Cather develops here. For example, the reference to *Der fliegende Holländer* suggests the differences between Senta and The Dutchman. The "Prize Song" from *Die Meistersinger*, the last piece before the intermission, suggests the triumph of Walther, which is a triumph of the noblest ideals of the Meistersingers; in addition, in Walther's winning the hand of Eva, Wagner "celebrates the perfect union and the double triumph of art and life" (Giannone 44). The last selection of the afternoon's program, Siegfried's funeral march, seems especially appropriate since both he and Georgiana suffer defeat, though his defeat is the stuff of heroic legend whereas hers is not. He is the great warrior; she is simply, in Thomas Gray's words, a flower "born to blush unseen and waste its sweetness upon the desert air." Interestingly, this story, like "The Garden Lodge," mentions laughter at its conclusion. The narrator of "A Wagner Matinée" tells us, "The concert was over; the people filed out of the hall chattering and laughing, glad to relax and find the living level again..." (241). Chatter and laughter are not possible for that sad woman who will again face hopelessness in the bleakness that awaits her back home.

Wagner's operas also play an important role in two of Willa Cather's novels, in one case implicitly and in the other very explicitly. Shortly after the publication of *One of Ours* in September 1922, Cather received a letter from Mr. Orrick Johns, who had written to inquire about a possible allusion to *Parsifal* in the novel. In her response Cather said she thought that she had buried the allusion to *Parsifal* so deeply that it might not be discovered. She revealed to Johns that she had thought about using the line, "The Blameless Fool, by Pity Enlightened," from Act I of *Parsifal* as the epigraph for the book (WC to Mr. Johns, 17 November 1922). Cather, in fact, apparently considered *Parsifal* not only the greatest of Wagner's operas but the greatest opera, period. Similarities between Wagner's medieval knight and Cather's World War I soldier are subtle but discernible.

In the novel Claude Wheeler, an idealistic young Nebraskan determined to do "something splendid" in his life, joins the American Expeditionary Force, goes to France to fight for the Allied cause, and is killed in action, his "beautiful beliefs" that he was fighting for a noble cause, intact (604). *One of Ours* evoked critical controversy immediately upon its publication, and debate continues. While a number of veterans wrote to Cather to praise her having captured their feelings and the war experience in remarkably true fashion, a number of literary critics, notably H. L. Mencken and Sinclair Lewis, condemned the novel as presenting an overly romantic and idealistic picture of the war. John Dos Passos' ironic and cynical novel *Three Soldiers*, which had appeared the year before, was, according to Mencken, the work against which all other World War I fiction must be measured.

Cather herself no doubt felt some ambivalence about the war: on the one hand, as a great Francophile and advocate of western civilization, she believed that the accomplishments, ideals, and values of the western tradition were being threatened by the German militarism that lay behind the war. On the other hand, she was by no means naïve as to the horror of the war itself or to the hypocrisy and corruption that accompany all wars. During the war, she seems to have believed the Allied war effort a noble cause; by the mid

Donald McIntyre as Klingsor in *Parsifal* at the Metropolitan Opera (photograph by Winnie Klotz).

1920s she had come to see things at least somewhat differently. Although the terms are those not of Cather but of her characters, in *One of Ours* the war effort is referred to as a "brilliant adventure" (413) and a "great enterprise" (422); in *The Professor's House*, published in 1925, the war is dubbed a "great catastrophe" (261). Complicating the question as to where, exactly, Cather stood as far as the war was concerned, is the fact that the novel, to a great extent, grew out of the actual experiences of one of Cather's cousins, G. P. Cather, who fought and died in France. Difficulties in determining how to read Cather's novel thus parallel in some ways the difficulty in interpreting *Parsifal*.

As was noted previously, one should avoid the temptation to try to find exact and extended parallels between *Parsifal* and *One of Ours*. However, some interesting similarities do exist. Cather's protagonist, Claude Wheeler, like Parsifal, is seen early on as a sort of innocent or fool, whose actions often bring trouble and disappointment. In Act I of Wagner's opera, Parsifal, not distinguishing it from other birds, shoots and kills the swan. Shortly thereafter, he is taken to observe the Grail ceremony, which he may or may not understand. The oracle, however, predicts that in time the naïf will be enlightened. Like young Parsifal, Cather's cousin also acted in ways that, while not malicious, were hurtful, especially to himself. As Cather told her friend Dorothy Canfield Fisher about six months before the novel was published, her cousin's life had been full of misery, and much of what he had done had been ridiculous or ugly (WC to DCF [8 Mar. 1922]). She would later describe G.P.'s fictional counterpart as "an inarticulate young man butting his way through the world" (Bohlke 78). Before he joined the military, Claude "troubled his mother and disappointed his father" (200); as he himself realizes, his life has been "one blunder after another" (345). Like his prototype, Claude Wheeler too experiences difficulties, in some cases the result of his own naiveté or incompetence and in others the result of his inability to adapt to a world in which traditional values are being challenged and disregarded.

What experience brings to both Parsifal and Claude Wheeler is the ability to see something greater than themselves. The oracular prophecy in Act I of *Parsifal* calls Parsifal a "blameless fool"; at the end of the opera he is redeemed by his realization of pity or compassion. The war provides Cather's Claude Wheeler the opportunity to make good his sense that "there ought to be something — well, something splendid about life" (79). In his involvement in the war effort, his sense of camaraderie with his fellow soldiers, and his dedication to what seems a noble cause, he dies believing that he has realized that desire.

Willa Cather's most explicit and significant use of Wagnerian opera in her works is in *The Song of the Lark* (1915). The novel, a *Künstlerroman* with a woman artist as its main character, is, especially in the section titled "Childhood Friends," the most autobiographical fiction Cather ever created (Woodress 266). *The Song of the Lark* traces the life of a young immigrant girl from Minnesota, who leaves the small town of Moonstone, Colorado (very obviously modeled on Cather's own Red Cloud, Nebraska), to study music in Chicago, and finally to experience artistic triumph on the stage of the Metropolitan Opera in the role of Sieglinde in Wagner's *Die Walküre*. While Thea Kronborg's art is music and Cather's was fiction, Cather's own artistic personality, struggle, and triumph are clearly reflected in her character.

The Song of the Lark, however, is not merely autobiographical. Cather drew upon a number of sources in creating her heroine. While the thoughts and feelings expressed by Thea are essentially Cather's own, a number of the details of her heroine's career are based on the artistic career of the great Wagnerian soprano Olive Fremstad. In her biography of Cather, Edith Lewis describes Cather's fascination with Fremstad:

We went constantly to the opera at this time [1905–1915]. "It was one of the great periods of opera in New York. Nordica and the de Reszkes, Melba and Calvé were still singing during our first years in New York. From 1905 on our old programmes continually list such names as Sembrich, Farrar, Chaliapin, Plançon, Destinn, Renaud, Mary Garden, Caruso, Amato, Homer, and Tettrazzini. Toscanini, not then half so famous, but at the height of his powers, was conducting two or three times a week at the Metropolitan. But the most thrilling, to us, of all the new stars that came up over the horizon was Olive Fremstad. We heard her nearly every time she sang" (89–90).

As managing editor of *McClure's* magazine from 1906 to 1913, Cather was often charged with writing non-fiction pieces for inclusion in various issues. Given her interest in singers, in early 1913 she chose to do interviews with and to write an article on Louise Homer, a leading contralto at the Met, most famous for her role in Gluck's *Orfeo*; Geraldine Farrar, best known for her performances in the operas of Verdi and Puccini; and Fremstad, the reigning diva, known for her Wagnerian roles.[3] As Cather biographer James Woodress points out, in "Three American Singers," published in *McClure's* in December 1913, Cather devoted only six paragraphs to Homer, significantly more space to Farrar, but over half the article to Fremstad (256).

The space devoted to each singer reflects the extent to which that singer did or did not dedicate herself to pursuing the ideal of greatness for which Farrar's teacher Lili Lehmann is seen to have striven. Homer was judged to be too devoted to her family to make the necessary sacrifices for artistic greatness. Farrar and Cather agreed that a family could prove detrimental to one's devotion to art, but Cather felt that Farrar nonetheless lacked the total dedication that was required. Cather quotes Farrar's admission that she has learned "that talents have limitations.... I do not long to, nor do I believe I can, climb frozen heights like the great Lehmann" ("Three American Singers" 42). According to Cather, only Fremstad had shown herself to be that artist who was willing to sacrifice everything else to art, which Cather declares is "the only thing that *remains* beautiful" in this world (42). As a young writer of eighteen, Cather, in her typically precocious fashion, had remarked, as Jehovah declares, "Thou shalt have no other gods before me"; Art cries, "Thou shalt have no other gods at all" ("Concerning Thomas Carlyle" 423). Twenty years later in Olive Fremstad Cather would find another artist who shared her sense of dedication to art and her willingness to make the sacrifices required of the truly serious artist.

As Woodress notes, "three glimpses of Fremstad a few days apart had a catalytic effect" on Cather's ideas for *The Song of the Lark* (254). In preparing to write about Fremstad for the *McClure's* article, Cather had made an appointment to interview her on March 12, 1913. When Cather arrived at Fremstad's apartment on Eighty-sixth Street, just off Riverside Drive, she learned that Fremstad's chauffeur had taken her out for a drive. When Fremstad returned, she seemed exhausted and obviously upset about something and was barely able to speak. Cather left, saying that she would do the interview at another time. That evening Cather and two friends were sitting in the house at the Met for a performance of Offenbach's *Tales of Hoffmann*, when the publicity director came on stage to announce that Mme. Duchene, who was scheduled to sing the role of Giulietta, would be unable to do so but that Mme Fremstad had agreed only minutes before the curtain was to go up to fill in for her. Upon hearing the announcement, the audience broke into wild applause. Twenty minutes after the desperate call to her apartment, Fremstad was backstage, preparing for her second-act entrance. After Fremstad's performance Cather was astounded, repeating again and again, "But it's impossible, it's impossible" (Lewis 91–92).[4]

Cather did interview Fremstad several days after this triumph, and she wrote to her friend

Elizabeth Shepley Sergeant a week after the meeting that she was fascinated with Fremstad (22 March [1913]), then in mid April that she was becoming acquainted with Fremstad but felt overwhelmed by her (14 April [1913]). In a letter written a week later, Cather told Sergeant that she would like to be able to convey in writing a mind like Fremstad's (22 April [1913]). The day before she had seen Fremstad as Kundry in *Parsifal*; although the two women knew each other at this point, Fremstad was so dazed and exhausted after her performance that she didn't even recognize Cather as she rushed to her waiting car. Cather was so impressed with Fremstad's having so given her whole self to the performance that the incident is recounted in *The Song of the Lark* exactly as it actually occurred (see pages 502–503).

A friendship between Cather and Fremstad continued to develop. Cather visited Fremstad at her summer place in Maine. On Christmas Eve 1913 Cather sent Fremstad a small orange tree, which was waiting in the singer's apartment when she returned from a performance of Isolde. Fremstad's thank-you letter, written that same night, evidences a deep sense of respect and fondness for Cather. In February when Cather was hospitalized with blood poisoning, Fremstad visited her on a regular basis, bringing gifts and encouragement. When *The Song of the Lark* appeared in February 1915, Fremstad, who had retired from the Metropolitan Opera in April of 1914, told Cather she was delighted with the book and the way in which she had been depicted in it (WC to Sergeant, 7 Dec. [1915]).

Before looking at the specific ways in which Cather used references to Wagnerian opera in *The Song of the Lark*, it is necessary at least to mention two other statements relevant to the topic. In a 1925 essay that served as the preface to a new edition to Gertrude Hall's *The Wagnerian Romances*, Cather declared, "I know of only two books in English on the Wagnerian operas that are at all worthy of their subject; Bernard Shaw's *The Perfect Wagnerite* and *The Wagnerian Romances* by Gertrude Hall" (60). In a 30 December 1899 review of Shaw's book, Cather had asserted that Shaw, so often known for his irony and cynicism, here seemed to have written "a thoroughly conventional book" ("The Perfect Wagnerite" 617). She particularly emphasizes Shaw's advice to those who might consider themselves "disqualified from enjoying the *Ring* by their technical ignorance of music": If the sound of music has any power to move them they will find that Wagner exacts nothing further. There is not a single bar of "classical" music in the *Ring*— not a note of it that has any other point than the single direct point of giving musical expression to the drama... (617).

Cather finds Hall's book a welcome departure from most "guide books" to the opera, which, she claims, have been written by "very unintelligent people, who know little about writing and even less about opera" (60). Hall's "rare gift," as Cather sees it, lies in her ability "to reproduce the emotional effect of the Wagner operas upon the printed page," "to reproduce the emotional effect of one art through the medium of another art" (61–62). While Cather singles out Hall's chapter on *Parsifal* for particular praise, she also cites Hall's essays on *Tristan und Isolde* and *Die Meistersinger*. Of the latter she asserts, "A mere literal translation of the written scene in which Walther for the first time sings before the Master-Singers, for instance, means very little. And the words of Walther's song, literally translated, without the feeling of the accompanying actions, mean almost nothing. Miss Hall's rendering of the scene is a brilliant piece of virtuosity" (64). Cather is particularly pleased that Hall's volume provides to "great numbers of people who have the intelligence to appreciate the Wagner operas but not the opportunity to hear them" a real sense of "those noble, mysterious, significant dramas" (65). Admitting that in writing *The Song of the Lark* she had relied heavily on *The Wagnerian Romances*, Cather says simply that she there paid Hall "the highest compliment one writer can pay another; I stole from her" (64–65).

Waltraud Meier as Kundry in *Parsifal*, Act 2, of the Otto Schenk production at the Metropolitan Opera (photograph by Winnie Klotz).

The Song of the Lark was thus created from a number of sources. Thea Kronborg's story is an amalgam chiefly of Cather's experiences growing up; her own thoughts and feelings about art and artistic careers; incidents from the career of Olive Fremstad; and Cather's fascination with Wagner's operas.[5] Thea Kronborg's rise from girlhood uncertainty and obscurity to the point at which she establishes herself as one of the operatic world's great divas is described in the first five parts of *The Song of the Lark*. At the end of Part five Thea is leaving to study in Germany. Part six, subtitled "Ten Years Later," presents a picture of Thea after her return and describes several triumphant performances in Wagnerian roles. An epilogue, set nearly twenty years after Thea left her hometown for the last time, provides a brief look at the common people of Moonstone, focusing especially on Thea's Aunt Tillie, who, bolstered by accounts of Thea's successes in New York and by a sense of the "noble pleasure" she has given to the world, "lives in a world full of secret satisfactions" (578).

Thea's early years are described mainly in terms of her youthful interest in music. In Part one, "Friends of Childhood," we see the extraordinarily sensitive Thea paired off against her rival, Lily Fisher, the blond, blue-eyed darling of the town, "the angel-child of the Baptists" (79), who, to Thea's chagrin, always manages to gain the greatest attention and win the most enthusiastic applause for her performances. It will be many years before Thea will come to realize that the more sophisticated, knowledgeable members of an audience in fact can appreciate real passion and talent, what lies behind mere looks, as the essence of artistic performance.

Thea's rise to success is marked by her relationships with a number of men, each of whom is a valuable friend. None of these men fully defines Thea's developing sense of self or artistic endeavor, but each significantly influences her future. Of the townspeople Doctor Archie nurses her through childhood illnesses and becomes a protective figure throughout the novel. "Spanish Johnny," a local Mexican musician, represents the most elemental love of and response to music. When Thea sings for Johnny and his friends, she experiences the appreciation of those for whom music is first of all simply an emotional experience. Ray Kennedy, a romantic who has made a comfortable life for himself in the railroad business, is the first of Thea's friends to believe in her potential. With his untimely death Thea inherits six hundred dollars, which will make possible her leaving Moonstone to pursue the development of her talent. Fred Ottenburg, "a florid brewery magnate," who pursues a romantic relationship with Thea, introduces her into Chicago society and provides the opportunity for her to realize her essential artistic self during a visit to the Southwest and the discovery of Native American Cliff-Dweller culture. Here, in the confrontation with the natural beauty of the landscape and that ancient culture, Thea finds the secret to artistic sensibility and creative power: "what was any art," she muses, "but an effort to make a sheath, a mould in which to imprison for a moment the shining, elusive element which is life itself..." (378).

Several music teachers also play major roles in Thea's artistic development. Her first piano teacher, Wunsch, gives Thea exactly what his name suggests: the *desire* to become a musical artist. During one of Thea's first lessons, the "sadly battered" man introduces her to Gluck's *Orpheus and Euridyce*, declaring it "the most beautiful opera ever made" (89). With Thea accompanying him, Wunsch sings Orpheus's lament, which begins with the lines, "*Ach, ich habe sie verloren/ All' mein Glück ist nun dahin.*" It is a fitting allusion: as his life moves toward its end, Thea's is just beginning. He laments his own loss of what she, as artist, will find. More than the other citizens of Moonstone, Wunsch realizes the potential that Thea possesses because she has the passion for musical expression essential to greatness: the secret, he declares to her, is "*in der Brust, in der Brust* it is [sic], *und ohne dieses giebt es keine Kunst, giebt es keine Kunst!*" (99).

Thea's move to Chicago to continue her study as a pianist takes her to Andor Harsanyi. It is he who discovers her talent as a singer and also adds another important element to her artistic development. If Wunsch had seen a passion for music as the key to genius, Harsanyi teaches Thea the importance of combining conception, "a beautiful idea," and technique with that passion to produce something truly artistic. Understanding the extent of Thea's talent but realizing that he can only "play" with Thea's voice, Harsanyi sends her to the finest voice teacher in Chicago, Madison Bowers. His instruction is cold and academic: "Bowers had all the qualities which go with a good teacher — except generosity and warmth" (315). Thea's experience as his student, however, prepares her for the next significant step in her career, her move to Europe to study and then to perform with the Dresden Opera Company.

In describing Thea's triumph in New York ten years later, in 1909, Cather focuses on her performances in several Wagnerian roles, each appropriate to her artistry and her career at this point. Thea's debut role, Elizabeth in *Tannhäuser*, is actually sung in Dresden. While visiting Thea's mother, Doctor Archie, one of Thea's old friends from Moonstone, notices a photograph of Thea "who must have been singing '*Dich, teure Halle, grüss' ich wieder*,' her eyes looking up, her beautiful hands outspread with pleasure" (492). As Giannone remarks, "Willa Cather's allusion here is perfectly clear and perfectly apt. The song, which is Elizabeth's entrance and [which] praises music itself, doubles as Madame Kronborg's artistic entrance into her personal Hall of Song. It is a joyous, symbolic debut..." (97). As she does generally throughout the novel, Cather quotes only briefly from the libretto. What follows is significant, however, for the passage in full reads:

> Oh, hall of song I give thee greeting!
> All hail to thee thou hallowed place!
> 'T was here that dream so sweet and fleeting,
> Upon my heart his song did trace.
> But since by him forsaken
> A desert thou dost seem —
> Thy echoes only awaken
> Remembrance of a dream.
> But now the flame of hope is lighted,
> Thy vault shall ring with glorious war;
> For he whose strains my soul delighted
> No longer roams afar [quoted in Giannone 97].

The passage, coming toward the end of the novel, signals Thea's triumph and is neatly juxtaposed to the earlier reference to the lines from Gluck's *Orpheus*, "*Ich habe sie verloren*," which is associated with the defeated and forlorn Wunsch (see also, Giannone 98).

Thea's next Wagnerian roles are as Elsa in *Lohengrin* and as Venus in *Tannhäuser*. In both cases she sings parts "not particularly suited to [her] voice at all" (512). With mention of these roles Cather suggests her familiarity with the competitive nature of the operatic world, a topic she had addressed earlier, for example, in her essay on Lillian Nordica's 1896–1897 dispute with Jean de Reszke over which singer, Nordica or Nellie Melba, would perform the roles of Elsa and Brünnhilde at the Met. (See Cather's essay, "Nordica," on this subject.) As it had earlier when she was given the role of Elizabeth in *Tännhauser*, "lucky chance" again plays a role when Thea, on incredibly short notice, is asked to finish the part of Sieglinde in *Die Walküre* after the singer scheduled for the role is unable to continue after Act I. (Cather changed the opera from *The Tales of Hoffman* to *Die Walküre*. See the incident recounted above in the discussion of Fremstad, pp. 20–21.) As noted previously, Thea's performance is extraordinary; as Fred Ottenburg, who has come to New York to see her, describes it, the audience's response at the end of the second act, "was something like a popular uprising" (530).

To her next role, Fricka in *Das Rheingold*, Thea, again apparently miscast, brings an interpretation that demonstrates both her uniqueness and her artistry. When Fred Ottenburg describes the role as "not an alluring part," Thea answers, "Then you've never heard it well done" (535). To the role, she brings "a distinct kind of loveliness ... a shining beauty like the light of sunset on distant sails. *Fricka* had been sung as a jealous spouse for so long that he [Fred] had forgot she meant wisdom before she meant domestic order, and that, in any event, she was always a goddess" (538–39).

The culmination of Thea's artistic journey comes with the opportunity to sing again the role of Sieglinde, this time from the beginning. Again Thea must deal with professional rivalries and personal jealousies, as well as preparing for the part. When the time for the performance arrives, the Metropolitan Opera House is filled with "an inspiring audience," including Thea's former teacher, Andor Harsanyi (565). Again quoting first lines of text to mark places in the story line, Cather takes the reader through Act I of the opera from Seiglinde's initial entrance and discovery of Siegmund, to their rapturous embrace upon their realization that they are brother and sister. Just as Act I ends with the themes of identity, coming together, possibility, and joy, so the "Kronborg" section of Cather's novel ends on the same notes. Thea has achieved her own artistic identity, all of the elements of her personality and training have come together, and her future is bright. Cather says finally of Thea's performance that it represents the synthesis of all those elements that finally make for genius: "Artistic growth," she declares, "is more than it is anything else, a refining of the sense of truthfulness. The stupid believe that to be truthful is easy; only the artist, the great artist knows how difficult it is. That afternoon nothing new came to Thea Kronborg, no enlightenment, no inspiration. She merely came into full possession of things she had been refining and perfecting for so long" (571).

* * *

Midway through *The Song of the Lark* Willa Cather describes Thea Kronborg's first exposure to the music of Wagner. The incident, which occurs shortly after Thea has moved to Chicago, doubtless echoes Cather's own experience when she first heard Wagner's works in the 1890s:

> She knew scarcely anything about the Wagner operas. She had a vague idea that "Rhinegold" was about the strife between gods and men; she had read something about it in Mr. Haweis's book long ago. Too tired to follow the orchestra with much understanding, she crouched down in her seat and closed her eyes. The cold, stately measures of the Walhalla music rang out, far away; the rainbow bridge throbbed out into the air, under it the wailing of the Rhine daughters and the singing of the Rhine. But Thea was sunk in twilight; it was all going on in another world. So it happened that with a dull, almost listless ear she heard for the first time that troubled music, ever-darkening, ever-brightening, which was to flow through so many years of her life [252].

Cather would come to see Wagnerian opera as the ultimate art form. Opera is, she declared in her essay on Gertrude Hall's *The Wagnerian Romances*, "a hybrid art,—partly literary to begin with. It happens that in the Wagnerian music-drama the literary part of the work is not trivial, as it is so often in operas, but is truly the mate of the music, done by the same hand. The music is throughout concerned with words, and with things that can be presented in language; with human beings and their passions and sorrows, and with places and with periods of time, with particular rivers and particular mountains, even..." (62). Cather believed that the scenes and characters in Wagner's operas — those "noble, mysterious, significant dramas in roughly made verse" (65–66) — were the essence of "the legendary beauty, the truly religious feeling that haunts [the operas] from end to end" (62).[6]

While Cather's taste in music would move from admiration of Wagner's grand operas to love of the more intimate works of Beethoven and Schubert, the discovery of Wagner's music played a significant role in the development of her artistic awareness. In some cases allusions to Wagner's works are explicit, as in "The Garden Lodge," "A Wagner Matinée," and *The Song of the Lark*; in other cases they are subtlety embedded as in her Pulitzer-Prize-winning novel *One of Ours*. Clearly, from early on, Wagner's music provided this literary artist with an awareness of the essence of great art and with a host of allusive possibilities.

NOTES

1. Richard Giannone's *Music in Willa Cather's Fiction* (1968) has long been the major study of Cather's use of musical references and themes in her works. Although a number of subsequent studies have explored ideas that Giannone did not mention or develop, his book is still considered the starting point for any consideration of the subject.

2. For a discussion of Cather's use of *leitmotif* in the story, see Todd Giles's article "Counterpoint, Memory, and Leitmotif in Willa Cather's 'A Wagner Matinée.'" Giles explores Cather's use of counterpoint (or juxtaposition) and notes that while Wagner did not originate leitmotifs, he "is well known for his liberal use of them in his operas, including dozens of them in the *Ring* cycle alone ..." (36). Giles demonstrates that both devices are used significantly in the development of the role of memory and remembrance in the story.

3. Cather was also acquainted with the great soprano Lillian Nordica, famous in large part for her performances in a number of Wagnerian roles. Cather originally saw her in a production of *Cavalleria Rusticana* with Campanini in 1893 and subsequently as a number of Wagnerian heroines. Cather interviewed her in the late 1890s. In an early journalistic piece Cather discussed Nordica's career with the Metropolitan Opera; in an open letter to Nordica, Cather noted that she preferred the diva in Wagnerian parts and praised her as the embodiment of "all that is best in American womanhood" (646). See "Nordica" and "An Open Letter to Nordica." Nordica was clearly the model for Cressida Garnet in Cather's story "The Diamond Mine," published in 1916.

4. Although the story of Fremstad's stepping into the role of Giulietta on short notice has long been seen as the genesis for a similar passage in *The Song of the Lark*, in a recent article Marvin Friedman notes another "substitution incident" that parallels the details of the substitution experience "much more clearly than the Fremstad episode" (53). This event, interestingly, involved Margaret Matzenauer's substitution for Fremstad in the role of Kundry in *Parsifal* on New Year's Day 1912. Freidman points out that a highly laudatory review in the *New York Times* on January 2 outlined "almost all the elements" of the incident as portrayed in Cather's novel (53). It is almost certain that Cather either saw the performance or read the review.

5. The title of the novel was suggested by Cather's having seen Jules Breton's painting by that name in the Chicago Art Institute. In the painting, as Cather describes it, there was "the flat country, the early morning light, the wet fields, the look in the girl's heavy face" (SOL 249), as she paused from her work in a field to listen more attentively to the song of a nearby bird. Thea told herself "that picture was 'right.' Just what she meant by this, it would take a clever person to explain" (249). In the preface she wrote for the 1932 edition of the novel, Cather provided an explanation: "The title was meant to suggest a young girl's awakening to something beautiful" (v).

6. For an interesting comparison of the operas of Mozart and Wagner, see Cather's essay "Three Operas" (*The World and the Parish*, II, 658).

BIBLIOGRAPHY

Bennett, Mildred R. *The World of Willa Cather*. New Edition with Notes and Index. Lincoln: University of Nebraska Press, 1961.

Bohlke, L. Brent, ed. *Willa Cather in Person: Interviews, Speeches, and Letters*. Lincoln: University of Nebraska Press, 1986.

Brown, E. K. *Willa Cather: A Critical Biography*. Completed by Leon Edel. New York: Knopf, 1953.

Cather, Willa. "Concerning Thomas Carlyle." *The Kingdom of Art: Willa Cather's First Principles and Critical Statements, 1893–1896.* Ed. Bernice Slote. Lincoln: Universtiy of Nebraska Press, 1966.

———. "The Garden Lodge." *Willa Cather's Collected Short Fiction, 1892–1912.* Lincoln: U of Nebraska P, 1965.

———. "Gertrude Hall's *The Wagnerian Romances.*" *Willa Cather on Writing: Critical Studies on Writing as an Art.* 1949. Lincoln: University of Nebraska Press, 1988.

———. "History in the Arts— Descent." *The Kingdom of Art: Willa Cather's First Principles and Critical Statements, 1893–1896.* Ed. Bernice Slote. Lincoln: University of Nebraska Press, 1966.

———. Letter to Dorothy Canfield Fisher. [8 March 1922]. University of Vermont.

———. Letter to Mr. [Orrick] Johns. 17 November 1922. University of Virginia.

———. Letters to Elizabeth Shepley Sergeant. Pierpont Morgan Library.

———. "Nordica." *The World and the Parish: Willa Cather's Articles and Reviews, 1893–* Ed. William M. Curtin. Vol. 1. Lincoln: University of Nebraska Press, 1970.

———. *One of Ours.* Scholarly Edition. Lincoln: University of Nebraska Press, 2006.

———. "An Open Letter to Nordica." *The World and the Parish: Willa Cather's Articles and Reviews, 1893–1902.* Ed. William M. Curtin. Vol. 2. Lincoln: University of Nebraska Press.

———. "Parlor Critics." *The Kingdom of Art: Willa Cather's First Principles and Critical Statements, 1893–1896.* Ed. Bernice Slote. Lincoln: University of Nebraska Press, 1966.

———. "The Perfect Wagnerite." *The World and the Parish: Willa Cather's Articles and Reviews, 1893–1902.* Ed. William M. Curtin. Vol. 2. Lincoln: University of Nebraska Press, 1970.

———. *The Professor's House.* Scholarly Edition. Lincoln: University of Nebraska Press, 2006.

———. *The Song of the Lark.* 1915. Sentry Edition. Boston: Houghton Mifflin, 1963.

———. "Three American Singers." *McClure's Magazine* 42 (December 1913): 33–48.

———. "Uncle Valentine." *Uncle Valentine and Other Stories: Willa Cather's Uncollected Short Fiction, 1913–1929.* Ed. Bernice Slote. Lincoln: University of Nebraska Press, 1986.

———. "A Wagner Matinée." *Willa Cather's Collected Short Fiction, 1892–1912.* Lincoln: University of Nebraska Press, 1965.

———. "A Week of Wagner." *The World and the Parish: Willa Cather's Articles and Reviews, 1893–1902.* Ed. William M. Curtin. Vol. 1. Lincoln: University of Nebraska Press, 1970.

Curtin, James, ed. *The World and the Parish: Willa Cather's Articles and Reviews, 1893–* 2 vols. Lincoln: University of Nebraska Press, 1970.

Giannone, Richard. *Music in Willa Cather's Fiction.* 1968. Lincoln: University of Nebraska Press, 2001.

Lewis, Edith. *Willa Cather Living: A Personal Record.* New York: Knopf, 1953.

Mencken, H. L. "Portrait of an American Citizen." *Smart Set* 69 (October 1922): 140–42.

Seibel, George. "Miss Willa Cather from Nebraska." *The Colophon* (September 1949): 195–208.

Woodress, James. *Willa Cather: A Literary Life.* Lincoln: University of Nebraska Press, 1987.

III. Wagnerian Opera in Performance

14

Michelle DeYoung: An Interview

John Louis DiGaetani

Michelle DeYoung, a Wagnerian mezzo-soprano, has sung some of the major Wagnerian mezzo-soprano roles at the Metropolitan Opera, the Wagner Festival in Bayreuth, the State Opera in Berlin, in Tokyo, and around the world. She is particularly famous at the Met for her Venus in *Tannhäuser* as well as Fricka in the Ring and Brangene in *Tristan und Isolde*. She has also sung these roles in Berlin and Japan with Daniel Barenboim and Seiji Ozawa. Her extensive discography includes Dido in the Grammy Award winning recording of *Les Troyens* with Sir Colin Davis and the London Symphony Orchestra.

JD: *Where were you educated?*
MD: My voice teacher is Trish McCaffrey from the voice department of the Manhattan School of Music. I have also attended other schools and studied with other voice teachers at Northridge University and San Francisco State University.
JD: *Are you from California?*
MD: No, I was born in Michigan and spent a lot of my childhood in Colorado and California.
Did you always want to be a singer, a singer of Wagnerian opera?
I originally wanted to teach, but while I was in college my friends and teachers convinced me that I should be majoring in music rather than education and so I switched and they really encouraged me to sing. I began singing in church choirs — my father was a minister — like a lot of professional singers, and also played many instruments including piano.
Which are your favorite Wagnerian roles and how are they different from each other?
The two Frickas in the Ring remain so interesting and so different. In *Rheingold* she is a young wife and very much in love with Wotan, though she is also very worried about her sister Freia. In *Die Walküre* she is an older woman, and much more bitter and angry. She has had to put up with Wotan's extramarital affairs over many years, and while she still loves Wotan she is also very resentful of his infidelities — and also his relationship with the bastard daughter Brünnhilde.

Brangene in Tristan is a totally different character . She is an assistant/maid to Isolde but Wagner does not specify her age. I think of her as a younger sister to Isolde — or maybe an old sister or aunt. In Francesca Zanbello's production of *Tristan* in Seattle I played her as a younger sister, and also clearly in love with Tristan herself. But she is in a very vulnerable position and engages in some very risky behavior in not following Isolde's orders. Brangene is also sometimes in a panic — specifically when Isolde orders her to get the death potion to murder both Tristan and Isolde as well. Brangene takes a terrible risk in switching the potions, but she is a very brave woman.

Which is the best approach to Brangene's character?

It has a lot to do with the director and his vision of the opera. Any character has many different sides, especially in Wagnerian opera. But Brangene refuses to follow stupid commands and goes out on her own — she does not just want to follow orders from Isolde.

What about Venus?

I just did the role with Ozawa in Japan, and earlier at the Met. She is so sexy and she keeps trying to seduce Tannhäuser and keep him with her in the Venusberg. Her music is so hard too — it keeps going up and up.

Are these your favorite roles?

I also enjoy Sieglinde and Kundry, which I did last year in Bayreuth.

I really enjoyed your Sieglinde at the Lyric Opera in Chicago with Placido Domingo as Siegmund. You were very sensual in the role, and your attraction to Siegmund was both immediate and desperate. It was interesting to watch your seduction of Siegmund and consequent liberation from a terrible marriage.

Well, poor Sieglinde is trapped in a loveless and brutal marriage to Hunding, and she senses something very familiar and very needy in Siegmund.

How did you like working in Bayreuth?

Well, Bayreuth is such a special place — appearing in the theater that Wagner himself designed for his operas becomes clearly a singular honor and opportunity. And the acoustic in that house remains so wonderful; with the orchestra under the stage it is easier for the singers to connect with the audience and just to be heard without so much volume. Also Bayreuth is much smaller than a house like the Met, where you really need the biggest voices to fill that very large theater. Bayreuth is a wonderful place to work and I really enjoyed doing Kundry there. The director, Christoph Schlingensief, was great to work with on this character, and he brought out different sides to her. He really opened my eyes to Kundry and how she operates through the three acts of the opera. She becomes both sexy and maternal in the second act, her big act.

It seems to me that in Wagnerian opera sexuality is usually connected with the search for mother. So many of Wagner's heroes are orphans because Wagner himself often felt like an orphan. He was pretty much without a father — even his step-father Ludwig Geyer (who might have been his biological father) died when Wagner was just a boy. And his mother was often rejecting and neglectful of him. I think Wagner was also bi-polar — or manic-depressive.

Well, certainly Kundry is both sexual and maternal with Parsifal. She sings lullabies to him as she tries to seduce him in the second act — and she succeeds and kisses him, at least for a while. I find Kundry fascinating because of her ways of manipulating the other characters in the opera, especially Parsifal. And she is clearly madly in love with him, rather like Venus is madly in love with Tannhäuser. But I find Venus much more difficult to sing than Kundry.

Why?

Venus is only in two acts of the opera, and most of her music is in the first act. She goes higher and higher and it is a very long first act for her. It is very difficult and she is a huge challenge.

You make it sound easy to the audience! And you are very sexy in the role as well.
Thank you but one has to be sexy when playing the goddess Venus. Kundry of course is the longer role since she appears in all three acts of *Parsifal*, but she has only two words, four notes, to sing in the last act. But she becomes a great acting challenge in the last act of *Parsifal*. She is also terrified of Klingsor, whom she must obey. She is certainly a complex character.

She is supposed to be a timeless and eternal woman.
But she is also a credible human being rather than just a monster.

What roles would you like to do in the future?
I would love to do, but probably won't, both Isolde and Brünnhilde. I have the notes already but not the tessitura. Both Venus and Kundry are called sopranos by Wagner. But I am truly a dramatic mezzo-soprano so shall leave these roles to my soprano colleagues.

Be careful! I think the main reason Jessye Norman had a short career in opera was that she was always really a mezzo-soprano and her doing soprano roles shortened her singing career.
She was so kind to me when we were both performing in *The Makropoulos Case* at the Met.

What do you think it takes to make a career singing Wagner?
You have to have a sizeable voice that does not sound pushed. You really need a big voice, especially if you want to sing Wagner in the large opera houses like the Met. In the smaller houses like Bayreuth you can sing Wagner even if you do not have a truly large, dramatic voice. Of course the orchestra is enormous in Wagner but some conductors make more demands than Wagner intended. You also have to have good German since a lot of the Wagnerian roles are really Sprechtstimme so your German diction has to be really good.

Are you of German descent?
I'm Dutch. So I had to work hard at my German with diction coaches at the Met and places like the Goethe Institute.

Where did you go to college?
I went to three colleges: (1) Calvin College in Michigan, (2) San Francisco State University, and then finally (3) Northridge University. My parents are Christian Reformed, as am I, and my father is a minister in that faith.

Do you think Wagner is very religious? Do you think he was a Christian?
There is a spiritual element in Wagnerian opera. He is constantly searching for religion but I do not think he ever finds it. I think he himself thought he was God so I think it was hard for him to believe in anybody else.

I myself think Wagner suffered from bi-polar illness—in other words, he was manic-depressive—and so fluctuated between suicidal depressions and manic highs. But I agree with you that he never really finds a satisfying religion, though he does seem to be looking. From an artistic point of view, the searching is more interesting than the finding since we are uncomfortable with art that is propaganda for a particular religion.
Yes, I agree with you that his constant searching makes his operas more interesting artistically.

What other music do you like to sing?
Well, I love Mahler and have been able to perform and record a lot of Mahler—symphonies and songs. I also was able to record one of my favorite roles, Dido in Berlioz' *Les Troyens*. She is such a fascinating role: Queen, seductress, rejected woman, suicide!

How do you deal with difficult conductors? You have worked with some of the best of them: James Levine, Daniel Barenboim, Colin Davis, Seiji Ozawa, etc.

Well, Wagner makes great demands on a singer but there are conductors who help and those who do not help. These conductors should help us! A singer needs time to breathe! We are human beings after all, and one needs conductors who will give you time to breathe and not drown you out! The orchestra in Wagner is enormous but we singers have only one pair of vocal cords. I particularly liked working on *Parsifal* with Pierre Boulez since he tries to keep the orchestra from overwhelming the singers. He really follows the score but he can sometimes be too quick. But James Levine and Daniel Barenboim have also been great to work with and are considerate of the problems of singers.

Which productions are you fond of?

I must admit to liking the realistic ones — like the Met's current production of the Ring cycle or *Tannhäuser*. Such gorgeous productions! The Met's Ring is really larger than life, it is both realistic and epic

In Germany in particular, realistic Wagner productions are dismissed as kitsch or as Nazi art. Unfortunately, realism in Wagnerian opera reminds many Germans of the realistic Wagnerian productions by Tietjens and other directors during the Nazi period. So many but not all of the German productions seem like Euro trash to many traditional Wagnerians. Speaking of Wagnerian opera and Venus, do you know the film Meeting Venus, which uses a very comic approach to Tannhäuser with Glenn Close playing a Wagnerian soprano. One of the notorious flops in opera history is Wagner's own attempt to stage Tannhäuser at the Paris Opera in 1861, and Meeting Venus is about another failed attempt to stage that opera in Paris.

Yes, I love that film and own a copy. But there are some German directors who do wonderful things with Wagner. The modern director approach can produce some wonderful results. Robert Carsen's production of *Tannhäuser* was wonderful , where all the Minnesingers were painters instead of singers, and the last act ended with all the great Venuses in Western art on stage — Titian's, Botticelli's, Raphael's etc. Such a new approach to Venus and *Tannhäuser* can produce some very interesting new insights into the opera and its major themes. In Germany Wagner is staged so often that often the public there wants something different, something new.

Of course, sometimes there is just shock value in new productions. I read of a production of Tristan und Isolde in Rio de Janeiro that began with Isolde masturbating.

Oh, no!

Yes. And the performances were sold out and received world-wide press attention. Shock value does sell tickets and gets a lot of press coverage while traditional productions tend to get ignored by the world press. In any case, what roles are in your future?

Well, I will be making my La Scala début as Brangene with Barenboim and I am certainly looking forward to that — plus singing in Japan and New York, also in Wagnerian roles.

You sing Wagner like an angel — and the best kind of angel, a sexy angel.

Thank you.

15

Ben Heppner: An Interview

John Louis DiGaetani

Ben Heppner, the great Canadian Heldentenor, was raised in Dawson Creek, British Columbia, is from a Mennonite family, and was one of nine children. Mr. Heppner was a music major at the University of British Columbia and a winner in 1979 of the Canadian Broadcasting Company Talent Festival. He also won the Birgit Nilsson Prize in 1988 at the Metropolitan Opera. He is considered one of the great dramatic tenors in the world today and he has sung most of the greatest dramatic tenor roles at the major opera houses around the world. He has sung at Milan's La Scala, the Vienna State Opera, London's Covent Garden, Munich's Bavarian State Opera, and New York's Met. He sang Walther von Stolzing in Wagner's *Die Meistersinger von Nürnberg* at the Metropolitan Opera in 1993 to standing ovations. He also recorded this role with the conductor Georg Solti as well as Maestro Wolfgang Sawallisch. He has also performed Lohengrin at the Metropolitan Opera under James Levine in Robert Wilson's production of the opera in 1998. He also sang the title role in Wagner's *Parsifal* at the Met. In 1999 he sang Tristan at the Met, a role he had sung the previous year at the Seattle Opera. He has also recorded most of these roles in complete opera recordings with major conductors. I spoke with Heppner during the summer of 2007 while he was vacationing at his home in Toronto.

JD: *How did you get interested in singing and in opera?*
BH: I sang in the church choir as a child and in high school, but a career in singing did not seem like anything real to me as a young person in Dawson Creek, British Columbia. I went to opera school in 1981 but Wagner was not on my list of composers that I ever sang. When I began studying voice with William and Dixie Neill in the fall of 1987, he was the one who told me I had a large tenor voice and could sing the young Heldentenor roles. My first big success in Wagner was as Walther in *Meistersinger*, still my favorite role, though I do not plan to continue singing it.
JD: *Why not, you are such a wonderful Walther, and you have sung the role often and so successfully at the Met and at other major opera houses.*
BH: Well, I want to go on to other roles. In 2006 I also sang Parsifal at the Met.
You certainly have. You have received standing ovations at the Met and at other opera houses for your performances in these very difficult roles.
Parsifal I find easy to do since the role is low for a tenor and not very long.

Ben Heppner as Walther in *Die Meistersinger von Nürnberg, Act 2,* at the Metropolitan Opera (photograph by Winnie Klotz).

Wagner had such trouble casting Siegfried that he made his final opera, Parsifal, *easier to cast. When Wagner himself staged the premiere of the Ring at Bayreuth in 1876, Siegfried was his most difficult role to cast. So Wagner composed the role of Parsifal with greater consideration for the tenor who must sing it. I notice that your most recent recording has been of excerpts of Siegmund and Siegfried.*

Yes, these are the roles I want to do in the future. In fact, I am scheduled to do my first complete *Siegfried* with Simon Rattle and the Berlin Philharmonic at Aix en Provence in 2008, and then in Salzburg in 2009. The *Götterdämmerung* Siegfried will follow at Aix en Provence later in the same year.

I am eager to hear you in these roles. What about your wonderful singing in the role of Tristan, often considered the most difficult Wagnerian tenor role.

Tristan is like climbing Mt. Everest to me since it is so long and so difficult. It really wears me out. Actually I enjoy singing Walther and Lohengrin more, but once I start performing Tristan the time flies and I feel the complex depth and suffering in Tristan, which make the role so compelling and rewarding to perform. The final act of the opera is so wonderful and compelling but also so difficult.

Do you think Isolde dies at the end of the opera, as Tristan so clearly does. Wagner's final stage directions for Isolde are rather vague since she is supposed to fall on his body.

Well, often in modern stagings of this opera Isolde does not die, but she does sing the Liebestod, which does suggest her death at the end. But I find greater joy in the role of Walther, though it is also very long and the quintet in the last act is so difficult.

And then you have to sing the Prize Song, which has been building up throughout the act.

Yes, but it is wonderful to have such a happy ending at the end of a Wagnerian opera, and *Meistersinger* provides that — the only Wagnerian opera which is a comedy.

And your Walther does not peter out at the end, and you sound fresh and forceful to the very end of the Prize Song, unlike most other tenors. That is also true of your Tristan, which also sounds fresh and wonderful in his final scene. What about Erik and Tannhäuser?

I have recorded Erik and performed it onstage, but I do not find it so interesting a role when compared to Lohengrin or Walther.

I wish you would record your wonderful Tristan since I have enjoyed you so much in that part.

It is available on DVD with the great soprano Jane Eaglen as Isolde with the Metropolitan Opera and with James Levine conducting. I was supposed to record the opera with Solti but alas he died before we could complete the project.

You have certainly worked with some fabulous conductors. Your Walther in Meistersinger *was conducted with Solti, your Lohengrin was under Colin Davis, your Tristan DVD was under James Levine, and now you will be performing Siegfried with Simon Rattle, certainly a major conductor though new to Wagner. Tannhäuser and Siegmund remain the only roles you have not performed.*

Yes, Tannhäuser remains a challenge for my future.

I am surprised you are first singing Siegfried and not Siegmund since the later role seems a bit easier for most Heldentenors to learn because it is lower.

Well, most Heldentenors were originally baritones who had to work on their high notes so most of them do Siegmund first and then Siegfried. But I was never a baritone but always a tenor so the high notes are more natural and easier for me. So I thought I would do the higher roles, Siegfried, first, and then Siegmund.

Your recording of excerpts of these two roles sounds quite compelling to me, and your high notes do not sound forced but open and natural, and I hope you will bring these roles to the Met, and soon. Your success as Parsifal suggests that perhaps that religious opera attracted you because of your own religious background as a Christian and a Mennonite.

Religion is important in my life, but I think of Wagner more as a mythic than a religious composer. Certainly *Parsifal* combines religion and mythology, but I see it more as a mythic work that has much more to do with Wagner and his conceptions of Schopenhauer than with Christianity.

One of the things I like about your performances is the excellence of your German diction. Are you of German descent?

Yes, I am. My father was born in the Ukraine in 1902 but his first language was a dialect of German and my mother's first language was also a dialect of German. But they never taught me German at home. I learned to sing proper German later on at University. In our house, only God spoke Hochdeutsch. But the dialect of German I heard at home did familiarize me with the sound of the language. I still have to struggle with it — for example, the final r in German words like "mir" and "hier" is different from initial r's in the language. I have to work hard at my German diction.

My German friends tell me your German diction is excellent. Would you say that Wagner is your favorite opera composer?

Yes, he is. But I do not only sing Wagner.

I certainly enjoyed your Andrea Chenier at the Met in 2007, and your Otello two years earlier. You gave those roles an Italianate sound so perfect for those parts.

Andrea Chenier seems so easy to me after singing Wagner — four arias and two short duets. It is a breeze to sing Andrea Chenier after the long Wagnerian tenor roles. I have also performed and recorded the tenor role of Aeneas in *Les Troyens*. I try to balance my singing by doing both German and Italian roles, though the greater demand is for the Wagner roles.

Those are the hardest roles to cast, and you do them so well.

I also sing Mozart — roles like Idomeneo — but I must confess that my favorite roles are Wagner's.

You remind me of another great Canadian tenor, Jon Vickers, who was also very wise about balancing his repertory. What does it take to sing Wagnerian opera?

Well, clearly, you have to have a big voice. You can sing Verdi, Puccini, or Mozart with a smaller voice since the orchestration is lighter with those composers. But length and endurance are also major problems in the Wagnerian Heldentenor roles — those are very long operas.

Tristan seems to be the longest and most death-obsessed of Wagner's operas. Both Tristan and Isolde seem to me so suicidal, and of course Tristan commits suicide at the end of the opera — after two earlier attempts.

The Wesendonck Lieder are also very death-obsessed. I will be performing them with the La Scala Orchestra and Riccardo Chailly.

Weren't these songs written for soprano?

Although they are most often sung by sopranos, they were not written specifically for the soprano voice, so tenors often sing them as well. Many of the musical themes in those songs were later developed by Wagner in *Tristan und Isolde*. Theirs certainly is a death-obsessed love, and their death is viewed by the lovers as a way of uniting them without any subsequent separation. Of course theirs is a hidden love, an adulterous love, a love under the cover of night, and night can be easily seen as a metaphor for death.

It has often seemed to me that Wagner himself suffered from depression and bipolar illness since

Ben Heppner as Tristan in *Tristan und Isolde* at the Metropolitan Opera (photograph by Winnie Klotz).

the highs and lows are so extreme in Wagner's operas, and these extremes also occurred in his life. Wagner went from being a pauper, sometimes even in debtors' prison, to having the King of Bavaria as his most generous patron.

Wagner also lived in the 19th century when the cult of personality became so prominent. Artists like Chopin, Liszt, and Wagner were allowed to be extravagant and crazy since that was the 19th century concept of the great artist, the great personality. These composers were indulged by the people around them during their time period.

Yes they were, at least by some people. Speaking of Tristan, a role you have performed so well, who is your favorite Isolde?

Jane Eaglen is a wonderful colleague and a wonderful Isolde. She was always so thoughtful and so perceptive during rehearsals, and she also has a great sense of humor. Deborah Voigt is wonderful as well — she has already performed the role in Vienna to great success and recorded it with Thielemann. I have also enjoyed working with Waltraud Meier and Deborah Polaski in this role.

Have you performed Erik in The Flying Dutchman? *I know you have recorded it.*

Yes, I did perform Erik with the Geneva Opera, and in Vienna, but I put the role aside since I find other Wagnerian tenor roles more interesting. The roles in my future will be Siegfried, Siegmund, and Tannhäuser. These are the challenges I want to face in the next decade.

You will have done all the great Heldentenor roles if you succeed in these roles as well, which I am sure you will. Will you emphasize a religious element in these later roles?

These parts seem more mythic to me than Christian. They share the mythology of even the Tolkien Ring, which has become so popular. Most of the countries in Europe or the ancient civilizations in the Americas have mythologies which present men looking for swords, for girlfriends, and for adventures while fighting the forces of evil. Clearly Tolkien's Ring learned a great deal from Wagner's Ring. These epics all provide great adventures for their epic heroes.

That sounds like Siegfried. Also that sounds a bit like Parsifal, arguably Wagner's most religious opera.

But is it Christianity? It seems more like Buddhistic transcendence than Christian theology to me.

Yes, you are clearly right. It has certainly been great fun talking to you — and it is even more fun to hear you sing.

Singing has been a great joy in my life. It is a blessing for me from God.

You make singing sound so easy!

It is not, but it sure beats working for a living!

16

The Silver Age of Wagnerian Singing

Barbara Josephine Guenther

Over a hundred years ago, after attending performances of *Parsifal, Die Meistersinger,* and *Tristan und Isolde* at Bayreuth, George Bernard Shaw wrote, "singers of genius, great Tristans and Parsifals, Kundrys and Isoldes, will not be easily obtained [in England] any more than in Germany; and when they are found, all Europe and America will compete for them" (213). Wagnerian singers engage in a high-stakes balancing act: infusing declamation with legato, meeting both interpretative and vocal demands, singing with an orchestra of unprecedented volume. It is no wonder that there are so few Wagnerian "singers of genius."

In Germany shortly after Wagner's death, there were a variety of competing styles — not only the Bayreuth style, but distinct vocal styles in Dresden, Munich, Berlin, and Vienna — and not until the period between the two World Wars was there a stylistic synthesis. David Breckbill finds two reasons for this synthesis: singers' increasing exposure to various styles, especially in London and at the annual Munich Wagner Festival, and the immense impact of Caruso's singing in Germany, which led to more lyricism being incorporated into German singing. This, he believes, is the reason that the interwar period was a golden age in Wagnerian singing.[1]

There is no reason, however, to see these two types of interaction as the only, or even the chief, reason for the remarkable singing during this period. One simply cannot deny the phenomenal talent of a few singers who remain today the most thrilling exemplars of Wagnerian singing: the Hungarian bass-baritone Friedrich Schorr, Norway's Kirsten Flagstad, and the Danish-American tenor Lauritz Melchior. Breckbill's admiration of the singing of this period leads him to believe that beginning in 1940 there was a prolonged and decisive decline in Wagnerian singing. "Prolonged" suggests a period of more than a decade, and if this is so, I choose to counter his assertion: the 1950s, '60s, and '70s can be considered the silver age of Wagnerian singing. This essay will deal with singers who were active internationally during most or all of this three-decade period.

A number of fine singers do not fit this framework but are worth mentioning at this point. Some — Siegmund Nimsgern, Bernd Weikl, Hildegard Behrens, Anna Tomowa-Sintow, Teresa Zylis-Gara, and the aptly named Siegfried Jerusalem, for instance — were too young for our time frame. Lucia Popp was performing during this period, but although she sang the *Götterdämmerung* Woglinde on Solti's mid–'60s recording of the *Ring*, she was for the most part singing soubrette and coloratura roles until the 1980s. Only then did she first sing the heavier lyric roles of Eva (1982) and Elsa (1989). English soprano Rita Hunter was singing Senta in the early '60s, but not until the 1970s, after a significant vocal change, did she come into her own. Even then she did not often fulfill the expectations created by her powerful Brünnhilde in Goodall's 1973 *Ring*, recorded live at the ENO.

Hunter's colleague on that recording, the English tenor Alberto Remedios, had a fine voice but sang in England for most of his career, performing non–Wagnerian roles in the U.S. in the 1970s. Helen Traubel sang a number of major Wagnerian roles with distinction, helping to fill the gap left between Flagstad's return to Norway in 1941 and the rise of Birgit Nilsson; however, she sang only in New York. The American tenor James McCracken, born in 1926, did have a notable international career but included no major Wagnerian roles until 1978. He had been asked to sing Tannhäuser a number of times, beginning with a 1961 offer from Karajan, but he did not choose to sing the role until 1978. The 1948 Covent Garden début of Swedish tenor Set Svanholm as Siegfried caused the London *Times* to hail him as the successor to Melchior. He continued to sing Wagnerian roles in a number of major opera houses, but ended his singing career in 1956, the year after his appointment as artistic director of the Stockholm Opera. Another singer who gave up the opera stage was Victoria de Los Angeles, who had successfully sung the lighter Wagnerian roles: Eva, Elsa, and, at Bayreuth in 1961 and 1962, Elisabeth. By 1969, however, she had chosen to sing only on the concert platform.

Svanholm and de Los Angeles had the luxury of making choices as they managed their careers; the Canadian-American bass-baritone George London did not. His career was cut short in 1967 by a partial paralysis of the larynx. London's early career included a tour in 1947 as part of the Bel Canto Trio (another member was Mario Lanza); his international career, beginning two years later, included engagements at Vienna, Glyndebourne, La Scala, and the Bolshoi (where he was the first non–Russian to sing Boris, in 1960) as well as the Metropolitan Opera (1951–56) and Bayreuth (1951–64). He sang just three Wagnerian roles: Amfortas, the Dutchman, and Wotan (including a 1962–64 Cologne performance in Wieland Wagner's *Ring*). Fortunately, Amfortas, the Dutchman, and the *Rhinegold* Wotan were all recorded twice.

Of the recorded performances, Ira Siff writes that London "was a singer of such intelligence, emotional power and stylistic grasp that virtually everything he touched turned to gold" (76). We also have the testimony of those who saw live performances, such as Martin Bernheimer, who recalled London's vocal and dramatic power and finesse as the Dutchman in a 1959 Bayreuth performance, a vivid 47-year-old memory at the time of writing (*Great First Nights* 136). Though London could no longer offer such memories after 1967, he made good use of his time and energy. He administered various arts programs in Washington, D. C. (the John F. Kennedy Center, the National Opera Institute, and the Opera Society), and staged the first complete English-language *Ring* in the U.S. (Seattle 1975).

Finally, although the singers discussed in this chapter vary in their vocal and dramatic gifts (not everyone can match Hotter or Nilsson), this chapter excludes singers of talent but lesser gifts. Welsh soprano Gwynyth Jones, for instance, superb as an actor, was uneven vocally. We must not forget, however, that singers like Jones and Rita Hunter, who were willing to tackle some of the most taxing roles in the entire operatic repertoire, enabled thousands to experience Wagner's great music.

When we look at the most gifted singers who had significant careers singing Wagnerian roles during the three decades of the silver age, we encounter almost two dozen exceptional performers. We begin with the lower-voiced men, who sang roles designated as bass, bass-baritone, and baritone. *And* is the operative word, for not one in this group limited himself to roles in only one of those designations. Five of our group of eight successfully sang in all three ranges during the same time period, and the rest in two. An expected pattern: baritones, in addition to the baritone roles (the Dutchman and Wolfram, for instance) often sang bass-baritone roles (Amfortas, Woton) as well as bass roles (such as Hans Sachs, Kurwenal, and Klingsor). Basses, however, did not sing baritone roles.

The German bass-baritone Hans Hotter, born in 1909 and making his début in 1929, would seem to be too early to be included in this group. However, his distinguished career spanned a remarkable sixty-plus years.[2] In fact, after retiring from the operatic stage in 1972, he continued to perform and record non–Wagnerian roles into the 1990's: Schigolch in *Lulu*, the Speaker in *The Magic Flute*, and *Sprechgesang* roles in Schoenberg works, inspiring reviewer Desmond Arthur to refer to him as "apparently indestructible" (84). (Hotter in his nineties was still teaching and adjudicating.) His fame, however, was based not on his longevity, but on his magnificent interpretations of Wagner. He was regarded as the definitive Wotan of his time, a worthy successor to the two greatest Wagnerian bass-baritones before him, Anton van Rooy and Friedrich Schorr. That role and Hans Sachs, first sung in 1948 at Covent Garden, in English, were his most acclaimed. Other Wagnerian roles included Wolfram, Pogner, Kurwenal, Amfortas, Gurnemanz, King Marke, and the Dutchman. His discography is extensive, including Titural in Solti's *Parsifal*; his King Marke, in Wieland Wagner's 1967 production of *Tristan und Isolde*, was released on video.

Hotter was not limited to the heroic Wagnerian mode; he was also a fine singer of lieder: Schubert (he recorded *Winterreise* four times), Brahms, Wolf, and others. He preceded Fischer-Dieskau in uncovering rare Schubert works, a debt acknowledged by the younger singer. Reviewers praise his delicately nuanced performances and his careful attention to the interaction between music and text. Without doubt, his ability to reduce his powerful voice to convey the intimacy and subtlety of lieder produced flexibility as he sang heavier, operatic music.

Hotter was an international performer: Prague, Germany (Bayreuth from 1952 through 1964, Hamburg, Munich, Berlin), Austria (Salzburg, Vienna), Paris, New York, Chicago, San Francisco, and Buenos Aires — in demand wherever Wagner was sung, with one curious exception. Despite Hotter's fine Metropolitan Opera début as the Dutchman (1950), Rudolph Bing felt that he was better suited for secondary roles. Hotter sang thirty-nine performances under Bing's tenure before Hotter left in 1954, but a great number of them were as the Grand Inquisitor in Verdi's *Don Carlo*.[3]

Nevertheless, for everyone except Rudolph Bing, Hotter was considered one of the greatest operatic artists of his time. In his Bayreth performances and recordings he was sometimes unsteady and even had to cancel performances because he suffered from hay fever.[4] Aside from that, however, reviewers were hard put to avoid repeating the same expressions of regard for this great singer: "sonorous," "noble," "powerful," "deep artistry," "lovely legato," "effortless tone," "immense conviction," "dignified elegance," "artistically excellent," "dramatic understanding"— in short, one of Shaw's "singers of genius."

Like Hotter, the German baritone Dietrich Fischer-Dieskau was a sensitive interpreter of lieder who left behind an extended discography of both song and opera. He sang Wagnerian roles in Germany (Berlin, Munich, Bayreuth), Austria (Vienna, Salzburg), and London. His earliest Wagnerian appearances were at Bayreuth, beginning with Wolfram in 1949, adding in the mid-'50s two smaller roles — the Herald in *Lohingrin* and Kothner in *Meistersinger*—

as well as Amfortas, first sung in 1955. He recorded those last two roles (Kothner under Cluytens, 1956; Amfortas with Knappertsbusch, in 1956; and again with Solti. in 1973) as well as four others: Kurwenal (Furtwängler), the Dutchman, Gunther (Solti 1958–61), and the *Rheingold* Wotan (Karajan, 1966–70). He hesitated before taking on the role of Hans Sachs — it is, after all a bass role (though high in tessitura), and Fischer-Dieskau was a baritone — but he finally sang it at the Deutsche Oper, Berlin, in the 1975–76 season, recording it at the same time.[5]

Fischer-Dieskau need not have worried about singing Hans Sachs. He was a sensation both on stage and on disc. *Opera*'s review of the performance, entitled "Fischer-Dieskau's Unforgettable Sachs," was as effusive as its title: "Fischer-Dieskau ... has achieved both as singer and actor a perfection such as was previously only equaled by Rudolph Bockelmann.... His performance made it difficult for the other singers to equal him" (Stuckenschmidt 458–59). At the same time that Deutsche Grammophon released the recording of *Meistersinger*, conducted by Jochum, London released its recording of this opera, conducted by Solti. Comparing the two recordings. *High Fidelity* reviewer David Hamilton finds Fischer-Dieskau's Sachs superior to that of the English baritone Norman Bailey. Hamilton prefers the German singer's beauty of tone, intonation, pacing, and intelligent phrasing.[6] He does note that Fischer-Dieskau is not in the tonal tradition of Schorr and Bockelmann, the two leading bass-baritones during the interwar years, for the voice is light. But he praises the skill with which Fischer-Dieskau uses his voice, "so that the climaxes really do count, and the delicate moments are unforgettable" (90).

Fischer-Dieskau's full, resonant voice was highly praised. Beyond the voice itself was the highest level of musicianship. Because of his extensive work with lieder (his repertoire included over a thousand songs performed all over the world), one is not surprised to hear his Wagnerian singing praised for its melding of words and text, for the fine effects of color and nuance of phrasing that he achieved, and for his ability to change timbre and color to fit the dramatic purpose.

After retiring from singing, Fischer-Dieskau turned back to conducting (which he had done briefly in the early '70s), sometimes with his wife, Julia Varady, singing. Both singer and conductor have been well received — for instance, high praise from *Fanfare*'s William Youngren for a 1998 recording of Wagnerian works. Fischer-Dieskau continues to write, having produced at last count nine books.

American baritone Thomas Stewart was active internationally for over forty years, singing in Germany (Berlin, Hamburg, Nuremburg, Bayreuth), Austria (Salzburg, Vienna), Paris, Rome, London (a regular guest at Covent Garden during the '60s and '70s), Buenos Aires, New York (192 appearances at the Metropolitan Opera from 1966 to 1980), and at San Francisco (1970–85). During the 1960s he had what felt to him like two careers; he told one interviewer, "For a while then, I was doing Wagner *only* at Bayreuth.... I had one career at Bayreuth and another elsewhere" (Jacobson 59).

During Steward's first summer at Bayreuth, in 1960, he sang Donner, Gunther, and Amfortas (replacing London); he later added Wotan, Wolfram, the *Lohengrin* Herald, and his first Dutchman. It was during the season of his first Dutchman and his first Rigoletto that he felt he had to end his dual-track repertoire.[7] Fortunately, he chose Wagner. Steward added Hans Sachs to his repertoire in 1971 and was successful in the role, though he excelled in portraying characters who were pained and conflicted: Amfortas, the Dutchman, Wolfram, and Wotan. After hearing Stewart's 1962 Bayreuth recording of Amfortas, Gary Grosporean wrote, "I was deeply moved.... His singing at the Grail shrine is plaintively lyrical. He sounds transformed by his pain, almost sanctified by it" (305). Stewart recorded this role again in 1970 (Boulez); he also recorded Sachs (Kubelik 1967), Telramud (1971), and the Dutchman.

Stewart's voice was more lyrical than dramatic, yet in the opinion of most reviewers, full enough to do justice to the heroic Wagnerian roles. The language of Stewart's reviews — "warmth," "nobility," "dignity," "intelligence," "sensitivity"— reminds one of reactions to Hans Hotter, and Stewart was indeed the successor to Hotter's Wotan. Hotter once put together a small book: a collection of animal photographs that he humorously captioned with quotations from the *Ring*. He gave a copy of the book to the younger singer, with this inscription: "The result of forty years of *Ring* experience passed on. From the old Wotan to the young one. August 1, 1970" (Jacobson, "Gift," 59).

After his retirement from a full schedule of singing, Steward, like Hotter, made the occasional appearance as a narrator of orchestral works. More importantly, he and his wife, singer Evelyn Lear, devoted themselves to educating and training young artists. The couple gave master classes at schools like Juilliard and at a number of professional companies in North America and Europe. In 1999 they established the Evelyn Lear and Thomas Stewart Emerging Singers program in partnership with the Wagner Society of Washington, D. C. The mission of the program was to identify singers with the potential for a career signing Wagner — perhaps in hopes of encouraging a second silver age of Wagner.

Theo Adam, a German, was one of the leading Wagnerian heroic bass-baritones of his time, though not as familiar to Americans as some others in our group because he focused his career on German houses. After singing in his native city of Dresden, he became a principal member of the Berlin State Opera, where he sang for many seasons. He had a long tenure at Bayreuth as well, starting with a small role in 1952, moving to King Henry (1954), Wotan (1963), and still later, the Dutchman, Amfortas, and Sachs. Though he sang so extensively in his native Germany, including Cologne, he was an international singer, performing in Austria (Salzburg and Vienna), London, where he made his Covent Garden début as Wotan in 1967, and in the U.S.: Chicago, San Francisco, and New York, with a Metropolitan Opera début as Hans Sachs in 1969.

Adam's recordings include Pogner (Bayreuth 1960), Sachs (Karajan), the *Götterdämmerung* Alberich (Haitink), the Dutchman, and Paolo Orsini in *Rienzi* (1976). Though he sang the baritone role of the Duchman and the bass-baritone roles of Wotan, Alberich, and Amfortas, Adam performed bass roles most frequently: Paolo Orsini, Pogner, King Henry, King Marke, Sachs, Gurnemanz. That last role, performed for the first time in 1976 at Bayreuth, is one that many listeners associate with a deep, dark bass, a fact noted by Alan Blyth in his review of this particular performance. Nevertheless, Blyth continued, Adam's "beautifully schooled and musical singing" resulted in a very satisfying performance (27). Adam had many successes throughout his career, but the role of Hans Sachs may have been his best. Writing of Adam's Cologne performance of that role in 1979, when he had been performing the role for about fifteen years, Harold Rosenthal asks, "Is there a finer Sachs today than Theo Adam? I think not.... The voice is as beautiful and fresh as ever, and there was never a moment of strain throughout the long evening." Referring to the first scene of the last act, which Rosenthal believes to be "possibly the most rewarding single scene in all Wagner," he sums up Adam's performance in one word: "superb" ("Memorable" 755–56).

Bass Karl Ridderbusch was Adam's colleague in age (younger by just seven years), nationality, and preference for German opera houses. His early career took place in Münster (1961), Essen (1963–65), and Düsseldorf, where he made the Deutsche Oper am Rhein his artistic base beginning in 1965. Later performances in Germany included Munich and Berlin. In 1967 he made two important débuts: at Bayreuth (Fasolt and Titurel) and at the Metropolitan Opera, as Hunding under von Karajan. For several years he was a favorite of Karajan, recording Fafner and Hagen in Karajan's *Ring* as well as King Henry (1975–76, 1981), King Marke, Pogner, and, in a Bayreuth recording of 1974, Hans Sachs, a role he sang under Karajan in the Salzburg Easter Festivals of 1974 and 1975. Recordings under other conductors include Titurel (Boulez, Bayreuth 1970), Daland (Bayreuth), and a second recording of King Henry (Kubelik 1971).

Ridderbusch was internationally recognized as one of the leading German basses of the '60s and '70s — famous enough that he could select where he sang. He ended his appearances at Salzburg because he disapproved of the rehearsal schedule, and he ended his long tenure at Bayreuth (1967–76) in protest over the controversial 1976 *Ring*. Besides singing in Germany, Austria (Salzburg and Vienna), and New York, he performed in Italy (Milan and Rome), Paris, Buenos Aires, and London (Fasolt, Hunding, and Hagen at Covent Garden, all in 1971).

Ridderbusch sang only one bass-baritone role in his career, the small role of Fasolt. All his other roles were firmly in the bass range: Fafner, Hunding, Hagen, Daland, Titurel, King Henry, King Marke, Pogner, Sachs. He had an extensive upper range, which helps account for his success as Sachs, a bass role that also requires firm high notes. Those hearing him either live or recorded remark on how equalized his tone was through his large range, as well as his richness in timbre and sonority. Alan Blyth felt that his tone "seemed to pour out of him in a natural, unfettered way that must have been the envy of colleagues" ("Karl Ridderbusch" 920).

The English baritone Norman Bailey began singing professionally in 1959 but did not sing a Wagnerian role in a major house until his London début as Hans Sachs in 1968 (in the London Coliseum with the Sadler Wells Company, which later became the ENO). Though his significant Wagnerian portrayals began late in terms of our time frame, he jumped into the Wagnerian repertoire with such vigor and such international success that he deserves our attention.

During the eight years before his London début (1960–68), Bailey performed Wagnerian roles in small houses (Linz, Wuppertal, Oldenburg, Bremerhaven): Klingsor, the Herald in *Lohingrin*, the Dutchman, Amfortas, and the *Walküre* Wotan. Then came the 1968 début as Sachs, followed in 1969 by débuts in the same role at Covent Garden, Bayreuth, Hamburg, Brussels, and Munich. He made U. S. débuts in that role at the New York City Opera in 1975 and at the Metropolitan Opera in 1976. Bailey was certainly not limited to the role of Hans Sachs; in 1975 alone he sang eight major Wagnerian roles: Wolfram, Klingsor, Kurwenal (all at Covent Garden; Kurwenal also at the Scottish Opera), all three Wotan/Wanderer roles (Sadler's Wells, at the Coliseum), Sachs (Saarbrücken), and Amfortas (Paris). Other roles included Gunther, first sung at Bayreuth in 1970, and a role added much later: *Tannhäuser's* Landgrave (Opera North, 1997).

Bailey's recordings of Hans Sachs (Solti 1975) and Wotan (Boulez 1976) are highly regarded, and reviewers praise his stage performances highly. In *Great First Nights*, Richard Fairman remembers Bailey in the ENO's first Ring as "titanic" (26). More than one reviewer has described his portrayals as three-dimensional, a compliment to his dramatic power and musical intelligence; he was also admired for his clear, firm timbre.

Like Bailey, British bass-baritone Sir Donald McIntyre, originally from New Zealand, was a compelling singing-actor. At Sadler's Wells (later, the ENO) between 1960 and 1968, he built up a repertoire of twenty-five roles, including the Dutchman. His Bayreuth début in 1967 was as Telramund. He appeared there through 1980, singing the Dutchman (1969), Klingsor (1970), Kurwenal and Amfortas (both in 1974), and Wotan (*Walküre* in 1971, the

Wanderer in 1972, complete cycles in 1973 and 1976 — the Centenary *Ring* cycle under Boulez). Other roles included Gunther, Hunding, Gurnemanz, King Marke, and Hans Sachs.

MaIntyre's stamina was remarkable. After his 1975 Metropolitan Opera début as Wotan, he would sing all three Wotan/Wanderer roles in a single week; in the weeks when he was not singing Wotan, he would sing Gunther. Perhaps this is not so unexpected in a world-class Wotan aged 41. However, a much older McIntyre still displayed a notable staying power. He sang the demanding role of Gurnemanz (first performed at the Welsh National Opera when he was 47, in 1981) as late as 1996, when he was in his early 60s. When he sang King Marke at the Los Angeles Opera in 1997, he was 63. He waited until he was 50 before singing Hans Sachs (Zurich 1984) and was still performing this demanding role when he was almost 60 (New York 1993). Of course, singing when one is older is in itself not laudable (we can all recall singers who sang long after they should have retired), but McIntyre was still delivering powerful performances in his sixties. *Opera News* editor Louise Guinther, who saw a dress rehearsal and then five performances of McIntyre's Sachs in New York, wrote of his "towering" interpretation, "a portrayal of such depth and dimension" that no subsequent Sachs performance measured up. What reverberated with that reviewer was not so much the voice (she found him to falter in Act III), but his ability to completely inhabit the role.

Fortunately, some of McIntyre's performances live on. He recorded Gurnemanz, under Goodall, and his strong, noble portrayal of Wotan, under Boulez, was recorded both on disc and on DVD (released in 1980 — the first digitally recorded version of the *Ring*). The strength of his voice through all registers was never in dispute; what he developed as he repeated various roles was his acting — not simply movement and gestures, but vocal renderings of the emotions of the character. Early in his career, writes Alan Blyth, his Wotan was "something of a dull dog"; as he worked with conductors such as Solti and Boulez, and producers such as Everding, Wolfgang Wagner, and Götz Friedrich, he became a superb singing actor, presenting, in Wotan, "a deeply considered, anguished reading of presence and power" ("Donald McIntyre," 535).

Like the Swedish tenor Set Svanholm, the great Finnish bass Martti Talvela chose to curtail his international career in order to devote himself to his own country's national opera. He scaled back his international career for months each year to direct and sing in the Savonlinna Festival (1972–79 — ending his Bayreuth appearances in 1970). He was also appointed general director of the Finnish National Opera but died shortly after that appointment, when he was only fifty-four years old. Nevertheless, in his 28-year career, he mastered fifty-five roles and achieved international recognition.

Like Karl Ridderbusch, Talvela sang only one bass-baritone role, Fasolt. All his other roles (including those outside the Wagnerian repertoire, notably Sarastro and Boris Godunov) were in the bass range: Hunding, Hagen, *Tannhäuser's* Landgrave, Daland, Titurel, Gurnemanz, King Marke. His recordings include a 1966 Bayreuth performance of King Marke and a 1976 Daland, under Solti.

Soon after his 1961 debut with the Swedish Royal opera, Talvela came to the attention of Wieland Wagner, which resulted in a Bayreuth début as Titurel, in 1962, the year he also joined Deutsche Oper, Berlin. Subsequent roles at Bayreuth included the Landgrave (1964), Fasolt and Hunding (1965), and King Marke (1966). Talvela also sang in Düsseldorf, Salzburg, Rome, New York, and London. His first appearances at Salzburg and at the Metropolitan Opera were in 1968. That year New York heard him as Fasolt and Hunding, with Karajan, and later (1974) as Hunding. In his Covent Garden début of 1970, he sang Hunding, and soon after, Fasolt and Hagen; in 1973, he portrayed his first Gurnemanz.

Talvela was a huge man, not only tall (6'7") but large-framed (his weight was estimated at 300 pounds). He used his size to great effect; reviewers noted his impressive stage presence, often described as "majestic" and "compelling." The voice, too, had an immense size and range, and though it could easily carry throughout a large house, Talvela could also sing with great sensitivity and tenderness.

Like his colleague Jon Vickers, Talvela felt he had an artistic-religious mission, doing the work of God. He spoke of "the human being who can see something mystical," and believed the drama of the opera "has something deep to say to people," something that he felt called to do: "I think I have to say something in this life to people" (qtd. in Steane I, 221, 224). This sense of being called to convey something mystical (found as well in the contemporary composers Henryk Górecki and Arvo Pärt) led Martti Talvela to use his formidable gifts to the fullest. He was a worthy representative of the silver age of Wagnerian singing.

As we have seen, the basses in our group, Talvela and Ridderbusch, did not sing high (with the one exception of the small bass-baritone role of Fasolt); the baritones and bass-baritones, however, sang in all three ranges when the tessitura of the bass role was not low. For women singing Wagner during these three decades, the situation was similar: regardless of how they described their voice, most sang roles in more than one vocal designation.

Like their male counterparts, women singers have three types of voice: soprano, mezzo-soprano, and contralto. One hears a true contralto less frequently, which led one commentator, Conrad Osborne, to claim that since the 1930's, the truly low female voice has virtually disappeared because of modern vocal methods and tastes ("Voices" 29). This is simply not the case. Human anatomy has not changed. (What a singer chooses to *call* herself is not the issue here.) It is true that voices at the extremes — true basses, contraltos, and tenors (one can add true coloratura sopranos) — are never as abundant as voices in the middle. Just as very tall or very short people of either gender are encountered less often than those between the extremes, so too with voices. Thus, one is not surprised that among women singers, there are indeed fewer contraltos — which is fortunate because the only Wagnerian contralto roles are Erda; Senta's nurse, Mary; and the First Norn. (Five of the Valkyries are designated as a group made up of mezzo-sopranos and contraltos; *Götterdämmerung*'s Waltraute is a mezzo.)

There are not even many major Wagnerian mezzo roles, only Fricka, Ortrud and Brangäne — and Conrad holds that Ortrud and Brangäne are "truly soprano parts" ("Voices" 29). It would seem that the singers agree with him, for six of our group of eight, whether they called themselves a soprano or a mezzo, were successful in dividing their Wagnerian singing between soprano and mezzo roles. (Helga Dernesch sang the contralto role of Erda as well.) To complicate matters further, Wagnerian soprano Astrid Varney states that it is common for a dramatic soprano to be categorized incorrectly as a mezzo. Certainly it is common, as Varney states, that Wagner's soprano roles include low notes of a mezzo quality (Jacobson, "Varney Revisited" 25).

The first two women in our group, Astrid Varney and Martha Mödl, were good friends and true colleagues, often linked by reviewers. (Martin Bernheimer wrote that Nilsson had virtually no Wagnerian rivals when she was singing in New York but mentioned that Mödl and Varney, "both more passionate," worked mostly in Europe (rev. "Birgit Nilsson" 85–86).

American soprano Astrid Varney, born in Sweden, was one of the singers who helped fill the gap between Flagstad's 1941 move back to Norway and the international activity of Birgit Nilsson. She began with a bang. Preparing for her Metropolitan Opera roles as Elsa and Elisabeth, both to be sung in January 1942, she made an unexpected début in early December 1941 as Sieglinde, replacing Lotte Lehmann on just a few hours' notice. She was only twenty-three, she had never sung on the operatic stage before, there was no time for a rehearsal, and her colleagues that evening included Melchior, Traubel, Schorr, and Kipnis, with Leinsdorf in the orchestra pit. Six days later she replaced Helen Traubel, again on short notice, as the *Walküre* Brünnhilde. The ability to retain her composure in taxing situations was a gift she was called on to continue exercising; in 1956, at Bayreuth, she was a last-minute replacement for Mödl as the Third Norn in *Götterdämmerung*, and Michael Tanner once saw her fetched from her hotel, between acts 1 and 2 of *Parsifal*, to sing Kundry, a role she had not sung for two years.

At the Metropolitan she sang from 1941 until 1956, and again during 1974–76, with her final performance there in 1979. During that first fifteen-year period, she sang a great number of Wagnerian roles: all three Brünnhildes, Sieglinde, Gutrune, Senta, Elsa, Ortrud, Eva, Elisabeth, Venus, Isolde, and Kundry. She once said that Ortrud is usually sung by a mezzo in order to provide vocal contrast to Elisabeth, but since the role of Ortrud has a high tessitura, the true contrast is in the coloring of the voice. She noted that she was able to darken her voice to portray successfully Ortrud, adding, "I was not an Elsa sound, really" (Jacobson 25–26).

She sang at Bayreuth for seventeen seasons, from 1951 through 1967, portraying Brünnhilde, Isolde, Ortrud, Kundry, and Senta, the First Norn, and the Third Norn. She also sang in Salzburg, Mexico City, Edinburgh, and London: at Covent Garden (as the *Siegfried* Brünnhilde in 1947) and at Sadler's Wells. After her husband died in 1955, she moved to Europe, joining the company at Düsseldorf and singing regularly in Vienna, Munich, Berlin, Zurich, Hamburg, and Stuttgart. Though her grief over her husband's death kept her from returning to New York until much later, she did sing in Paris and Great Britain: in Covent Garden's 1958 and 1959 productions of the *Ring*; in Edinburgh as Isolde in Wieland Wagner's 1958 production of *Tristan*, with the Stuttgart Company; and at Sadler's Wells as Ortrud in Wieland Wagner's 1962 production of *Lohengrin*, with the Hamburg Company. In what she calls "a second international career," she began in 1962 to perform mezzo roles, including Strauss's Herodias, Klytämnestra (sung 121 times), and Elektra (sung 81 times)—roles that a grateful Metropolitan Opera Company was happy to have her sing. After Varnay's last performance at the Metropolitan, in 1979, she continued to appear in opera with some frequency well into the 1980's, singing smaller character parts. Her last performance, as the Nurse in *Boris Godunov*, was in 1995, when she was seventy-seven.

Varney's Wagnerian recordings are limited to roles recorded live at Bayreuth: all three Brünnhildes (Keilberth 1951; *Walküre* also recorded under Knappertsbusch in 1957), Ortrud, and Senta (recorded twice in 1955, with Knappertsbusch and with Keilberth). Her 1956 substitution for Martha Mödl as the Third Norn in *Götterdämmerung* (conducted by Knappertsbusch) meant that she sang both that role, in the first act, and then, as the curtain went up on the second act, Brünnhilde. Reviewer Sunny van Eaton, praising Varnay's "undiminished vigor and power," describes the performance of this "inexhaustible " singer as "vocal heroism indeed!" (rev. of *Götterdämmerung* 272). One wishes that Varnay had recorded more extensively, for the reviewers of those Bayreuth discs celebrated her for much more than her stamina, praising her as "vibrant," "radiant," "dynamic," "expressive," sensitive," and "intelligent." Reviewers of her performances on stage found the same qualities. Gifted with a large vibrant voice and the ability to use her fine vocal technique in the service of truly inhabiting each role, she is a worthy representative of the silver age of Wagnerian singing.

The German singer Martha Mödl became a legend of music theatre, with a stage career spanning fifty-seven years. She began as a mezzo and she began late, not making her début until she was thirty years old, which she felt accounted for her longevity. (She sang the Countess in *The Queen of Spades* when she was 87 and the Nurse in *Boris Godunov* when she was 89, a few months before her death.) By the time she joined the Hamburg State Opera in 1949, seven years after her début, she had become a dramatic soprano, though she continued to sing mezzo roles as well.

Not until 1951, in a major breakthrough in her career, did she sing a major Wagner role, when Wieland Wagner elected her to sing Kundry at the first postwar Bayreuth Festival. (She and her friend Astrid Varney shared roles at Bayreuth during the same sixteen-year period: 1951–67.) At Bayreuth she sang Brünnhilde in the entire *Ring* five times between 1953 and 1958, as well as the roles of Isolde, Sieglinde and Gutrune; later, when she returned to the mezzo repertoire, she sang Waltraute and Fricka. Mödl was proud of having undertaken all three female leads in *Walküre*: Fricka, Sieglinde, and Brünnhilde.

Mödl sang at the Metropolitan Opera only between 1957 and 1960, performing a dozen roles, five of them Wagnerian: Isolde, Kundy, and the three Brünnhildes. Because of its high tessitura, the *Siegfried* Brünnhilde is the most taxing of the three; unfortunately, that was Mödl's Metropolitan début role. Reviewers praised her moving performance and the richness of her voice, but felt that her top notes did not have freedom and brilliance.

At Bayreuth, Mödl sang every important female role in the *Ring* as well as Kundry and Isolde; elsewhere she also sang Ortrud and Venus. She did not sing Brangäne, though the role would have suited her, and, understandably, she did not sing the lighter soprano roles: Senta, Elisabeth, Elsa, and Eva. Besides singing at Bayreuth and at the Metropolitan, she sang at La Scala and Covent Garden, and in Paris, Vienna, Buenos Aires, Edinburgh (with the Hamburg company), and in her native country: Berlin, Stuttgart, Hamburg, Düsseldorf, and Munich.

Praised for her fine voice and for her ability to project emotional intensity not only with her face, carriage, and movement but also with the way she colored the text, Mödl was regarded as the finest Isolde and Brünnhilde between Flagstad and Nilsson. This gap between the two greatest Wagnerian sopranos of modern times would leave us grateful for a singer of merely modest gifts. Fortunately, Mödl's gifts were much more than merely modest.

The soprano that every lover of Wagner had been waiting for finally arrived in the person of the great Swedish singer Birgit Nilsson. She began slowly, with a 1946 operatic début at the Royal Opera in Stockholm and a performance in 1951 at Glyndeburne. She did not perform a Wagnerian role until eight years later, 1954, when she was thirty-six — and what a year that was. She sang Elsa at Bayreuth and at the Vienna State Opera; the *Götterdämmerung* Brünnhilde at Sweden's Royal Opera; and all three Brünnhildes in Munich. After that, the pace of the débuts leaves one breathless: in 1955, Isolde in Buenos Aires; in 1956, the *Siegfried* Brünnhilde in Florence, and the *Walküre* Brünnhilde in San Francisco; in 1957, all three Brünnhildes at Covent Garden, under Kempe, and the *Walküre* Brünnhilde at Chicago's Lyric Opera; in 1959, at the Metropolitan Opera, Isolde — a role she was eventually to perform over 208 times.

In addition to Elsa, Brünnhilde, and Isolde, Nilsson's Wagnerian roles included Senta, Venus, Elisabeth, and Sieglinde. Though she performed in many houses, including La Scala, most of her considerable energies were given to Bayreuth (1954, 1957–70) and to the Metropolitan (1959–75, 1979–83). Her discography is extensive, with multiple recordings of Brünnhilde (a Bayreuth recording on the Philips label, and others with Leinsdorf and with Solti) and Isolde (the second of which, from Bayreuth in 1966, is regarded as especially thrilling).

Nilsson was a force to be reckoned with — perhaps the only soprano to call Turandot her "vacation role." The story is often told of a January 1960 performance at the Metropolitan, sometimes dubbed the "three-tenor" performance of *Tristan und Isolde*. The scheduled tenor, Chilean Ramón Vinay (who had called Nilsson a "Tristan killer") told general manager Rudolph Bing the day before the performance that he was not well. Both the first and the second covers for the role pleaded illness as well, so Bing convinced each tenor to sing one act. Nilsson's final performance was in October 1983, as a participant in the Metropolitan Opera's 100th anniversary gala. After her retirement from public performance, she devoted herself to giving master classes.

When one considers the phenomenal nature of Nilsson's voice — the volume, the ease with which she flung out high B's and C's, the pure, shining tone so often remarked upon — and when one considers her impressive acting ability, with one solid, serious interpretation following another, combined with a variety and subtlety of vocal expression, one would assume that she had been blessed with talented teachers. Amazingly, she was not. In her Covent Garden master classes, she said that her teachers did not even teach one of the most basic of vocal techniques: support ("I just breathed when I wanted air," she said — qtd. in Steane I, 133). She was simply left to work it out for herself — and work it out she did, memorably and magnificently.

Austrian soprano Leonie Rysanek, who performed for almost fifty years, was singing when Nilsson did. However, even though both sopranos sang four of the same roles — Senta, Elsa, Elisabeth, Sieglinde — they were almost on two different Wagnerian tracks. Nilsson's Wagnerian energies were spent less on those four roles than on Brünnhilde and Isolde, two roles that the Rysanek did not perform.

Early in her career, shortly after a 1949 début, Rysanek sang Senta and Sieglinde at Saarbrücke, taking those roles to Bayreuth (a début as Sieglinde in the first postwar festival, in 1951; in 1959, Senta). The 1951 performance was said to have created a sensation; the 1959 performance, with George London as the Dutchman, was successful even beyond Wieland Wagner's expectations. During her long association with Bayreuth she also sang Elsa (1958), Elisabeth (1964), and Kundry (1982). In her 1959 début season at the San Francisco opera, she again sang Senta and Sieglinde. After her 1959 début at the Metropolitan Opera, she sang most of the time either at the Metropolitan, her favorite house, or at the Vienna State Opera, with guest appearances at Covent Garden, Marseilles, Munich, Paris, and, in 1985, the Australian Opera. Like Varney and Mödl before her, she continued to sing late into her career. When she was seventy years old, two years before her death in 1998, she sang the Countess in *The Queen of Spades* at the Metropolitan and, that summer, Clytemnestra at the Salzburg Festival.

Rysenek credits her longevity on stage in part to knowing when to give up roles at the right time. Sometimes this was a vocal issue; sometimes, a dramatic one. In an interview with Alan Blythe, she explained why she had exchanged Senta and Sieglinde for Ortrud (Metropolitan Opera 1986):

> I could have gone on singing Sieglinde much longer but I wouldn't have anyone writing that she could be Siegmund's grandmother.... When I gave up Senta, many people said I was crazy — but I knew it was time to stop. I'm my own severest critic, and I know when the time has come to say goodbye to a part when I knew I was not as good as I had been in it — though I can tell you it broke my heart to abandon Senta, Sieglinde and the Kaiserin. Then I thought my voice is still too good to give up altogether, so I tried Ortrud ["Rysanek" 18].

It is typical of Rysanek's attentiveness to selecting roles that, although she would have liked to have sung Isolde and was actually engaged to sing it at Bayreuth, under Kleiber, in

1975, she cancelled her agreement. She met her mentor, Karl Böhm, while still studying the role and he was insistent that she not sing a role that, he felt, was vocally too low for her.

Rysanek's recordings of her major roles include Senta (Bayreuth, 1959; and for London, 1960) and Sieglinde: under Furtwängler, again under Böhm, and Act 3 under Karajan; she leaves us as well a fine record on film of Elsa (Levine 1986). The beauty of her voice, with its thrilling upper range, combined with great interpretive powers, led reviewers to describe her performances as eloquent, riveting, and incandescent.

Eloquence also suits the French soprano Regine Crespin. She sang Elsa as her first part on any stage (Mulhouse 1950) and repeated the role the following year at the Paris Opéra. Believing that work in the French provinces would allow her to build up a comprehensive repertoire in German, French, and Italian roles, she spent five years mastering a number of roles, including Sieglinde (sung in French), returning to Paris in 1956. Wieland Wagner was eager to bring young French singers to Bayreuth, and engaged both Crespin and Belgian soprano Rita Gorr to début at the festival in 1958. It was assumed that Gorr would be Mödl's successor as Kundry and that Crespin would sing Sieglinde. However, in a bold and successful move, Wieland Wagner selected Crespin to sing Kundry (Gorr sang Fricka). Reviewing the recording of that performance, Gary Grosporean notes the "novel casting" of Crespin in this role; he found that her lyric voice brought "an uncharacteristic brilliance and delicacy to Kundry's high notes" (305).

In addition to Elsa, Sieglinde, and Kundry, Crespin's Wagnerian roles included Senta, Elisabeth, and the *Walküre* Brünnhilde, first sung at the 1967 Salzburg Easter Festival. That was another role that came as a surprise. When Karajan told her he wanted to present *Walküre* at the festival, she assumed he wanted her to sing Sieglinde. She was shocked when he said "I want Brünnhilde"; he explained, "I want a woman's voice, not a trumpet. I want a human being" (qtd in Innaurato 36). She gave up that role after just a few performances,[8] perhaps because she was beginning to experience something that was evident by the early '70s: serious vocal difficulties in her upper register. She took time off, retrained her voice, and began to undertake non–Wagnerian mezzo roles, which she sang until she retired in 1989.

Though she sang fewer Wagnerian roles than our previous three sopranos, she sang them beautifully. Reviewers consistently praised her extraordinary expressiveness, marked by her finesse in diction and phrasing, and her ability to use her flexibility in tone color to underscore text. She was particularly gifted when meeting one of the most daunting of a singer's challenges: high soft singing that matches the beauty of tones in lower registers.[9] The rich darkness of the voice that could so successfully sing Kundry was matched by a lyric warmth that made her so notable as Sieglinde. Crespin has left behind an extensive discography, but not a great deal in Wagnerian roles. Her performances as Kundry and Sieglinde were recorded twice: in addition to the Bayreuth recordings, she can be heard as Kundry on the Philips label (1962) and as Sieglinde in Solti's *Ring* (1958–65).

The Belgian singer Rita Gorr had such a rich timbre that, though usually referred to as a mezzo-soprano, she moved Holland's most knowledgeable opera critic, Leo Riemans, to exclaim in 1957, "Here at long last is a real French contralto" (qtd. in Rosenthal 77). Labels aside, she consistently delivered exciting performances, drawing on her two-octave range that had no breaks between registers.

Gorr's 1949 début in Antwerp was in an important Wagnerian role, *Walküre*'s Fricka. That same year she made an unexpectedly early début at Strasbourg, singing Brangäne on short notice to replace an ailing singer. She stayed there for three seasons, adding Venus to her repertoire, and then, in 1952, joined the Paris Opera, in the début role of Magdalena.

She was given no role with more scope than that minor role in *Meistersinger* during her three seasons with the Opera; her decision to leave the company was important in leading to a distinguished international career not many years later.

In her first season at Bayreuth, in 1959, she sang both Frickas, roles she performed that same year in her first season at Covent-Garden (in Hotter's production of the *Ring*, conducted by Solti). She stayed at Covent Garden until 1971, making débuts in a number of other houses: the Rome Opera (1958, as Kundry), La Scala (1960), the Metropolitan Opera (1962, as Elsa), Lisbon, Edinburgh, and the Opéra Comique.

All of her Wagnerian roles except the two Frickas and Waltraute have been outside the *Ring*: Magdalena, Venus, Elsa, Ortrud, Brangäne, and Kundry. Audiences can no longer enjoy her performances that were described as a tour-de-force, a virtuoso rendering, and grandly exciting. Fortunately, however, Gorr's two recordings under Leinsdorf—the *Walküre* Fricka, in the early '60s, and Ortrud, in 1965—allow today's listeners to enjoy her rich, warm voice.

German mezzo-soprano Christa Ludwig had a successful 45-year career, singing a fine farewell lieder concert at age sixty-five in 1993. Her longevity was due in part to wise decisions at two important points in her career. After a 1946 début in Frankfurt, where she sang for three years, followed by two years in Darmstadt studying stagecraft and acting, she joined the company at Hanover, where she first sang Wagnerian roles: Ortrud, Waltraute, Fricka, Venus, and Kundry. Only twenty-six years old, she came to the attention of Karl Böhm, the music director of the Vienna State Opera. Ludwig's good musical sense made her uneasy about singing such heavy roles in the larger house; Böhm, who understood the voice (his wife was a singer), agreed, and Ludwig sang Mozart and other lighter roles for several years, resuming the heavier roles with Karajan.

Böhm was not the only person careful of Ludwig's vocal development. Her mother was a mezzo who had sung Elektra with Karajan and who had damaged her own voice by mixing low mezzo and soprano parts without spacing them properly. It was a lesson that Ludwig never forgot, but one that did not apply to her at the very beginning of her career, for during her Frankfurt days, she had not yet developed her upper register. Her mother, who was her only teacher, worked with her—like the good mother, reassuring her; like the good teacher, reminding her that as she strove to develop the top notes, she must be careful not to force them. "Every six months," Ludwig later said, "I gained a further semitone" (qtd. in Osborne, 220). Even when she joined the Vienna State Opera, she was missing one or two top notes, which Böhm noted. Ludwig and her mother continued to work, and the top notes eventually did come.

During her early years in Vienna, Ludwig added two Wagnerian roles to her repertoire: Adriano Colonna in *Rienzi*, and Brangäne, her 1966 début role at Bayreuth. She made débuts in non–Wagnerian roles at Salzburg (1954), Chicago (1959), and Covent Garden (1968). In that year it was announced that she would sing Brünnhilde at the next Salzburg Festival, as well as Isolde, with Karajan. Another wise decision: a year later Ludwig announced that she had changed her mind and would abandon dramatic soprano roles. Personal and medical problems led to vocal problems in the early 70's, when she was only in her mid-forties. A new marriage, medical treatment, taking a year off, and changing her repertoire restored her voice. She continued to sing Fricka and Waltraute, but stopped singing the more vocally demanding roles in Strauss, Beethoven, Berg, and Wagner: Ortrud and Kundry.

Although she sang in a number of cities, including Paris, San Francisco and Tokyo, she divided most of her time for over thirty years between two companies: the Vienna State Opera (1955 until the late '80s) and the Metropolitan Opera (1959–90). She also gave many concerts—lieder, Brahms's *Alto Rhapsody*, and others—which of course reinforced her ability to heighten the interaction between word and music when singing on the operatic stage.

Ludwig has left us an extensive record of her artistry. In addition to her many recordings of lieder and non–Wagnerian roles, she recorded several roles under Solti: the *Walküre* Fricka and the *Götterdämmerung* Waltraute (1958–65), Venus (1971), and Kundry (1973). Other recorded roles include Adriano Colonna (Kreps 1960), Brangäne (Karajan, in the early '70s), *Meistersinger*'s Magdalena (Jochum 1977), and Ortrud (Kempe).

Her recordings bear out the assessments of her live performances. Her rich, voluptuous tone is seamless as she moves between registers with flexibility and a sense of ease. The expressiveness that one finds in the recordings was certainly evident on stage as well. No one who has seen her sing Ortrud can forget the extraordinary power and menace she brought to that role. We are fortunate that several of her roles in the *Ring* were captured on film, in the 1990 Otto Schenk production of the *Ring*, conducted by Levine: both Frickas and the *Götterdämmerung* Waltraute. Her remarkable expressiveness and sumptuous voice were captured not only in memory but electronically as well. The singing of this contributor to the silver age of Wagnerian singing is unlikely to be forgotten.

Austrian soprano Helga Dernesch began as a soprano, in 1961, but began singing mezzo-soprano roles in 1978. After three years in Berne (1961–63) and Wiesbaden (1963–65), she moved to Cologne, where she sang from 1965 to 1968. It was after the mid–60's that her international career began.

Her début at Bayreuth was in small roles: one of the Flower Maidens in *Parsifal*, and the second Rhinemaiden. During the next two summers, 1966 and 1967, she performed as one of the Rhinemaidens. If she needed any encouragement that she would soon move beyond such small roles, she received it from Wieland Wagner. Always wanting to hear promising young singers, he asked to hear a tape of the first act of *Die Walkürie* as he lay in a hospital bed in 1966. He engaged her for the proposed Bayreuth visit to Osaka, but unfortunately died shortly after making this decision. Nevertheless, this encouragement was a sign that her career was moving upward. In 1968 she sang Gutrune at the festival, and later, Freia and Eva.

The Bayreuth performance of Gutrune was not her first; earlier that same year she sang the role in her début with the Scottish Opera, a company that became one of her favorites. She later sang the *Walküre* and *Siegfried* Brünnhildes there, and, in 1973, Isolde. The other of her favorite venues was Salzburg. She first became associated with the festival in 1969 after meeting Karajan. She subsequently sang both the *Siegfried* and the *Götterdämmerung* Brünnhildes there as well as Isolde (1971).

Dernesch made her Covent Garden début as Sieglinde in 1970 and has also performed in Vienna (début in 1971), Berlin, Hamburg, and the Metropolitan Opera. She did not sing in the New York house until 1994, after her 1978 decision to move to mezzo roles, including Fricka and Erda. Some sopranos move to the mezzo repertoire as they move into the last years of their career; Dernish, however, was not yet forty when she made the change.

Her earliest recording, on Solti's 1958–65 *Ring*, was as one of the Valkyries designated for a soprano, Ortlinde. Later recordings include her two Brünnhildes and her Isolde from Salzburg (Karajan, the early '70s), and Elisabeth (Solti, the early '80s). Reviewers described her tone as beautiful. One reviewer of her recorded Isolde found her timbre "uncannily reminiscent of Christa Ludwig's" (Gurewitsch 289), who sings Brangäne on that recording Those seeing her on stage noted her compelling performances (perhaps helped by the fact that, at six feet, she looked heroic) and the great power and richness of her voice.

Born in 1940, Anja Silja would seem too young to be included with singers performing during the '50s, '60s, and '70s. But, as *Opera*'s Wolfram Schwinger wrote in 1969, "The case of Anja Silja has no parallel on the international operatic stage of today" (194). This is a singer who, at the age of twelve, made a concert début at the Hamburg Musikhall and during the following four years gave eighty concerts in Germany, Denmark, and Finland. In 1954, when she was fourteen, she sang the Queen of the Night at the Aix-en-Provence Festival; one year later, at age fifteen, she made her operatic début, at Brunswick, as Rosina (1955). There she also sang the coloratura role of Zerbinetta in *Ariadne auf Naxos* a few weeks before she turned seventeen.

None of this suggests a career in Wagner, yet that is what happened. Her idol was the great Wagnerian soprano Astrid Varnay, so she traveled to Bayreuth determined to perform Wagner herself, singing for Wieland Wagner every time he held his annual auditions for new voices. Asked to audition again for the current musical director at Bayreuth, Wolfgang Sawallisch, and yet again for Wieland Wagner in March 1960, Silja was sent a contract, in May, to sing all performances of Senta that summer.

The artistic collaboration between singer and director was deep and lasted until Wieland Wagner's death in 1966. During the next seven years, when she sang Elsa (1961), Elisabeth, Venus, Eva, Freia, and Venus, Silja became one of the most controversial singing actresses in postwar Bayreuth. The turmoil was probably due to a number of things: the productions themselves, the relationship between singer and mentor, the eroticism underlying Silja's portrayals, and Silja's voice, which had as individual a timbre as the voice of her early idol Maria Callas.

Controversy did not affect the partnership. From 1960 on, there was no new Wieland Wagner production without Anja Silja, whether at Bayreuth or in Paris, Brussels, Cologne, Stuttgart, or Frankfurt — and whether Silja was singing Wagner, Strauss, or Berg. Silja honored her commitments but would accept no further engagements that did not involve the man who more than any other musical figure was most responsible for her artistic development. Under her mentor's guidance, she added the heavier soprano roles of Isolde (Brussels) and Brünnhilde (Cologne).

Before her association with Wieland Wagner, Silja had made a 1963 London début at Sadler's Wells with the Frankfurt Opera. After his death she made débuts at Covent Garden (1967), San Francisco (1968), Glyndebourne, the Metropolitan Opera (1972), Vienna (1976), and Boston (1986).

Among her recordings of Wagnerian roles, the 1962 recording of Elisabeth (from Bayreuth, under Sawallisch) received a review that points up an issue with this singer. William Huck writes,

> As Elisabeth, Anja Silja offers a fresh voice her admirers might point to with pride. Her detractors, conversely, will say that they can hear the future problems. Silja never adequately supported her upper register, and though she is here accurate, the top is thin and artificial [269].

It is true that Silja studied with her grandfather, who — utterly astonishing to any trained singer — was a great enemy of diaphragmatic support in singing. He advocated bringing the tone to the frontal cavity, rotating it between the upper teeth and the forehead (Schwinger 194). The kind of support that Birgit Nilsson and virtually every other trained singer worked so assiduously to develop was something that Silja was told not to do. Speculation about how she managed is fruitless, for what matters is the singer's ability to produce powerful, beautiful singing without damaging the voice.

One cannot claim that Silja damaged her voice, for she was still singing successfully in the twenty-first century — and by the time she reached her sixties, she had sung in public for at least a decade longer than any other singer reaching that age, man or woman. There remains the question of the quality of the voice. No one who can sing Berg's Marie in her forties with a review like the following can be said to have anything but a top-level instrument: "Anja Silja possesses precisely the voice Berg must had had in mind for Marie — a range of utilitarian scope that encompasses an earthy contralto as well as the prescribed supple soprano" (Ellsworth 155). Some might argue that Silja's sensationally magnetic stage presence caused that reviewer to be distracted from what he was hearing, but the review was of a recording.

Anja Silja was a phenomenon. Like Callas, her individual timbre made her controversial. She was nonetheless a gifted and highly recognized Wagnerian singer, a colorful contributor to Wagner's silver age.

As we have seen, voices at the extremes are rare. One of the reasons that Anja Silja's career is so unusual is that she began as one of the rarest types of woman's voice: the coloratura soprano. Another voice in short supply is the contralto. Wagner wrote very few contralto roles, and since most of them were secondary roles — Senta's nurse, Mary; one of the Norns; some of the Valkyries — a dramatic mezzo-soprano could negotiate those roles without the listener feeling shortchanged. Even the role of Erda, hardly a secondary role, can be managed by many mezzo-sopranos. That substitution might leave an experienced listener wishing for the rich contralto sound, but the feeling will not last long since the role, though important and highly dramatic, is short.

Listeners, then, can deal with the dearth of contraltos. The same is true with the lowest of the men's voices, also in short supply. In our group of eight men singing the lower Wagnerian roles, only two were true basses: Karl Ridderbusch and Martti Talvela. Bass-baritones could and did sing some of Wagner's bass roles; the high tessitura of Sachs allowed every baritone and bass-baritone in our group except the short-lived George London to sing the role successfully; and though Gurnemanz lies much lower, the great Hans Hotter, a bass-baritone, was splendid in the role. So, although the true bass voice is relatively rare, lovers of Wagner's music do not suffer from the rarity.

They do suffer, through, from the short supply of true tenors. Tenors of any type — dramatic, spinto, lyric — are a relatively small group, and Wagner's tenors, who are almost expected to do the impossible, are perhaps as rare as counter-tenors. Wagner expects his tenor to be able to lighten his voice almost like the lyric tenor of Italian bel canto opera, yet the roles often assume a strength and richness in the lower notes that is found in a baritone. It is a difficult balancing act, as John Steane points out: "The extra weight that the true heroic tenor brings to bear has to do with the breadth of timbre and the openness of high notes at a point where the lyric-dramatic types will start to 'cover'" (I, 74). Add to this the extraordinary stamina required to sing Tristan and Siegfried, and it is no wonder that some divide the universe of Wagnerian singing into pre–Melchior and post–Melchior, a singer who seems to one reviewer "more and more like some genetic aberration" (Miller 269). Our group of silver-age tenors is our smallest of our three groups, but it does contain two true Heldentenors: Jon Vickers and Wolfgang Windgassen.

Windgassen was the leading postwar (which means post–Melchior[10]) tenor singing heroic Wagnerian roles to international acclaim. Comparisons are inevitable: he did not have both the dramatic weight and the beauty of Melchoir — no one did. Between Melchoir and Windgassen came the notable Max Lorenz, but though he had the power, he did not have the beauty. Windgassen, originally a lyric tenor, grew into the Heldentenor category. After his first Wagnerian role, Walther, he took on the great heroic characters one by one and spaced his roles very carefully. Between Lohengrin and Parsifal, for instance, he studied a role with an entirely different character, Mozart's Tamino. Windgassen's careful but steady progression can be seen in two comments by the perceptive critic Andrew Porter. Speaking of the tenor's first Bayreuth Lohengrin in 1953, Porter wrote, "Wolfgang Windgassen is almost certainly the best Wagnerian tenor on the stage today. For the part of Siegfried he still lacks sheer vocal stamina (though almost all other qualities were his), but his Lohengrin was strong, noble, sweet and lyrical." One summer later, Porter wrote, "Without losing any of the youthful freshness in his voice, Wolfgang Windgassen has developed new heroic resources since last year's Siegfried, and gives an eminently satisfying account of the role" (qtd. in Rosenthal 210).

Windgassen's vocal acumen came in part from his father, a leading tenor at the Stuttgart State Opera. Fritz Windgassen told his son, "Sing Mozart as often as you can, even if it is not the most suitable role for your voice As long as you can sing Tamino with ease you can be sure that your voice is in order" (qtd. in Honolka 592).[11] Long before such advice was even needed, when Wolfgang was fourteen, he worked at his father's theater as a technical apprentice, training as a carpenter and electrician. His studies with his father led to a début at a provincial house, and, after military service, an association with the Stuttgart State Opera — where his roles included Cola Rienzi — that quickly led to an international career.

He had a long association with Bayreuth, from 1951 through 1970. He sang every Tristan at that festival from 1957 through 1970 except 1959, when he needed a substitute. Other Bayreuth roles were Parsifal and Froh (both in 1951), both Siegfrieds and Lohengrin (1953), Tannhäuser and Eric (1955), Siegmund and Walther (1956), and Loge (1965). In addition to his summers at Bayreuth, he has sung for significant periods of time at several houses: Stuttgart, where he sang from 1945 until 1972, when he was appointed director; Covent Garden, from his 1954 début as Tristan until 1966; and Vienna, initially with Karajan. He has also sung in a number of German houses, Belgium, Milan, Naples, Barcelona, Lisbon, Belgium, San Francisco (début as Tristan, 1970). And what of New York? As with the great Hans Hotter, so with Windgassen. In 1957 Rudolf Bing engaged the tenor to sing in just seven *Ring* performances with the Metropolitan Opera (one of them out of town). Once again, as in his estimation of Hans Hotter, Bing leaves us puzzled: he preferred the essentially inferior through competent Karl Liebl.

Windgassen certainly did not need to worry about the opinion of Rudulf Bing; he was in great demand everywhere else, particularly requested as Tristan. As of 1962, he had sung the role 150 times, including the over 80 times that his Isolde was the great Birgit Nilsson. He recorded the role more than once, most notably under Böhm, and also recorded Walther (1956, Clutens; 1960, Knappertsbusch), Tannhäuser (1962, Sawallisch), and Siegfried (several Bayreuth recordings as well as Solti's *Ring*). As Tristan he can also be seen on the DVD of the 1967 Wieland Wagner production, conducted by Boulez.

Martin Bernheimer aptly summarizes Windgassen's place in the history of Wagnerian tenors:

> ... for a couple of decades after World War II, Windgassen set Wagnerian standards, vocal and expressive. In the process, he redefined the nature of the heroic beast. He proved that intelligence, suavity, stamina and slender tone could compensate for any lack of superhuman power [62].

Only two of our six silver-age tenors, Windgassen and Vickers, were Heldentenors. Wagner's musical mansion, however, had more than one chamber for tenors; the Hungarian lyric tenor Sándor Kónya took up residence in the room marked Lyric and performed with distinction.

After performing in regional German houses in the early 1950s, he made a series of international débuts. One was as Parsifal (La Scala 1960); four were as Lohengrin: Bayreuth (1958), Paris (1959), the Metropolitan Opera (1961), and Covent Garden (1973). Of his three Wagnerian roles — Walther, Lohengrin, Parsifal — it was Lohengrin for which he was best and for which his strong, appealing, flexible voice was so well suited. Reviewer Kurt Moses, who finds Kónya's rendering of the role "an object lesson on how to sing this part," believed there to be no better Lohengrin in the second half of the twentieth century.

Kónya's voice lay between the lyric-spinto and the dramatic; he had an easy, unforced delivery and could achieve vocal power without straining. He was welcomed wherever he sang — Paris, San Francisco, Florence, Berlin, Milan — but especially at the venues where he performed for the longest periods of time: Bayreuth (1958–67) and the Metropolitan Opera (1961–75), where he sang 287 performances of twenty-two roles.. Although he sang only three Wagnerian roles, he was in great demand: for some fifteen years the leading choice in most major houses for those roles.

American tenor James King began as a baritone. When he was 31, he realized that he was a tenor, and after retraining, made his début as a tenor when he was 35, singing Cavaradossi in Florence (1961). After a début in San Francisco (1961), he became principal tenor at the Deutsche Oper, Berlin (1961), where he sang his first Wagnerian role, Lohengrin (1963). In the 1960's he made a number of important débuts: Salzburg (1962), Vienna (Lohengrin 1963), Bayreuth (Siegmund 1965), Covent Garden and the Metropolitan Opera (both in 1966), and Milan (1968). He moved his base from Berlin to Munich in the mid 60s, with continental Europe remaining as the focus of his career, although he performed internationally — for instance 114 appearances in 13 roles at the Metropolitan.

King was a versatile singer, but his greatest successes were in the German repertoire. Like Kónya, he sang Wagner's more lyrical roles: Eric, Siegmund, Walther, Lohengrin, and Parsifal. He wanted to sing Tannhäuser, but circumstances never allowed it, and he avoided the heavier role of Siegfried. Perhaps because of the baritone quality lingering in his voice, King was able to sing Tristan, though only in concert. He had accepted Bayreuth's invitation to sing the role, but cancelled the performance, probably remembering the counsel of Böhm, who had warned him off the role. In an interview, King noted that Tristan is twice as long as Otello (which he had performed), and Otello "is long enough" (James 16). He waited until he was in his fifties to sing the role in concert, including a Tanglewood performance under Bernstein.

Virtually everyone assessing King's career notes his remarkable stamina. In 1990, at the age of 65, for instance, he sang Lohengrin four times in eight days, and he was singing — and singing well — into his seventies, almost to the end of the century. His stamina was probably constitutional though he credits his long career to having started as a baritone.

King's Wagnerian recordings include Lohengrin (Kubelik), Siegmund (in the *Ring* cycles of Böhm and of Solti), and Parsifal (Bayreuth 1970, Boulez). The discs bear out the assessments of those hearing him on stage: an easy top voice, lyrical yet strong, a pure, bright tone.

One reviewer categorized King as a "lyrical heldentenor," but this seems a contradiction in terms. A true heldentenor, like Melchior and even Windgassen, would not avoid the heavier roles. It was King's Canadian contemporary Jon Vickers who exemplified this rare type of voice.

After a Canadian début in 1954, Vickers first performed at Covent Garden (on tour in Cardiff) in 1957. He came to international attention when he made his Bayreuth debut at Bayreuth one year later, as Siegmund. In 1959 there were débuts in Vienna and San Francisco, and in 1960, the Metropolitan Opera, where he was to sing for over twenty-five years. Her sang Tristan and Siegmund at the Salzburg Festivals of '66, '67 and '68, under Karajan. Throughout a massive career and in a variety of roles, he sang as well in France, his native Canada, at La Scala, and at the Chicago Lyric Opera (début, 1961).

His many recordings include Siegmund and Tristan. The live recording of the latter role, with Birgit Nilsson and Karl Böhm, exists on DVD; the early '70s recording under Solti, elicited this response: "Jon Vickers gives what is without questions the most profound and handsome account of Tristan's music since the advent of high fidelity" (Gurewitsch 289). Such reactions were typical, and those who love this opera can only wish they could have experienced the only Metropolitan production to feature Vickers and Nilsson. Listeners certainly recall the size and intensity of his voice, but he also had an exciting timbre, singing with assurance and a heroic ring. Like the great bass Martti Talvela, Vickers felt a kind of religious calling as a dramatic singer. For that reason there were some roles that he would not perform, notably Tannhäuser. He had studied the role for thirteen months, preparing for new 1977 productions at Covent Garden and the Metropolitan. Not until he had memorized all the role except for the Rome narrative did he finally decide to cancel those performances. He said that he was offended by Tannhauser's making a saint of Elisabeth, therefore allowing her to come between him and his God (qtd. in Steane I, 214), and he elaborated on his aversion to the role in a later interview with Carl Halperin:

> The bottom line is that I *wouldn't* sing Tannhäuser because it attacks the very basis of my Christian faith. The arrogance of Tannhauser, the self-pitying arrogance of the guy, the superiority of his believing that everybody else walked with shoes and he walked in the ice and snow with his bare feet — oh, my gosh, I just puked trying to learn it. I simply couldn't swallow that crap [16].

Vickers was not completely comfortable with the character of Parsifal, which he called "blasphemous," and even less comfortable with Tristan as well, saying of him, "What a coward! You can't face the shame, and so you not only kill yourself, you ask her to follow you. It's ludicrous!" However, Vickers was able to rationalize these objections: "I don't think Tristan is a nice person, and I don't think Isolde is, either. I ignored what he was doing to is own reputation, what Isolde was doing to herself and what the two of them as human beings were doing to themselves" (Halperin 16). Fortunately for the world of opera, Vickers was able to perform the role. No one who was fortunate enough to experience his final performances of Tristan at Chicago's Lyric Opera in the mid–80's can forget his impassioned dramatic presence and the thrilling electricity of that magnificent voice.[12]

The distinguished but short career of the American Jess Thomas illustrates the dangers that some Wagnerian roles pose for a singer who is not a Heldentenor. After a San Francisco début in 1957 followed by three years in a regional German house, Thomas was selected by Wieland Wagner to sing Parsifal at Bayreuth in 1961, returning there in 1966 to sing Tannhäuser. He made his Metropolitan Opera début in 1962 as Walther, a role he sang at Covent Garden in 1969, and sang in Munich, Vienna, and Berlin during the early sixties.

The trouble began when he assumed the heavier roles: Siegfried and Tristan. He sang the title role of Siegfried in the Salzburg Easter Festival of 1969 and Tristan in 1971 at Covent Garden (with Nilsson and Solti). He continued to sing the latter role at Covent Garden and at the Metropolitan. His voice began to deteriorate in the mid–70's; when he returned to Bayreuth in 1976 for the centenary *Ring* cycle, he performance as the *Götterdämmerung* Siegfried was described by Alan Blyth as "a sad coda" to his career ("Jess Thomas" 1416).

When he was at his peak, he was praised for his intelligent interpretations and for his eloquent singing, particularly in long and taxing monologues. In retrospect, one sees the prescience of some reviewers who thought the role of Siegfried was "a shade heavy" for him, or who noted a certain diminishment of freshness and ease due perhaps to the strain of the heavier roles. His vocal deterioration is all the more poignant when one reads early reviews, for instance, the following comments about his 1962 recording as Parsifal: "Jess Thomas's voice has the clarion purity to make us believe his Parsifal. His revelation, the empathy with Amfortas, and the realization of his mission seem to have bypassed his brain and been burnished into his soul" (Grosporean 304).

René Kollo encountered some of the problems that Thomas did, but was able to preserve his voice. After singing in regional houses in his native Germany, beginning in 1965, he made his Bayreuth début as the Steersman in 1969. Until then, his only Wagnerian role had been Froh, but bigger roles were soon to come. While singing at Munich, Hamburg, Berlin, and Vienna, he added three roles: Eric, Parsifal, and Walther. At Bayreuth he sang Lohengrin in 1971 and Walther in 1973. At the Salzburg Festival, under Karajan, he sang Walther in 1974 and the next year, Lohengrin (one performance only: illness produced a weak first performance which garnered negative reviews, which led to his departure).

Three notable achievements took place in 1976: a début at the Metropolitan (Lohengrin), a Covent Garden début (Siegmund), and the title role in *Siegfried* at the Bayreuth centenary *Ring*. In time he was to add the roles of Tannhäuser, the *Götterdämmerung* Siegfried, Tristan (Zürich; then Bayreuth, under Barenboim, 1981) and Rienzi (Munich 1983). Kollo recorded most of his Wagnerian roles: with Solti he recorded Eric, Tannhäuser (1971), and Parsifal (1973). He also recorded Lohengrin (Karajan, 1975–81) Eric (1976), Tristan (Kleiber), and Rienzi (Hollreiser).

Recording a role is less taxing than singing it on stage; engineers can adjust the vocal-instrumental balance, and singers have breaks between sections. (Hence, for instance Domingo's Tristan, recorded but never sung live in its entirety). We would expect, then, that reviews of Kollo's recordings would not emphasize the strain on his voice. However, with the exception of Kollo's recording of the small role of Eric, which a reviewer found to be strong and virile, reviewers of Kollo's recordings detect distinct limits to his voice. Of his early (1971) recording of Tannhäuser, for instance, one reviewer praises his ability to project a sense of youthfulness, but notes that the tenor "has to force unpleasantly" at musical climaxes (Lee 268) Another finds the tenor "seriously overextended" when singing Lohengrin (Harris 253). After noting that *Rienzi* requires "heroic, iron-lunged singers," William Moran writes of Kollo's difficulties with the "massive title role," most of which is "simply too heavy for his essentially lyric voice" (262, 63). Reviewing Kollo's recording of Tristan, Thomas Rimer expresses the paradox of an essentially lyric voice singing such a heavy role. On the one hand, he welcomes Kollo's lyric sound: "it is welcome ... to find a Tristan who avoids altogether that beefy, unsubtle sound that so often characterizes performances of this most demanding of roles." Yet he also states that "as the recording continues, act by act, the listener's suspicion that this tenor could never sing the role well in the opera house becomes a felt certainty" (292).

Once again we are reminded of the extraordinary demands that Wagner makes of his singers.[13] Fortunately, as Kollo used his lyrical voice while performing heavier roles, he did not damage his voice as Jess Thomas had done. The bright timbre and firmness still remained. Alan Blythe writes that although Kollo was "not blessed with a voice of old-style Wagnerian proportions ... he sings [Tristan] with such musicality and understanding as to make one forget the missing decibels" ("Postscript 103). That, really, is all we can ask.

George Bernard Shaw was right when he said that "singers of genius" will not be easily found. However, during this silver age of Wagnerian singing there were a few such singers and a fine group surrounding them who enabled listeners to experience the thrill of Wagner's music.

Notes

1. See Breckbill's overview in "Singing," in *Wagner in Performance* (356–58) as well as his chapter "Wagner on Record," in the same book (153–67). He sees the interaction described above as leading to "a natural summit in the history of Wagner singing" ("Wagner on Record" 156).

2. Hotter's repertoire was extensive even for a career that spanned sixty years. Besides 118 roles in 82 operas, he performed in three operettas, a number of oratorios, and gave many lieder recitals.

3. Hotter would not have sung this role over five hundred times in his career if he had not enjoyed singing it. Nevertheless, he must have felt constrained at singing so little Wagner at the Met. Bing's idea of a good Wagnerian role for Hotter was Pogner (*Meistersinger*), which could also explain Hotter's relatively short tenure at the Met.

4. Hotter was not eager to cancel. Soprano Leonie Rysanek recalls one time when he wanted to cancel during one of his hay-fever bouts; Karajan persuaded him to perform, promising to support him—"and so he did," said Rysanek, "carrying him like a mother" (qtd. in Blyth 21).

5. Sachs is a bass role, but its tessitura is high—a fact that caused the deeper-voiced Hotter to limit his stage performances of the role to twenty-five.

6. In fairness to Norman Bailey, one should note that the reviewer also writes that "Bailey is an always interesting performer in this part—but on records he is only partially successful" (90).

7. No Wagnerian performer sings *only* Wagner; most are aware of the importance of alternating between the heavier roles of Wagner and roles that make different kinds of demands on the voice, and even when Stewart chose to specialize in Wagner, he continued to sing other roles. Until the early '70s, however, he seems to have compartmentalized his two separate seasonal repertoires.

8. Innaurato writes that Crespin performed the role nine times, three of them at the Metropolitan; Robert Connolly quotes Crespin as saying that she sang it only six times (72).

9. Every singer finds it far easier to sing loudly than to sing softly. The great Verdi baritone Sherrill Milnes, for instance, was told by teachers at Drake University that he would never have a successful solo career because he "bellowed." At Northwestern University as a graduate student, he studied with the great Hermanus Baer, whose goal was to enable Milnes to achieve the finesse that he later exhibited throughout his international career. Baer tells of a conversation with Milnes after one of his performances at Chicago's Lyric Opera, in which the singer asked, "Did you notice that final pianissimo at the end of act 2?"

10. Although Melchoir was singing after the war—he sang Siegmund with the Danish RSO in 1960 to celebrate his seventieth birthday—he was most active on the international operatic stage from the mid-'20s until 1950, the year he left the Metropolitan Opera.

11. Windgassen's mother was a singer, and his aunt was the original Octavian, in the 1911 Dresden première.

12. Vickers would not record Gerontius, telling an unhappy record-producer that he could not now conscientiously sing Newman's words (*now* suggests that Vickers had initially agreed to the recording—qtd. in Steane I, 214).

13. Most—like Wagner himself—are aware that singers performing Wagner's roles must deal with an increase in orchestral forces, which is why the orchestra at Bayreuth is sunken and covered. Many, however, are not aware that pitch was not yet standardized in Wagner's day. Wagner's preferred pitch was a' = 435, and in many German cities he could specify that the orchestra tune to that pitch. The difference between that pitch and today's, standardized to a' = 440, is less than a half-step. That may not seem like much, but singers who have been producing sound for hours while contending with a large orchestra would certainly welcome the lower pitch. Wagner was known to have complained bitterly on behalf of his singers when he was forced to tune his orchestra higher.

For a detailed discussion, see Clive Brown's chapter "Performing Practice" in *Wagner in Performance*, edited by Barry Millington and Stewart Spencer, pp. 99–119.

Bibliography

Arthur, Desmond. Rev. of *Lulu*. CD. *American Record Guide* (May–June 1999): 84–85.
Baker, David J. Rev. of "Régine Crespin." CD. *Opera News* (October 2003): 67.
Baustian, Robert. Rev. of *Götterdämmerung*. CD. *Opera Quarterly* 1:3 (Autumn 1983): 272–73.
_____. Rev. of *Die Meistersinger von Nürnberg*. CD, *Opera Quarterly* 1:3 (Autumn 1983): 273–74.
Berg, Gregory. Rev. of *Classic Archive: Régine Crespin*. CD. *Journal of Singing* (November–December 2003): 211–13.
Bernheimer, Martin. "Bayreuth, 1959: *Der Fliegende Holländer*." *Opera* (2006 supplement: *Great First Nights*): 136–37.
_____. "Martha Mödl." *Opera News* (March 2002): 97.
_____. Rev. of "Birget Nilsson," "Wagner Arias and Duets" [Nilsson and Hotter], Schubert's *Winterreise* [Hotter]. CDs. *Opera News* (April 2001): 85–86.
_____. Rev. of *Der fliegende Holländer*. CD, *Opera News* (November 2006): 70.
_____. Rev. of *Götterdämmerung*. CD, *Opera News* (May 2007): 85.
_____. Rev. of *Das Rheingold*. CD. *Opera News* (February 2007): 63–64.
_____. Rev. of Wolfgang Windgassen. CD. *Opera News* (August 2007): 62–63.
Blyth, Alan. "Donald McInntyre." *Opera* 26 (1975): 529–36.
_____. "Great Voices: Alan Blyth Talks to the Great German Bass-Baritone Hans Hotter." *Gramophone* (March 1991): 1649–50.
_____. "Gwyneth Jones Talks to Alan Blyth." *Gramophone* (June 1972): 26.
_____. "Hans Hotter at Ninety: Alan Blyth Surveys His Discography." *Opera* 50 (1999): 36–42.
_____. "James King." *Opera* 57 (2006): 166–68.
_____. "Jess Thomas." *Opera* 44 (1993): 1415–16.
_____. "Karl Ridderbusch." *Opera* 48 (1997): 919–20.
_____. "Leonie Rysanek." *Opera* 45 (1994): 15–24.
_____. "Lucia Popp." *Opera* 33 (1982): 132–38.
_____. "Martti Talvela." *Opera* 40 (1989): 1067–68.
_____. "Postscript." *Opera* 26 (1975 Festival Issue): 103.
_____. "Reputations: Hans Hotter." *Gramophone* (July 1999): 48–49.
_____. Rev. of *Parsifal*. *Opera* 27 (1976 Festival Issue): 26–27.
_____. "Rita Hunter, 1933–2001." *Opera* 52 (2001): 814–16.
_____. "Sándor Kónya." *Opera* 53 (2002): 1073.
Bourgeois, Jacques. "Rita Gorr." *Opera* 12 (1961): 637–40.
Breckbill, David. "Singing." *Wagner in Performance*. Ed. Barry Millington and Stewart Spencer. New Haven, CT: Yale University Press, 1992.
Brown, Clive. "Performing Practice." *Wagner in Performance*. Ed. Barry Millington and Stewart Spencer. New Haven, CT: Yale University Press, 1992.
Chakwin, Stephen D., Jr. Rev. of "Twilight of the Gods." CD. *American Record Guide* (November–December 2001): 208–09.
Clark, Andrew. "Prospero: Theo Adam." *Opera* (2004 supplement *Great Singers in Great Roles*): 62–63.
Connolly, Robert. "Régine Crespin." *Stereo Review* (November 1973): 70–72.
Conrad, Jon Alan. Rev. of *The Valkyrie*. CD. *Opera News* (May 2001): 73.
[Cutts, Paul]. "Rita Hunter." *Gramophone* (July 2001): 21.
Davis, Peter G. "Das Lied von der Ludwig." *Opera News* (October 2007): 34–37.
Driscoll, F. Paul. "James King." *Opera News* (February 2006): 77.
_____. "Thomas Stewart." *Opera News* (December 2006): 84.
Ellsworth, Oliver B. Rev. of *Wozzeck*. CD. *Opera Quarterly* 1:2 (Summer 1983): 155–56.
Fairman, Richard. "London, 1973: The Ring of the Nibelung." *Opera* (2006 supplement: *Great First Nights*): 26–27.
Fath, Rolf. Rev. of *Queen of Spades*. *Opera* 50 (1999): 1458–59.
Forbes, Elizabeth. "James King." *Opera* 37 (1986): 758–63.
_____. "Norman Bailey." *Opera* 24 (1973): 774–80.
_____. "Rita Hunter." *Opera* 27 (1976): 14–20.
Fox, Gerald S. Rev. of *Das Lied von der Erde*. CD. *American Record Guide* (January–February 2000): 123–24.
Grosorean, Gary. "Hans Knappertsbusch at Bayreuth: *Parsifal*s. Rev. of 3 CDs. *Opera Quarterly* 1:3 (Autumn 1983): 301–05.
Guinther, Louise T. "Spoilers." *Opera News* (April 2008): 84.

Gurewitsch, Matthew. "Looking Back on Karajan's Wagner Experiment." Rev. of *Ring, Tristan, Meistersinger, Parsifal, Lohengrin.* CDs. *Opera Quarterly* 1:3 (autumn 1983): 285–91.
Halperin, Carl. "Jon Vickers in Black and White: The Tenor Speaks His Mind." *Opera News* (10 April 1993): 14+.
Hamilton, David. "Wagner's Masters Get Their Due." *High Fidelity/Musical America* (February 1977): 89–91.
Harris, Dale. Rev. of *Lohengrin*. CD. *Opera Quarterly* 1:3 (Autumn 1983): 250–53.
Hawn, Harold G. Rev. of *Parsifal*. CD. *Opera Quarterly* 1:3 (Autumn 1983): 305–06.
Honolka, Kurt. "Wolfgang Windgassen." *Opera* 13 (1962): 590–95.
Huck, William. Rev. of *Tannhäuser*. CD. *Opera Quarterly* 1:3 (Autumn 1983): 269–70.
Innaurato, Albert. "To Live: Régine Crespin's Life Experiences Are Reflected in Her Art." *Opera News* (May 1996): 34+.
Jacobson, Robert. "The Gift to Be Simple: Thomas Stewart's Philosophy for Success." *Opera News* (June 1983): 8+.
_____. "Varney Revisited." *Opera News* (December 1974): 24–26.
James, Jamie. "American Hero." *Opera News* (2 March 1991): 16–17.
Kayser, Beate. "René Kollo." *Opera* 40 (1989): 1415–21.
Knutsen, Arvid J. Rev. of *Tristan und Isolde*. CD. *Opera Quarterly* 1:3 (Autumn 1983): 296–98.
Lee, M. Owen. Rev. of *Tannhäuser*. CD. *Opera Quarterly* 1:3 (Autumn 1983): 266–68.
Leslie, Murray. "*Lohengrin*, Karajan, and Kollo." *Opera* 26 (1975 Festival Issue): 626–29.
_____. Rev. of *Die Meisinger von Nürnberg*. *Opera* 26 (1975): 547–48.
Loveland, Kenneth. "Gwyneth Jones." *Opera* 21 (1970): 100–06.
MacMillan, Rick. Rev. of *Der Ring des Niebelungen*. DVD. *Opus* (Fall 2002): 29.
Martin, Thomas. Rev. of *Der Ring des Niebelungen*. CD. *Opera Quarterly* 1:3 (Autumn 1983): 279–82.
Matheopoulos, Helena. *Diva: Great Sopranos and Mezzos Discuss Their Art*. Boston: Northeastern University Press, 1991.
_____. *Divo: Great Tenors, Baritones, and Basses Discuss Their Roles*. New York: Harper, 1986.
Miller, James. Rev. of *Götterdämmerung* [2 versions]. CDs. *Fanfare* (February 1993): 268–70.
Milnes, Rodney. "Hans Hotter." *Opera* (2004 supplement: *In Character: Great Singers Sing Great Roles*): 76–77.
Minter, Drew. Rev. of *Met Legends: Régine Crespin*. CD. *Opera News* (April 2001): 84–85.
Moran, William R. Rev. of *Rienzi*. CD. *Opera Quarterly* 1:3 (Autumn 1983): 262–64.
Moses, Kurt. Rev. of *Lohengrin*. CD. *American Record Guide* (January–February 1999): 201.
_____. Rev. of *Martha Mödl*. CD. *American Record Guide* (July–August 2002): 229–30.
Movshon, George. Rev. of *Lohengrin*. *High Fidelity/Musical America* (February 1977): MA-23–24.
_____. Rev. of *Die Meistersinger von Nürnberg*. *High Fidelity/Musical America* (February 1977): MA-24–25.
Osborne, Charles. "Christa Ludwig." *Opera* 24 (1973): 216–22.
Osborne, Conrad L. "Voices from the Festspielhaus." *Opera News* (August 1976): 28–31.
Prag, Robert. Rev. of *Tistan und Isolde*. DVD. *Opera Quarterly* 12 (Summer 1994): 114–17.
Rasponi, Lanfranco. *The Last Prima Donnas*. New York: Knopf, 1984.
Rauch, Rudolph S. "Astrid Varnay." *Opera News* (November 2006): 77.
Richards, Denby. "Rita Hunter." *Musical Opinion* (September 2001): 202–03.
Rimer, Thomas. Rev. of *Tristan und Isolde*. *Opera Quarterly* 1:3 (Autumn 1983): 291–92.
Rosenthal, Harold. *Great Singers of Today*. London: Calder, 1966.
_____. "Memorable *Meistersinger*." Rev. of *Die Meistersinger von Nürnberg*. *Opera* 30 (1979): 755–57.
_____. Rev. of *Die Meistersinger von Nürnberg*. *Opera* 26 (1975): 1146.
Russell, Thomas E., III. Rev. of *Parsifal*. CD. *Opera Quarterly* 1:3 (Autumn 1983): 299–301.
Schmitz, Claude M. Rev.of *The Flying Dutchman*, CD. *Opera Quarterly* 1:3 (Autumn 1983): 265–66.
Schwinger, Wolfram. "Anja Silja." *Opera* 20 (1969): 193–98.
Shaw, George Bernard. "Wagner in Bayreuth." *The Wagner Companion*. Ed. Raymond Mander and Joe Mitchenson. London: Allen, 1977.
Shengold, David. Rev. of *Boris Godunov*. CD. *Opera News* (May 2008): 82–83.
_____. "Thomas Stewart." *Opera* 57 (2006): 1443.
Siff, Ira. Rev. of George London: *Spirituals*. CD. *Opera News* (December 2006): 78.
_____. "The Right Stuff." Rev. of *Un Ballo in Maschera*. CD. *Opera News*. (August 2008): 52–53.
Simpson, Harold. *Singers to Remember*. [Lingfield, England]: Oakwood, [1972].
Smillie, Thomson. "Helga Dernesch." *Opera* 24 (1973): 407–12.
Sollis, Todd B. Rev. of *Hans Hotter: Memoirs*. *Opera News* (September 2006): 92–93.

Steane, J. B. *Singers of the Century*. 3 vols. Portland, OR: Amedeus, 1996, 1998, 2000.
Steane, John. Rev. of *George London: Great Singers of the Century*. CD. *Gramophone* (January 2001): 102.
Stuckenschmidt, H.H. "Fischer-Dieskau's Unforgettable Sachs." *Opera* 27 (1976): 457–59.
Tanner, Michael. "When Does the Next Swan Go?" Rev. of *Fifty-Five Years in Five Acts: My Life in Opera*, by Astrid Varnay with Donald Arthur. *Gramophone* (January 2001): 106.
Thomason, Paul. Rev. of *Siegfried*. CD. *Opera News* (August 2001): 53.
Tubeuf, André. "Régine Crespin." *Opera* 15 (1963): 227–32.
Tumbleson, J. Raymond. Rev. of *Die Meistersinger von Nürnberg*. CD. *Opera Quarterly* 1:3 (Autumn 1983): 298–99.
Turok, Paul. Rev. of *Parsifal*. CD. *Fanfare* (September–October 1982): 389.
Van Eaton, Sunny. Rev. of *Götterdämmerung*. CD. *Opera Quarterly* 1:3 (Autumn 1983): 272–73.
_____. Rev. of *Siegfried*. CD. *Opera Quarterly* 1:3 (Autumn 1983): 284.
Varney, Astrid. "Valhalla on the Hudson," excerpt from *Fifty-Five Years in Five Acts: My Life in Opera*, by Astrid Varnay with Donald Arthur. *Opera News* (June 1997): 18+.
White, Edward. Rev. of *Tristano e Isoletta*. CD. *Opera Quarterly* 1:3 (Autumn 1983): 295–96.
Youngren, William. Rev. of *Der Fliegende Holluander*. CD. *Fanfare* (September–October 1982): 387–88.
_____. Rev. of *Lohengrin*. CD. *Fanfare* (January–February 1999): 271–73.
_____. Rev. of *Die Meistersinger von Nürnberg* [2 versions]. CDs. *Fanfare* (July–August 1998): 265–68.
_____. Rev, of *Parsifal*. CD. *Fanfare*. (September–August 1993): 270–72.
_____. Rev, of *Tannhäuser*. CD. *Fanfare* (January–February 1988): 235–37.
_____. Rev. of Wagner selections cond. Fischer-Dieskau. CD. *Fanfare* (November–December 1998).
_____. Rev. of *Die Walküre*. CD. *Fanfare* (September–October 1988): 300.

A Manichean Conclusion

John Louis DiGaetani

Was Richard Wagner a Manichaean? Manichaeism was a very early medieval belief, considered by the Catholic Church a heresy, though it always had its followers. Wagner of course set most of his operas in exactly this period so naturally this "heresy" was part of Wagner's historical setting for his operas and would clearly reflect his chosen period. The early Christian church fought long and hard against all heresies, especially this ancient one.

There actually was a man named Mani who founded this heresy; he was a Persian who lived from A.D. 216 to 277, and he was obsessed with the problem of evil and the problem of suffering, especially the suffering of the innocent. If a group of school children were murdered by a deranged terrorist, the Manichaean would wonder how God could allow such a thing to happen? Those children were totally innocent; if God loves us and is concerned for us and remains all powerful, how can He allow those children to be slaughtered and how can those parents endure so much suffering as a result?

The Manicheans concluded that the reason the innocent sometimes suffer is because God quite frankly lacks the power to stop that suffering. The Manicheans saw the world as controlled by two opposing forces, both equally powerful, God and the Devil — or the spiritual (light) and the material (darkness). God won some battles and the Devil won others, but neither of these two forces was omnipotent and the struggle between them would continue for all eternity in an eternal cycle.

Wagner's operas often reflect the beliefs of the Manicheans, especially his more overtly religious works. We see this philosophy most clearly in the Ring cycle, where Wotan lacks the omnipotent powers to eliminate the machinations of Alberich, but in the non–Ring operas this view of two cyclical forces of good and evil struggling forever often occurs. One would think that as the head of the gods, Wotan would have the power to control events, just as the Christian God allegedly can. But Wotan's powers are clearly not omniscient and Alberich and his evil followers win some battles and can outsmart Wotan.

We can see this conflict more clearly in *The Flying Dutchman* where the Dutchman has made a pact with the devil and repeatedly calls for redemption and freedom from this evil pact. Senta is torn between her desire to help the Dutchman and her love of her fiancé Erik, who seems to symbolize married life and the normal forces of good. What complicates matters is Senta's desire to offer her own life to save the Dutchman, which she does by the end of the opera.

In *Tannhäuser* as well, the Roman goddess Venus seems as powerful as St. Elizabeth, and they both seem to be struggling with each other for the possession of the Minnesinger Tannhäuser. And while Venus and Elizabeth are often presented in polar opposition, they are actually bipolar sisters. While Venus seems to represent pagan sexuality, she clearly has a spiritual interest in Tannhäuser's art and a maternal interest in his character. While Elizabeth seems to represent the Christian concept of chastity, she also clearly has a sexual interest in Tannhäuser and wants to marry him.

Can they be symbols of bipolarity, Wagner's bipolar reality? Or are they symbols of the Manichean concept of God and the Devil in eternal struggle and both equally powerful? Both perhaps. Clearly Wagner presents his audience with cyclical conflicts in his operas — neither side clearly right or clearly wrong. Vico's concept of life controlled by conflicting cycles seems to be suggested here.

In *Lohengrin* we see the medieval belief in God and his Christian followers, but Ortrud obviously believes in the old Germanic gods Wotan and Fricka and is clearly determined to outsmart the Christian God and his followers. In her monologue in the second act of the opera, Ortrud proudly proclaims her belief in those old gods and calls upon them to assist her in her determination to outsmart those naïve Christians and their powerless God.

The opera reflects this conflict as well. When Lohengrin enters in the first act on a boat, drawn miraculously by a swan, he proclaims to be from God and from heaven, and sent by the Grail knights to help poor Elsa in her hour of need. She has been accused of murdering his brother Friedrich, and Lohengrin announces that he will defend her innocence. All he asks in return is that she does not ask him any personal questions about his name and ancestry, which she quickly agrees to. But we find out in the last act, from Ortrud, that that swan that was leading Lohengrin's boat was actually Elsa's brother Friedrich, whom Ortrud has turned into a swan through her magical powers. If God is omnipotent, which according to Christian belief he is, how could he not know that his messenger from heaven was being lead by a magical swan controlled by Ortrud and her evil, pagan gods?

The implications are clearly Manichean: the Christian God is not all powerful and the Devil, or the German god Wotan, is just as powerful and can outsmart the Christian God and sometimes does.

We can see this again in *Parsifal*, where the Grail brotherhood's leader, Amfortas, has been wounded by the evil magician Klingsor. If Amfortas is a representative of the Christian God, and if that Christian God is omnipotent, surely a prayer to Him would end any power that Klingsor wields. According to Christian belief, God is omnipotent and can easily outsmart the Devil and all his evil works. But in *Parsifal* we see Wagner's characters struggling through a cyclical force of two equally powerful forces. While Parsifal appears triumphant by the final scene of the opera, one can not help wondering how long his power will endure.

Wagner's operas are eternally fascinating because just when we feel we understand them, another possible interpretation becomes apparent. Wagner clearly knew how to insure that his operas would be mysterious and as a result eternally fascinating. If we totally understand a work of art, Wagner clearly knew, we would quickly lose interest in that work of art and it becomes dull and mechanical. Wagner insured that this would never happen to any of his operas. They can be approached many different ways because they suggest and include many different meanings, and opera directors of the last fifty years have tried to explore all these different meanings in their various new productions of Wagner's operas through what the Germans call Regietheater — director's theater.

Was Wagner personally a Manichean? There does not seem to be much evidence of that.

Peter Hofmann as Parsifal in the Metropolitan Opera production (photograph by Winnie Klotz).

But Wagner clearly knew about this medieval heresy, and he also knew that as a dramatist any omnipotent force would be less dramatically interesting than two forces of equal strength struggling. The essence of drama is conflict, as Wagner knew from Aristotle, and the Manichaeism struggle became a theatrical reality in Wagner's operas. Who is right? Who is wrong? Who is good? Who is evil? Not even God knows in Wagnerian opera.

Appendix: Discography and Videography of Recommended Performances

Die Feen

• CD •

Otvos: Teatro Communale di Cagliari with Patchel, Korhonen, Sirkia (Dynamic)

Das Liebesverbot

• CD •

Sawallish: Bavarian State Opera with Prey, Hass, Coburn (Orfeo)

Rienzi

• CD •

Krips: Vienna Philharmonic with Svanholm, Ludwig (Bravissimo)

Der Fliegende Holländer

• CD •

Levine: Metropolitan Opera with Morris, Voigt (Sony)
Nelsson: Bayreuth Festival with Estes, Balslev (Philips)

• DVD •

Sawallisch: Bayreuth Festival with McIntyre, Ligendza, directed by Vaclav Kaslik (Deutsche Grammophon)

Tannhäuser

• CD •

Barenboim: Berlin Staatsoper Orchestra with Eaglen, Meier, and Seiffert (Teldec)
Gerdes: German Opera Berlin with Nilsson, Windgassen (Deutsche Grammophon)
Haitink: Bavarian State Opera with König, Popp, Meier (EMI)
Sinopoli: Royal Opera House with Domingo, Studer, Baltsa (Deutsche Grammophon)
Solti: Vienna State Opera with Kollo, Dernesch, Ludwig (Decca)

• DVD •
Davis: Bayreuth Festival with Jones, Wenkoff— directed by G. Friedrich (Deutsche Grammophon)
Levine: Met Opera with Cassilly, Martin, Troyanos, directed by Otto Schenk (Deutsche Grammophon)
Welser-Most: Zurich Opera with Seiffert, directed by G. Fredrich (Teldec)

Lohengrin

• CD •
Barenboim: German State Opera with Seiffert, Magee, Polaski (Teldec)
Davis: Bavarian State Opera with Heppner, Sweet, Marton (RCA Victor)
Karajan: Berlin Philharmonic with Kollo, Tomowa-Sintow, Vejzovic (EMI)
Kempe: Vienna Philharmonic with Thomas, Grümmer, Ludwig (EMI)
Leinsdorf: Boston Symphony Orchestra with Konya, Amara, Gorr (RCA Victor)
Sawallisch: Bayreuth Festival with Thomas Silja, Varnay (Decca)
Solti: Vienna Philharmonic with Domingo, Norman, Randova (Decca)

• DVD •
Levine: Met Opera with Peter Hofmann, Eva Marton, Leonie Rysanek, directed by August Everding (Deutsche Grammophon)
Nelsson: Bayreuth Festival with Peter Hofmann, Karan Armstrong, Elizabeth Connell, directed by G. Friedrich (Initel)

Tristan und Isolde

• CD •
Barenboim: Berlin Philharmonic with Meier, Jerusalem (Teldec)
Bernstein: Bavarian State Opera with Hofmann, Behrens (Philips)
Böhm: Bayreuth Festival with Nilsson, Windgassen (Deutsche Grammophon)
Furtwängler: Royal Opera House with Flagstad, Suthaus (EMI)
Karajan: Berlin Philharmonic with Vickers, Dernesch (EMI)
Kleiber: Bayreuth Festival with Brillioth, Ligendza (Opera D'Oro)
Pappano: The Royal Opera Orchestra with Domingo, Stemme (EMI)
Thielemann: Vienna State Opera with Voigt, Moser (Deutsche Grammophon)

• DVD •
Barenboim: Bayreuth Festival with Jerusalem, Meier, directed by Heiner Müller (Deutsche Grammophon)
Barenboim: Bayreuth Festival with Kollo, Meier, directed by Jean-Pierre Ponnelle (Philips)
Böhn: Orange Festival with Birgit Nilsson, Jon Vickers, directed by Pierre Jourdan (Kultur)

Die Meistersinger von Nürnberg

• CD •
Jochum: Deutsche Opera Berlin with Fischer-Dieskau, Ligendza, Domingo (Deutsche Grammophon)
Solti: Chicago Symphony Orchestra with Mattila, Heppner, Jose van Dam (Decca)
Varviso: Bayreuth Festival with Cox, Bode, Ridderbusch (Philips)

• DVD •
Levine: Met Opera with Morris, Mattila, Heppner, directed by Otto Schenk (Deutsche Grammophon)

Parsifal

• CD •

Barenboim: Berlin Philharmonic with Meier, Jerusalem (Teldec)
Levine: Metropolitan Opera with Domingo, Norman (Deutsche Grammophon)
Solti: Vienna State Opera with Kollo, Ludwig (London)
Thielemann: Vienna State Opera with Domingo, Meier (Deutsche Grammophon)

• DVD •

Gergiev: The Kirov Opera, St. Petersburg with Domingo, Urmana, Salminen, directed by Tony Palmer (Kultur)
Jordan: The Prague Philharmonic with Reiner Goldberg, Yvonne Minton, directed by Hans-Jürgen Syberberg (Corinth)
Levine: Met Opera with Jerusalem, Meier, directed by Otto Schenk (Deutsche Grammophon)

About the Contributors

Mary Cargill is a reference librarian at Columbia University who has been writing about dance since the early 1990s. She has published articles and reviews in *Dance View, Ballet Alert, Dance Magazine,* and *Ballet Review.* She has recently edited a biography of the famous Martha Graham and Broadway dancer Yuriko, which will be published by the University Press of Florida.

Steven R. Cerf is a professor of German at Bowdoin College in Brunswick, Maine. He received his Ph.D. in Germanic languages and literatures from Yale University. His areas of specialization are Thomas Mann, opera as literature, and the Holocaust.

John Louis DiGaetani is a professor of English at Hofstra University. He received a B.A. from the University of Illinois, his M.A. from Northern Illinois University, and his Ph.D. from the University of Wisconsin. His books include *Richard Wagner and the Modern British Novel*; *Penetrating Wagner's Ring: An Anthology*; *Wagner and Suicide*; *Carlo Gozzi: A Life in the 18th Century Venetian Theater, an Afterlife in Opera*; *Puccini the Thinker*; *A Search for a Postmodern Theater*; and *An Invitation to the Opera.* His most recent book is *Stages of Struggle: Modern Playwrights and Their Psychological Inspirations.*

Lisa Feurzeig is a musicologist whose central interest is interpreting vocal music in its historical and intellectual contexts. Her research has explored Schubert, Wagner, German folksong in the Napoleonic era, and the Viennese popular theater of the late eighteenth and early nineteenth centuries. She has prepared two critical editions: *Deutsche Lieder für Jung und Alt* and (with co-editor John Sienicki) and *Quodlibets of the Viennese Theater.* She is also a singer specializing in art song, whose performances have ranged from Perotin to *Pierrot Lunaire.* Lisa is associate professor of music at Grand Valley State University in Michigan.

Barbara Josephine Guenther has degrees in music and in English literature from Nazareth College, the University of Michigan, and the University of Wisconsin (Ph.D.). She teaches courses in writing and in Romanticism at the School of the Art Institute of Chicago. She is active as a singer in a number of choral groups, including the Green Lake Festival Chorus (Wisconsin) and the Apollo Chorus of Chicago, which sings with its own Baroque orchestra and, in the summers, with the Chicago Symphony Orchestra.

Richard C. Harris is the John J. McMullen Professor of Humanities and assistant dean at Webb Institute on Long Island. He has published extensively on Willa Cather in a number of journals, including *Cather Studies, Studies in American Fiction, The Journal of Narrative Theory,* and the *Midwest Review*. Two recent articles deal with Cather and Franz Schubert. Harris was also the volume editor for the scholarly edition of Cather's Pulitzer Prize–winning novel *One of Ours* (University of Nebraska Press, 2006).

James K. Holman is the author of *Wagner's Ring: A Listener's Companion and Concordance*. He is chairman of the Wagner Society of Washington, D.C. He is a former trustee of the Washington National Opera and is on the board of the American Friends of the English National Opera. He writes and lectures on Wagner and resides in Washington. His most recent book is *Wagner Moments*.

Gregory Kershner is a professor of German at Hofstra University. His Ph.D. in German is from the University of California at Davis, and he has a master's degree in international affairs from Columbia University. His specialty is German literature of the nineteenth and twentieth centuries, and he has taught and lectured on these topics in the New York City area.

John J. H. Muller teaches music history at the Juilliard School and is a former department chairman. He lectures frequently on Wagner and other opera composers for the Metropolitan Opera Guild.

Yvonne Nilges studied German, English, and American literature at the University of Heidelberg and at Harvard University. She received her Ph.D. from Harvard in 2006; her doctoral thesis was titled *Richard Wagner's Shakespeare*. She is a Powys Roberts Research Fellow at the University of Oxford in the United Kingdom.

Hans Rudolf Vaget is professor emeritus of German studies and comparative literature at Smith College in Northampton, Massachusetts. He received his academic training at the Universities of Munich, Tübingen, and Columbia University. He has published widely in the field of German studies from the eighteenth century to the present, focusing primarily on Goethe, Wagner, and Thomas Mann.

Nicholas Vazsonyi is a professor of German and director of the German Studies Program at the University of South Carolina. He has published extensively on German literature and culture from the eighteenth to the twentieth centuries. His books include *Lukacs Reads Goethe: From Stalinism to Aestheticism, Searching for Common Ground: Diskurse zur Deutschen Identitat 1750–1871,* and *Wagner's Meistersinger: Performance, History, Representation*.

Hilan Warshaw is a writer and filmmaker living in New York. His writing and video editing credits include documentaries broadcast on PBS and other networks. He recently co-edited and researched *Shadows in Paradise,* a documentary about the artistic refugees who fled Hitler and settled in Los Angeles, which was broadcast on PBS and ARTE. He has also written about music for Carnegie Hall and other organizations. He has a B.F.A. in film and television from New York University and an M.F.A. in music theater writing also from New York University; he was a conducting major at Mannes College of Music.

Index

Adam, Theo 230
Appia, Adolphe 29
Arlaud, Philippe 47

Bach, Johann Sebastian 157
Bailey, Norman 232
Barenboim, Daniel 217–220
Bartók, Béla 188
Barzun, Jacques 115
Basile, Giambattista 10
Bayreuth Festival vii, 5, 27–30, 34, 37, 45, 47, 50, 67, 111, 125, 130, 135, 143, 145, 162, 180, 185, 191, 200
Bechstein, Ludwig 40, 43, 45, 48
Beethoven, Ludwig van 3, 143, 151, 189
Behrens, Hildegard 26, 109, 113, 114
Bellini, Vincenzo 55
Berlin, Germany 25, 29
Berlioz, Hector 24, 151, 187
Bernstein, Leonard 151, 154
Billinghurst, Sarah 1
Bing, Rudolf 229
Bloom, Harold 54
Boehm, Karl 245
Brecht, Bertolt 191, 195
Brendel, Wolfgang 163
Brentano, Clemens 43, 52
Brontë, Charlotte 58
Bulwer-Lytton, Edward 18–20

Campbell, Joseph 190
Cassilly, Richard 44, 109
Cather, Willa 199–215
Chicago, Ill. 200, 212, 213, 218
Close, Glenn 219
Coleridge, Samuel Taylor 59–60, 188
Commedia dell'arte 9–11
Coppola, Francis Ford 194–195
Cramer, Carl Gottlob 94–98
Crespin, Regine 238

Dahlhaus, Carl 59–64, 67, 71, 90
Dalayman, Katharina 112
Darwin, Charles 103, 115
Davis, Colin 217
Deathridge, John 80, 105, 106
Dernesch, Helga 240
DeYoung, Michelle 217–220
Diaghilev, Sergei 180, 181
Domingo, Placido 5, 84, 164, 170, 182
Dresden, Germany 3, 7, 21, 25, 41, 227
Duncan, Isadora 178
Dürer, Albrecht 125
Dvořák, Antonín 199

Eichendorff, Joseph 102
Einstein, Albert 141–144, 150–154
Eisenstein, Sergei 192–194
Engels, Friedrich 18
Eschenbach, Wolfram von 158
Estes, Simon 56
Everding, August 33, 76, 93, 116

Die Feen 9–13
Feuerbach, Ludwig 57, 68, 117
Fischer-Dieskau, Dietrich 229, 230
Flagstad, Kirsten 234
Der Fliegende Holländer 23–39
Fremstad, Olive 207–209
Freud, Sigmund 32, 34, 38

Geyer, Ludwig 158
Giannone, Richard 212ff
Goethe, Johann Wolfgang von 11, 18, 51, 95
Goldoni, Carlo 9, 10
Gorr, Rita 238
Gozzi, Carlo 3, 9–12
Greek Drama 148
Gregor-Dellin, Martin 159
Grimm, Jakob 90

Hagegaard, Hakan 69
Halevy, Fromenthal 24
Haneke, Michael 194–195
Hanslick, Edward 125
Harris, Dale 176
Hegel, Georg Wilhelm 57, 61
Heine, Heinrich 53, 74, 179
Heppner, Ben 221–226
Herder, Johann Gottfried 96, 126, 134–136
Herheim, Stefan 162
Herrmann, Bernard 188, 195
Hitchcock, Alfred 195
Hitler, Adolf 1, 193
Die Hochzeit 9
Hoffmann, E.T.A. 63
Hofmann, Peter 62, 73, 253
Hotter, Hans 229ff
Hugo, Victor 58, 63
Hunter, Rita 228
Huyssen, Andreas 124

Jackey Club 176ff
Jones, Gwynyth 228

Keats, John 68, 70, 71
King, James 244
King Ludwig II of Bavaria 145ff
Klemperer, Otto 29
Kochno, Boris 180
Kollo, Rene 246
Konya, Sandor 243–244
Korngold, Erich 192

Laban, Rudolf von 179
Labarre, Theodore 176
Lang, Fritz 191
Leipzig, Germany 94
Lessing, Gotthold 126
Levine, James 219
Lewis, M.G. 63
Das Liebesverbot 13–18
Liszt, Franz 17, 66
Lloyd, Robert 182

Lohengrin 55–104
London, George 228
Ludwig, Christa 239
Luther, Martin 45

Magee, Bryan 59
Mahler, Gustav 188
Mann, Heinrich 191
Mann, Thomas 191, 195
Marthaler, Christoph 117
Marton, Eva 62, 73
Marx, Karl 115
Mattila, Karita 131
McIntyre, Donald 131, 206, 232, 233
Meier, Johanna 65, 107
Meier, Waltraud 210
Die Meistersinger von Nürnberg 122–156
Melba, Nellie 212
Melchinger, Ulrich 30
Melchior, Lauritz 242
Mendelssohn, Felix 187, 199
Metropolitan Opera Co. 33, 44, 56, 101, 131, 132, 149, 152, 161, 163, 167, 170, 182
Meyerbeer, Giacomo 24
Millington, Barry 59, 68, 159
Mödl, Martha 234, 235
Morris, James 20, 149
Moshinsky, Elijah 59
Mozart, Wolfgang Amadeus 141, 154, 199
Munich, Germany 7, 12, 178, 227
Muybridge, Eadweard 184–185

Napoleon I 45
Napoleon III 176
Naubert, Christiane 95, 99, 100
New York City 208, 211
Nietzsche, Friedrich 103
Nilsson, Birgit 234–245
Nordica, Lillian 212
Norman, Jessye 42, 164, 170, 182
Novak, Kim 188
Novalis 102

Ozawa, Seiji 217

Paris, France 24, 25, 175–178
Paris Opera 175–179, 238
Parsifal 157–173
Petipa, Lucien 176
Poe, Edgar Allan 63
Ponnelle, Jean-Pierre 30

Ridderbusch, Karl 231–232
Riefenstahl, Leni 192
Rienzi 17–21
Ring Cycle 1, 5, 58, 107, 142, 153, 158, 199, 203
Rome, Italy 4, 19
Rossini, Gioacchino 55
Royal Opera, London 59, 228–230
Rysanek, Leonie 167, 237, 238

Saxony, Saxon State Opera 17–21
Schenk, Otto 132, 133, 152, 182
Schiller, Friedrich 189
Schlegel, Friedrich von 59
Schleicher, Erasmus 97–99
Schneider, Herbert 130
Schoenberg, Arnold 188, 191
Schopenhauer, Arthur 108, 158, 189, 190
Schubert, Franz 199
Schumann, Robert 17, 199
Scott, Walter 102
Shakespeare, William 3, 11–16, 72
Shaw, George Bernard 227, 247
Shelley, Percy Bysshe 66–68
Silja, Anja 240–242
Smith, Patrick 115
Smith, Robert Dean 111, 119
Solti, Georg 221ff
Spencer, Stewart 72
Spotts, Frederick 178
Steiner, Max 192
Stewart, James 188
Stewart, Thomas 230–231
Strassburg, Gottfried von 112
Syberberg, Hans-Jürgen 193

Talvela, Martti 233
Tannhäuser 40–79, 175–183
Tchaikovsky, Peter Ilyich 176
Theorin, Irene 111, 119
Thomas, Jess 245–246
Tieck, Ludwig 40–51
Tolkien, J.R.R. 190
Tristan und Isolde 105–12
Troyanos, Tatiana 46, 64, 113, 161

Varnay, Astrid 234–235
Venice, Italy 5
Verdi, Giuseppe 103
Vickers, Jon 172, 224, 243, 244
Vienna, Austria 227
Vogler, Christopher 190
Vogt, Klaus Florian 145
Von Karajan, Herbert 240–41

Wagner, Cosima Liszt 27, 52, 91, 178
Wagner, Johanna 158–159
Wagner, Katharina 125, 129, 130, 135, 143, 145
Wagner, Minna 23, 106
Wagner, Siegfried 178–179
Wagner, Wieland 233–241
Wagner, Wolfgang 194
Weber, Carl Maria von 43–45, 55
Weber, Veit 99
Weimar, Germany 4, 96
Wesendonck, Mathilde 105–111
Wesendonck, Otto 105–111
Wilson, Robert 221
Windgassen, Wolfgang 242–243
Wordsworth, William 188ff

Zucchi, Virginia 177–178